# CREATING GRAPHICS FOR LEARNING AND PERFORMANCE

*Lessons in Visual Literacy*

*Second Edition*

**Linda L. Lohr**

University of Northern Colorado

PEARSON

Merrill
Prentice Hall

Upper Saddle River, New Jersey
Columbus, Ohio

**Library of Congress Cataloging-in-Publication Data**

Lohr, Linda.
   Creating graphics for learning and performance : lessons in visual
literacy / Linda L. Lohr.—2nd ed.
     p. cm.
  Includes bibliographical references and index.
  ISBN-13: 978-0-13-219158-6
  ISBN-10: 0-13-219158-X
  1. Visual literacy.  2. Visual learning.  3. Visual communication—Technique.  4. Graphic
arts—Study and teaching.  I. Title.
  LB1068.L65 2007
  370.15′23—dc22

                                  2007020656

**Vice President and Executive Publisher:** Jeffery W. Johnston
**Senior Editor:** Darcy Betts Prybella
**Editorial Assistant:** Nancy Holstein
**Development Editor:** Christina Robb
**Production Editor:** Kris Roach
**Production Coordination:** Aptara, Inc.
**Design Coordinator:** Diane C. Lorenzo
**Cover Designer:** Terry Rohrbach
**Cover Image:** Linda L. Lohr
**Production Manager:** Susan Hannahs
**Director of Marketing:** David Gesell
**Marketing Coordinator:** Brian Mounts

This book was set in Garamond Book by Aptara, Inc. It was printed and bound by Edwards
Brothers. The cover was printed by Phoenix Color Corp.

Pearson Education Ltd.
Pearson Education Singapore Pte. Ltd.
Pearson Education Canada, Ltd.
Pearson Education—Japan
Pearson Education Australia Pty. Limited

Pearson Education North Asia Ltd.
Pearson Educación de Mexico, S. A. de C.V.
Pearson Education Malaysia Pte. Ltd.

10 9 8 7 6 5 4 3 2 1
ISBN 13: 978-0-13-219158-6
ISBN 10:    0-13-219158-X

# DEDICATION

*To Gary and Kelly*

# Brief Contents

# CONTENTS

## Chapter 3  Visuals and Learning     45

## Chapter 4  ACE It with Principles, Actions, and Tools     71

# PART II    PRINCIPLES    97

## Chapter 5  Selection Principle: Emphasizing Figure and Ground   99

## Chapter 6  Organization Principle: Working with Hierarchy   119

## Chapter 7   Integration Principle: Gestalt     157

# PART III     ACTIONS AND TOOLS     191

## Chapter 8   Actions: Contrast, Alignment, Repetition, and Proximity     193

# PREFACE

I wrote this book to help teachers, students, and practitioners create effective visuals—visuals that are clear, communicate well, and help people learn and/or perform their jobs better. As both an instructional design teacher and a practitioner in the field, I work with many professionals—teachers, computer programmers, graphic artists, instructional designers—in a number of arenas. These individuals have extensive knowledge of their discipline, but they lack either knowledge or skill in visual design or think these principles are too complicated and time consuming to integrate into their daily practices.

These professionals have voiced many concerns:

- "When it comes to design, I just start grabbing any book I can, but I don't really know what I'm looking for."
- "There is an abundance of advice out there; it's hard to know what to pay attention to or where to begin."
- "I know something such as contrast is a good thing, and I'm supposed to teach contrast, but I don't even know what good contrast is. Is there enough or too little?"
- "There seems to be this giant invisible step between analysis and creating something visual."

These comments are not surprising when we consider that most people receive years of training in verbal communication but almost no assistance in the art and science of communicating visually. Technology makes creating visuals easier than ever, yet mastering these tools is not the same as using them wisely. Teachers, students, and practitioners everywhere need a resource that clearly and quickly explains why limiting the number of fonts is important, why using all capital letters in copy is not desirable, why it is important to go easy on the "bells and whistles," and how to make charts and graphs understandable.

## THEORETICAL FRAMEWORK

*Creating Graphics for Learning and Performance* uses cognitive load theory to provide the framework for visual literacy. Students are not required to learn countless principles that will soon be forgotten.

Instead they learn about cognitive load theory and three almost intuitive principles (selection, organization, integration) that they begin to apply immediately. Helping readers think about design, not just apply strategies, is the underlying purpose of the book. By increasing their understanding, their thinking moves to a higher level where design principles make intuitive sense. They will find themselves trying to implement the actual design of images rather than trying to recall particular abstract principles.

The principles learned are gradually reinforced in different contexts as readers explore tools such as color, type, and shape. They learn to reduce extraneous load, and increase germane load by facilitating the mind's tendency to seek figure/ground distinctions, hierarchical arrangements, and gestalt. Underlying each chapter is the idea that effective visuals should support cognitive processes through selection, organization, and integration.

## COVERAGE

*Creating Graphics for Learning and Performance* is organized using a Principles, Actions, and Tools framework. Principles of perception are the heart and soul of this book. These chapters cover, among other things, research-based rules for creating tables and charts, strategies for working with color, symbols, symmetrical and asymmetrical balance, etc., and the theory behind designing the instructional interface. The reader learns the actions and tools needed to influence how the learner will "see" or perceive instructional information.

Actions are manipulations made to type, shape, color, depth, and space (the tools). By adjusting contrast, alignment, repetition, and proximity, students learn to make an image more aesthetically pleasing and more instructionally efficient as well. Richard Mayer's (2001) multimedia principles provide the backdrop for understanding why these actions work.

Tools are the basic elements of design and include type, shape, color, depth, and space. The tools chapters cover research on typography; descriptions of different typefaces; the difference between a type family and a font; how to use different shapes to unify, separate, and chunk information; how to use color effectively; how to put research on color to work; and how to use texture, depth, and space to focus attention.

Early in the book an analyze, create, and evaluate process—presented in the context of traditional and nontraditional instructional design models—explains how visuals are imagined, created, and tested for usability. This chapter covers synectic and other strategies for visual design, helpful advice (such as the diamond and snowman approach to design iteration explained in Chapter 4), and basic rules for usability testing.

A Resources section at the end of the book provides a quick guide to the tools of graphic design including hardware, software, books, and Web resources. Helpful job aids cover a variety of topics: the 80/20 rule and software options, ten tips for composing images, how to avoid the font problem, steps for creating a table, and more.

## BOOK FEATURES

Throughout *Creating Graphics for Learning and Performance* a delicate but user-friendly balance between theory and practice is maintained. In keeping with the book's theme, more than 600 instructional graphics are included to demonstrate the application of theory to real-world applications. Contexts for K–12, higher education, business, and performance are equally represented.

To afford the reader the best opportunity to learn theory and practice, the book is set up to teach the knowledge and skills from both a collaborative and a constructivist orientation. While the book works in both face-to-face and distance learning environments, its style is particularly effective in distance settings.

Chapter activities engage students and motivate them. Typical student comments are enthusiastic and positive at the end of the course or semester:

- "I don't look at visuals the way I used to."
- "The book has changed the way I work."
- "This is one class that I can really use."
- "I have told my friends to take this class or buy the book."

## BOOK ORGANIZATION

From the first chapter, readers are prompted to involve themselves in a series of visual design situations. They are asked to immediately apply the principles in the end of chapter web and challenge activities. Relevant discussion questions are posed for each chapter.

This book is divided into three parts, moving from theory to practice. Part I covers the theory behind visual design for learning. Part II covers visual design principles derived from research on learning. Part III covers the tools and actions you will use to implement the principles. Here are some specifics:

### Part I: Foundations

Part I covers:

Definition and need for visual literacy (Chapter 1)
Getting started (Chapter 2)
General theories that support the book's approach (Chapter 3)
The ACE process (Chapter 4)

### Part II: Principles

Part II is the heart and soul of the book. This section thoroughly describes the principles that you'll use or manipulate to create effective instruction. This section focuses on ways to increase:

Learner "selection" (helping the learner see critical information) (Chapter 5)
Learner "organization" (helping the learner see hierarchy in information) (Chapter 6)
Learner "integration" (helping the learner see the big picture) (Chapter 7)

### Part III: Actions and Tools

Employing actions and tools by adjusting contrast, alignment, repetition, and
    proximity (Chapter 8)
Using tools such as type (Chapter 9), shape (Chapter 10), color, depth, and space
    (Chapter 11)

### Resources

The Resources section following Chapter 11 presents information on hardware, software, and training support that you might want to have around to help you work more efficiently and effectively. You will find a number of job aids that will help you complete the chapter practice activities. Jump ahead to Figure R-1 in the Resources section to see a chart showing all of the job aids and the chapters that directly use them. For example, before starting the activities at the end of each chapter, it would be helpful to read through Figure R-1 and the text related to it.

## CHAPTER FORMAT

The chapters in *Creating Graphics for Learning and Performance* are presented as follows:

- Notes about the opening visual, a section in which the reader learns what the artist was thinking while he or she created the chapter opening design.
- Focus questions
- Key terms
- Introduction, in which one of four book characters is involved in a real-life chapter-related project
- Many visual examples in each chapter, both in education (K–12 and higher education), training, and performance contexts (businesses and government)
- Summary
- End-of-chapter practice activities
- A Companion Website that provides links, extensive examples, and additional student practice activities (http://www.coe.unco.edu/LindaLohr)
- Discussion questions that generate a meaningful exchange of ideas
- K–12 student activities that provide an opportunity for K–12 teachers and students of any discipline to learn visual composition skills together
- A learner-friendly writing style that is easy to understand

## MATERIALS AVAILABLE WITH THIS BOOK

An extensive Companion Website at http://www.coe.unco.edu/LindaLohr complements the textbook. This website includes end-of-chapter exercises:

- Web Activities that present visual problems for readers to solve both in the text and on the Companion Website.
- Challenge Activities that provide additional hands-on activities allowing readers to practice their visual skills. Readers can see student solutions to the problems.
- A Links section that allows the reader to explore related websites.

## NEW TO THIS EDITION

A number of new features are included in this edition:

- Conceptual groupings of images that make visual examples easier to understand and reference.
- A four-page color insert for the chapter on color.
- K–12 student and teacher examples and activities clearly identified.
- New examples of graphic design.
- Chapter by chapter visual examples of student solutions to practice activities that help students think about practice activities and expectations right away.
- A cognitive load theory framework that integrates Mayers' multimedia theory, Baddeley's episodic buffer theory, and Cowan's memory capacity research.
- Chapter reorganization to cover principles first.
- Retitled chapters that emphasize cognitive strategies of selection, organization, and integration and clarify the separation of gestalt principles of perception.
- Flexible chapter sequencing strategies that allow teachers to adapt the text to their teaching styles.

- Job aids that provide practical advice such as the 80/20 software rule (the 20 percent of the tools that are used 80 percent of the time), posting projects in a distributed learning environment, and composing and editing photographs.
- References to new research, books, websites, and professional organizations.
- Integration of the ACE and PAT process that streamlines the design process.
- Ideas and examples for how the Resources section can be used for end of chapter activities.
- A greater distinction between education and performance applications within a universal design context.

## ACKNOWLEDGMENTS

I would like to thank the many people involved in producing this book, especially my editor Debra Stollenwerk and the reviewers of this edition. They are Cheryl Foltz, William Woods University and Southwest Baptist University; Susan Jane Britsch, Purdue University; Robert Atkinson, Arizona State University; Anthony Flinn, Eastern Washington University; Jim King, University of Nebraska Lincoln; and Eric Smith, Wilkes University.

A special thanks to the students at the University of Northern Colorado who provided many of the illustrations on the Companion Website and in the text. The unique work of Aadil Askar, Dalia Alyahya, Diane Kasselhut, Erin Hunt, and Henry Wang is appreciated. I also appreciate the feedback, encouragement, and idea exchange that I received from Jackie Dobrovolny and her students at the University of Colorado, Denver. The educational technology faculty (Jeff Bauer, David Falvo, James Gall, and Heng-yu Ku) supported me throughout the process with goodwill and patience.

Underlying the ideas that are key to this book was the inspiration of many individuals. For that I would like to thank Carol Eikleberry for her friendship, encouragement, and brilliant ideas on creativity; Bill Hinson for his life-changing typography class; Diane Horgan for helping me see the connection between cognitive psychology and instructional visuals; and Gary Morrison and Steve Ross for their scientific approach to instructional design. Finally, I would like to thank Bea Doyle, Bill and Lois Eikleberry, and Gary and Kelly Lohr.

# PART I

## Foundations

# CHAPTER 1

## Visual Literacy for Educators and Performance Specialists

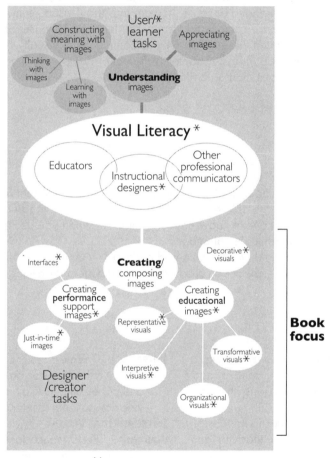

✳ = key term

Visual literacy is defined as the ability to understand and use images, including the ability to think, learn, and express oneself in terms of images.

*Roberts Braden*

## NOTES ABOUT THE OPENING VISUAL

The first visual you see in each chapter relates to a central idea or theme within the chapter. On the previous page the opening visual shows a concept map for the term *visual literacy,* the focus of this chapter.

I used this image for a number of reasons, all relating to sections of this book: The image explains the organization and relationship of topics in the chapter (see *organizational visual* in the Key Terms). Simple shapes in this image convey meaning (see Chapter 10 to learn why the lines and oval shapes used here are effective). Type is used to show relationships. Notice how the words "Visual Literacy," "Understanding," and "Creating" are the largest, most noticeable words. They are large to catch your attention first to establish the importance of those words in the overall context of the image. Observe how subordinate information is presented in a smaller typeface. Chapter 6, Organization, and Chapter 9, Type, explain hierarchy and typography's role in establishing importance.

Words are used because they are important visual elements, and this chapter explains why text can be considered visual. You learn at the onset of this textbook that text-based words are often the quickest way to communicate visually. Words are encouraged when they clarify an image. Chapter 5, Selection, helps you learn how to use words to effectively focus attention on critical information.

## FOCUS QUESTIONS

- What is visual literacy?
- Why is visual literacy important?
- What is an educational context and how is it different from a performance context?
- What is the difference between an instructional image and a performance image?
- Do you have to know anything different when you design a performance image versus an educational image?
- Is a printed word considered a visual?
- Why does the design of educational and performance images involve both art and science?

## KEY TERMS

**DECORATIVE VISUAL** A visual that does not have a strong association with the instructional content, generally added for aesthetic or other reasons; the most frequently used type of instructional visual.

**EDUCATIONAL DESIGN** Similar to instructional design but focusing on creating materials for learning and long-term memory. Transfer of knowledge to new and novel situations is the ultimate goal.

**ELECTRONIC-SLIDES** Electronic slide display software (such as Microsoft PowerPoint®) used in business and educational settings.

**INSTRUCTIONAL DESIGN** Design that encompasses educational and performance design; the art and science of solving instructional problems and identifying their solution.

**INSTRUCTIONAL DESIGNER** A professional who analyzes instructional problems and their solutions and creates, implements, and tests appropriate interventions.

**INTERFACE** The message or cue between a system and a user, such as a link or button on a computer screen, or headings and page numbers in a document. These cues tend to provide navigational assistance to the user/learner.

**INTERPRETIVE VISUAL** A visual that helps explain content.

**JOB AIDS** Performance tools that help people perform a task at the time of need.

**JUST-IN-TIME** Instructional or task support available at the moment of need. (Think of instructions on the gas pump or automatic bank teller, or pop-up spelling corrections as you type using a word processor.) Job aids are considered just-in-time support.

**LITERACY** A broad term describing the ability to be knowledgeable about a particular subject, traditionally that of reading and writing.

**ORGANIZATIONAL VISUAL** A visual that strengthens the structure and hierarchy of information and helps integrate information.

**PERFORMANCE DESIGN** Design that helps people perform a task or job immediately.

**PERFORMANCE SUPPORT** A tangible product that helps people do something at the moment of need (just-in-time). Maps, recipes, and instructions on a gas pump are types of performance support.

**POWERPOINT** An electronic slide software tool from Microsoft®.

**REPRESENTATIVE VISUAL** A visual that carries the same information as the text or clearly identifies information to make it more concrete.

**SLIDE-WARE** Electronic slide display software (such as Microsoft PowerPoint®) used in business and educational settings.

**TRANSFORMATIVE VISUAL** Visuals that supplant new information into memory by making the information more memorable.

**TYPOGRAPHY** The art and science of the letterform.

**UNIVERSAL DESIGN** A usable design of products and environment, accessible to all people. Recently the term *universal design* has been used to address the larger context of design. Universal design employs design principles (visual and otherwise) to create environ-ments accessible to as many people as possible. Skills in visual literacy rely on a number of principles that also fall under the universal design umbrella.

**USER** The receiver of a message, also considered the audience. Learners are considered users when they interact with instructional messages.

**VISUAL LITERACY** A group of acquired competencies for interpreting and composing visible messages. A visually literate person is able to (a) discriminate and make sense of visible objects as part of a visual acuity, (b) create static and dynamic visible objects effectively in a defined space, (c) comprehend and appreciate the visual testaments of others, and (d) conjure objects in the mind's eye (Brill, Kim, and Branch, 2001, p. 9).

**VISUAL LITERACY FOR INSTRUCTION AND PERFOR-MANCE SUPPORT** The ability to work with tools (type, shape, color, depth, and space) and actions (contrast, alignment, repetition, and proximity) to influence learning and performance. More specifically this could be described as the tools (type, shape, color, depth, and space) and actions (contrast, alignment, repetition, and proximity) necessary to facilitate cognitive processes of selection, organization, and integration.

## INTRODUCTION

"I am a visual learner." "I have to see it." "Would you draw that for me?" "I need to draw it first." Most of us have heard comments like these that suggest the importance of visuals in learning and communicating. It should not be surprising then that visual literacy is now a required competency in K–12 education. Although it might seem an obvious need, the subject of visual literacy still catches people off-guard, not knowing what it really is, and requiring effort to understand.

## THE NEED FOR VISUAL LITERACY

**Visual literacy** is defined as the ability to understand, use, and create with images effectively (Braden, 1996). You know from your own experiences that you must be visually literate to navigate through life. Daily existence is full of information that must be identified, processed for meaning, and sometimes remembered. There is so much information that visuals become a convenient way of reducing the cognitive complexity of information: the "a picture is worth a thousand words" phenomenon.

As a teacher, trainer, instructional designer, or professional who needs to communicate visually, you have two types of visual responsibilities: (1) you must interpret visual messages, and (2) you must create visual messages. Thus, you take on two roles: (1) you are a user, and (2) you are a designer. Both of these roles are illustrated in the conceptual drawing of visual literacy for this chapter's opening visual.

This book focuses on how to become more visually literate in the composition sense. You learn how to tap into the visual ability that most of us have, even if we are not artists. You will also learn from reading this book that creating instructional visuals involves both art and science. Many of the principles covered here (the science) lead to visuals that are not only easier for people to understand but also aesthetically appealing (the art). The art of visual design has a long history and most people associate the word *visual* with art. This book, however, also addresses the science of visual design for learning. The science of how we learn is based on the way the mind processes information. In the coming chapters you will learn how the brain's short-term, working, and long-term memory stores and processes visual data. By learning this science of brain behavior, you learn the "whys" and "hows" behind visual information design.

Disciplines such as advertising have long used the power of visuals to persuade and motivate while the field of education has lagged behind. "If visual literacy is so important, why is this the first time we have heard of it?" teachers and designers ask in my introductory teacher preparation and instructional design courses. It is my goal that after a few chapters you will wonder why the topic is not considered more important and why it is not treated as an everyday survival skill. Better yet, you will be able to communicate visually and help others (perhaps students at all levels) do so as well.

# THE CONTEXT: EDUCATION AND PERFORMANCE

This book focuses on creating and understanding graphics for two overall situations: (1) training/education and (2) performance. These settings are reflected in the title: *Creating Graphics for Learning and Performance*. You will learn within these pages how to design graphics for educational or training settings as well as for performance support.

## Education and Visual Literacy

Most of us know the world of education, that world of imparting knowledge and skills—even attitudes—that takes place when we go to school, be it, elementary or high school, community colleges, trade/technical schools, or universities. When we design for educational goals (**educational design**), the design focuses on making information meaningful and memorable so that it can be used at a later date. In this chapter you see many examples of educational images.

## Performance and Visual Literacy

The world of **performance support,** however, is a little less familiar to us, although as students and professionals we are using visual forms of performance support all the time. Performance support, as it relates to visual literacy, is something observable and often tangible (e.g., a worksheet, recipe, gas station or bank machine instructions) that helps people do some task at the exact moment that they need help performing that task.

Think of creating a quick set of directions to tell new students or employees where to park prior to school or work. Those directions are considered performance support. You are helping (supporting) these students/employees as they find (performance) the parking lot. You want to make your directions clear enough that they can use them while driving. Whenever you create for other people, we consider your audience to be **users**. Throughout this book, the term *users* is used to identify the audience of your training or performance materials.

Creating simple directions might seem a mindless task, but, if you really want to do a good job, you think about your users' perspectives, and how they are likely to perceive the information you present. On your end, creating things like parking directions involves analyzing the tasks performed by users as they enter, park, and exit the parking lot. A performance design for this type of situation might be distinct in several ways:

- extra large type for legibility while driving
- a paper size and weight that is easy to place on a car dashboard or car seat
- information on permitted parking locations
- information on parking fees or parking tag display locations
- directions to school or work entrances

Thus, when you create clear directions, you give users a tangible product they can reference when they need it (called just-in-time support or a **job-aid**), although they might later throw away the directions or file them until they need them again. Providing clear direction or instruction is worthwhile because it preserves the user's mental energy for the important information rather than wasting that energy on access to the information.

## Differences in Education and Performance Support

Designing visual messages for performance and education or instruction is different in some basic ways. A good performance support product can have stand-alone features that help users without the presence of a live person. Performance support rarely involves fully educating someone—that is, actually making a person go through all the things that need to happen to remember and learn and apply a message or task. Rather, performance support helps someone at the time of need. Once performance support has been used, it tends to disappear until it needs to be used again, as in our parking example when the parking instructions are either thrown away or stored for later use.

When you design for performance settings, you become very task oriented. You ask questions like this: What information is critical to this job? How do I make that crucial information the focus of attention? With performance design, you focus on immediate recognition for quick access to information. Your goal is to make that information quick and easy to understand—not to make it memorable.

Another way to understand the difference between education and performance settings is to think about the difference between recall and recognition. *Recall* involves long-term memory and is usually the objective of educational contexts. *Recognition* involves quick identification but not necessarily long-term memory, and it is typically needed to navigate throughout a day.

### Performance Support in an Educational Setting

At a recent teacher job fair, recruiters were asked these questions: What can we do to improve the job fair experience for you? What about this job fair is working well, and what is not working well? Ninety percent of the responses made by the recruiters suggested the need for greater visual support:

> *"The orientation materials did not tell us which building to go to."*
>
> *"Make the applicant job tags legible from a distance. I am from a small school district. I have to be very aggressive to attract students to our booth. I scan the crowd for math majors and science majors. Be sure that you print the names and majors on their name tags really big so I can see them at a distance."*
>
> *"I find it embarrassing to be squinting at an applicant's chest (where the name tag is) in order to recall their name. Printing the names using a computer and large font is better than having the applicant fill out the label in thin pencil [that requires squinting]."*
>
> *"We loved that you provided us with maps of our districts. Many students do not know where Guam is, and the map helped them decide if they should interview or not, given that Guam is so far away."*

All of these comments relate to performance tools or visual messages that need to make sense on the spot to help the job fair recruiters do their job effectively.

Once again we see that performance design is important for access issues, which are important to help users get to something they need. What good is having a job fair if recruiters can't see potential candidate names or majors?

For that matter, what good is an instruction when users can't access it? Think of the countless electronic slide **(PowerPoint)** presentations that obscure important instructional content because too many cute but irrelevant fonts and clip-art images are used? Or, the message that gets lost because it is buried in a stream of so many bullet points that you lose all context?

Teachers and trainers will find that there are countless situations where they need to create easy access to important content. In other words, they have to create visual cues that lead a user toward instruction or support.

## Combining Educational and Performance Support Through Universal Design

Recently the term *universal design* has been coined to address all design issues that influence people as they learn and perform in life. The goals of universal design focus on making information and learning accessible in the broader sphere of life for all people. While this is a lofty goal, there are a number of universal design principles that make it easier to do this. This book shares those principles that relate to the visual aspects of universal design.

When visuals are considered in a universal design context, they address the visual interface between a person and a larger system. All the visual cues that help people perform and function are considered. For example, instructions at the gas pump make use of a number of visual cues between the user and a system. Not only are printed words and pictures used in that visual interface, but the physical design of the product itself, which is visual, is carefully designed to help the person do the task. For example, the gas pump nozzle is shaped in a way that helps people know exactly what to do when they pick it up, without thinking. When we squeeze the handle, the gas is dispensed.

Although design of the physical product itself is beyond the scope of this book, a more tangible and relevant example is design of static visual elements in a learning environment. There are many ways we can use visuals to make a learning environment more accessible to all, as addressed in the teacher job fair example. Many of those strategies involve visuals, the focus of this book. As you read the chapters ahead, you gain knowledge of visual literacy for instructional and performance support.

# EXAMPLES OF EDUCATION AND PERFORMANCE NEEDS

So far, I've suggested that you will learn the art and science behind visual literacy skills. I've also suggested that you will use these skills in two general settings: (1) education settings (the traditional school) and (2) performance settings (places where people have some task or job that needs to be done and they need quick, just-in-time information).

## Three Education and Performance Stories

Three stories, all of them based on real experiences, will demonstrate why it is important to develop visual literacy. When you read these stories, try to identify what a designer could have done to improve the outcome. Think about the role of both the designer/teacher and the user/learner. It might help to use a chart such as the one shown in **Table 1–1.** Ask yourself, who experiences the problem? Is some type of hardship created for this person? What is wrong with the design? Think in terms of this chapter's opening visual and the definition of visual literacy. Where do you see the story characters having problems interpreting an image? What were flaws in the message composition?

### Story 1: Hamburger World

The story begins one evening when a busy aunt, after a tiring day at work, takes her nieces to a local mall to do some shopping. Being hungry, they head toward a fast-food restaurant

**TABLE 1–1**   *User and Designer Issues in Three Stories*

| Story | User issues | Designer issues |
|---|---|---|
|  | Is there a problem understanding or interpreting an image? If so, describe how the user interpreted the image and experienced a hardship. | What is the likely composition challenge? What did the designer do or not do that created the hardship experienced by the user? |
| 1. Burger World | ? | ? |
| 2. Teacher Training | ? | ? |
| 3. The Writing Project | ? | ? |

in the food court—partly because there are not any people waiting in line. When they arrive, the clerk motions toward a computer display (see **Figure 1–1**) and asks the aunt to enter her order. She begins looking for a mouse then flounders a bit until the clerk informs her "you need to touch the screen." When the order arrives, the aunt discovers she has ordered four burgers (she wanted three) and a surprise (a plastic toy), which truly was a surprise.

## Story 2: Teacher Training

Seventy plus teachers sit in a large room of 10 perfectly spaced round tables [see Figure 1–1 (continued) on next page]. They are assembled to learn how to use the district's new e-mail system. While the district's computer technician sets up the presentation computer, the teachers talk among themselves, not minding the delay since they rarely get the chance to visit. When the computer is ready, the technician stands proudly by the screen as a lengthy animation of the words "E-mail Training" and the names of all the individuals responsible for the training roll onto a display screen at the front of the room. Several repetitions of an upbeat song fill the room while the animations play out. The teachers are initially interested in the animations but eventually resume their conversations and ignore what is happening in front of them.

The computer technician clears his throat to get their attention, then sits in front of his computer. With his back to the teachers he says, "There's nothing to this new e-mail system. Just click here." He then clicks somewhere. His movements are projected onto a screen that displays the e-mail **interface,** but most of the audience cannot see where he is clicking because the buttons and fields used are too small to be seen from a distance. "I doubt that you'll have much trouble with this system," he assures them, "because what you're supposed to do is pretty obvious." For a moment he is silent and some movement in the interface is detected, but most onlookers have no idea what has taken place. "Don't forget to sign in with your password," the technician laughs, "but that's basically all you need to know. I told the principals there really wasn't much to it." The technician then goes on to show the teachers other e-mail features that he thinks make sense to cover, such as a calendar that reminds teachers about meetings and a junk mail folder. When the teachers leave the room, they raise their eyebrows as if to say "yet another useless in-service."

## Story 1—The burger order screen

Burger looks like it might be smaller than Burger Jr., but is it?

Why would you ever click on No? Maybe to cancel?

This should say **"calculate total"** or something that doesn't make the user think they have to add everything up.

This is customer service? Not only do customers have to enter their orders, they have to figure out the computer screen. This does not make sense when nobody is standing in line. Ordering a burger on a screen is unfriendly and confusing. Technology is not helping here.

**FIGURE 1-1**   Questionable uses of technology

## Story 2—Teacher training

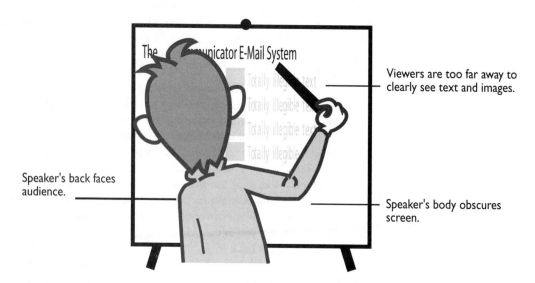

The Communicator E-Mail System

Totally illegible text
Totally illegible te
Totally illegible text
Totally illegibl

Viewers are too far away to clearly see text and images.

Speaker's back faces audience.

Speaker's body obscures screen.

Teachers could not see the training. Text and images were too small to be visible at a distance, and the speaker's body covered the display. Technology is not helping much here either.

**FIGURE 1–1**   (Continued)

### Story 3: The Writing Assignment

Mrs. Umber's seventh grade students are writing reports about Egypt. To encourage their visual literacy, she asks them to write the report in PowerPoint. Students spend a lot of time with the graphics tools to make each screen visual. Keith, a good student, makes his report especially attractive with images of pyramids and rivers that rival that of a graphic artist in training. After a week of working on the report Mrs. Umber reviews the students' work, beginning with Keith's presentation (see **Figure 1–2**). His report shows six slides of beautiful artwork with approximately one sentence per page. Some of the slides do not contain sentences, but they do contain labels. For example, an abstract river and plants are labeled on the second slide. Keith abbreviates words wherever he can, simply to have room enough to show his picture. On the second to last slide, titled "Summary", Keith writes extensively about Egypt introducing many ideas and concepts that were not covered in the previous slides.

## What Is Wrong, Designwise, with These Stories?

If you filled out the chart in Table 1-1 on page 8, compare your ideas with the following observations. Did you notice these issues?

### Story 1: Hamburger World, Design Problems

There are two problems with the Hamburger World order screen. The first is that Hamburger World has decided to ask customers to place their own orders. Managers of this fast-food chain must be pretty enamored with technology to think that the user-unfriendly order entry screen will improve customer service, especially when the counter person isn't even busy taking orders from other customers.

The second problem is that the visual design of the screen is too confusing. Is Burger smaller than Burger Jr., or is it a medium-sized burger? Why were the words "Enter total" used for a button that calculates the total? Presumably the Y and N are used for Yes and No, but why would anybody select No? If No is used to allow the user to back out of a decision, wouldn't the word cancel be more accurate? Notice how there isn't much space between

## Story 3—The writing assignment

Mrs. Umber asked her 7th grade students to write reports on Egypt using a PowerPoint package. Keith, one of the top students, turned in the report shown here.

**The Egyptians** were one of the earliest civilizations.

Slide 1

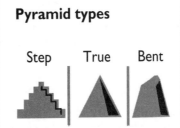

**The Nile** was the giver and taker of life. It gave water for crops, but sometimes it gave too much water, causing floods.

Delta

Cataract

Slide 2

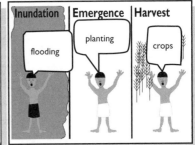

Inundation | Emergence | Harvest

flooding    planting    crops

Slide 3

**The pyramids** are the most well-known part of Egypt.

Slide 4

**Pyramid types**

Step    True    Bent

Slide 5

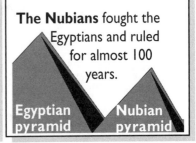

**The Nubians** fought the Egyptians and ruled for almost 100 years.

Egyptian pyramid     Nubian pyramid

Slide 6

### Note to the teacher

Thank you for letting us do our reports this way. I think I deserve an A because I spent a lot of time on the layout.

Summary: The Egyptians settled along the Nile River and started to farm. Eventually they decided they needed a ruler to lead

Slide 7

them and make the gods happy with them. The new rulers were Pharaohs. To please the gods they built pyramids for their pharaoh's tomb. The Nubians lived south of Egypt. For a while the Egyptians and Nubians lived in peace but soon got to fighting. The Nubian King Kushte conquered upper Egypt and his son King Piankhi conquered Lower Egypt.

Slide 8

Note how most of the content for the report is introduced in the summary (not a recommended strategy). Although the graphics are very good, they seem to be the student's focus instead of the critical information. If the teacher's objective is to teach writing skills, the effectiveness of this format would be questionable.

**FIGURE 1–2**   More questionable uses of technology

choices, making it hard to select something without accidently pressing on and selecting something else as well. General design principles of contrast, alignment, repetition, and proximity (you will learn about these in Chapter 8) could have made this computer screen much more usable, but they were for the most part ignored.

## Story 2: Teacher Training, Design Problems

Story 2 has problems that are similar to those in Story 1. Why is a technician responsible for training? The lack of expertise in teaching causes the technician to make several mistakes:

He spends too much time on an animation that was fun for him but bores the teachers in his audience; he starts the training by saying everything is easy (easy for him maybe); by not facing his audience he puts all of the attention onto the computer screen; and the text and links that are projected are illegible from a distance. Perhaps the worst of these mistakes is that his back is to the teachers during the entire presentation. Not only can they not hear him, but he cannot read their faces to gather important nonverbal feedback—something that technology has not yet figured out how to do. This story thus illustrates how poor use of technology and visuals impedes learning.

## Story 3: The Writing Assignment, Design Problems

Story 3 introduces a new problem. What happens when students use technology to communicate? In this story we assume the student had so much fun creating artwork that one of the main goals of the instructional activity—writing—was mostly ignored, until time ran out. The emphasis of the presentation was on the visuals, not the content. Introducing all of the content in a summary is bad writing. Here again, as in the previous two stories, technology and visuals that are not used well can impede learning.

# Universal Design Issues

Underlying the three stories discussed here is the concept of universal design. The settings might relate to **performance design** or **educational design,** but the solution to those problems rests on design principles that are most likely to work for a majority of the population.

## Performance Setting in Story 1

The purpose of the visual, the burger order screen, is to help customers do the job of ordering a burger. The purpose of the visual is not to teach the individual so much about ordering food as getting them to remember how to order food next week. The design is considered to be **just-in-time**—a concept that refers to training that presents itself when it is needed. The design here was not understandable at the time of need and resulted in a number of user errors.

## Educational Setting and Performance Elements in Story 2

The purpose of the projected display was to educate teachers on how to use the e-mail system, but the visuals were too small to see. This story also represents a situation where a good interface would likely prevent the need for the training in the first place. A good interface includes so many cues and signals to the user (such as envelope symbols meaning "send" and trash can symbols meaning "delete") that training is not needed. When users learn e-mail as they use the e-mail system, they are benefiting from a type of performance support. The images in the interface "tell" them what to do. If the interface does a good job, is the workshop training really needed? Again the failure of the design to work for a majority of the audience indicates that its design was flawed.

## Educational Setting in Story 3

The purpose of the student project was to teach students to write and illustrate a report on Egypt. The activity could have been a good one, however, the problem was that students emphasized graphics and clip art over good writing skills.

Poorly designed information can have life or death consequences. Edward Tufte's (2003) review of a PowerPoint presentation made during the 2003 NASA Columbia accident found a number of problems that may have influenced poor decision making. During the January 2003 takeoff of the Columbia, debris from the fuel tank hit and broke through the shuttle, causing a hole that led to Columbia's destruction on reentry to the earth after two weeks in orbit. During that critical two-week time period, when it might have been possible to prevent the accident, Tufte demonstrated how information formatted to accommodate the spatial limitations of PowerPoint prevented a focus on the critical data. These restrictions include the need to abbreviate, the breaking of messages across slides, and the unwise use of up to six levels of bulleted hierarchies. If an already abbreviated message is six levels deep, how could anybody remember the first and second levels? If thinking is fragmented and obfuscated by unmemorable bullets, what value is generated?

Tufte's comments about the use of **slide-ware** in schools is especially relevant to K–12 educators. Of concern is the adoption of PowerPoint as a writing tool for students and the likelihood that it inadvertently leads to poor composition skills. Again the spatial limitations of PowerPoint prevent students from writing in complete sentences. According to Tufte, elementary school PowerPoint exercises (as seen in teacher guides and in student work posted on the Internet) typically consist of 10 to 20 words and a piece of clip art on each slide in a presentation of three to six slides—a total of perhaps 80 words (15 seconds of silent reading) for a week of work!

All of the examples discussed so far—from the teacher job fair to slideware student reports—demonstrate settings where visual messages were not used effectively. In some settings the situations were not highly critical, as was the case with name-tag legibility at the teacher fair. In other settings, such as the Columbia incident, the outcome was a life or death matter. Note too how technology was not used optimally and contributed to less than positive outcomes in all three story examples. Given the overall failure of the designs to work for the majority of user populations, the universal design could have been better.

## Visual Literacy Defined

Universal design is a broad term referring to design issues that encompass almost everything that affects learning and performance. We will significantly narrow that field by focusing on visual messages. As you read in the previous stories, better visual design was needed. Underlying that need is another need: the need for visual literacy—the ability to understand, use, and create with images effectively (Braden, 1996). Let's explore this term in greater depth.

### What Exactly Is a Visual?

A visual is typically thought of as a form of communication that is not verbal. Braden (1996) identifies five categories of visuals that have been studied by educational researchers:

- semiotics and film/video conventions
- signs, symbols, and icons
- images and illustrations
- multi-images
- graphic representation

We will focus on the definition of visual on the fifth type of graphic listed above, graphic representation.

### *Saunders' Definition*

The connotation for the word *visual* in this book is closest to the definition given by A. C. Saunders (1994), who explains graphics as a prepared form of visual communication. Visuals can appear in many forms:

- symbols (pictographic or abstract)
- maps
- graphs
- diagrams
- illustrations or rendered pictures (realistic to abstract)
- models
- composite graphics (multi-images)
- photographs (still or moving)

## *Adding Typography to the List*

We will use Saunders' definition with one exception; we will add **typography**—the art and science of the letterform—to the list. In general, typography takes place when a word or letter is presented in a particular way to form a message. For example, words like "wave" and "bold" (look ahead to the bottom of Figure 1–4) can be made to look like their meaning. In this case, both the words and the presentation are considered visuals. A section titled "Visual Language: Text as Visuals" is included in Braden's (1996) review of research on visual literacy, suggesting that others consider text to be a graphic or visual element. Misanchuk (1992) also considers text having a visual connotation since he describes design decisions about typeface selection and page layout as graphic design. If you read through the pages of this book, you will see many examples where text could be classified as a visual according to these definitions.

## **What Is Literacy?**

### *A Broad Definition*

**Literacy** is broadly defined in the traditional sense as "the condition or quality of being literate, especially the ability to read and write…the condition or quality of being knowledgeable in a particular subject or field" (American Heritage Dictionary, 2005).

### *More Specific Definitions*

Other definitions of literacy are more specific and include a number of connotations important to this book. These definitions involve three types of literacy:

- *Information literacy*: The ability to locate, evaluate, use, and communicate using a wide range of resources including text, visual, audio, and video sources.
- *Workforce literacy*: The ability to meet the demands of the workplace. The Workforce Investment Act of 1998 defined literacy as "an individual's ability to read, write, speak in English, compute and solve problems at levels of proficiency necessary to function on the job, in the family of the individual and in society" (National Institute for Literacy, 2006).
- *Visual literacy*: The ability to create meaning, analyze and evaluate aesthetic merit, grasp the affective impact, and make decisions regarding the integrity of the information displayed (Bamford, 2003; Hughes, Mcavinia, & King, 2004; Lacy, 1987.) By understanding visual composition skills (including an understanding of research and the ability to effectively use technical (computer graphic programs) and nontechnical (pencils, paints, rulers, compasses, etc.) tools, you are able to influence the ability of others to make sense of images.

## **Visual Literacy for Instruction and Performance Support**

We are now at the point of precisely defining visual literacy for learning and performance, the focus of this book. Defined in the context of instruction and performance, visual literacy is described as the ability to work with tools (type, shape, color, depth, and space) and actions (contrast, alignment, repetition, and proximity) to influence learning and performance. More specifically, visual literacy can be described as the tools (type, shape, color, depth, and space) and actions (contrast, alignment, repetition, and proximity) necessary to facilitate cognitive processes of selection, organization, and integration. The rest of this book will help you acquire this literacy.

### *Four Characters in Search of Education and Performance Support*

This book is for anybody responsible for creating or using instructional or performance materials. If you are in a front-line position where the information you create or manage has an important, instructional or performance goal, then this book is for you. As you read this material, you will become familiar with the stories of four characters who are looking for ways to make their training or instruction more visual:

**Antonio, the Sixth Grade Teacher**  Antonio wants to create highly visual, self-paced instruction for his science classes. He also creates bulletin boards, student worksheets, and overhead transparencies.

**Sylvia, the Instructional Designer/Trainer**  Sylvia works for clients who demand that her instruction is not only excellent but also exciting and contemporary. Sylvia creates all types of training materials and environments: print-based instruction, computer and Web-based training, electronic presentations, job aids, and traditional overhead transparencies.

**Zack, the Computer Programmer/Graphic Artist**  Zack works with Sylvia and is frequently in conflict with trying to express himself, test graphics applications, create understandable navigation systems, and make Sylvia and others happy with his work. Zack programs computer and Web-based training and creates the instructional graphics and interfaces.

**Latisha, the Community College Instructor and Part-time Technical Writing Contractor**  Latisha creates classroom overheads, electronic slide presentations, class handouts, and print and computer-based documentation. She would like to be able to create graphics that enhance her technical writing contract work. Since Latisha is about to teach an online course, she is interested in knowing how to design materials for the Web as well.

### Professions Involved in Visual Literacy for Instruction and Performance Support: Is This Book for You?

Since you are browsing through this book, I assume you are somewhat like Antonio, Sylvia, Zack, or Latisha, and I hope that you will relate to one or more of the visual tasks they handle. You want to know more about how to create visuals specifically for learning and performance environments. My guess is that you represent any number of professions:

- an education or instructional design major in college
- a K–12 teacher (Look for the bolded words **K–12 Relevant Examples**).
- a corporate trainer or manager
- an instructional designer who creates and develops computer-based or Web-based training, distance learning environments, and performance support tools
- a technical writer who wants to compose instructional visuals to enhance your writing
- a graphic artist who wants to know more about the special requirements of educational graphics
- a computer scientist or Web designer who creates icons and interfaces for software

It is possible you do all of these tasks: train, develop instruction, create graphics, program computers, design interfaces, and write. Whatever you do, whether you are a college student, a professional who designs training for others, or a manager who oversees the design process, you will find this book filled with information and inspiration on creating visuals that help people learn and perform.

## SOME EXAMPLES OF INSTRUCTIONAL AND PERFORMANCE IMAGES

Now that you know specific definitions of the words *visual* and *literacy,* let's review how visuals are used in instructional settings. Several researchers (Alesandrini, 1984; Duchastel & Waller, 1979; Levie & Lentz, 1982; Levin, 1981; Reiber, 1994) have classified the instructional value of illustrations into taxonomies or categories. In this book, we use the classification of visuals used by Levin (1981), who identified five instructional functions for graphics: (1) decoration, (2) representation, (3) organization, (4) interpretation, and (5) transformation. Levin's functions help us think of what we hope to accomplish in the learner's mind. Figures 1–3 through 1–10 show examples of these different types of visuals.

## Decorative Visuals

**Decorative visuals** are used to make instruction more appealing and motivating (see **Figure 1–3**). They typically do not have a strong association with the instructional content. In a study of sixth grade science textbooks, Mayer (1993) found that more than 85 percent of the illustrations fell into the decorative category.

### K–12 Example
Language Arts

This ornamental typeface is used to make text passages more appealing.

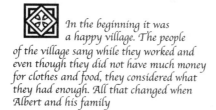

### K–12 Example
Publications

This is the first page of a web-based typography lesson for a high school publications class.

This decorative graphic is used as an opening image for a customer service seminar.

**FIGURE 1–3**   Using decorative visuals to make instruction more appealing and motivating

## Representative Visuals

**Representative visuals** are used to make information more concrete (see **Figure 1–4**). They are used to convey information quickly and easily. The words in a representative visual are likely to be the same words that are used in accompanying text.

### K–12 Example

Art

These representative visuals are used for an art textbook. The words in the image are the same as the words in the text it accompanies.

### K–12 Example

Science

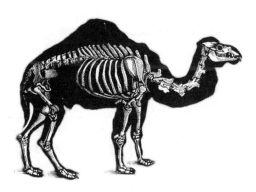

This representative visual makes it possible to see a camel's skeletal structure.

Universal symbols:

Red Cross          Bus          No Smoking

Here the words look like their meaning

**FIGURE 1–4**   Using representative visuals to make information more concrete

## Organizational Visuals

**Organizational visuals** help learners understand the structure, sequence, and hierarchy of information and help integrate that information (see **Figures 1–5** and **1–6**). Charts, graphs, and displays that help people see relationships between elements are considered organizational visuals.

### K–12 Example
Computer Applications

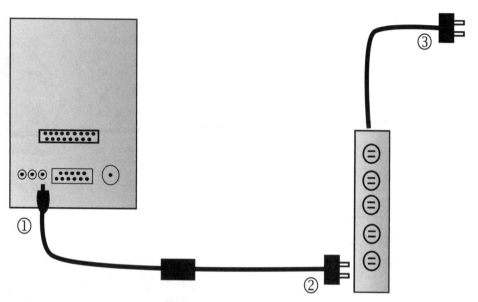

This image is posted in an elementary school computer lab. No words are needed to show the sequence of steps to follow when plugging in the computers.

### K–12 Example
Career Counseling

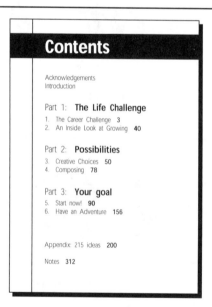

A table of contents for a high school career counseling textbook is an organizational visual because it logically organizes career selection information.

**FIGURE 1–5**  Using organizational visuals helps learners understand the structure, sequence, and hierarchy of information and helps integrate that information

## K–12 Example
History

Edward Tufte (1997) shares an excellent example of an organizational visual in his book *Visual Explanations*. Tufte describes how in 1854 John Snow effectively used a map with symbols to communicate that a polluted water well was causing a cholera epidemic.

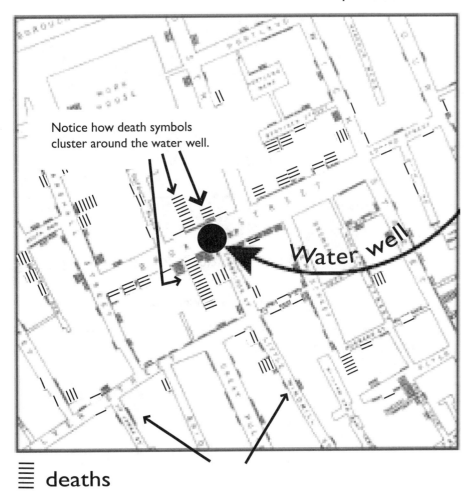

1854
Section of Snow's Cholera Map

Because the death symbols were not as thickly represented in any other part of the map, Snow was able to visually communicate that water from that well was causing the cholera. When the health officials shut down the well, the epidemic stopped.

**FIGURE 1–6**   Using organizational visuals such as charts, graphs, and displays helps people see relationships between elements

## Interpretive Visuals

**Interpretive visuals** help learners understand difficult and ambiguous content (see **Figure 1–7,** and **Figure 1–8**). In general, they help make information more comprehensible. Examples of interpretive visuals include models of systems and diagrams of processes.

In this text, interpretive graphics are those that challenge working memory and work the hardest to interact with long-term memory.

**K–12 Example**
Business

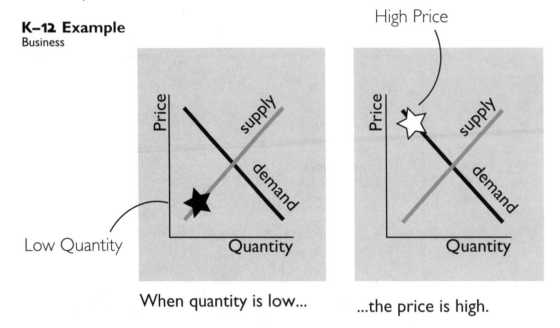

When quantity is low...          ...the price is high.

This interpretive visual helps explain the relationship between supply and demand.

**K–12 Example**
Math

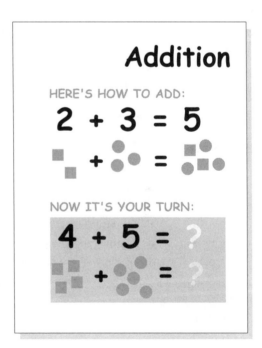

The blocks and circles help children make connections between numbers and quantity.

**FIGURE 1–7**   Using interpretive visuals to help learners understand difficult and ambiguous content

## K–12 Example
Language Arts

### Although he tried, Christopher Columbus never managed to circumnavigate the earth.

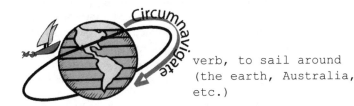

verb, to sail around (the earth, Australia, etc.)

Now create your own vocabulary illustration for one of the following words: circumference, circumambulated, circumscription, circumvent. Also write a sentence that demonstrates the meaning of the word you choose.

This interpretive visual helps explain the word *circumnavigate*.

## K–12 Example
Language Arts

### The retrospective museum exhibit displayed artifacts describing the Civil Rights movement in the 1960s.

adj., looking back on past experiences or events

Now create your own vocabulary illustration for one of the following words: retrograde, retroactive, retrogress, retrorocket.
Also write a sentence that demonstrates the meaning of the word you choose.

This interpretive visual helps explain the word *retrospective*.

**FIGURE 1-8**  Using interpretive visuals to help learners understand words
*Source: Both images created by Krista Brakhage. Used with permission.*

## Transformative Visuals

**Transformative visuals** (see **Figures 1–9** and **1–10**) make information more memorable. This book uses Fleming and Levie's definition, which describes this type of visual as a tool to facilitate the thinking process. A transformative visual focuses more on helping the learner understand than on presenting the content. It might help to think of transformative visuals as images that supplant or support cognitive processes.

Transformative visuals affect long-term memory because they rely on analogy, or previous experiences stored in memory, as devices to help people learn. Thus, many visual analogies are considered transformative. Transformative visuals are images that are unconventional and often difficult to find in educational materials. Some believe that the learners, not the designers, gain the most from generating transformative visuals.

So what do all these categories mean to you? Hopefully they have provided a richer understanding of how graphics are used in instructional settings.

### K–12 Example
Math

This image shows how to teach numbers using counter points. The circles help children use sections of a number to visualize values.

### K–12 Example
Biology

How Chlamydia **Changes Form** as It Advances Through a Cell

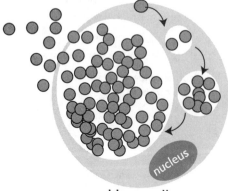

1. The **infectious form** of Chlamydia enters the host cell.

2. Chlamydia replicates inside a vacuole and becomes the **replicated form,** using the cell's amino acids, energy, and possibly the help of the newly discovered protein, Cap 1.

3. Chlamydia **reverts to its infectious form** when the cell can no longer tolerate the growing vacuole. The cell bursts, releasing infectious particles, ready to spread through other healthy cells.

**FIGURE 1–9**   Using transformative visuals to make information more memorable

## K–12 Example
Language Studies

SHI                 STOP

This Japanese pictograph (Kanji) is a transformative visual. By comparing the normal underlying shapes the word *stop* is learned.

---

## K–12 Example
Language Studies

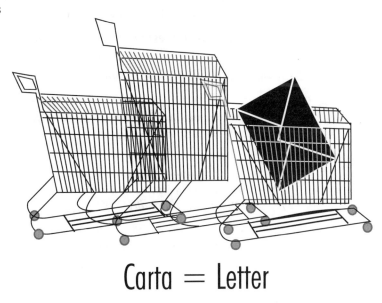

# Carta = Letter

Showing a letter in a grocery cart helps students remember the Spanish word for letter.

**FIGURE 1-10**  Using transformative visuals to have an impact on long-term memory through analog or previous experiences

## SUMMARY

Today's information-rich world increasingly requires visual literacy skills, defined as the ability to understand and use images, including the ability to think and express oneself in images. Teachers, trainers, and those who design instruction, manuals, and programs all depend in part on visuals to communicate.

Two types of visuals, performance visuals and education visuals, are introduced. Performance visuals help users at a time of need and are considered just-in-time support. Recipes, maps, labels, and any visual that helps someone on the spot are examples of performance visuals. Design for almost instant recognition is important for performance visuals. Educational visuals are used to help students learn information for the long-term and are designed to improve long-term memory and problem solving down the road. Design for recall is more important in educational visuals. As such, the designer's task is to present information in ways that will help learners when they must recall that information. Both types of visuals are needed in everyday life and fall under a broader category of universal design.

## PRACTICE

Each chapter ends with a number of activities. Use the Resources to help you complete these exercises. For additional activities and examples of student work, visit the Companion Website for this book at *http://www.coe.unco.edu/LindaLohr*.

## Resource Activities

The Resources section at the back of this book contains basic technical information that will help you create instructional graphics with greater confidence and ease. Learn what is in the Resources section by finding the answers to these questions:

1. *Name a website address where you can find credible information on copyright laws.* _____

2. *Name a book on the Books and Training page that sounds interesting to you.* _____

3. *What type of graphics program (Paint or Draw) would allow you to use an eraser tool to remove pixels from clip art or a digitized photograph?* _____

4. *The author recommends that you learn how to use text boxes, also called text blocks. Why would you create a separate text block when programs like PowerPoint provide them automatically?* _____

5. *If you find a graphic image on the Internet that does not show a copyright symbol, can you use it for class projects? Why or why not?* _____

6. *Locate directions for finding, downloading, and inserting images into PowerPoint or Illustrator.* _____

7. *Using Figure R-1 in the Resources section, list the figures or job aids that are especially relevant to this chapter.* _____

## Web Activity

Use a browser to locate examples of universal design that address performance issues in an instructional context. For example, try search terms such as *universal design instruction*. Locate an example of universal design that relates to visual literacy. An example of a design solution is shown here.

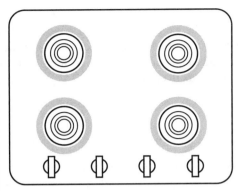

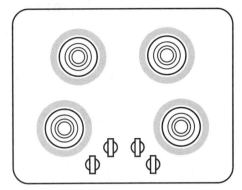

Which control goes with which burner?

This design is better because it is easier to see which burner goes with which control.

## Example of Justification

When I searched for a visual example of universal design related to instruction, I came across a Simple and Intuitive principle, described as design that is easy to understand, regardless of the user's experience, knowledge, language skills, or current concentration level.

This description made me think of controls for range-top cooking. I found an image showing range top control knobs placed on the stove top in a way that would communicate to most people easily. I consider this design as visual because the knobs provide a visual cue (page 18) that is easily perceived due to their relative location on the stove top. The design is universal because it is likely to appeal to a majority of individuals. The cues are visual, not verbal, and thus allow communication that cuts through language barriers. I think it is interesting that not only were the knobs placed in a more intuitive location, but also the burner arrangement was changed.

Universal design attends to physical access issues too (page 8). Placing each knob immediately adjacent to the burner would create a situation where people might accidentally burn themselves when they reach for the control knob. Placing the knobs in front of the burners, near the edge of the range top, minimizes the chance of burning.

# Challenge Activity

This chapter discusses the difference between performance support visuals and educational visuals. Skim through the book and the Companion Website for this book at *http://www.coe.unco.edu/LindaLohr* to locate three examples of performance support visuals and three examples of educational visuals. Briefly describe why each image falls into your assigned category.

## Independent Activity

Take one day and record how many performance support and educational visuals you encounter as part of your normal activities. Describe how visuals of each type you encountered, and describe the best and worst for each category. Take care to identify features that contributed to or detracted from the visual's effectiveness.

## Justification Activity

Write a justification paper for the activity you select. Describe the following:

- *Your users and the assumptions you make about them (such as age, reading level, and assumed skills).*
- *Why you think your solution will work; include at least two ideas from the book, including page numbers and your interpretation of the passage used.*
- *What you learned from a "user-test" (have someone look at the image and verbalize their thoughts while looking at the image).*
- *The changes you will make based on user comments (or create a revised image).*

## Discussion Questions

1. Find a performance support visual and an educational visual and post these in the threaded discussion or meeting space on the companion website. Identify the type of educational visual (representative, organizational, interpretive, or transformative).

2. Provide a recent example of a poor visual design and how it impeded performance or learning.

3. Provide a recent example of good visual design and how it facilitated performance or learning.

## K–12 Student Activities

Use any of the Web Activities and Challenge Activities in this chapter to generate similar ideas for K–12 students. Learn visual literacy skills with your students as they create images (such as maps of their neighborhood, directions to interesting places, classroom rules) or instructional visuals (such as historical timelines, vocabulary posters, illustrated poems).

## REFERENCES

Alesandrini, K. L. (1984). Pictures and adult learning. *Instructional Science, 13,* 63–77.

*American Heritage Dictionary of the English Language* (4th ed.). (2005). Boston, MA: Houghton Mifflin.

Anglin, G. J., Towers, R. L., & Levie, W. H. (1996). Visual message design and learning: The role of static and dynamic illustrations. In D. H. Jonassen (Ed.), *Handbook of research for educational communications and technology* (pp. 755–794). New York: Simon & Schuster.

Bamford, A. (2003). *The visual literacy white paper.* Uxbridge, MA: Adobe Systems Incorporated, Waterview House.

Beauchamp, C., Braden, R. A., & Baca, J. C. (Eds.), *Visual literacy in the digital age.* (ERIC Document Reproduction Service No. ED 370 602). Blacksburg, VA: International Visual Literacy Association.

Braden, R. A. (1996). Visual literacy. In D. H. Jonassen (Ed.), *Handbook of research for educational communications and technology* (pp. 491–520). New York: Simon & Schuster.

Brill, J. M., Kim, D., and Branch, R. M. (2001). Visual literacy defined: The results of a Delphi study—Can IVLA (operationally) define visual literacy? In R. E. Griffen, V. S. Williams, & J. Lee (Eds.), *Exploring the visual future: Art design, science and technology* (pp. 9–15). Blacksburg, VA: International Visual Literacy Association.

Duchastel, P. C., & Waller, R. (1979). Pictoral illustration in instructional texts. *Educational Technology, 19(11),* 20–23.

Fleming, M., & Levie, W. H. (Eds.). (1993). *Instructional message design: Principles from the behavioral and cognitive sciences* (2nd ed.). Englewood Cliffs, NJ: Educational Technology.

Hughes, J., Mcavinia, A., & King, T. (2004). Visual literacy: What is it and do we need it to use learning technologies effectively? *ReCALL, 16(1),* 85-102.

Lacy, L. (1987). *Visual education.* Minneapolis, MN. Minneapolis Public Schools.

Levie, W. H., & Lentz, R. (1982). Effects of text illustrations: A review of the research. *Educational Communications and Technology Journal, 30(4),* 195-232.

Levin, J. R. (1981). On the functions of pictures in prose. In F. J. Pirozzolo, & M. C. Wittrock (Eds.), *Neuropsychological and cognitive processes in reading* (pp. 203-228). New York: Academic Press.

Mayer, R. E. (1993). Illustrations that instruct. In R. Glaser (Ed.), *Advances in instructional psychology* (Vol. 5, pp. 253-284). Hillsdale, NJ: Erlbaum.

Misanchuk, E. R. (1992). *Preparing instructional text: Document design using desktop publishing.* Englewood Cliffs, NJ: Educational Technology.

National Institute for Literacy. Retrieved August 23, 2006, from *http://www.nifl.gov/nifl/faqs.html.*

Reiber, L. P. (1994). *Computers, graphics, and learning.* Dubuque, IA: Brown & Benchmark.

Saunders, A. C. (1994). Graphics and how they communicate. In D. M. Moore, and F. M. Dwyer (Eds.), *Visual literacy, a spectrum of visual learning.* Englewood Cliffs, NJ: Educational Technology Publications.

Tufte, E. R. (2003) *Wired,* pp. 183-92. Retrieved May 25, 2005, from *http://www.wired.com/wired/archive/11.09/ppt2.html.*

Workforce Investment Act of 1998. 112 Stat 936 codified as Section 504 of the Rehabilitation Act, 29 U.S.C. § 794d.

# CHAPTER 2

## Getting Started

Make mistakes
Play a little
Get inspired
Revise a lot

Just do it

*Student*

Due to cost, pictures and images may not always be on the same page.
Whenever possible, images are placed as close to their reference as possible.

## Focus Questions

- Why are skills in visual literacy difficult to come by?
- How does the book help you overcome the plethora of advice out there?
- What is edu-junk and why should it be avoided?

## Key Terms

**Edu-junk** Educational junk that involves the overuse of clip art, borders, shading, all-capitalized text, all-centered text, and Word Art.

**Eye candy** Decorative design features that catch the eye.

**Human factors** A discipline that studies people's relationship to machines (including interfaces among other things).

**Instructional message design** The art and science of the format of communication for instructional purposes.

**Learner-friendly** A description of design that focuses on making instruction effective, efficient, and appealing to the learner.

**Multimedia** More than one media, including paper-based graphics with text.

**Technocentric** A description of design that is driven by technical rather than functional features.

**Word art** A feature available in some word processing packages that allows distortion of text for decorative purposes.

## Introduction

In Chapter 1 you learned about the importance of visuals in educational and performance settings and the growing need for visual literacy—the ability to understand, use, and create with images effectively (Braden, 1996). The chapter established the focus of visual literacy in this book as a focus on visual composition skills.

Because the purpose of this book is to help you create effective visuals, you will be asked to start creating instructional or performance visuals from this chapter forward. As you create, you learn visual composition skills. For many students, this is a difficult and intimidating process. For years we learn verbal composition skills and the importance of writing. Learning to compose visually is a different thing entirely. Outside of general art classes, most of us have never been taught how to write with visuals. How do we create visual messages that mix words and images together? How do we make the two interact in a way that is meaningful and easy for learners to access? The purpose of this chapter is to get you started.

## The Importance of Visual Communication Skills

Although you might think that people who study education and cognition—educators, trainers, and even instructional designers—would be knowledgeable about creating effective visuals, many are not. These professionals are often gifted at verbal forms of communication that make information memorable and useful, but they are not as comfortable with nonverbal formats, such as visuals. **Figure 2–1** shows a devastating example of poor visual communication and how it might have played a role in the Challenger disaster. The important message was not communicated by the data display used. As you can see in the left side of Figure 2-1, it is difficult to understand that low temperatures and O-ring damage are related. Had this relationship been more visually evident, the danger of launching during low temperatures would have been more obvious.

## K–12 Example
Social Studies, History, Publications

Tufte's book *Visual Explanations* shows examples of the communication that occurred the night before the Challenger explosion. Below is a sketch of how Tufte presented the information design problems in his book. To experience the powerful impact of the original charts and redesigns by Tufte, see pages 38–50 of *Visual Explanations*.

**The type of data that was presented**

CONCLUSIONS
·
TEMP OF O-RING IS NOT ONLY
PARAMETER CONTROLLING BLOW BY
·
·
·
AT ABOUT 50 DEG. F BLOW BY COULD
BE EXPERIENCED
·
·
TEMP FOR SRM 25 ON 1-2-86 LAUNCH
WILL BE 29 DEG. F 9:00 AM, 38 DEG F
2:00 AM

RECOMMENDATIONS:
O-RING TEMP MUST BE GREATER THAN
53 DEG. F AT LAUNCH

**The type of data that MIGHT have been presented**

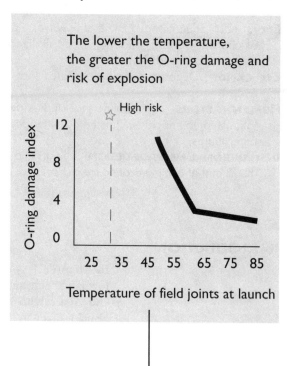

Do you see a relationship between low temperatures and O-ring damage in these data?

This chart **shows a causal relationship** between temperature and O-ring damage and more effectively communicates the need to delay a launch when temperatures are low.

**FIGURE 2–1**    The Challenger disaster

Part of the problem stems from a common belief that anything visual is "easy." We tend to assume that pictures are self-explanatory and serve to make information effortless. Unfortunately, this is not always true and especially so with complex scientific information (Lowe, 2000), such as that related to the Challenger example.

Although many people are aware of their design limitations and want to improve their visual literacy skills, they lack confidence. At a recent conference, a member of a work session expressed her dilemma this way: "I'm not an artistic person, so even though I know that something like contrast is a good thing, I'm not really sure what good contrast is. Does something have the right amount of contrast, or does it need more or less contrast?" Several people in this workshop nodded in agreement. Another person summarized a similar frustration: "I'm supposed to teach visual literacy, yet I'm not really visually literate myself." Using visuals to communicate is simply not a natural skill for most people.

Feeling visually illiterate may not have mattered much in the past. Today's world, however, is increasingly information-oriented. To be effective as well as competitive requires skill in presenting and communicating, verbally and visually, since visuals can condense vast amounts of information into formats that are easy to understand.

# WITH ALL THE TECHNOLOGY, WHY THE CHALLENGE?

Because new software for electronic presentations, newsletters, Web pages, and computer-based education are more accessible, it would seem that creating visuals for learning would be easier than ever. After all, even simple word-processing programs now feature graphic tools for creating shapes, changing colors, experimenting with visual layouts, and importing clip art or photographs.

The challenge, however, is using these tools effectively. Knowing how to use a tool technically is not the same thing as knowing how to use the tool for instructional purposes. Technical skills and design skills are two completely different things. Most people can master the technical skills, but fewer people know how to use the tools effectively. In all likelihood there are more bad than good designs today simply because more people are creating visuals without a good background in design. Their design skills are developed mostly from using a tool, without considering the learner or user. Therefore, many visual designs have a technocentric quality. The following section describes technocentric ways of thinking and an overwhelming number of principles that get in the way of learning visual design.

## Technocentric Thinking

Design that is **technocentric** is driven by technology. Usually this is not a good thing. The Hamburger World example described in Chapter 1 is a perfect example of a technology-driven product that was not designed well from either a practical or a visual perspective. Design that is **learner-friendly** is driven by instructional goals. That is a good thing. The designer's focus is more on the instruction than on using the tool to create the instruction. Take a look at the two computer-based training menus in **Figure 2–2.** Which one do you think is more learner-friendly?

Note how changing the wording is part of the redesign in Figure 2–2. Throughout this book you will notice instructional makeovers that use different words and images in the redesigned visual. The purpose of a makeover, or redesign, is to make the visual more understandable. Sometimes it is necessary to change words along with the visual elements. Many times this involves a reorganization of the message, moving toward a rearrangement of all of the elements in a visual.

Examples of technocentric design similar to Figure 2–2 are easily found. I see technocentric work every day in lessons from beginning instructional designers who create instructional units that employ inconsistent grid systems, too many boxes and drop shadows, multiple font sizes and types, and numerous colors and color schemes. When students "play" with too many features of the technology, they mark themselves as a novice. This habit is so prevalent that I now believe that most people need to work through a technocentric stage—that is, they need to play with all of the features before they learn how to use them wisely. Even after students have read this chapter, about half of their projects will be full of garish combinations that took hours to create. Students think that the extra effort and time involved will be rewarded with a good grade. This is technocentric thinking because all of the added "extras"—from drop shadowing and **word art** to boxes, arrows, and colors—obscure the message and make the work not only look bad also communicate poorly.

## The Blind Belief That a Picture Is Always Worth a Thousand Words

Aside from a tendency toward technocentrism, there seems to be a widespread belief that all pictures are valuable. The cliché "A picture is worth a thousand words" makes sense some of the time, as in the case of the Snow cholera map (Figure 1-6) in Chapter 1. But just because something is visually composed does not necessarily mean it is easy to understand. Too often

Here are two menu designs for the same Web-based tutorial. Notice the difference between the technocentric menu (A) and the learner-friendly menu (B). Menu B was created to improve the usability of the tutorial when users were unable to use Menu A. Notice too how the text has been changed in Menu B.  Words like "Learn How To" help establish the purpose of the menu.

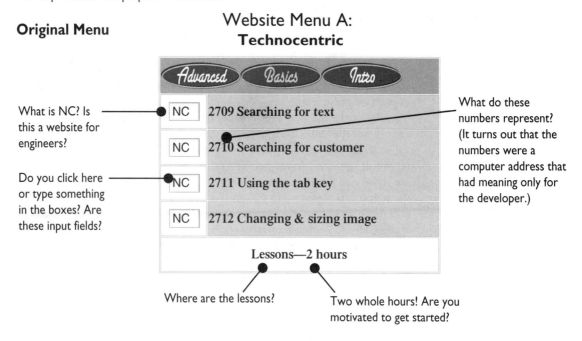

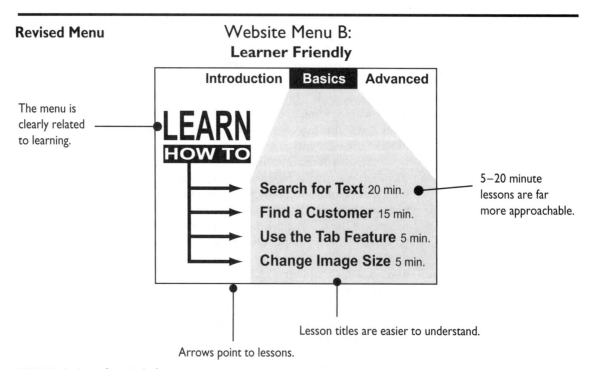

**FIGURE 2-2**   Before and after training menus

## Before

This image is not worth a thousand words. The arrow does not quite communicate what to do. Does that swirl in the arrow mean that the user is supposed to rotate the page and turn it somehow?

## After

The words "turn scannable image face down" and the image of a sheet of paper with the words facing down in the bottom image do a better job of communicating.

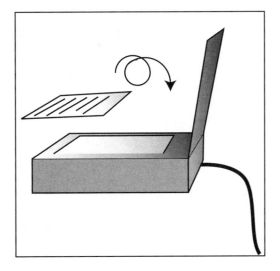

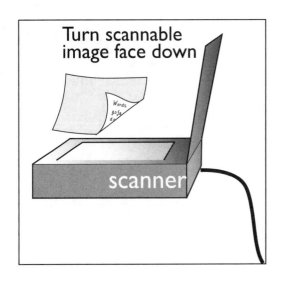

What is this arrow telling you to do?

Words and graphics help to make this clear.

*Please note:*

It is OK to change the wording in an image when you are trying to improve and revise it. Throughout this book, you will see many Before and After images that allow a change in wording as part of the redesign.  If the original text is not working, then its composition should also be part of the makeover.

**FIGURE 2–3**   Before and after scanner instruction

poorly designed instructional materials impede rather than facilitate instruction or performance. We can all relate to the poorly designed instructional manuals that accompany children's toys, appliances, and other new products. For example, look at the instructions to place the image face down on the scanner shown in **Figure 2–3.** The image on the left is not really worth a thousand words; in fact, it confused people.

## Before

This computer-training disk arrives with a new software product. Most users did not know what the disk was. For one thing, they don't know what CBT stands for (computer-based training), and consequently they do not use the training.

## After

A redesign of the disk makes the training more successful. Notice how the disk's purpose (training) is clearer in this redesign.

Is this a software CD?

This label communicates the purpose of the disk—training.

**FIGURE 2–4**   Before and after CD training labels

Another example of technocentric design is illustrated by the CD training labels in **Figure 2–4.** The original label in the image created so much confusion that customers thought it was part of a software program they had just purchased. The customers were not sure what the CD did so most of them put it aside. When customers did not use it, they lost the opportunity for important training. When the label was changed to "Training Disk," customers knew what to do with the disk. The call volume to the customer support center dropped significantly after the new label was used. Two simple words, "Training Disk," made a huge difference in the customer experience.

## A Plethora of Design Guidelines, Many That Overlap and Contradict

You have learned that technocentric design and a falsely optimistic faith in the instructional power of visuals are not the way to proceed. Where, then, do you begin to learn, and where do you turn for advice to avoid the problems mentioned so far? Although it might seem that good design information is scarce, the truth is that the opposite is true. There are almost too many design recommendations. As expressed by a student recently, "There's this plethora of advice and design guidelines. Which ones should I go with and where do I begin?"

To illustrate this point, **Table 2–1** lists the terms used to guide design from disciplines of **human factors,** graphic design, and **instructional message design**. These are classified into

**TABLE 2-1**   *Design Terminology: Some of These Words Mean Roughly the Same Thing*

| Discipline | Efficiency<br>Ways to make a visual or product easier to understand and use | Appeal<br>Ways to make a visual or product attractive and motivating |
|---|---|---|
| ***Human Factors*** | **Galitz (1997)**<br>Compatibility, clarity, recovery, responsiveness, consistency, configurability, efficiency, and forgiveness | **Galitz (1997)**<br>Aesthetic appeal |
| | **Nielsen (1993)**<br>Minimization of user memory load, consistency, feedback, clearly marked exits, shortcuts, good error messages, prevention of errors, help, and documentation | **Nielsen (1993)**<br>Simple and natural dialogue (using words that are immediately familiar) |
| ***Graphic Arts*** | **Mullet and Sano (1995)**<br>Simplicity (achieved through unity, refinement, and fitness) | **Mullet and Sano (1995)**<br>Elegance (achieved through unity, refinement, and fitness), scale contrast and proportion (achieved through clarity, harmony, activity, and restraint) |
| | | **Williams (1994)**<br>Contrast, alignment, repetition, and proximity |
| ***Instructional Message Design*** | **Schwier and Misanchuk (1993)**<br>Simplicity, consistency, clarity, time, and minimal memory load | **Schwier and Misanchuk (1993)**<br>Aesthetic considerations (balance, harmony, unity), and white space |
| | **Reilly and Roach (1986)**<br>Sequence and emphasis | **Reilly and Roach (1986)**<br>Proportion and balance |
| | **Hartley (1985)**<br>Repetition, outlining, and spacing | **Hartley (1985)**<br>Reward, novelty, and sensory experiences |

two categories: terms that relate to making a product or a visual easier to understand (the efficiency column) and terms that relate to making a product more visually or aesthetically attractive (the appeal column). Which do you follow? If you are working on a computer program, do you follow the suggestions of human factors experts, or do you follow graphic designers? When should you follow the advice from instructional message designers?

Universal design, a term introduced in Chapter 1, provides an umbrella term for all these variables and disciplines. Even so, identifying which variables to focus on remains complicated. We are, however, going to simplify the process considerably.

## HOW THIS BOOK HELPS

Rather than trying to teach all of the critical principles, this book will make the whole process of creating visuals for learning and performance easier by focusing on just three learner-driven principles of design: (1) selection, (2) organization, and (3) integration. Because these principles are based on the cognitive processing of information, they have a learning focus that other design principles do not emphasize. Using these three principles to guide your design will help you create better electronic presentations, instructional handouts, job aids, performance support tools, computer and Web-based training, and paper-based training. We are not going to cover these principles just yet. If you are interested though, you can skip ahead to Chapters 5, 6, and 7 to learn more.

Employing selection, organization, and integration principles will help you create instruction based on what the learner is likely to perceive. Graphic arts books, information design books, and instructional message design books stress these three principles, but they use different terms and often have a different goal. These principles can be observed time and again in the work of many disciplines, attesting to their underlying consilience. You will also see that once you understand these principles, you will start to recognize their power everywhere. As a result, you will find it easier to create instruction that is based on the learner and that the learner is more likely to perceive in a way you intended.

## Learn by Doing

You might think "but I don't need to do the visuals. I can work with images that someone else designs." This is true, and you can also use the knowledge gained in this book to help you select effective instructional visuals. One problem you might encounter though is that many graphic designers are more artists by nature than designers. Their goal is more self-expression than communicating to as wide an audience as possible. Many graphic artists do not have a learner-centered approach—that is, they do not focus on learning or the learner. This problem can also be compounded by the need to market and sell instructional materials. To some extent, the public demands **eye candy**—decorative design features that catch the eye.

This demand is in part due to the exceedingly high standards people apply to **multimedia**—more than one media, including paper-based graphics with text. They compare everything to what they see in professionally produced, color-enhanced publications or on television or at the movies. When using training products, learners do complain when a page is not catchy or visually embellished (Lohr, 1999). This presents real problems to instructional designers who rightly want the instructional content to be the emphasis. Although it is difficult to compete with the million dollar budgets of the television and movie industry, the instructional designer must consider the possibility that the audience will reject instruction, or be less enthusiastic about its merits, simply based on its appearance.

### Three Approaches to Creating Good Design

You can take three approaches to creating a good design:

1. *Leave the design to a professional graphic artist.* Managers of instructional products, such as teachers and corporate trainers, are likely to take the first approach and leave everything up to a graphic artist. If this is you, this book will help you understand the goals of instructional visuals and select products or hire people who can get the job done correctly.
2. *Become a better graphic artist yourself.* This approach is likely to be taken by those who do not have the budget to outsource the work, or by those who simply want to learn the skills. If this is you, this book has many tips, techniques, and practice exercises to get you started.
3. *Become a better designer in order to communicate with a professional designer.* Many instructional designers choose this strategy because it allows them to take a strong role in the conceptual design of information. The closer the designer can come to the visual goal, the easier it is to communicate with the artist about what is needed to keep things instructionally optimal.

This book will help you in whatever direction you take as long as you have a strong interest in the learner. Rather than having a technocentric focus (attention to the media, not the instructional message), you will need to develop a learner-centered focus and understand what makes visuals instructionally effective. Regardless of which approach you take, the three principles covered in this book all deal with learner perception and are an excellent way to approach design.

Knowing how people process information and learn is the key to creating effective visuals for learning and performance. Thus, when you work with designs, you look at them with the learner in mind. You think about what learners notice first, what stands out to them, how they perceive the relationship of elements in an image, and the overall gestalt.

In this book, you will see numerous examples of good, bad, and evolving design. As you read, you will find yourself getting better at spotting good and bad designs. You will be able to practice your developing skills as well. In the process you will become a better artist, or someone who knows how to talk effectively with an artist.

## Do You Need Computer Skills?

Many of you will ask, "Are computer skills necessary?" Technically they are not. You can learn about good design without a computer. You can learn basic design information with traditional tools of the trade such as pencils and pens, T-squares, and protractors. If you want to implement the information in this book, however, you will find that knowing how to use a computer will make the job easier.

To do basic design work, you need to be able to experiment with type, shape, color, white space, and dimension. The computer allows you to work with all of these elements easily. You will most likely find that computer-generated examples are easier and more satisfactory to manipulate.

If you are unfamiliar with the computer, this book will explain how to do some basic tasks. The Resources section describes the basic functions performed by most software applications. These descriptions assume a rudimentary level of knowledge and are thus not overly detailed. If you lack basic computer skills, the Resources section will also help you access introductory self-paced training that can help you get started (some of it is free on the web).

## Just Do It!

You will learn by doing and reflecting using Web and Challenge Activities at the end of each chapter of this book. These activities have been tested by graduate students who report that the problems are not only educational but fun. What's more, you can compare your visual solutions to the work of others on the Companion Website for this book at *http://www.coe. unco.edu/LindaLohr*. You will be amazed at how many ways a visual problem can be solved.

If you feel some anxiety at this point— "I'm not ready for exercises yet" or "I don't know how to use a computer"—just take a few deep breaths! At some point you just have to jump in and get started. It feels risky, but one of the first steps to learning anything new is to take a risk. Most of your learning will come from doing anyway.

It is also good practice to create visual instructions whenever you can, just to get practice. Make advertisements, flyers, and simple things first. As you experiment, keep four important rules in mind: (1) don't be too hard on yourself when you make mistakes, (2) play a little, (3) get inspired, and (4) revise a lot (get used to doing things over and over). Let's look at each rule in more detail.

### Don't Be Too Hard on Yourself When You Make Mistakes

Although the purpose of this book is to alleviate as many mistakes as possible, you still need to be open to learning from visuals that may not be as effective as you planned. In the world of art education, students are encouraged to make their first 100 mistakes as soon as possible to learn their first 100 lessons. Book knowledge helps, but to become proficient you need to do design and watch how people react to your instruction. The reactions of others will teach you. Your "mistakes" teach you. Your analysis of what works and what does not work teaches you. Even though the overriding purpose of this book is to eliminate as much trial and error as possible on your journey to good design, you will want to analyze carefully what does and does not work.

## Play a Little

Have fun, especially when undertaking low-risk projects (those that do not put your career at risk). Although this book simplifies and explains why certain techniques are better than others, quite often designs that "work" theoretically should not work. These designs are often more interesting and are more likely to happen if you are relaxed.

## Get Inspired

If you want to be original and come up with creative ideas, don't forget that the best work often comes from inspiration. Seeing other people work, or things another person does, can inspire you to create completely original work. Look at what professional graphic designers have done in books, magazines, brochures, flyers, and websites. Think too of how artists throughout history had tremendous influence on each other's work. I was surprised to learn that talented art students often start by practicing with images created by someone else. By the time they are finished with their work, the image is completely different.

One student told me she learned the most from the previous paragraph while using this book. She summarized it as "It is OK to cheat a little." By that she meant it was OK to use designs, clip art, and other things that made her job easier.

A word of caution though: Copyright laws make a distinction between illegal copying and inspiration. It is unlawful to represent any form of someone else's image or visual as your own. Inspiration is considered a suitable degree of departure from an original work. What is considered suitable is open to legal interpretation, so my advice is to be sure to make your work really different from your inspiration piece. More on copyright is found in the Resources section.

## Revise a Lot

Get used to creating prototypes or quick copies of your work that you can get feedback on immediately. The prototyping process involves analyzing (planning) a design, creating it, and evaluating and changing the design—what we call the ACE process (which will be described in Chapter 4 but there is no reason you cannot get started on it now). As we created the examples for this book, we often used what we originally thought were good examples as our "bad" examples. This is because even though we were using all the theory, things did not quite go right when we showed our work to others. The prototyping process is what made our work acceptable. Remember, rarely will your work be good enough on its first draft.

You can compose your solutions to these problems in a variety of ways. You can simply sketch the solution on unlined paper if you do not have skills using a computer. Or you can use a word-processing program that allows you to insert graphics and position text. If you know how to insert graphics and create text blocks, you can make professional-looking images in a simple word-processing program.

The Resources section includes some of the more popular software tools available and tutorials to help you learn these packages. Students in my classes use Microsoft Word, Microsoft PowerPoint, Adobe Illustrator, and Adobe Photoshop. Most of my students use PowerPoint, but Adobe Illustrator and Adobe Photoshop are advanced tools that are worth the effort to learn. Consult the Resources section for freeware alternatives to Illustrator and Photoshop. Since these programs are free of cost, the instructions for using them are limited.

A final tip before you start: Try to minimize the use of clip art, word art, centered text, borders, and all the other design features that tend to get overdone. Think of these as **edu-junk,** elements that "junk" up a message. Focus on your message and what you want to communicate. Do not be afraid of using words in your images.

## SUMMARY

Chapter 2 introduced the growing importance of visual literacy to teachers and performance specialists. Using visuals effectively, however, is not a natural skill for many people. Although tools for design are more accessible than ever, many people have too much of a tools or technocentric focus—that is, they let the features of a particular technology drive the design of their message, often to the detriment of their instruction.

Likewise, there is a popular opinion that any visual is worth a thousand words; many images are therefore created without the awareness that they may or may not be understood, often depending on the skill of the designer.

Learning visual literacy represents a number of challenges. Although design advice abounds—from diverse fields such as graphic arts, information design, computer science,

interface design, human factors, and message design—this plethora of rules often confuses people instead of helping them. While universal design principles appear to collapse the principles together into one framework, the number of relevant principles does not change. In other words, there are just as many, if not more, universal design principles.

This book reduces confusion by simplifying the number of learner-driven principles of design to three: (1) selection, (2) organization, and (3) integration. By considering such principles of human cognition and perception as critical design elements, this book takes a learner-centered rather than technocentric approach to design. The chapters that follow in Part I address the theories underlying visual design for learning and suggest processes to assist novices with visual design.

## PRACTICE

For additional activities and examples of student work, visit the Companion Website for this book at *http://www.coe.unco.edu/LindaLohr*.

### Resource Activities

The Resources section contains basic technical information that will help you create instructional graphics with greater confidence and ease. Learn what is in the Resources section by finding the answers to the following questions:

1. *Why do the fonts (computer text) you use in a document sometimes appear differently on other people's computer screens?* _____

2. *What type of graphics program (Paint or Draw) allows you to create shapes and images that are outlined shapes, outlined and filled shapes, or filled shapes only?* _____

3. *Name a book on the Books and Training page that sounds interesting to you.* _____

4. *If you want to learn Illustrator but do not have it, you have the option to download an open source software program similar to Illustrator for free. How would you find the download site? What name would you use in a Web search engine?* _____

5. *What type of graphics program (Paint or Draw) allows you to scale images without losing any resolution or clarity?* _____

6. *What type of graphics program (Paint or Draw) would allow you to change the color of a digitized image using a bucket tool?* _____

### Web Activity

The Web Activity is likely to be the easiest project and best for beginners. The assignment posted here asks you to make simple instructions for hot chocolate. Examples of student work that are "good" and "needs improvement" are shown here. More examples are found on the Companion Website for this book at *http://www.coe.unco.edu/ LindaLohr*.

Here are two solutions to the Chapter 2 Web Activity, which asks students to create instructions for making a cup of hot chocolate. Students were given the cup and spoon clip art.

## (a) A good solution and justification

**Audience:** A middle-school student who knows how to read and how to heat milk.

I decided to make the hot chocolate instructions free from distracting clip art so used only the spoon and cup clip art. The text states that technocentric design focuses on the technology, not the message (p. 31). Computer technology makes it easy to use lots of pictures and fun type, but I thought those would be too distracting. I used numbers because I think they help make the content easier to understand. This makes the image an organizational visual because it shows the sequence of steps (p. 31).

**User test:** I showed this to middle-school students. They thought the image worked but suggested two changes: (1) show the words "1 Tablespoon" on the spoon to make sure that the right measuring spoon is used. (2) The little squares are confusing. Are they supposed to be the chocolate?

**Changes:** I will put the word "Tablespoon" on the spoon handle. I will put the word "cocoa" over the chocolate.

Chapter 2 Web Activity

## (b) A solution and justification needing improvement

**Audience:** Anyone who can read.

The computer made this project really fun because I could copy the cup and resize it, as I did for the border. I think the cup border does a good job of making the image more attractive and also helps the focus. I also used stars to give the cup more pizzazz and again to improve the focus. The milk carton needed to be identified so I labeled it and made it look like it was pouring milk. Because three tablespoons are needed, I showed three spoons.

**User test:** I showed this to my mom and she really liked it.

**Changes:** Since my mom liked it I didn't change anything.

# Challenge Activity

The Challenge Activity asks you to be a little more brave. One of these activities asks you to create visual instructions to help students learn the days of the month. Use your knuckles activity on page 42 shows a "good" and a "needs improvement" sample of student work.

# Independent Activity

The Independent Activity asks you to pick your own project. You are encouraged to try this one because the information will be more meaningful and thus is likely to be more motivating. Here are some ideas: Make a map showing directions to your house or apartment; create a poster for your office door; design a job aid to help your great aunt use her new cell phone; create a poster teaching rules for surfing the Web (how to use quotes, AND, and OR).

# Justification Activity

Write a justification paper for the activity you select (see the justification in the Web Activity on page 40). Describe the following:

- *Your users and the assumptions you make about them (such as age, reading level, and assumed skills).*
- *Why you think your solution will work; include at least two ideas from the book, including page numbers and your interpretation of the passage used.*
- *What you learned from a "user-test" (have someone look at the image and verbalize their thoughts while looking at the image).*
- *The changes you will make based on user comments (or create a revised image).*

# Discussion Questions

Describe a recent encounter with technocentrism in enough detail that others will understand why your particular example could be considered technocentric. Discuss as a group the similarity and differences in the experiences and examples described.

# K–12 Student Activities

Use this chapter's Web Activity and Challenge Activity to generate similar ideas for use with K–12 students. Some student examples are shown here on page 43.

1. *Ask students to create simple visuals such as the following:*
   *Hallway passes*
   *"Quiet" signs for the library*
   *Forms for the principal or office managers*
   *School posters*
2. *Create a copyright poem or story to emphasize the meaning of copyright.*
3. *Encourage students to work from an inspiration!*

Here are two solutions to the Chapter 2 Challenge Activity, which asks students to create instructions to help people remember the number of days in each month.

## A good solution

Student justification not provided (see the Web Activity on page 40 for an example of how to write a justification)

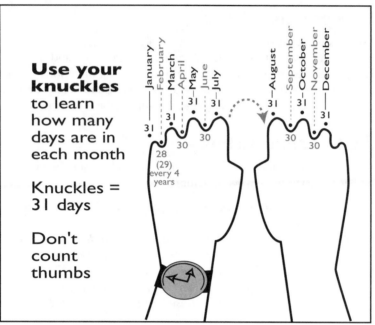

If students can remember that their knuckles represent 31 days, they can easily recall the rest. This is likely to work since hands are familiar to students. Because hands serve as a "cue" for months and their dates, they are more likely to trigger memory than if the cue is absent when memory needs to be recalled.

## A solution needing improvement

Student justification not provided (see the Web Activity on page 40 for an example of how to write a justification)

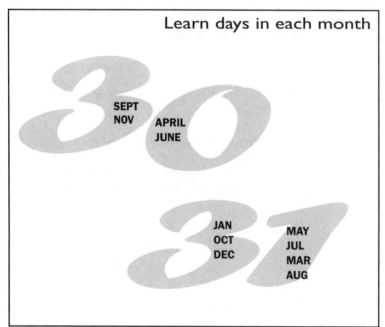

This is likely to be harder to remember than the example above. Students have to remember that September, November, April, and June = 30 days. The other months are 31. February is the odd month with 28 days, 29 every 4 years. This probably requires more mental effort to remember than the example above. The abbreviated month names are also harder to recognize.

Chapter 2 Challenge Activity

Below are two activities to try with K–12 students.

## K–12 Example
### (a) Create school posters

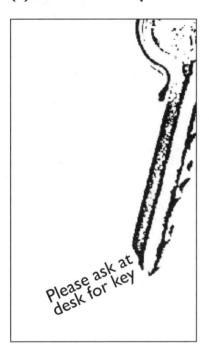

Chapter 2 K–12 Student Activities

### (b) Write a copyright poem

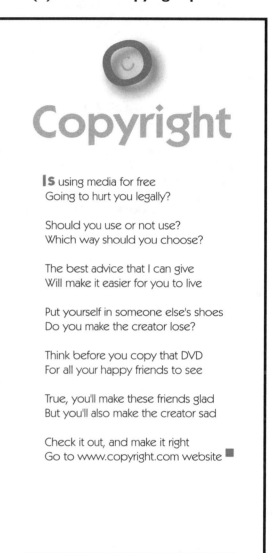

# REFERENCES

Braden, R.A. (1996). Visual literacy. In D. H. Jonassen (Ed.), *Handbook of research for educational communications and technology* (pp. 491–520). New York: Simon & Schuster.

Galitz, W. O. (1997). *The essential guide to user interface design: An introduction to GUI design principles and techniques*. New York: Wiley Computer Publishing.

Hartley, J. (1985). *Designing instructional text.* New York: Nichols.

Hughes, J., Mcavinia, A., & King, T. (2004). Visual literacy: What is it and do we need it to use learning technologies effectively? *ReCALL, 16(1),* 85–102.

Lohr, L. (1999). Development of a procedure for GUI design. In R. E. Griffin, W. J. Gibbs, & B. Wiegmann (Eds.), *Visual literacy in an information age: Selected readings from the Annual Conference of the International Visual Literacy Association,* Athens, GA, October 21–24, 225–233.

Lowe, R. (2000). Visual literacy and learning in science. *ERIC Digest.* ERIC Clearinghouse for Science Mathematics and Environmental Education, Columbus OH ED463945

Mullet, K., & Sano, D. (1995). *Designing visual interfaces: Communication oriented techniques*. Englewood Cliffs, NJ: Prentice Hall PTR.

Nielsen, J. (1993). *Usability engineering*. Boston: Academic Press.

Reilly, S. S., & Roach, J. W. (1986). Designing human/computer interfaces: A comparison of human factors and graphic arts principles. *Educational Technology, 26(1),* 38–40.

Schwier, R.A., & Misanchuk, E. R. (1993). *Interactive multimedia instruction*. Englewood Cliffs, NJ: Educational Technology.

Tufte, E. R. (1997). *Visual explanations: Images and quantities, evidence and narrative.* Cheshire, CT: Graphic Press.

# CHAPTER 3

## *Visuals and Learning*

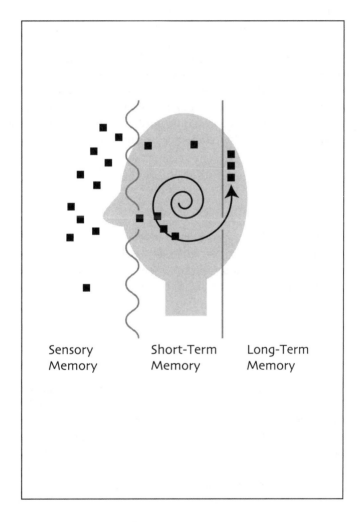

Sensory Memory   Short-Term Memory   Long-Term Memory

Perceiving and thinking are indivisibly intertwined.

*Rudolf Arnheim*

## NOTES ABOUT THE OPENING VISUAL

The words and simple shapes on the chapter-opening visual represent information processing theory. There are three reasons why words and simple shapes are being used here.

Words are used because they can be the easiest and clearest graphic tool available. Too much effort is spent trying to come up with clever metaphors and analogies when simple words do the job and are often easier to understand. Words also make an image appealing by providing texture, a topic you will learn about in Chapter 11, which focuses on color, depth, and space. Texture (an example of depth) refers to visual characteristics that give an object a tactile quality. As stated in Chapter 1, visual literacy is both an art and a science and texture is one of those artistic elements that you will explore in chapter activities throughout this book.

The second reason is that words and simple shapes are easily accessible. Most of us do not have a lot of time and find that simple shapes are an easy way to communicate. For the opening visual I used an oval, a rectangle, and a freeform tool that allows me to draw freehand shapes (such as the nose).

The third reason for using words and simple shapes as graphics is because the letters (shapes) that make up the words themselves are copyright free, an important consideration that will save you time. You can use fonts (a typeface like Arial and Times New Roman) and simple shapes without seeking permission from the typeface designer, something that could take time and cause considerable delay in your development. You will learn more about type and shape in Chapters 9 and 10.

## FOCUS QUESTIONS

- What are three types of cognitive load?
- Why should designers focus on working memory?
- What is the relationship between selection, organization, and integration and figure-ground, hierarchy, and closure?

## KEY TERMS

**CHUNKING** A design strategy that groups information into smaller units.

**COGNITIVE LOAD THEORY** A theory that describes mental energy and its reaction to various loads, including intrinsic, extrinsic, and germane load.

**EXTRANEOUS LOAD** The type of cognitive load that is based on content irrelevant to the important message.

**FIGURE-GROUND PRINCIPLE** A perception principle that describes the mind's tendency to see edges and in doing so to separate figure elements from ground elements.

**GERMANE LOAD** The type of cognitive load that is based on content that has meaning for the learner.

**GESTALT THEORY** A perception principle that describes how the whole is greater than the sum of its parts.

**HEURISTICS** Rules of thumb that do not apply in all situations.

**HIERARCHY** The layering of information into categories that have an order of importance.

**INFORMATION OVERLOAD** When the quantity of information exceeds a person's capacity to process that information.

**INFORMATION PROCESSING THEORY** A theoretical perspective that focuses on the specific ways in which individuals mentally think about and "process" the information they receive.

**INTEGRATION** The simultaneous presentation of text and images to facilitate cognition.

**INTRINSIC LOAD** The type of cognitive load that is based on content complexity.

**LONG-TERM MEMORY** The component of memory that holds knowledge and skills for a relatively long period of time.

**MULTIMEDIA** More than one media, such as pictures and words.

**MULTIMEDIA PRINCIPLE** The theory that people learn better from words and pictures than from words alone.

**ORGANIZATION**  A cognitive process in which learners find connections (e.g., forming categories, identifying hierarchical relationships) among the various pieces of information they need to learn.

**PICTURE SUPERIORITY EFFECT**  The belief that pictures are superior to words in terms of recall.

**REHEARSAL**  A cognitive process in which information is repeated over and over as a possible way of learning and remembering it.

**SCAFFOLDING**  A successive construction of knowledge whereby instructional support is presented for new content when support for learned content is gradually withdrawn.

**SCHEMA**  The representation of knowledge in memory.

**SELECTION**  Attending to particular information for cognitive processing.

**SENSORY MEMORY**  A component of memory that holds incoming information in an unanalyzed form for a brief period of time (probably less than 1 second for visual input and 2 or 3 seconds for auditory input).

**SHORT-TERM MEMORY**  A term used to describe both sensory and working memory.

**VERBAL MEMORY**  Information that is encoded verbally, or in words.

**VISUAL MEMORY**  Information that is encoded pictorially, or in pictures.

**WORKING MEMORY**  A component of memory that holds and processes a limited amount of information; also known as short-term memory. The duration of information stored in working memory is believed to be approximately 5 to 20 seconds.

**ZONE OF PROXIMAL DEVELOPMENT**  The point where a learner moves from understanding to a higher level of expertise and requires instructional assistance or support.

## INTRODUCTION

Before getting started with this chapter, you should be aware of the possibility that the information presented here will be complex and hard to absorb in a meaningful way. To guide your reading, I have divided the chapter into three sections. The first section starts with this introduction and continues to the next section on theory. The last section discusses strategies for putting all of this information together.

You determine how much time to take between each section. It might be a good idea to wait until you think you have a solid grasp of what you have read before moving on. Rereading the section should help increase your understanding.

## SECTION 1: SYLVIA AND THE NEED FOR RESEARCH SUPPORT

### Sylvia's Multimedia Experience

Sylvia, the instructional designer described in Chapter 1, is in charge of a multimedia-training project on customer service skills. She develops a project plan for her design team, which includes a storyboard with several interactive sections using video clip segments of customer calls, then delegates some of the work to her development team.

After a few days, one of Sylvia's designers shows her a prototype of the project along with a storyboard (see **Figure 3–1**). Sylvia is dismayed; too much information is presented on the computer screen, none of it synchronized. The animated graphics do not make sense and are out of sync with the narration. To make matters worse, her manager and her design team think the prototype is great. Sylvia guesses they are just responding to flashy animation and graphics rather than the instructional value of the material.

Fortunately, Sylvia knows of research on visual learning that addresses her concerns. She summarizes recent books (Clark & Lyons, 2004; Mayer, 2001) as well as a number of research studies (Mayer, 1993; Mayer, Steinhoff, Bower, & Mars, 1995; Moreno & Mayer, 2000). This literature explains the importance of well-designed visuals in the learning process. The research she cites shows that learning improves when text and graphics are presented in close proximity in a synchronized, simultaneous manner rather than in the disjointed style of the prototype (Mayer, 2001). She also shares Reiber's (1989; 1994) guidelines to use animation when the content warrants it, particularly when motion or direction are parts of the learning task. When asked to look at the prototype more directly from a learning and research perspective, Sylvia is able to convince the design team that the prototype could be improved.

Sylvia objects to the animated text on the storyboard, Screen 5. When the words "Is the representative clear?" move from the top right to the bottom left of the screen the audio track is also saying "Did I hear you say the bolt is missing?" Sylvia thinks this nonsynchronization is confusing.

The same problem takes place in Screen 6. The text and the audio are not synchronized, the scrolling bulleted list and the animated question mark (which does not look like a question mark) are distracting.

**FIGURE 3-1**   Sylvia's storyboards

Many people react to **multimedia**—the use of more than one media—the way Sylvia's team did. They assume that because instruction is visual or flashy and because many media are used, then the instruction is effective. As we discussed in Chapter 1, pictures are not always worth a thousand words.

Because visuals are expensive to produce, it is important to understand the theories and research related to visual learning. As Sylvia's situation demonstrates, it often helps to have a rationale for design decisions and critiques.

## Multimedia Research Principles

We are like Sylvia's team in that most of us think images and multimedia do contribute to learning. Significant research shows that many individuals have a better memory for images than for words (Anglin, Towers, & Levie, 1996; Braden, 1996.) The **picture superiority effect** refers to the improved recall that people have for images over words after 30 seconds of exposure to images and words (Lidwell, Holden, & Butler, 2003). The combination of words and visuals appears to help learning especially when the pictures are related to the textual information (Levie & Lentz, 1982; Levin, Anglin, & Carnay, 1987).

Mayer (2001) introduced a number of multimedia principles, two of which relate directly to Sylvia's concerns. The temporal contiguity principle suggests that words and pictures be presented simultaneously. If words reference a picture, but that picture is several pages away from the words, then it is difficult for the learner. Placing text in a different location than the image it references makes the learner spend cognitive resources to mentally group or connect the text and image.

The redundancy principle suggests that animations be accompanied by narration but not by narration and text. Using narration along with printed words that directly mimic the narration creates split attention. It is much more efficient for the learner to hear words and see a corresponding animation than to read words, hear the narration, and try to also "read" the narration at the same time.

Both of these principles address the need for design to compensate for the limitations of a learner's short-term memory. Although not related to Sylvia's example, Mayer's research supports a number of other design heuristics, including the following recommendations:

- If possible, use instructional pictures, because words and pictures are more effective than words alone (the multimedia principle).
- Reduce any extraneous information because nonessential media may create a split attention effect (the coherence principle).
- Use images to help learners that have a low prior knowledge or high spatial ability (the individual differences principle).

Mayer's multimedia principles are important for every designer of educational/instructional materials. The purpose of this book is to help you think about design in a way that makes sense of the heuristics.

# SECTION 2: THEORY

The overall purpose of this chapter is to explain how research in learning can be applied to the design of instructional materials. As such, general learning theory applies.

We will cover a number of learning theories, starting with cognitive load theory (CLT) and ending with Mayer's multimedia theory, **Figure 3–2**. At the top you see CLT, what we will consider our macro theory. Everything you see under CLT is related. Some of these are extensive theories in their own right and are covered in entire books. For our purposes, however, we will consider them within the context of CLT, and as such they take the position of being in a supportive role.

## An Overview

Starting with **information processing theory,** which focuses on basic memory structure, you then move to Pavio's (1965, 1990) dual coding theory, which introduces separate visual and auditory memories. You then learn about specific components of working memory introduced by Baddeley (2000). This takes you through a number of design principles on which this book is based—including Mayer's (2001) theory of multimedia, which you have just read about. Think of your progression through these theories this way.

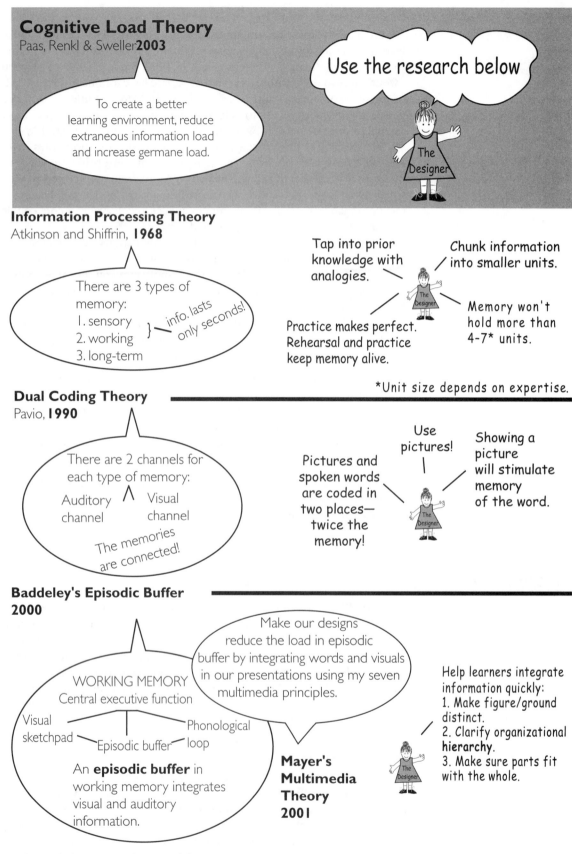

**FIGURE 3–2**   Memory theory and design tips

The overall goal of **cognitive load theory** is to make learning easier and to understand the importance of designing instructional visuals to match as closely as possible the learner's cognitive structure, or way of thinking. If you make a visual too easy or basic, you miss out on germane (meaningful) learning, because you do not add anything new to the way the learner thinks about instructional content. If you make a visual too complex, learners will not see enough of a connection between the image and what they already know, and you miss out on germane learning again. Cognitive load theory helps you understand the importance of presenting content in a way that fits with a learner's **schema**—his or her way of understanding that content.

Information processing theory describes the three parts of memory that you will be working with: (1) sensory, (2) working, and (3) long-term. It reinforces the importance of making that match between learners' current understanding and where you hope to move them (the zone of proximal development). Information processing theory stresses the importance of making that match or connection as quickly as possible usually through careful scaffolding of information.

Pavio's and Baddeley's theories explain different channels of memory within the three parts of memory introduced by information processing theory, and they give you increasingly specific advice on how to present verbal and pictorial content. You learn the importance of designing both visual and auditory content in ways that make the connection between them as strongly as possible, and as such strengthen memory because of two representations, rather than one, in memory.

Mayer's multimedia theory explains how to make that visual and auditory connection as strong as possible. Mayer promotes a number of principles to help you make design decisions.

Each of the theories, from the macro CLT to Mayer's prescriptive theory, helps you understand the larger context of images and their importance to learning. When you understand these theories and how they interact, you begin to think of design in a new way that does not rely on your memory of specific principles that are fairly easy to forget. Instead, you change the way you think and see, and it is this underlying understanding that helps you design.

## THEORY

## Cognitive Load Theory: Our Macro Design Theory

Cognitive load theory describes the mental energy needed to think about or process information. Attention to cognitive load is a critical concern for designers of instruction, particularly when a learning context and its content are complex. If the cognitive load for a student is too high, learning is not effective. Too much information, irrelevant information, complex information, and the like can all result in a high cognitive load. If the cognitive load is too low, learning is not efficient. Too little is covered to make a difference, or the mind does not engage in information in a way that allows learners to remember and use the information later when they need it.

As the term *load* would connote, information can be thought of as having a weight that places demands on memory. At any point in time, human memory holds only seconds of information before it is either passed on to a long-term storage area of the brain or simply lost. We will cover this topic next, in the information processing theory section of the chapter. For now, it is best to consider memory as a bottleneck in the flow of information within the brain. If we present information in a way that is compatible with the individual learner, those seconds may be used optimally. You can think of **chunking**—organizing content into units—as a type of presentation strategy useful when considering optimal load.

It might help to think of instructional design this way. On one end, you have the information that should be learned. On the other end, you have the learner's mind. As a designer, you are in the middle, trying to create an optimal presentation of the information. If you do your job well, the information will almost snap into place, and new information will make sense. You have essentially optimized the cognitive load. Skip ahead to Figure 3-9 to see a visual reinforcement of this information.

Designers use a number of strategies to help create that optimal presentation. Stories, analogies, presentation sequence, and more are all part of an instructional designers tool kit, and they are used to create an optimal load.

## Categories of Cognitive Load

The research on cognitive load describes three categories of load: (1) intrinsic load, (2) extraneous load, and (3) germane load (Paas, Renkl, & Sweller, 2003). Understanding each category assists in the identification of potential instructional strategies.

**Intrinsic Load**   **Intrinsic load** refers to the nature of the content and its level of complexity. Complexity can be defined in terms of element interactivity, or the extent that a learner must understand instructional content that overlaps and interacts with other instructional content. High content interactivity describes content that can be understood or studied only when an understanding of many different factors is taken into account. Low content interactivity describes content that is more easily understood in isolation, because it requires an understanding of fewer elements. For example, learning concepts would be more likely to involve high element interactivity than learning facts, which would involve low element interactivity.

**Extraneous Load**   **Extraneous load** can be thought of as the noise or superfluous elements of communication that act as barriers to learning due to the increased load they place on memory. For example, using a large number of fonts in a section of text does not add to the content, but rather adds to the extraneous load as the reader attempts to assign meaning to the various typographic changes.

**Germane Load**   **Germane load** can be thought of as those things that a designer can do to facilitate optimal learner load. For example, textual techniques that reinforce the content, such as chunking content, sequencing it, and providing analogies can help people understand new information more quickly.

## Summary of Cognitive Load Theory

Up to this point we have learned that an instructional designer's job is to reduce undesired information load and to increase germane load. This makes sense, and a number of instructional strategies support this advice—from sequencing and schema construction strategies to the use of analogies, visuals, and stories. The effectiveness of these strategies depends on the prior knowledge and experiences of the learner.

Cognitive load theory provides a clear direction for instructional designers by emphasizing the importance of optimizing load. Simply applying strategies that theoretically should work, is not enough. In order to design that information, we must consider how the memory will actually work with our designs. Presenting information for optimal load depends upon the structure of memory and how it is likely to process our design (or how we chunk content, as shown in **Figure 3–3**). Individual differences in previously constructed knowledge, attitudes, and skills makes chunk size different from one person to another. An analysis of that prior experience and knowledge is critical to success. Knowing how experiences and understanding are represented in memory, and how to address different levels of expertise, is perhaps the best way to proceed. Understanding information processing theory is a good way to start.

# Information Processing Theory

Information processing theory describes how information travels through memory (Atkinson & Shiffrin, 1968; Broadbent, 1984; Lockhart & Craik, 1990; Norman & Bobrow, 1975; Waugh & Norman, 1965). Atkinson and Shiffrin proposed a model of memory based on two types of memory: (1) short-term memory (including sensory and working memory)

When we chunk content, we are basically organizing the content into smaller units. How small do you go? Try to match your chunk size to what the learner already knows. You want to plant information in a way that helps the learner move to the next level of understanding.

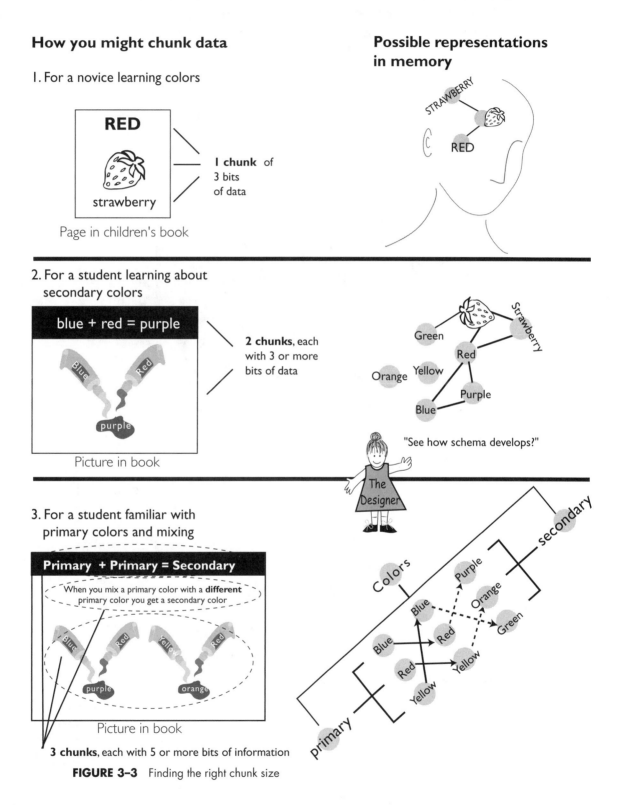

## How you might chunk data

## Possible representations in memory

1. For a novice learning colors

**RED**

strawberry

**1 chunk** of 3 bits of data

Page in children's book

STRAWBERRY

RED

2. For a student learning about secondary colors

blue + red = purple

Blue    Red

purple

**2 chunks**, each with 3 or more bits of data

Picture in book

Strawberry

Green    Red

Orange   Yellow

Purple

Blue

"See how schema develops?"

The Designer

3. For a student familiar with primary colors and mixing

**Primary  + Primary = Secondary**

When you mix a primary color with a **different** primary color you get a secondary color

Blue    Red    Yellow    Red

purple        orange

Picture in book

**3 chunks**, each with 5 or more bits of information

Colors

secondary

Blue    Purple

Red    Orange

Yellow    Green

primary

**FIGURE 3–3**   Finding the right chunk size

Learning is attributed to the successful transfer of important information from one type of memory to the next. Sensory memory transfers some information to short-term memory; short-term memory transfers some information to long-term memory. Notice in the diagram below how some of the information has not been transferred between sensory, working, and long-term memory. When information is not transferred, it is considered lost or forgotten.

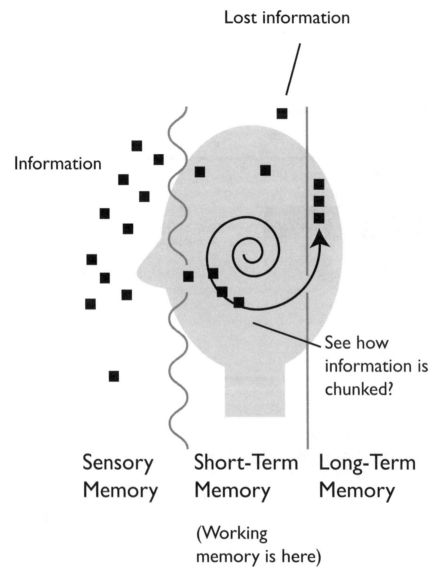

Lost information

Information

See how information is chunked?

Sensory
Memory

Short-Term
Memory

Long-Term
Memory

(Working
memory is here)

**FIGURE 3–4**  Information processing model

and (2) long-term memory. This dual-store model of memory is commonly referred to as in-formation processing theory (see **Figure 3–4**) and it explains how **short-term memory** is limited to seconds, which explains why humans have difficulty remembering things long enough to perform simple tasks, or long enough to understand (learn).

A component of short-term memory is **working memory,** a system that performs in an executive capacity by managing and manipulating information. Working memory is where we as designers must focus our efforts. We must structure information to "stay alive" in memory, long enough to make it to long-term memory.

**Long-term memory** is unlimited, capable of holding an infinite amount of data for an indefinitely long time. It is theorized that once information makes it to long-term memory, it stays there forever. This would be great if most people could find that information when they wanted it! The problem in retrieving information from long-term memory resides in how that information was stored—in other words, in how effectively and efficiently the learner stored the information. This is the part that designers can help with.

## Understanding Short-Term Memory

It is important to understand sensory and working memory when we design support and instructional materials. A big problem with most training and educational contexts is the lack of attention to the perception and learning barriers created by the limitations of sensory and working memory. Again, sensory memory holds an unlimited amount of information, but just for a few seconds.

If you are not convinced, stop for a moment and think about everything that your sensory memory is taking in now. Try to hear sounds around you that you have been ignoring. You might hear a fan, the compressor in a refrigerator, the hum of a printer, the voices of neighbors, or any number of sounds. Because you have decided to pay attention to your environment, you are suddenly conscious of things you were unaware of just seconds before. Look back at this page now. Your sensory memory is taking in a lot of information on this page; it sees individual letters, words, paper, your hand, the edges of your book. Much of what you sense you ignore because your sensory memory has a filter that directs your attention only to certain things. For example, you do not really pay attention to individual letters within a word; instead you attend to the word.

**Sensory Memory**   Selection, or the process of attending to specific information and ignoring other information, is a key part of **sensory memory.** Fortunately as the exercise above just illustrated, your mind does filter out a lot of unnecessary information, freeing you up to focus on only the most relevant, satisfying, or interesting information.

**Working Memory**   The information in working memory may not stay there long because it is a part of short-term memory and does not have a large capacity. (Remember, it only holds information for seconds.)

Miller (1956) found that working memory holds anywhere from 5 to 9 units (7 plus or minus 2) of information. Cowan (2001) has presented research suggesting 4 units, and he suggests that as designers we may need to be even more concerned about finding ways to limit information overload.

Both Miller and Cowan use the term *unit* to describe information that is chunked together. What comprises a unit varies according to how much information can be chunked together and still have meaning. It becomes very important to help learners/performers work with units that make sense to them. In other words, we want to create appropriate chunk sizes. This is where we begin to address individual differences, which we have identified as critically important to assessing optimal cognitive load.

Novices typically need smaller information units (or chunks) than experts. Think of how a beginning reader first has to focus on small chunks (individual letters that make up simple words). Reading materials for young children usually consists of very small chunks of information. Each page has only one or two words.

Experts, however, are able to use page-sized chunks that are subdivided into sentence- and paragraph-level chunks to help them process the content. If you comprehend this passage, it is because your mind chunks letters into words so quickly that you do not notice the words as much as their meaning in the context of a sentence. This is also true of sentences, which experts tend to process in terms of the meaning of sentences rather than individual words. Greater expertise requires greater chunk sizes.

## *Understanding Long-Term Memory*

Moving information from working memory to long-term memory is usually the biggest challenge. Rehearsal increases the chance that information remains in memory, but the best bet for getting information into long-term memory is by making the rehearsed information meaningful to the learner.

Analogies and metaphors have long been used to do just that. By comparing new information to something the learner already knows, the learner is more likely to understand the new information. Whenever you can make connections to things within your audience's experience, they are more likely to remember it.

## *Your Job as a Designer*

Your job as a designer is to design information with the three types of memory (sensory, short-term, and long-term) in mind. In order to do this, you must help learners notice the important information (selection in sensory memory); think about and work with information that has been selected (rehearsal in working memory); and associate new information with their previous experiences to make learning meaningful (working with long-term memory).

Two strategies help you do this. The first asks you to provide learner cues for each type of memory. The second asks learners to generate their own cues. Learner-generated understanding is considered by many to be the optimal strategy, because the learners' construction of meaning essentially requires them to increase germane load.

To demonstrate the two strategies (learner generated and designer generated), we will illustrate how content can be presented both ways with some specific examples.

### You Provide the Cues for Short-Term and Long-Term Memory

*Task:* Remember the number 120719411945.

*Strategy:* The strategy assumes that the learner knows the dates of Pearl Harbor and World War II (12/07/1941–1945) and that their schema (memory) looks like **Figure 3–5.**

- To begin, you might simply show the learner the familiar dates:

    12/07 1941–1945 (Pearl Harbor and World War II)

- Directly under that you show the learner the unfamiliar numbers:

    120719411945

*Strategy Rationale* Schema is similar to the flowchart in Figure 3–5, which represents memory for certain World War II facts. The boxes represent information nodes in memory, and the lines represent the connections or relationships between the different nodes. These connections provide access to and from different parts of memory, and as such are traceable. It is this traceable characteristic that allows for recall or the ability to remember.

Consider each node of the schema as a potential trigger that could lead memory down the required path for recall. The more you help learners think about new information and hook it into their schemas, the more entry points they will have for retrieval purposes (recall) later. Words like "War," "WWII," "Pearl Harbor," once read or heard, could activate and trigger those nodes in memory as well as their path toward a specific date. Access to the date should help them recall the numbers.

### You Ask Learners to Generate the Cues for Short-Term and Long-Term Memory

*Task:* Remember the number 120719411945.

Memory is set up as a network with many paths leading to the same information. The more ways you think of information, the more "triggers" you'll have to recall that information later when you need it. Here the words "Wars," "WWII," and "Pearl Harbor" could all provide the appropriate path to the number 120719411945.

# Schema

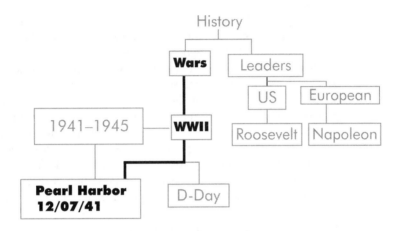

Any part of the schema that leads to the desired information can be considered a trigger. Here the WWII path was a trigger. Remembering the dates 1941–1945 could also have been a trigger.

**FIGURE 3–5**   The schematic structure of memory

***Strategy:***   To help learners move those numbers into long-term memory, you ask them to create personal meaning to the numbers. You could share the example "I lifted 120 pounds when I lived in area code 719. Now that I'm 41, I lift 194 pounds 5 times a week."

Aside from making this information meaningful, notice too how numbers have been chunked into five units (120, 719, 41, 194, 5). By grouping the 12-digit number into chunks, you have made it easier to remember.

***Other Types of Content:***   Although the examples here are limited to factual information, information processing theory works with higher levels of learning like concepts, principles, procedures, and attitudes. Remember that learners are limited information processors, especially when it comes to short-term memory. They are not computers that can store vast amounts of information. You thus need to facilitate the learner's (1) attention to the most important information, and (2) ability to process information in a way that is meaningful. Many strategies to help you do this are presented in the pages that follow.

## Summary of Information Processing Theory

Information processing theory suggests that instructional designers consider three types of memory when they create learning materials. The first two types of memory, sensory and working memory, have an extremely limited capacity for information. The third type of memory, long-term memory, is theoretically infinite in its capacity to store information.

Given the limitations of short-term memory, access to and from long-term memory becomes the designer's greatest challenge. By creating organized and meaningful instruction, designers are able to reduce the load placed on working memory.

## Pavio's Dual Coding Theory

Pavio (1990) proposes that rather than just one sensory memory, one short-term memory, and long-term memory, as might be implied by information processing theory, there are two separate memory systems for different types of information: one for verbal information and one for imaginal. (There are other types of memory as well, including memory of how things feel, taste, and smell.)

Pavio broadly defines **verbal memory** as information related to language systems (auditory and speech), and **visual memory** as information related to pictures, sounds, tastes, and nonverbal thoughts (imagination).

Verbal and imaginal memories are very different. Verbal information moves from sensory memory to verbal processors. Visual information moves from sensory memory to visual processors. Information in either processor can activate the information in the other processor. In other words, images can activate verbal information and vice versa.

The power of images can be explained by the ability of concrete words (words that can easily be visualized, such as people, places, objects, tastes, touch, and smell) to stimulate nonverbal memory (images). Words that are abstract (emotions, ideas) are less likely to stimulate nonverbal memory and are less likely to be remembered, because the chance of learning is much greater when two memories, rather than one, are involved (see **Figure 3–6**).

### Summary of Dual Coding Theory

Humans have different short-term, working, and long-term memory systems for verbal and imaginal information. Because verbal and imaginal systems are connected, learners have greater access to content when they need to remember it later. Showing an image of a word will likely

Concrete words such as "cat" will stimulate visual representations. Abstract words such as "distinct" are less likely to generate an image. Because some verbal representations are stored only in verbal memory, the theory argues for a "picture superiority effect" (Levie, 1987). Pavio's (1965) research, showing better memory for concrete rather than abstract word pairs, backs up this theory.

The word "cat," when spoken or read, will trigger an image of a cat.

**FIGURE 3–6**   The visual power of concrete words

activate both memories, or twice the recall, due to these extended memory traces. Designers can strengthen memory by using imaginal (pictures) and verbal (sounds) instruction.

## Baddeley's Episodic Buffer Theory

Baddeley's (2000) research identifies new capacities within working memory (see **Figure 3–7**). Working memory is composed of a central executive function that is involved in focusing attention, switching attention, and dividing attention. The executive function monitors a visual sketchpad (visual and spatial memory), a phonological loop (auditory memory),

The long-term memory characteristic of the episodic buffer allows new representations to form as well as memory to be retrieved within working memory. This mixing may explain some aspects of problem solving and creativity via the unique juxtaposition of information in the episodic buffer.

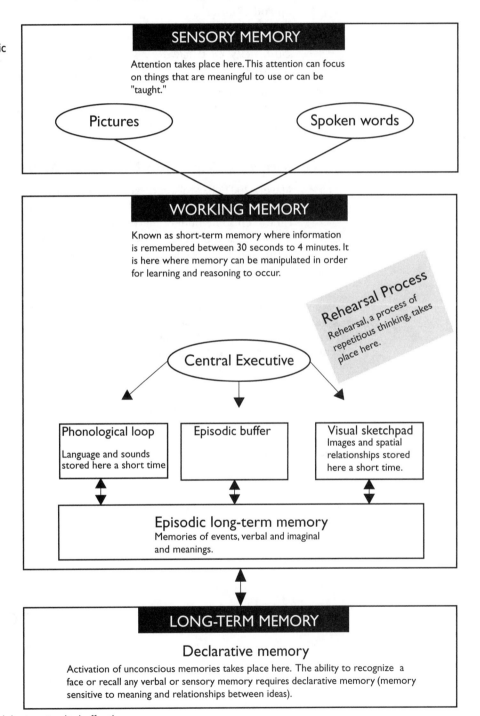

**FIGURE 3–7**   Baddeley's episodic buffer theory

and an episodic buffer. The episodic buffer is the area that interfaces with the visual sketch-pad and the phonological loop and binds or integrates this information.

It is of particular interest to designers that this buffer is not considered part of long-term memory. We may be able to design information for the buffer by integrating information so that the buffer spends less time doing so. One positive consequence of this is that cognitive energy can be spent for learning. Working memory can retrieve information from the episodic buffer creating relatively new representations while at the same time retrieving information from long-term memory. This may explain some aspects of problem solving and creativity via the unique juxtaposition of information in the episodic buffer.

## Summary of Baddeley's Episodic Buffer

Baddeley contributes to memory theory by promoting a deeper understanding of working memory. The relationship between the visual sketchpad, phonological loop, and episodic memory may some day provide insights into how designers can tap into an extended working memory.

## Mayer's Cognitive Theory of Multimedia

Mayer (2001) has to some extent identified strategies for extending memory using his multimedia design principles and he is interested in how visual and verbal memories interact (in the episodic buffer). Mayer's research suggests that visuals and words are most likely to facilitate learning when they are designed to help people select, organize, and integrate information in ways that are meaningful (see **Figure 3–8**.)

Processes of selection, organization, and integration are closely connected with information processing theory. When you help the learner select, organize, and integrate, you are helping information move from sensory to working to long-term memory. As you read this information, you may think it similar to what you've already read. It is! Where information processing theory focuses on the structure of memory, Mayer's theory focuses on facilitating memory.

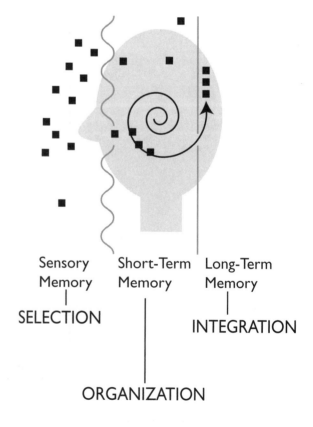

Sensory Memory    Short-Term Memory    Long-Term Memory

SELECTION        INTEGRATION

ORGANIZATION

**FIGURE 3–8**   Selecting, organizing, and integrating

## Selection

As we've just seen, the information processing model describes information moving through sensory memory into working memory in the early stages of learning. During this process, the mind acts as a filter. This selective perception is the mind's way of reducing **information overload.** What is interesting is that your mind is also selecting things of which you are unaware, and this has tremendous implications for design and the power that designers can exert.

**Unconscious Selection**  Though we tend to think of perception as highly influenced by past experiences, a certain degree of perception is predetermined. Research in artificial intelligence gives us insight into this type of predetermined perception. By programming computers to "see," scientists have studied how people "see" and have learned that features and boundaries of an image are detected first. The mind then progressively fills the image until it represents "generalized cones" that are recognized (Marr, 1982).

If you were driving and saw in the far distance an octagonal outline at an intersection, what would you do? You'd probably prepare to stop without thinking about it much. Your mind would fill in the outline to be an octagonal shape, which by past association means "stop." Suppose that shape were filled with four letters such as "SLOW." What do you think you would do if you saw this from a distance? Many people would stop anyway, not even noticing the word "SLOW."

Winn (1993) explains the implications of Marr's research:

> Perceptual organization strongly predisposes people to make one interpretation of what is seen rather than another. The net result is that, in spite of top-down influences that operate once attention is brought to bear, preattentive organization is a powerful determinant of what is actually understood in the perceived message. These include, but are not limited to, the relative placement, size, and dominance of objects in the visual field, and the way the eye is "led" over the image by various techniques of composition. The message designer cannot assume that people will see what they are told they are looking at, and cannot easily compensate for a poorly designed message with instructions on how it is to be perceived. (p. 56)

This is an important statement because it encapsulates the importance of understanding theory in order to create effective visual instruction (see **Figure 3–9**). Basically Winn is saying learners are more likely to think about your visuals the way you want them to if you organize or present information in a way that the mind is predisposed to grasp.

Consider this example. We know from Marr's research that the mind seeks out the edges of an image; the mind is programmed or predisposed to do that. Although there may be many objects in any given image, the mind will seek out those objects that have the most distinct edges. As the mind fills in these edges, it begins to understand what the image is. This activity describes the **figure-ground principle,** which states that during perception the mind seeks to identify and separate figure and ground elements in an image. As a designer, you can manipulate an image so the edges are easier to detect since you know the mind is likely to be looking for edges. For example, if you want a particular shape to show up, you just make sure that the edges of the shape are distinct from everything else.

**Conscious Selection**  We've been exploring what takes place unconsciously and in sensory memory. Selection also takes place consciously. Meaningful learning begins when pictures and words move from sensory memory to working memory. As you have already learned, working memory is limited in capacity, able to process 7 plus or minus 2 units of information (Miller, 1956), or 10 to 20 seconds of information. During that time, the learner must select relevant information from visuals to store in visual memory, and relevant information from words and sentences to store in verbal memory. Mayer refers to this process as building mental representations. Learners essentially reconstruct what they see into their own representations. They do so in two ways—verbal and visual—in a process Mayer calls *organization.*

Learners are more likely to think about your visuals the way you want them to if you organize or present information in a way that the mind is predisposed to grasp.

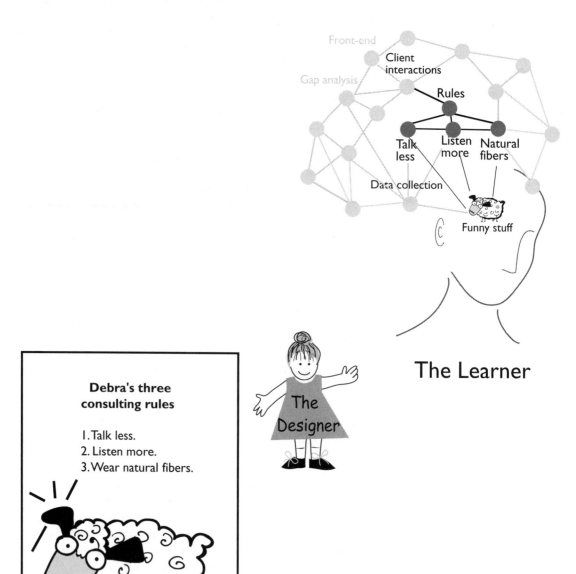

The Learner

The Designer

The Lesson

**FIGURE 3–9**  An important sentence

## Organization

**Organization** takes place when information in verbal and visual memory is categorized and ordered by the learner to make more sense. Organization involves building representational connections in the information. For example, learners may try to structure the information sequentially, hierarchically, or according to past experiences. They might arrange things in a list or imagine parts of an image in a certain format. This process is termed **rehearsal,** a cognitive activity that is important because the more learners think about or organize the information, the more likely they will remember it.

## Integration

**Integration** takes place when related visual and verbal representations are held in working memory at the same time. You might show the learner a diagram of a person perspiring on the top floor of a building; in the same diagram you would depict a person on the bottom floor wearing a sweater. The words "warm air rises" would be displayed close to the two floors. This integration of visual and verbal information makes it more likely to transfer into long-term memory because it is more meaningful to the learner. Unlike short-term memory, long-term memory has an unlimited capacity for information.

Mayer's (2001) research supports this interpretation of integration. In a series of experiments, he found that a verbal description of information during animation was better for learning than was a verbal description following the animation. In another experiment he found that the combination of animation and narration was better than the combination of animation and on-screen text. He suggests that narration was processed in a separate memory channel and did not overload visual memory the way the on-screen text did. In another experiment music was added to an audio narration and compared to narration alone. The results of this experiment found that the addition of music impeded learning, suggesting that the auditory portion of verbal memory was overloaded.

## Summary of Mayer's Research

Mayer suggests that the design of instructional information should be based on the cognitive processes of selection, organization, and integration. These three processes map well to the structure of short-term, working, and long-term memory. However, integration is in part a function of working memory—that is, the episodic buffer. When visual and verbal messages are integrated using the six principles that Mayer identifies, working memory is extended.

As designers, our job is to try to create an optimal structure that is similar enough to activate long-term memory but designed to integrate new information into long-term memory and thus strengthen understanding.

# SECTION 3: HOW DO YOU PUT IT ALL TOGETHER?

It is time to put everything together and use this information to create instructional visuals. You have learned that people have both visual and verbal memory systems. You have also learned that the combination of text and visuals is a powerful learning strategy. Several theories explain why either visuals alone or the combination of visuals with verbal information make for effective learning strategies.

Stemming from the research related to these theories is Mayer's suggestion that visuals be designed so that they support cognitive processes of selection, organization, and integration. By using principles of design, you can, to some extent, help learners do these things more easily. By making some things stand out more than others, you help them select information. By showing hierarchies and creating pathways through information, you help them organize. By repeating elements and themes (such as simultaneously showing pictures and related words), you help them see the big picture and integrate information.

It is important to realize that a visual does not always warrant attention to all three of these processes. This is an important distinction to make because many visuals are used as support and performance tools, not as learning tools. When you are creating a support or performance tool, you do not need to design information for long-term learning. You just need to make it easy to understand and access. Understanding does rely some on integrative processes because recall of memory is an important element in selection or recognition. Design, however, does not always need to focus as much on creating schemas as on accessing them.

For some situations, you may want to focus design on selection, perhaps when you just want someone to notice something. This may be true for decorative, representative, or organizational visuals.

For other situations, you may choose to focus design on selection and organization because you want to present organized information to a person, as is the case for organizational visuals such as telephone numbers and recipes. In these situations the visuals support a performance task but do not teach anything so that it can be recalled later.

There may be yet other situations where you want to go all the way and design for selection, organization, and integration because you want the person to learn the information and be able to recall it later. Representation, transformation, and interpretation visuals may require attention to all three of these processes. For example, Mayer's work focused on all three processes because he was interested in designing interpretive visuals.

## Three Design Principles

You will use three cognitively based design principles to create better visuals: (1) selection, (2) organization, and (3) integration. These principles are directly related to the three parts of learner memory: short-term memory, working memory, and long-term memory.

### Selection: Helping the Learner Notice Important Information

The selection principle is similar to the gestalt figure-ground principle, which addresses the mind's tendency to organize information into figure and ground categories. The goal of each designer of instruction is to make figure-ground distinctions as clear as possible in order to reduce the amount of information that memory needs to process. When designers make the most important information really noticeable, they make it easier for the learner to pay attention to the relevant content.

The figure-ground principle is widely recognized in many professional disciplines. For example, the information design literature focuses on emphasizing content; to information designers, information is king. Edward Tufte (1990), an information designer, stresses the importance of emphasizing the instructional information (the data) over the data container. Tufte describes a $1 + 1 = 3$ phenomenon—the visual effect that takes place when two elements are combined and produce a third ($1 + 1 = 3$) element, which may or may not communicate. **Figure 3–10** shows an example of a figure-ground problem. Notice how all of the arrows and fills make the message hard to read. In the bottom text box, you see one element (text) plus another element (a gradient fill) that equals a third image (a combination of text and fill that is almost illegible).

The graphic design literature focuses on creating optimal contrast. According to Mullet and Sano (1995), "contrast is essential for differentiating elements from one another—for allowing form to emerge from the void" (p. 52).

The message design literature describes perceptual processes that are at work in the learner's mind separating important from nonimportant information. Fleming and Levie (1978) suggest that "distinguishing between figure and ground is one of the most basic perceptual processes. Early perceptual processes are active in figure/ground organization" (p. 59).

There are many visual distractions on this page. We have a case of "boxitis" going on. The gradient fill in the last box makes the text too hard to read. This is a 1 + 1 = 3 example because you have words (one element), graphics (another element), and convoluted message (the third element that is not really a good combination of the words and the graphics on the page).

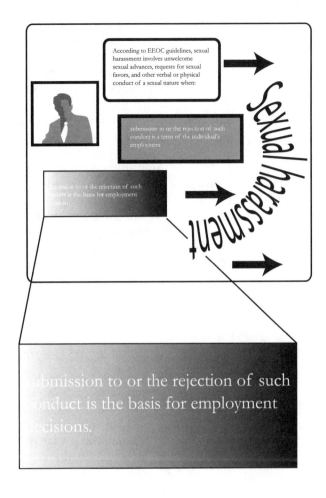

**FIGURE 3-10**  The 1 + 1 = 3 Principle

The common theme of these different sources of advice is to make important information stand out. Loud backgrounds, competing typography, and clashing colors detract from the important information rather than enhancing it.

In the chapters that follow you will learn how to use tools such as depth, color, and type, and actions such as contrast to create optimal figure-ground compositions. You will also learn more about figure-ground principles in Chapter 5.

### Organization: Helping the Learner Structure Information

The organization principle is based on the mind's tendency to process and remember "chunks" of information that in turn are arranged hierarchically. To facilitate this process, it is the designer's job to shape information structures to show subordinate, superordinate, and coordinate relationships, including those related to time and direction. The use of outlines, arrows, and lists are common ways to establish hierarchy in a visual.

As with selection, organization is considered a critical design principle by other disciplines. The information design literature speaks of layering and stratifying information. Tufte (1990) provides many examples of data enhanced by effective layering and separation, terms he uses to describe the relative organization of information:

> Among the most powerful devices for reducing noise and enriching the content of displays is the technique of layering and separation, visually stratifying various aspects of data. (p. 53)

The graphic design literature addresses the creation of pathways through content. According to Mullet and Sano (1995), "organization and visual structure provide the user with the visual pathways needed to experience a product in a systematic way" (p. 89). The same authors note, "Organization begins with classification, which involves grouping related elements and establishing a hierarchy of importance for elements and groups" (p. 93).

The message design literature stresses the importance of chunking information, suggesting that the designer may influence perception by organizing information in a way that essentially saves the mind from doing the same work. Fleming and Levie (1978) suggest that "early processing organizes perceptual units into groups, and groups into other groups in a hierarchical manner" (p. 63). When a designer chunks the information up front, that theoretically leaves less mental work for the learner.

This literature encourages the organization of information into hierarchical levels. Learner disorientation is prevented with clear hierarchical structures, implying subordinate, coordinate, and superordinate relationships and a sense of direction. Aligning coordinate information, using different intensities of color to designate importance, and using space to chunk content into distinct categories are all methods used to achieve a greater sense of hierarchy. In the chapters that follow, you will learn to use these tools and others to improve organization, and you will learn more about hierarchy in Chapter 6.

## Integration: Helping the Learner See the Big Picture

The integration principle is based on the **gestalt theory** that the whole is greater than the sum of its parts. A person's prior experience allows him or her to see that whole, even if they are only presented with a part.

The integraton principle deals with how information comes together in a meaningful way. As with selection and organization, its importance is found throughout the design literature. Information design literature stresses the importance of content and detail presented in a manner that is easy to understand. Tufte (1990) espouses the importance of detail, culminating into a larger coherent structure. Integration can be thought of as the ability to see how parts create a whole. As such it is similar to the gestalt closure principle—the belief that you can easily see the whole, even if you are only given part. Too often people have interpreted this to mean that detail should thus be avoided, the "can't see the forest for the trees" problem. Good design, however, uses detail in a way that richly provides access to the whole. Simplicity is not the lack of detail but an organization of detail that makes the information meaningful and clear.

Graphic design literature stresses the importance of experiencing a product systematically in order to make the information easy to understand. Experiences with a systematic design allow a person to use a product more easily. Graphic artists promote the use of grid structures for organizing information and providing the big picture (seeing the whole by integrating the parts). Grid structures facilitate the development of consistent designs that users can experience in a harmonious way.

Instructional message designers stress the importance of grouping items into meaningful units. Greater understanding is achieved when parts, or elements of a message, are attended to as a whole, not selectively.

Mayer (2001) provides the most specific integration advice with his six principles of multimedia design. These principles focus on the importance of presenting information in ways that require less cognitive effort from the learner—in other words, that reduce cognitive load.

All four sources of advice—information design, graphic arts, instructional message design, and instructional research—address the importance of creating a clearly understandable whole or big picture from individual parts. Disorientation may be prevented when the learner has a firm sense of the relatedness of the overall environment and the lay of the land. Repeating graphic elements and colors, using shapes to connect items, and placing items close together or far apart are all methods of integrating content to create a whole.

In the chapters ahead you will learn to use tools such as type, shape, color, depth, and space and actions such as alignment repetition, and proximity to create better integration. You will learn more about integration in Chapter 7.

## SUMMARY

In the previous chapters you learned that although the instructional world increasingly relies on visual communication, in many cases visuals do not help learning or performance. In all likelihood the belief that a picture is worth a thousand words has been interpreted too loosely, giving people the false confidence that any picture will do. A strong need exists for instruction related to creating visuals for learning and performance.

This chapter helps you build expertise in instructional visual design by sharing and explaining the research on learning from visuals. Significant research shows that learning is positively influenced by visuals. Cognitive load theory provides the overarching principles from which to understand information processing theory, Pavio's dual-coding theory, Baddeley's episodic buffer theory, and Mayer's multimedia theory.

Overall, the suggestions presented here are designed to reduce cognitive load. By focusing design of instruction and instructional visuals on the three types of memory—sensory, short-term, and long-term—you should be able to support the cognitive functions of selection, organization, and integration. These three principles will help you design images that are perceived the way you want them to be perceived. The chapter that follows moves from theory to application by describing the analyze, create, and evaluate (ACE) design process.

## PRACTICE

For additional activities and examples of student work, visit the Companion Website for this book at *http://www.coe.unco.edu/LindaLohr.*

### Resource Activities

Use Table R–4 in the Resources section to help you complete the challenge activity.

### Web Activity

> The Web Activity asks you to identify an example of a document or image with high intrinsic load (complex content). Describe why the design does either a good job or a poor job of the intrinsic load. Provide specific examples.

### Challenge Activity

The Challenge Activity asks you to create a drawing, table, or diagram to help you reduce the intrinsic load of this chapter. For example, you might create a drawing that shows the relationship of information processing theory and Baddeley's episodic buffer. Focus your efforts on developing meaningful chunks.

### Independent Activity

The Independent Activity asks you to pick your own project. You are encouraged to try this one because the information will be more meaningful and thus is likely to be more motivating. For example, create a job aid (a one-page "cheat" sheet) for content that needs to be more understandable. Describe how you decrease the cognitive load and increase the germane load. One student recreated a website evaluation rubric and then wrote a justification paper on it, as shown below.

## Website Evaluation Rubric                    *Your name:*

| Website 1 | Not Proficient `1-2` ☐ | Partially Proficient `3` ☐ | Proficient `4` ☐ | Advanced `5` ☐ |
|---|---|---|---|---|
| | Does not answer questions. | Answers questions insufficiently and some left blank. | Answers all questions, some more complete than others. | Answers all questions sufficiently. |

| Website 2 | Not Proficient `1-2` ☐ | Partially Proficient `3` ☐ | Proficient `4` ☐ | Advanced `5` ☐ |
|---|---|---|---|---|
| | Does not answer questions. | Answers questions insufficiently and some left blank. | Answers all questions, some more complete than others. | Answers all questions sufficiently. |

## *Justification*

I chose to recreate the rubrics used for a website evaluation activity. The original rubric was simply described in the syllabus as follows:

```
Evaluation of 3 website rubrics
For each website you are evaluated on a 5-point scale. Answering all
questions listed on the guide sheet will result in a score of 5 points.
Answering some questions, but not all, will result in one point less. Poorly
answering questions and not answering some questions results in one less
point. Anything worse than that will result in a score of 2 or less.
```

The easiest way to describe my revision of this rubric is to point out that the original rubric is one chunk with lots of content. The revised rubric is clearly separated into two immediately recognized chunks. I think the separation of content decreases the intrinsic load (complexity of content, page 52) by creating manageable chunks. As stated in the textbook, it is important for the teacher to prompt the student with meaningful learning cues. I created check boxes to clearly separate different score values and their meaning. In the end I had chunks within chunks. For example, there is a website chunk, a score-by-score chunk, and within each score category the check boxes are chunked with point values. Overall, these things should increase germane load (page 52) by improving the perceived relationship between the elements in a chunk.

Chapter 3 Independent Activity

## Justification Activity

Write a justification paper for the activity you select. Describe the following:

- *Your users and the assumptions you make about them (such as age, reading level, and assumed skills).*
- *Why you think your solution will work; include at least two ideas from the book, including page numbers and your interpretation of the passage used.*
- *What you learned from a "user-test" (have someone look at the image and verbalize their thoughts while looking at the image).*
- *The changes you will make based on user comments (or create a revised image).*

## Discussion Questions

Try any of the following to generate discussion:

1. The underlying assumption of this chapter is that visuals support learning because they facilitate memory processes. Software companies have made extensive use of this belief by designing icons based on the user's previous experience. Provide an example and describe why the icon should work.

2. Describe an image that was especially effective in helping you organize information in a way you could remember. For example, the food pyramid uses the triangular shape to convey that foods at the base of the pyramid (the wide part) should be eaten in greater quantity than the foods at the top (the narrow part) of the pyramid. Describe how characteristics of the image that you select worked for you.

3. Share a chunking strategy that you have used to remember information. For example FBIUSACIA might be hard to remember until you chunk it into meaningful units: FBI USA CIA. The FBI is part of the USA intelligence world, as is the CIA.

## K–12 Student Activities

Use this book's Web and Challenge Activities to generate similar ideas for use with K–12 students. For example, try the Challenge Activity on page 67 by asking students to create a job aid (like a cheat sheet) to help them study for an upcoming test. Ask the students to focus on chunking the information into memorable units.

## REFERENCES

Anglin, G. J., Towers, R. L., & Levie, W. H. (1996). Visual message design and learning: The role of static and dynamic illustrations. In D. H. Jonassen (Ed.), *Handbook of research for educational communications and technology* (pp. 755–794). New York: Simon & Schuster.

Arnheim, R. (1969). *Visual thinking.* London: Faber & Faber.

Atkinson, R. L., & Shiffrin, R. M. (1968). Human memory: A proposed system and its control processes. In K. W. Spence, & J. T. Spence (Eds.), *The psychology of learning and motivation: Advances in research and theory* (Vol. 2, pp. 89–195). New York: Academic Press.

Baddeley, A. D. (2000). The episodic buffer: A new component in working memory? *Trends in Cognitive Sciences, 4(1),* 417–423.

Braden, R. A. (1996). Visual literacy. In D. H. Jonassen (Ed.), *Handbook of research for educational communications and technology* (pp. 491–520). New York: Simon & Schuster.

Broadbent, D. E. (1984). The Maltese cross: A new simplistic model for memory. *Behavioral and Brain Sciences, 7,* 55–94.

Clark, R. C., & Lyons, C. (2004). *Graphics for Learning: Proven guidelines for planning, designing, and evaluating visuals in training materials.* San Francisco: Wiley.

Cowan, N. (2001). The magical number 4 in short-term memory: A reconsideration of mental storage capacity. *Behavioral and Brain Sciences, 24,* 1.

Egan, K. (1986). *Teaching as story telling: An alternative approach to teaching and curriculum in elementary school.* Chicago: University of Chicago Press.

Fleming, M., & Levie, W. H. (1978). *Instructional message design.* Englewood Cliffs, NJ: Educational Technology.

Levie, W. H., & Lentz, R. (1982). Effects of text illustrations: A review of the research. *Educational Communications and Technology Journal, 30(4),* 195–232.

Levin, J. R. (1981). On the functions of pictures in prose. In F. J. Pirozzolo & M. C. Wittrock (Eds.), *Neuropsychological and cognitive processes in reading* (pp. 203–228). San Diego: Academic Press.

Levin, J. R., Anglin, G. J., & Carney, R. N. (1987). On empirically validating functions of pictures in prose. In H. A. Houghton, & D. A. Willows (Eds.), *The psychology of illustration* (pp. 51–86). New York: Springer-Verlag.

Lidwell, W., Holden, K., & Butler, J. (2003). *Universal principles of design.* Gloucester, MA: Rockport Publishers.

Lockhart, R. S., & Craik, F. I. M. (1990). Levels of processing: A retrospective commentary on a framework for memory research. *Canadian Journal of Psychology, 44,* 87–112.

Marr, D. (1982). *Vision: A computational investigation into the human representation and processing of visual information.* San Francisco: Freeman.

Mayer, R. E. (1993). Illustrations that instruct. In R. Glaser (Ed.), *Advances in instructional psychology* (Vol. 5, pp. 253–284). Hillsdale, NJ: Erlbaum.

Mayer, R. E. (2001). *Multimedia learning.* Cambridge, England: Cambridge University Press.

Mayer, R. E., Steinhoff, K., Bower, G., & Mars, R. (1995). A generative theory of textbook design: Using annotated illustrations to foster meaningful learning of science text. *Educational Technology Research and Development, 43,* 31–43.

Miller, G. A. (1956). The magic number seven, plus or minus two: Some limits on our capacity for processing information. *Psychological Review, 63,* 81–97.

Moreno, R., & Mayer, R. (2000). A learner-centered approach to multimedia explanations: Deriving instructional design principles from cognitive theory. Retrieved from http://imej.wfu/articles/2000/2/muex.asp

Mullet, K., & Sano, D. (1995). *Designing visual interfaces: Communication-oriented techniques.* Englewood Cliffs, NJ: Sunsoft Press.

Norman, D. A., & Bobrow, D. G. (1975). On data-limited and resource-limited processes. *Cognitive Psychology, 7,* 44–64.

Ormrod, J. E. (1995). *Human learning.* Upper Saddle River, NJ: Merrill/Prentice Hall.

Ormrod, J. E. (2000). *Educational Psychology: Developing Learners.* Upper Saddle River, NJ: Merrill/Prentice Hall.

Paas, F., Renkl, A., & Sweller, J. (2003). Cognitive load theory and instructional design: Recent developments. *Educational Psychologist, 38(1),* 1–4

Pavio, A. (1965). Abstractness, imagery, and meaningfulness in paired-associate learning. *Journal of Verbal Learning and Verbal Behavior, 4,* 32–38.

Pavio, A. (1990). *Mental representations: A dual coding approach* (2nd ed.). New York: Oxford University Press.

Reiber, L. P. (1989). A review of animation research in computer-based instruction. *Proceedings of selected research papers presented at the annual meeting of the Association for Educational Communications and Technology,* Dallas, TX (ERIC Document Reproduction Service No. 308–832).

Reiber, L. P. (1994). *Computers, graphics, and learning.* Dubuque, IA: Brown & Benchmark.

Smith, P. L., & Ragan, T. J. (2004). *Instructional Design* (2nd ed.). Upper Saddle River, NJ: Merrill/Prentice Hall.

Tufte, E. R. (1990). *Envisioning information.* Cheshire, CT: Graphics Press.

Vygotsky, L. S. (1978). *Mind and society: The development of higher mental processes.* Cambridge, MA: Harvard University Press.

Waugh, N. C., & Norman, D. A. (1965). Primary memory. *Psychological Review, 72,* 89–104.

Winn, W. (1993). Perception principles. In M. Fleming & W. H. Levie (Eds.), *Instructional message design: Principles from the behavioral and cognitive sciences* (pp. 55–126). Englewood Cliffs, NJ: Educational Technology Publications.

# CHAPTER 4

## ACE It with Principles, Actions, and Tools

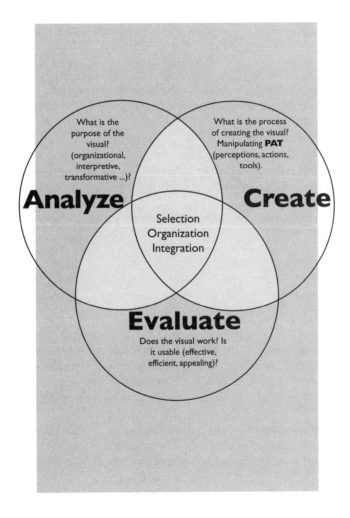

Design is inherently a messy process. It's ironic that the end result is about creating order.

*Tom Mecklen*

## NOTES ABOUT THE OPENING VISUAL

The opening visual is a Venn diagram of the analyze, create, and evaluate (ACE) design model that you will learn about in this chapter. The model uses circles to represent the cyclical (ongoing and repetitive) and overlapping process of creating instructional visuals. The diagram communicates an abstract process, the intersection of *analyze*, *create*, and *evaluate*. Notice how the intersection becomes a separate space. This is effective because analyzing, creating, and evaluating tend to happen at the same time, and the Venn diagram captures that phenomenon by showing this intersection as something distinct. Shading is used to visually separate the overlap. The background rectangle represents the additional context of the design process.

## FOCUS QUESTIONS

- What is the ACE process, and how does it work?
- How does a designer move from analysis to concrete form, from the invisible to the visible?
- What is the PAT model?
- What does CARP stand for?
- What is the relationship between PAT, CARP, and ACE?
- Why are the concepts of contrast, alignment, repetition, and proximity considered actions?
- Do you use all four actions in every visual?

## KEY TERMS

**ACE (ANALYZE, CREATE, EVALUATE) MODEL**   A model that explains how to create instructional visuals.

**ACTIONS**   What you do with tools; actions include contrast (as in contrasting colors), alignment of type and visuals, repetition, and proximity.

**ADDIE (ANALYZE, DESIGN, DEVELOP, IMPLEMENT, EVALUATE) MODEL**   A generic instructional design model.

**ALIGNMENT**   Lining elements up along an edge or imaginary path.

**APPEAL**   A measure of user satisfaction and confidence toward an instructional product, as well as the degree of confidence and relevance perceived by a user.

**CONTRAST**   Making elements different, such as making the shape or color distinct.

**EFFECTIVENESS**   A measure of instructional and educational quality.

**EFFICIENCY**   A measure of how easy an instructional and educational product is to access and use.

**INSTRUCTIONAL MESSAGE DESIGN**   A plan for the physical form of instructional communication.

**PRINCIPLES**   The rules explaining how the mind processes information using selection, organization, or integration subprocesses.

**PROXIMITY**   The placement of elements close together or far apart.

**REPETITION**   The reuse of elements or the use of similar elements.

**SYNECTICS**   A set of strategies used to enhance creativity through analogy and metaphor.

**TOOLS**   The basic elements of design, including type, shape, color, depth, and space.

**USABILITY TESTING**   Asking a small group (approximately 5) of representative users to evaluate the effectiveness, efficiency, and appeal of your instructional product.

# INTRODUCTION

Antonio (a teacher) and Latisha (a community college instructor) find themselves creating many instructional visuals, but they have no idea of how they are "supposed" to be doing them. Typically they "just do it." They don't even think about what they are doing. Sylvia (the instructional designer) and Zack (the graphic artist) both have training in design and, to some extent, have learned about the creative process. When it comes to creating instructional visuals, though, neither of them has thought much about a separate design process to facilitate learning. For Zack, creating an instructional visual is the same as creating any other type of visual. For Sylvia, the step where analysis takes on a concrete form has always seemed a little vague. She analyzes instructional needs and—poof!—they take on a concrete form. The step between analysis and actual development has always seemed a little like magic. She is not really sure how she does it and has a hard time explaining the step to others.

Antonio, Latisha, Zack, and Sylvia all have the same questions:

- How do I get started?
- How do I know that the visual works the way I want it to work?
- How do I get comfortable with design if I do not have artistic skills?

This chapter will answer these questions. Look again at the opening quote by Tom Mecklen. Why does he say that design is a messy process? What does that mean? Perhaps the easiest way to understand this quote is to think about making a cake from scratch for the first time. You may not know what order to measure out ingredients, you may be rushing all over the kitchen finding different measuring and mixing tools, and the floors and counters may become a sticky mess. When the cake is finally in the oven baking, you can stop and take a bird's eye view of the kitchen. You will see pans, bowls, mixing spoons, and utensils of every sort piled into the kitchen sink. The room looks like a storm passed through. In the end though, a cake is produced. The making of that cake was a messy process, but in the end something was created. This analogy works only to a point because a cake usually comes with a recipe, specific ingredients and instructions and a sequence to follow. With visual design, we never really have exact rules. What we do have is **heuristics**, which are rules of thumb that do not apply to every situation. This chapter provides you with heuristics to guide you through the messy process.

We have quite a bit to cover here because the process is complex. **Figure 4–1** shows the chapter topics covered. (Test yourself: what type of visual is Figure 4-1?) Remember Levin's classification scheme for instructional visuals (decorative, informative, representational, transformative, and organizational). The answer is at the bottom of Figure 4-1.

# GETTING STARTED WITH ACE

We use the **analyze, create, and evaluate (ACE) model** to explain the design process. The three cyclical components of the ACE model—analyze, create, and evaluate—together do a good job of explaining the design process for an instructional visual, but they do not really describe where you start or how you get started, often the toughest part of all. The best example I like to provide for getting started comes from *Finding Forrester,* a movie about a famous (but fictitious) author (Forrester) who befriends a young writer to teach him how to write. When a typewriter is placed in front of the young writer, he freezes. "I need to think" he says. Forrester says something along these lines, "Don't think—write. If you can't think of anything to write, copy something already written. Type that, and keep typing until the words become your own. You save thinking for when you edit, and that is when you really need to think." Along the way, you should find yourself somewhere within the ACE process.

The ACE process involves many other sub-processes. The outline below will help you navigate the chapter

Use these icons to keep track of where you are in the process.

## A.  Analyze

    1. Identify instructional function.
    2. Identify content classification.
    3. Consider artistic  or heuristic approach.

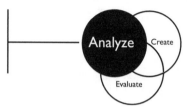

## B.  Create

    1. Generate the visual idea.
    2. Work with Principles, Actions, and Tools (PAT).

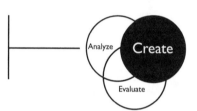

## C. Evaluate

    1. Assess effectiveness.
    2. Assess efficiency.
    3. Assess appeal.

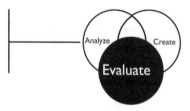

## D. The Context

    1. Instructional design models
    2. ADDIE

## E. Practice

    1. Computer skills
    2. Taking risks

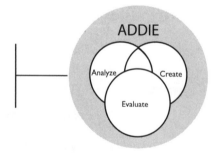

This is an organizational visual.

**FIGURE 4–1**  Chapter organization

## Analyze

During the analyze phase, you identify the purpose of the instructional visual. This analysis is greatly influenced by the purposes of the overall instructional or performance context, as identified in the ADDIE process. For example, based on what you have learned by conducting analysis for the overall instructional context, you will already have an idea of the audience, their task, and the overall instructional objective for the visual.

During the analyze phase, you consider selection, organization, and integration at a high level. You want to make the instructional objective clear (selection), provide well-organized and comprehensive information (organization), and create an environment or context where the overall message and organization are easy to understand (integration). You may want to consider the instructional functions of visuals identified by Levin (1981 and covered in Chapter 1):

- Decoration (to improve aesthetic appeal)
- Representation (to make information more concrete)
- Organization (to make information easier to understand logically)
- Interpretation (to explain difficult information)
- Transformation (to change your visual representation of something in order to help you remember it)

Clark and Lyons (2004) take the analysis phase a step further by introducing a content classification scheme for visuals. Most instructional design models include a step whereby instructional content is analyzed and categorized as procedures, facts, concepts, principles, and processes. Clark and Lyons (2004) prescribe specific categories of visuals to each classification. When illustrating procedures, use transformational visuals. When illustrating facts, use representational and organizational visuals. When illustrating principles, use interpretive visuals. When illustrating processes, use transformative visuals. No advice is given for conceptual visuals.

Although Clark and Lyons (2004) content classification approach can be used for instructional design analysis as well as information mapping purposes, I do not use or recommend it for visual design for several reasons. The problem I have with the content classification approach stems from liking it in theory but not finding it helpful in practice. For example, if you were creating visual directions to your house or apartment, you would probably think of creating a map. Would you start out by analyzing "map"? Is a map a fact, or is it a concept, maybe a principle, or is it a process? You might decide to give up there. However, if you really wanted to give it a chance, you might equate a map with a process. According to Clark and Lyons, a process involves use of a transformative image. Would it help to know this? Would you remember what a transformative image is, and if not would you take the time to look it up? Probably not.

The analysis approach of the book is to start by thinking about how your friend is going to interpret your map. You will ask questions such as the following:

1. What parts of the map do I want to emphasize in order to help my friend identify the critical information?
2. What is the best way to organize the details?
3. How do I make the map relevant and familiar in order to make it easy for my friend to follow?

These three questions directly relate to the following chapters:

1. Chapter 5, Selection
   (What do you want the learner to focus on?)
2. Chapter 6, Organization
   (How do you organize the information?)
3. Chapter 7, Integration
   (How do you provide a context to make the information meaningful?)

## Create

During the create phase, you translate analysis into physical form, something that might be visual, auditory, or kinesthetic. You essentially take your goals and objectives and make them into something you can see. For example, use the three questions posed during the analysis phase of map-making above. For each question, create something concrete.

1. What parts of the map do I want to emphasize in order to help my friend identify the critical information? (Perhaps you will draw a big X on the map to locate your residence.)
2. What is the best way to organize the details? (You might create a North/South orientation arrow and create thick lines for major streets and thinner lines for less major streets.)
3. How do I make the map relevant? (Here you might create small icons of places your friend is familiar with, such as schools, churches, shopping centers.)

The create phase involves moving design from a conceptual form to a physical form. This book, with its emphasis on perception, actions, and tools, is all about the create phase. Of all the phases, the create phase is the most complex, encompassing many details (**Figure 4–2**). Two overall tasks describe the create phase: (1) generating the visual idea, and (2) working with the PAT model.

### Generating the Visual Idea

Everyone faces the daunting blank sheet of paper or the blank computer screen. You have knowledge of design, tools beyond the dreams of previous generations, and the opportunity to edit and revise easily. It is easier than ever to create, right? Maybe, maybe

---

The create phase is complex and includes the information in the outline below. Note that later chapters cover some of this information in greater detail.

Use this icon to keep track of the many parts of the create phase. This particular icon indicates content related to the repetition action of the create phase.

I. Generating the visual idea (this chapter)

2. Working with the PAT model

  A. Principles

    a. I  Selection (Chapter 5)
    a. 2 Organization (Chapter 6)
    a. 3 Integration (Chapter 7)

  B. Actions (Chapter 8)

    b. I Contrast
    b. 2 Alignment
    b. 3 Repetition
    b. 4 Proximity

  C. Tools

    c. I Type (Chapter 9)
    c. 2 Shape (Chapter 10)
    c. 3 Color, Depth Space (Chapter 11)

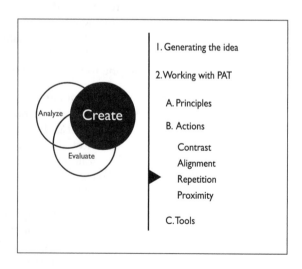

**FIGURE 4–2**   The create phase

not. Regardless of relative ease, the task is still challenging. Where do you come up with an idea for an interface that is visual, or a suitable theme for instruction, or a clever advance organizer?

In the example at the start of this chapter, Forrester tells his young student to "just start typing"—even if it means copying someone else's work and typing until the words became his own. Even Picasso is credited with saying, "Good artists copy. Great artists steal." The idea for using inspiration has been around for a long time. Most artists work from inspiration, and you should too. You'll see examples of good graphic art everywhere, from advertisements in magazines, on the Web, and on television to billboards on the highway and direct mail you receive at home. Keep in mind that you do need to be aware of copyright laws (see the Resources section at the end of the book). You want to use the work of others to get you started, but your final product should look very different. If what you end up with looks exactly like the source of inspiration, you may be violating copyright laws.

**Ideas for Developing a Visual Concept**   Landa (1998) suggests becoming thoroughly familiar with the concept you are trying to communicate. Here are some suggestions for getting visually unstuck:

- Think through your topic, to the point of looking words up in a dictionary in order to fully understand concepts.
- Make a comprehensive list of anything related to your content (ironically, most visuals start with words, sentences, even paragraphs).
- Look everywhere and at everything you can think of pertaining to your subject (paintings, book covers, websites, toys, posters).
- Give your subconscious a chance by putting the idea away and allowing your mind to work on the problem without pressure.
- Try lots of directions or approaches, including taking notes; analyzing great books, movies, and advertisements; fooling around; talking to people; and taking your list and brainstorming with it.

**Synectics**   Brainstorming can be exceptionally effective when employing a strategy that involves synectics—a set of strategies used to stimulate and enhance creative thought (Gordon, 1961), derived from the Greek roots *syn* (bring together) and *ectics* (diverse elements). The primary tool of synectics is the analogy and metaphor, which are used to help you "break set" and explore new ideas. You use this approach to enter the world of "soft thinking," where the illogical and emotional aspects of a topic are emphasized (vonOech, 1983). The synectics model is based on the belief that creativity can be developed in most people but is often stifled by the "hard thinking" norms of logic and rationality. By sparking new ideas and associations, they can sometimes solve problems. The route to this type of problem solving is through divergent, preferably generative, thinking, as Weaver and Prince (1990) suggest:

- Divergent thinkers consider relevant material, but often discard it and look for widely different, even seemingly irrelevant, connection-making material.
- Generative thinkers are open to divergent beginnings but eagerly search for connections that make things workable. (p. 380)

The synectic strategy encourages divergent and generative thinking through activities that encourage the development of metaphors. When brainstorming visual ideas, you might try one of two recommended metaphor-provoking exercises: (1) making the familiar strange (see **Figure 4–3**) and (2) making the strange familiar (see **Figure 4–4**). These examples get you to think of metaphors that give you some distance from the topic and allow you to think about it in a different way.

## K–12 Example      Science

This strategy involves visualizing familiar things in an unfamiliar way. The following steps (Joyce & Weil, 1986) take you through this process. This strategy is used to make the familiar (King Henry VIII) strange (similar to a virus).

What is compact, hard, logical, and dedicated to making copies of itself?

A virus is made of membranes, proteins, and one or more DNA or RNA strands. These strands allow the virus to replicate. A virus is "compact, hard, logical, totally selfish, and dedicated to making copies of itself." (Preston, 1994)

| | | |
|---|---|---|
| **1** | Think through the situation or concept and define it as it is now. Describe in as few words as possible what you are trying to teach. | "Viruses are keenly bent on multiplying themselves, and they are deadly." |
| **2** | Think up analogies that relate to the concept. Ask yourself what the idea/concept is similar to. You try here to think about the idea/concept in a new way; thus, it doesn't matter how close your comparison is to the real thing. | "A virus is like a war. A virus is like the plague. A virus is initially unobservable—it is lurking unseen, like a thief."<br><br>"A virus is a greedy Scrooge counting its copies as Scrooge counted his money, not happy with what he had, always wanting more, regardless of who he hurt." |
| **3** | Select one of your analogies and become it. Think about the idea/concept as if it were you. Try to empathize with the ideas being compared. | "If I were a greedy virus, I'd want gold copies of my power, like Scrooge's gold coins." |
| **4** | Create a compressed conflict. Think of a two-word description of the idea/concept where the words conflict with each other (friendly fire, beautifully repulsive). | "Golden destroyer, kingly sadist" |
| **5** | Create another direct analogy. Think of an analogy based on your compressed conflict. | "A golden destroyer is like a king who killed many, like King Henry who wanted sons (dedicated to his own duplication) and had his wives beheaded if they bore him daughters." |
| **6** | Reexamine the task. Think through your concept again and recycle as needed. | "The King Henry analogy works, so I will go with it." |

**FIGURE 4–3**   Making the familiar strange

## K–12 Example   Science

You often need to teach something that is a new idea, and to do this you need to think of something the learner already knows. The following steps ( Joyce & Weil, 1986) take you through this process. Bea Doyle used this strategy when she designed this graphic to teach the concept of choice.

*Source: Bea Doyle. Used with permission.*

| | | |
|---|---|---|
| **1** | **Review information.** <br> Explore the idea or concept. | "People must make choices throughout their lives, choices about who they become, who they marry, what career they pursue, what values they uphold, what houses they buy, how they invest their money, and more. Though it seems simple, choice isn't always so easy. Choosing requires nonbiased education about alternatives. |
| **2** | **Think up analogies that relate to the concept. Ask yourself what the idea/concept is similar to. You try here to think about the idea/concept in a new way; thus, it doesn't matter how close your comparison is to the real thing.** | "Choice is like a fork in the road." |
| **3** | Select one of your analogies and become it. Think about the idea/concept as if it were you. Try to empathize with the ideas being compared. | "I am standing in front of a fork in the road. I have two ways to go. The directions are marked." |
| **4** | **Compare similarity of analogies.** <br> Identify how the personalized analogies match the idea or concept. Identify specific points that are similar. | "There are alternative ways to go, directions to take, just like in real life." |
| **5** | **Explain the differences.** <br> Identify how the personalized analogies do not match the idea or concept. Identify specific points that are not similar. | "There are only a few clearly marked options available and the decisions are thus fairly informed. In real life there are many more options and they are more ambiguous." |
| **6** | **Reexamine the task.** <br> Think through your concept again and recycle as needed. | "I'm standing in front of a decision, there are several alternative decisions that can be made. The alternatives are all attractive. I like the opportunity of each and don't know which to take. I'm like a child in a toy store. I am like a child in a candy store. I like the candy analogy." |

**FIGURE 4–4**   *Making the strange familiar*

Hopefully you can use some of the suggestions in this section to come up with visual ideas. Once you have those ideas, you need to arrange them for whatever media you plan to use: paper, computer screen, electronic slides, perhaps even a flip chart.

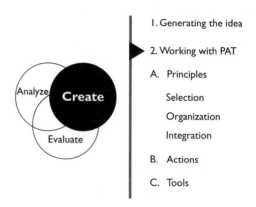

1. Generating the idea

2. Working with PAT

   A.   Principles

        Selection

        Organization

        Integration

   B.   Actions

   C.   Tools

## Working with PAT

The concepts of principles, actions, and tools form the PAT design framework. Creating visuals for learning and performance involves starting with the goal of facilitating learner perception through the use of actions and tools. You can jump ahead to Figure 4-8 to see the chapter-opening visuals for the rest of the chapters in this book. PAT components are addressed individually. Through abstract concepts, the rest of the book is dedicated to helping you understand principles, actions, and tools and how you can use them to improve your design.

**Principles**   **Principles,** the P of PAT, were discussed in Chapter 3, where we saw that there are three principles most critical for instructional designers: selection, organization, and integration. **Figure 4-5** shows two images with selection problems, as well as re-designed images to improve selection problems. The first set of images were created to help a third-grader make hot chocolate. Which image would you consider to have visual problems?

In case you have forgotten, rework of a design often involves the use of different wording (see Chapter 2). This is okay! The goal is to make something easier to understand, not to reuse all of the elements of the original design. **Figures 4-6** and **4-7** show problems with organization and integration.

The importance of keeping design simple is addressed in information, graphic, and message design literature for selection, organization, and integration principles of perception. In a nutshell, selection is the principle that supports the importance of visually separating important from less important information. Organization is the principle that endorses developing designs with clear directional cues. Integration is the principle that advocates the importance of helping learners perceive the "big picture" and the relationship of the parts to the whole.

**Actions**   **Actions,** the second component of the PAT model, deal with the changes or movements that have been made to instructional information or to the elements of information assembled to convey an idea. **Figure 4-8** (the opening visual of Chapter 8) emphasizes the four actions within the PAT framework: contrast, alignment, repetition, and proximity (CARP). Simply contrasting, aligning, repeating, and spacing elements close together or far

Which image do you think would cause selection problems?

**K–12 Example**    Practical Arts

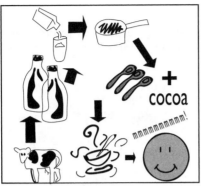

This one might cause selection problems. Too many graphics.

This one should work.

The text below is too hard to read. Although the clipart used has been softened to 30 percent black, it is not enough to make the text easily readable.

This image reads well and uses minimal graphics. The image would also look fine without graphics.

**Buying Guide For Blender Beverages**

Buy pineapples that have a raised diamond texture with a bright yellow color underneath the scales. Make sure you smell a sweet aroma. Avoid pineapples with brown and dried leaves.

Buy strawberries that smell sweet and are not moldy. Avoid berries with fine white hairs covering the skin near the top of the berry.

Buy bananas in any stage of ripeness. Bananas that have a slight fragrance and have small brown spots are best for blender beverages.

The Buying Guide For **Blender Beverages**

Buy **strawberries** that smell sweet and are not moldy. Avoid berries with fine white hairs covering the skin near the top of the berry.

Buy **pineapples** that have a raised diamond texture with a bright yellow color underneath the scales. Make sure you smell a sweet aroma. Avoid pineapples with brown and dried leaves.

Buy **bananas** in any stage of ripeness. Bananas that have a slight fragrance and have small brown spots are best for blender beverages.

**FIGURE 4–5**   Selection problems

## K–12 Example Science

The second most common visual problem I see is related to a lack of organization in information. Many designs are difficult to "read" with no organizational cues to show relationships or provide direction.

This image lacks organizational design, which makes it tougher for the reader to understand the relationship of the solar system to the galaxy and universe.

Showing the galaxy as a part of the universe and the solar system as part of the galaxy improves understanding.

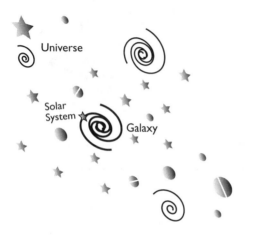

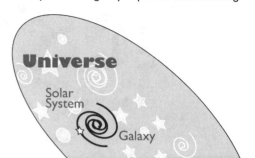

Organizational cues can be overused though. In this image you see too many boxes, arrows, and ornamental text. The designer intended you to read the image from the top left to the bottom right, but the subject, sexual harassment, is placed in a location most likely to be read last. Where do you start? Does your eye easily follow the path of the boxes and arrows, or does it tend to jump around? There are selection problems here as well. Who is the person in the top-left corner, and what relationship does he have to the boxes of text?

This image does a better job of unifying the image and providing organizational direction by reducing the use of unneeded graphics.

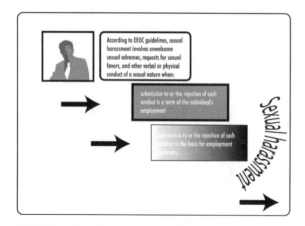

**FIGURE 4–6**   Organization problems

Here the images and tools (such as typography, color, or shape) do not match the instructional theme. For now think of integration simply as "creating a whole or harmony." Many visuals do not have any harmony or unified theme, making them difficult to understand.

This website did not look right. The palette images did not match the workshop materials. The typeface seemed pretty conservative for a creative topic.

The workshop materials looked like this.

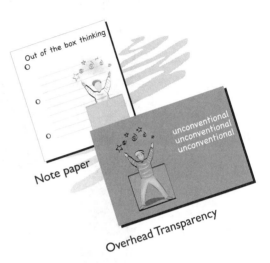

This image matched the workshop materials better. Notice how it uses the jack-in-the-box character as well as a typeface that is more informal.

**FIGURE 4–7**  Integration problems

Chapters 5 through 11 use the graphic below to show how all the elements of PAT (principles, actions, and tools) interact. This version of the graphic emphasizes the CARP (contrast, alignment, repetition, and proximity) tools. Try to guess where each action took place in the graphic.

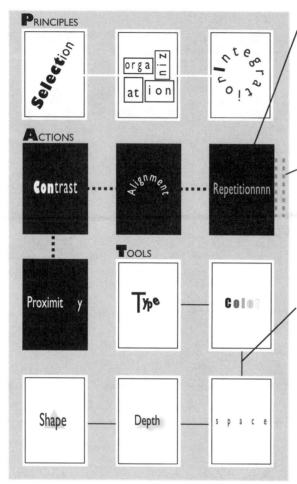

Each Action is on a highly **contrasting** black background, which clearly separates action icons from tools and perception icons. *Instructional benefit? The action icons grab your attention. You see where they fit within the bigger picture.*

The icons are **aligned** with the edges of the light gray background and with each other. *Instructional benefit? All icons appear to be connected by invisible lines.*

Each icon uses typography to express its meaning, *Instructional benefit? The* **repetition** *of typography increases the simplicity of the design and increases the sense of relationship between elements.*

Related icons are in close **proximity.** *Instructional benefit? The learner sees groupings, or a unified message.*

Although this image uses all four actions, you do not always need to use all four actions in an image. Sometimes you'll just use one or two, because that is all you need to improve your message.

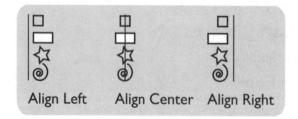

Most Draw, Paint, and Desktop publishing tools use alignment tools such as these. Be sure to visit the Companion Website for this book at http://www.coe.unco.edu/LindaLohr, to learn more about using these tools.

**FIGURE 4–8**   CARP (contrast, alignment, repetition, and proximity)

apart can be powerful methods of improving visuals for learning and performance). Chapter 8 will teach you more about CARP.

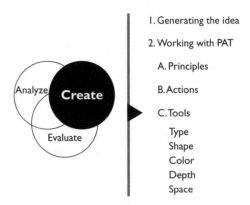

**Tools** Tools, the third and last element of the PAT model, are survival basics. They are the core elements of design, the things that people reach for first instinctively without even thinking. Color is intuitively used to highlight information, a circle is used to show a cyclical process, a line is used to connect thoughts or concepts. Color, simple shape, depth, space, and typography are all tools that are accessible and are frequently used by most trainers and educators.

Tools can be thought of as the basic design elements important for all designers. They can be manipulated using actions (contrast, alignment, repetition, and proximity), or they may influence perception directly. When designers become skilled, tools alone help achieve their design goals without even thinking of actions or principles—because they have cognitively automated the design process.

**Figure 4–9** shows how all five tools (type, shape, color, depth, and space) are used to create two images that teach rules of grammar. The bold property of type is used to focus attention. Several shapes (a cartoon character, ripped paper, and curved arrows) are used to provide context and meaning. Color is used to create contrast in the images. Depth is used in the shadow of the torn paper to provide both contrast and realism. Space is used to disconnect content and to group headings with content.

If you are still somewhat confused about the relationships between organizations, actions, and tools, some analogies might help. For example, think of something simple like hanging a picture on a living room wall. You usually grab a nail (a tool) and hammer it (an action) into either a stud or a molly to view and appreciate the picture (perception). Or think about an instruction that does not read well because the two main colors clash and interfere with legibility. You might choose a new background color (a tool) to create better contrast (an action) to influence selection distinctions (a principle of perception).

## K–12 Example Grammar, Writing, Composition

Type, shape, color, space, and depth are tools that help communicate instructional materials. Below are two examples of these tools used to teach grammar.

**Type** is used to emphasize instructional content. Bold words focus attention on important information.
**Shape** is used in the cartoon and ripped paper.
**Color** is black, white, and shades of gray.
**Space** is used to separate and emphasize different types of instructional content.
**Depth** is achieved using hat, cloak, and paper shading.

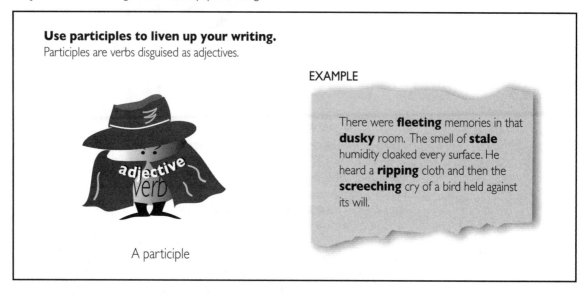

**Type** is used to emphasize instructional content. Bold words focus attention on important information.
**Shape** is used in the arrows and ripped paper (the example) to help the reader make connections.
**Color** is black, white, and shades of gray.
**Space** is used to separate and emphasize different types of instructional content.
**Depth** is achieved using paper shading and advancing arrow.

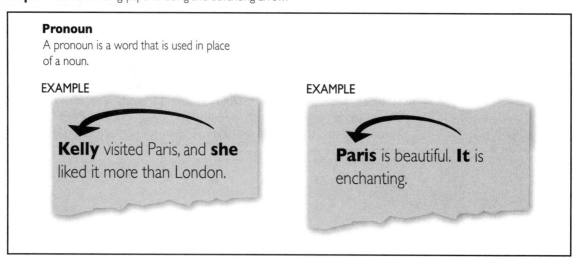

**FIGURE 4–9**   The tools

# Evaluate

During the evaluate phase, you carefully edit your work and learn what you need to change. Notice the assumption that you will be changing your visual? Rarely are visuals perfect the first time through. Because as a society we are not schooled in visual syntax, you can expect that people will interpret your visual in a variety of unexpected ways. You can count on it!

You can evaluate effectiveness of your instructional visuals (Lohr & Eikleberry, 2001) by asking three questions:

1. Do cues in the visual help perception of selection, organization, and integration?
2. Is the visual learner-friendly?
3. Have you weeded out the extraneous data?

## Teacher and Learner Cues

Start by looking over your visual with your learners in mind. Would the visual make sense to them? Do you need to add or take away elements to increase understanding? Your essential elements are type, shape, color, depth, and space and their arrangement. Do these elements form cues that do things a good teacher would do, such as help direct attention to important information (selection)? Do they let you know what to do next (organization)? Do they provide an orientation and overview (integration)? Likewise, does the visual anticipate the types of questions learners typically have? Does the visual help the learner answer questions like these: What am I supposed to do with this visual? Am I interpreting this in a way that helps me understand instructional content?

## Learner-Friendly Visuals

There are three usability criteria that will help you determine the learner-friendliness of your instructional visuals: (1) effectiveness, (2) efficiency, and (3) appeal. There are two approaches to evaluation, and both are important: (1) go through the visual yourself and self-edit its effectiveness; (2) after you are satisfied, test the visual with a target audience.

## Testing Out the Visual

Try answering the following set of questions as you assess your work:

# Effectiveness

- *Does the visual work instructionally?*
- *Does the visual cover the correct content?*
- *Does the visual cover an optimal amount of information (not too much or not too little content)?*

# Efficiency

- *Does the visual make important information (selection) easy to perceive?*
- *Is the visual organized (organization) so that information is easy to access?*
- *Does the visual help the learner relate (integrate) the information to the overall learning or performance context?*

# Appeal

- *Does the appearance of the visual motivate the learner to look at it?*
- *Is the information in the visual relevant and important to the learner in the learning context?*
- *Is the visual clear enough to convince learners that they will understand it?*

## Usability Testing with a Target Audience

Up until this point, the process of **usability testing** has been directed or structured around specific criteria of interest, and you have been the sole editor of your work. This final step—perhaps the most important in the entire process—is unstructured and involves other people. If you do this step correctly, you will get the chance to see problems or learner confusion you had not even envisioned, perhaps because you are too close to the design to see the problem, or you just do not have the unique perspective of the learner.

During this step, you ask the learner to use the visual in a realistic context, if possible. For example, if the visual is to accompany a set of instructions, you would want to provide the learner with the instructions and any materials that are mentioned in the instructions. If your situation is not readily observable, you can ask learners to share what they are thinking when they look at the visual. Ask them what the visual communicates. Try not to tell learners what you were hoping the visual would do, because you'll bias their perspective. You want to get information about how they really are seeing your visual so you can change it and make it better.

How many people should you use? Try to get up to five people. The more eyes on your visual, the better. Nielsen (1993) suggests a minimum of three to five users for Web usability testing. Although this falls short of sample size requirements learned in basic research methods and statistics courses, this rule of thumb is a real-world number that fits with the demands of most development environments, where time and money are always key drivers of design. Perhaps a better way is to consider three to five users per iteration. Try the design out on this group. If these users indicate a few problems, then redesign and retest with three to five new users. When you get to the point where you are not seeing any new comments, you can consider yourself ready to implement.

**Figure 4–10** provides a usability test worksheet that might be helpful.

---

## LEARNER-TEST

### A   SET UP YOUR TESTING ENVIRONMENT

*Setup*        learning environment (load software, assemble any other instructional artifacts)

*Set*          your chair at a 45 degree angle to users. *(This way the users won't feel like you are staring at them, but you will be able to see what they are doing and what they are looking at.)*

### B   FILL IN THIS INFORMATION

Name of interviewer:            Name of interviewee:            Time completed:
Date:                           Time started:

### C   START THE OBSERVATION

*Explain the Purpose*

For the next few minutes I'm going to ask you to describe what you think each image that I show you means. Your opinion is very important in helping me design visuals that make sense. You will not hurt my feelings when you say that you don't like or understand the image. We are evaluating the image, not evaluating you. When you have trouble understanding a visual or get mixed up, it means my design is the problem, not you.

If possible, I'd like you to think aloud while you are looking at this product. Tell me what you are thinking as you "read" the image. Tell me what you like and don't like. Tell me if what you see seems relevant to you. Does it make you curious? Does it bore you? Share all of these reactions with me.

### D   RECORD YOUR OBSERVATIONS

### E   CONCLUDE YOUR USABILITY TEST   This concludes your review. Thank you for your time.

---

**FIGURE 4–10**   Usability worksheet

## Weeding Out Extraneous Design Elements

Of all the advice in this book, the following suggestion is likely the most important: Take out visual elements that do not add anything. It is hard to make yourself do this, especially if you spent a long time creating something and find it is not needed. Your ability to remove unneeded elements makes you an effective designer. Peterson (1996) describes the design process as diamond-shaped. You begin with your idea and build it up to a certain point (using tools such as type, shape, color, depth, and space) where it makes sense. You then eliminate all but the most essential elements. You stop when you have removed any of the elements that do not add anything to your design. The process looks like the diamond shape shown in **Figure 4–11**. At the start of the process you have few ideas, you are at the top of the diamond. As you create, you add more and more elements until you reach a point where you have added all the elements you think are necessary. At this point you are at the middle of the diamond. You then begin to take away elements, until you end up at the bottom of the diamond. At this point, your design is considered complete.

Students in one of my classes came up with a similar model, which they named "the snowman" model to represent the same process but showing the iterations (see again Figure 4–10). After several iterations, you stop either because you have a successful design or have run out of time or resources.

The best way to get good at removing design elements (it's a hard step) is to start doing it. If you bitterly regret not being able to include an element you spent hours designing, try to think of that element as moving you toward your visual solution. All was not lost. You might even save the element to use for another project.

### The Diamond Design Process

The X's represent the tools used: type, color, shape, space, and depth. During the design process, you add tools. At some point you have too much going on and your ideas or instruction is obscured. You now begin to take elements away until the message is clear.

### The Snowman Design Process

The snowman design process is an adaptation of the diamond process. The repetitive circles represent iterative phases where new ideas or adaptions of the previous cycle are implemented and continue the process. Theoretically there are as many cycles as time and resources permit.

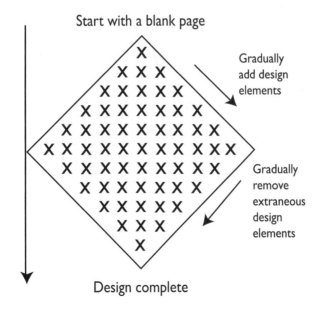

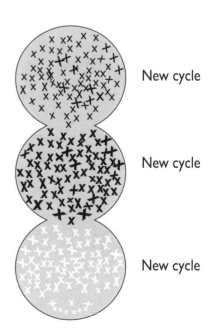

**FIGURE 4–11**  Removing the extraneous

## Cycle 1

The ACE process is used to create a visual teaching the 80/20 rule. This rule explains how numbers seem to reflect reality and can be used to help people manage their resources more effectively.  For example, people seem to spend 80% of their time on only 20% of the tasks they need to complete.  The ACE process below shows how an 80/20 image was analyzed, created, and evaluated. The image created is shown in the create circle. Because the image did not seem to explain the concept clearly, the designer decided to try another approach, hoping it would make more sense and also be a little more appealing.

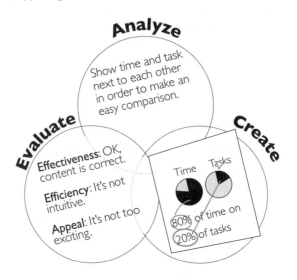

## Cycle 2

The designer is happier with the results of the second round of ACE.

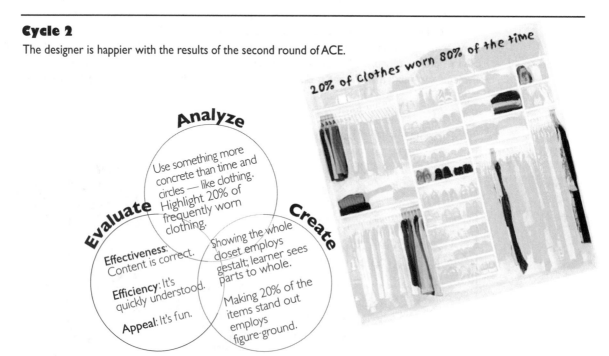

**FIGURE 4–12**   ACE in action (designing the 80/20 rule)
*Source: Closet image created by Erin Hunt. Used with permission.*

## Putting It All Together

**Figure 4–12** shows two cycles of the ACE process that is used to create a graphic describing the 80/20 rule. Keep in mind that not everything covered in the book and this chapter will be employed—just the points that were relevant to the 80/20 graphic. For example, you will not see a storyboard because this is a single visual and does not require extensive documentation.

# THE CONTEXT: USING INSTRUCTIONAL DESIGN MODELS

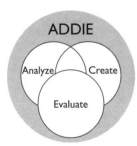

We have discussed ACE, a fairly micro-level model—a design model that deals with relatively small artifacts or products, in our case a single visual or set of visuals in a lesson. However, visuals are one of many design elements of instruction. The design of instruction is a macro-level process—a model that involves more of a systems orientation. ACE, a micro model, fits within a larger macro model.

A number of instructional design macro models are used to help create instruction, including, but not limited to, the Dick and Carey (2004) model, the Smith and Ragan (2005) model, and the Morrison, Ross, and Kemp (2004) model. These models help designers visualize all the discreet and often invisible steps that take place when analyzing an instructional problem and delivering its intervention.

Each of these models has its own strengths. The Dick and Carey (2004) model is widely used and has a long history of success in business and military projects. The Smith and Ragan (2005) model is known for its extensive focus on the development of instructional strategies based on information processing theories. The Morrison, Ross, and Kemp (2004) model is known for its application across business and academic settings and for its non-linear approach. Although covering all of these models in any depth is beyond the scope of this book, **Figure 4–13** does show how three of these models share an underlying structure called ADDIE, which we discuss here briefly.

## The ADDIE Model

The acronym ADDIE is derived from the key stages of the instructional design process: (1) analysis, (2) design, (3) development, (4) implementation, and (5) evaluation. Let's first look at how instruction is likely to move through the five ADDIE stages:

- During the analysis stage, you determine if any instructional problem needs an intervention. This analysis involves conducting needs assessments, determining learner characteristics, and evaluating tasks and content.
- During the design stage, you decide about how information should be presented or taught depending on your analysis. Considerations include type of learner and content, learning philosophy, instructional or performance goals and objectives, and instructional or performance context.
- During the development stage, you take all your analysis and design and make it tangible or visible. You create storyboards and prototypes, and you design the message. You also write code, use an authoring package, write text, and create graphics or animation. If you are thinking that development is where instructional message design takes place, you are right (although some think it belongs in design).
- During the implementation stage, you plan for the execution and management of the instructional product in increasingly realistic contexts. Considerations such as delivery platforms, training, and resources take place during this stage.
- During the evaluation stage, you test your visual to see if you can make it better and to determine how effective, efficient, and appealing it is.

What is interesting about ADDIE is that it can be interpreted on macro and micro levels. It can help you design entire curriculums and lessons as well as the tiniest element of

| | Dick and Carey (2004) | Smith and Ragan (2005) | Morrison, Ross, and Kemp (2004) |
|---|---|---|---|
| **A**nalysis | ■ Identifying an instructional goal<br>■ Conducting a goal analysis<br>■ Conducting a subordinate skills analysis<br>■ Identifying entry behaviors and characteristics | ■ Analyzing learning context<br>■ Analyzing learners<br>■ Analyzing learning task | ■ Identifying the need for instruction (needs assessment, goal analysis, performance assessment)<br>■ Conducting learner and contextual analysis<br>■ Task analysis |
| **D**esign | ■ Writing performance objectives<br>■ Developing criterion-referenced test items<br>■ Developing an instructional strategy (based on content classification) | ■ Creating instructional strategies (organizational, supplantive, generative, macro, and elaboration strategies)<br>■ Developing an instructional strategy (based on content classification) | ■ Determining instructional objectives (based on content classification)<br>■ Designing the instruction (sequencing, strategies, message design, advance organizers) |
| **D**evelopment | ■ Developing instructional materials | ■ Designing delivery and management strategies (media characteristics and selection)<br>■ Production of instruction (print, computer, video, teacher, time, and cost) | ■ Developing instructional materials |
| **I**mplementation | ■ Planning and managing implementation | ■ Designing delivery and management strategies | ■ Planning for instructional implementation<br>■ CLER model (configuration, linkages, environment, and resources) |
| **E**valuation | ■ Formative evaluation<br>■ Revising instructional materials<br>■ Summative evaluation | ■ Assessing learner performance | ■ Formative evaluation<br>■ Summative evaluation<br>■ Confirmative evaluation |

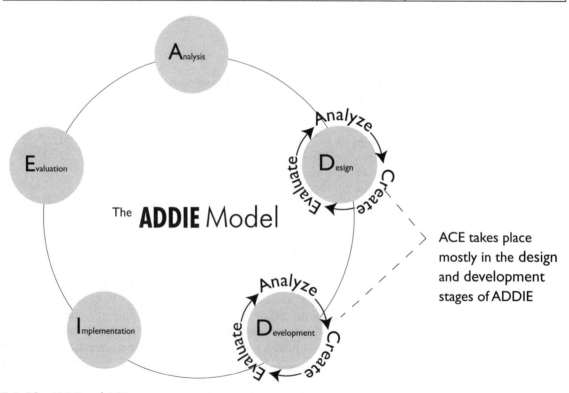

**FIGURE 4–13**   ADDIE and ACE

an instructional visual. As you cycle through ADDIE, you may find yourself recycling through ADDIE. Sounds confusing? That is probably why design is called a "messy process."

Consider this example. Suppose you are creating management skills training using the ADDIE model. During the design stage of ADDIE, you come up with different strategies to teach managers how to set priorities as well as the visuals to go along with them. You soon find yourself analyzing what the visual should say, designing the visual on paper by sketching it out, developing it in PowerPoint, testing (implementing) it with a sample audience, and revising (evaluating) it. You've just cycled through ADDIE while you are technically using ADDIE to create the larger management training. I've simplified this description of the inner instructional design process for visuals to focus on ACE: analyze, create (which includes designing and developing), and evaluate (which includes implementation and evaluation).

As you can see from this example, the ACE model is a micro process within the larger macro ADDIE process. Of all of the instructional design models, the Morrison, Ross, and Kemp (2004) model explains the nature of ACE most directly because it uniquely addresses an instructional message design component (see the design section of Figure 4-13). Designing the instructional message is the phase where you decide the format of your instruction. Is it going to be visual? Auditory? Kinesthetic? A combination of these? What specific cues and signals will you include to focus and direct attention?

Although attention to message design principles is not a major component of many design models, you can assume that it typically takes place in both design and development phases of the ADDIE model. During design you may sketch out your visual, and during development you use tools to refine and strengthen it. As Figure 4-12 shows, you cycle through three steps: (1) analyze (plan for design), (2) create (sketch or develop using a tool), and (3) evaluate (assess the visual's effectiveness). You continue through this process until the visual is satisfactory.

## The ACE Model

The ACE model is derived from Reigeluth and Nelson's (1997) analysis, synthesis, evaluation, and change (ASEC) model of instructional design. I've reduced the four stages of ASEC to three because based on my research (Lohr, 2000), these three phases (analyze, create, and evaluate) capture the core activities that take place, with the added benefit that they are easy to remember. Though each phase is described earlier in this chapter, the following overview will give you an idea about what takes place. I'll first explain how ACE was used to create Figure 4-13, which shows ADDIE and its relationship to common instructional design models.

During the analyze phase, I identified the purpose of the visual. My instructional objective was to teach the concept of instructional design models. My instructional strategy was to show the similarity between models and to also show the details of each model. I made quick notes during the analysis phase.

During the create phase, I sketched the rows and columns I'd need to show similar steps of ADDIE and specific details of each model. After the sketch I focused on what I wanted to be seen and perceived instantly (selection). A table format seemed right because it would clearly illustrate the data and its relationships. I worked mostly with text, shape, space, alignment, repetition, and proximity. I also wanted to establish an order of importance (organization). Because I considered the underlying ADDIE structure to be important, I made the words *Analysis, Design, Development, Implementation,* and *Evaluation* larger and bolder than the rest of the text.

During the evaluate phase, I made several changes to the table based on how effectively I thought the image was working. I asked myself if the image met its objectives. Did the image show the underlying similarity of the different design models? Did it show the detail sufficiently? I evaluated the image as I was creating it and afterward I considered the first draft complete. I then showed the image to a group of students.

While this description may seem fairly linear, I wasn't really thinking or performing as clearly as I describe here. In reality I was working on many of these decisions at once. I was constantly adjusting the space between columns and lines of data (proximity). I was making some lines bolder and thicker than others (contrast).

## SUMMARY

The first three chapters of this book focused on the need for visual literacy skills and the theory behind the design of effective visuals. This chapter describes how to do this using an ACE (analyze, create, evaluate) model that integrates the PAT (principles, actions, and tools) model.

During the analyze phase, you review the purpose of the visual and consider the goals and objectives of the overall instructional context as well as the purpose of the visual. Is the visual used for decoration, representation, organization, elaboration, or transformation? Instructional visuals are usually part of a larger instructional design project; therefore, much of the analysis that takes place when designing for the larger training or performance context influences the analysis that goes into a visual.

During the create phase, you transform your analysis into something visual. This phase involves generating and representing ideas. Several strategies are suggested to help you open your mind, including brainstorming and using synectic strategies. The create phase incorporates a principles, actions, and tools (PAT) approach to design. Principles refer to the cognitive processes of selection, organization, and integration referred to in the theory chapter. Actions include contrast, alignment, repetition, and proximity (CARP), which is discussed in Chapter 8. Tools refer to type, shape, color, depth, and space, topics that are discussed in the final chapters of the book.

During the evaluate phase, you critically edit your work using two approaches: (1) reviewing your design and (2) having others review it. When you conduct your review, you attempt to see the visual as the learner would. When you have others review your visual, you observe representative users or learners as they interact with it, a process called *usability testing*. Of the two approaches, the usability approach is a better way to get a true picture of how well your visual communicates.

Often you'll find that communication improves when you remove some of the elements you added. Though a difficult step to implement, it is a critically important one. The ability to take away, or subtract, often clarifies the message and increases its simplicity.

## PRACTICE

For additional activities and examples of student work, visit the Companion Website for this book at *http://www.coe.unco.edu/LindaLohr*.

### Resource Activities

1. *Figures R-14 and R-15 show software icons that are the most important for activities in this book. Use them to help you complete the website activities in this chapter as well as others.*
2. *The Resources section contains a job aid (Figure R-16) showing books and training materials related to the text. Look over the list to identify books that might be of interest to you.*

### Web Activity

> Take one of the images you created for Chapters 1 through 3 and user-test it using Figure 4-10.

### Challenge Activity

The 80/20 rule is defined as "80 percent of the effects generated by any large system are caused by 20 percent of the variables in that system" (Lidwell, Holden, & Butler, 2003, p. 12). The 80/20 rule is often used to illustrate how numbers seem to reflect reality and can be used to help people manage their resources more effectively. For example, people seem to spend 80 percent of their time on only 20 percent of the tasks they need to complete. Or, 80 percent of sales are made by 20 percent of salespeople, and 20 percent of your clothes are worn 80 percent of the time. Create an image that demonstrates the 80/20 rule.

## Independent Activity

Many public facilities have been extensively user-tested to help people navigate the environment with minimal assistance. Visit an airport or any large structure that is used by the general public, such as a football or baseball stadium or a large conference hall. Identify as many visual cues as you can for the environment. For example, the airport uses restroom, arrival and departure, and baggage area symbols, to name a few. Describe the symbols and cues in the setting that demonstrate high levels of usability and justify why you find them to be especially effective. Do the opposite as well. Identify cues and symbols that are not effective and do not appear to have been user-tested. Describe the reasons why these symbols are not useful, and suggest potential solutions.

## Justification Activity

Write a justification paper in which you describe the following:

- *Your users and the assumptions you make about them (such as age, reading level, and assumed skills).*
- *Why you think your solution will work. Include at least two ideas from the book, including page numbers, and your interpretation of the passage used.*
- *What you learned from a "user-test" (have someone look at the image and verbalize their thoughts while looking at the image.)*
- *The changes you will make based on user comments (or create a revised image).*

## Discussion Questions

1. Describe an image that does a good job of gaining your attention. Based on what you know so far about tools and actions, which tools and actions were used most effectively in this image? Put your thoughts and impressions into words.
2. Describe an image that does a good job of helping you synthesize or integrate content in a way that was meaningful. Based on what you know so far about tools and actions, which tools and actions were used most effectively? Put your thoughts and impressions into words.

## K–12 Student Activities

Use the chapter Challenge Activities to generate similar ideas for use with K–12 students.

- Eighty percent of the noise comes from 20 percent of students.
- Twenty percent of the food in a lunchbox creates 80 percent of enjoyment.
- Twenty percent of classes generate 80 percent of homework.

## REFERENCES

Clark, R. C., & Lyons, C. (2004). *Graphics for learning: Proven Guidelines for Planning, Designing, and Evaluating Visuals in Training Materials*. San Francisco: Wiley.

Dick, W., & Carey, L. (2004). *The systematic design of instruction*. New York: HarperCollins.

Gordon, W. J. (1961). *Synectics*. New York: Harper & Row.

Grabowski, B. L. (1995). Message design: Issues and trends. In G. J. Anglin (Ed.), *Instructional technology, past, present and future* (pp. 221–231.) Englewood, CO: Libraries Unlimited.

Joyce, B., & Weil, M. (1986). *Models of teaching* (3rd ed.). Englewood Cliffs, NJ: Prentice Hall.

Landa, R. (1998). *Thinking creatively: New ways to unlock your visual imagination*. Cincinnati, OH: North Light Books.

Levin, J. R. (1981). On the functions of pictures in prose. In F. J. Pirozzolo & M. C. Wittrock (Eds.), *Neuropsychological and cognitive processes in reading* (pp. 203-228). San Diego, CA: Academic Press.

Lidwell, W., Holden, K., and Butler, J. (2003). *Universal Principles of design: 100 Ways to Enhance Usability, Influence Perception, Increase Appeal, Make Better Design Decisions, and Teach Through Design*. Glouster, MA: Rockport Publishers.

Lohr, L. (1999). Development of a procedure for GUI design. In R. E. Griffin, W. J. Gibbs, & B. Wiegmann (Eds.), *Visual literacy in an information age: Selected readings from the Annual Conference of the International Visual Literacy Association* (pp. 225-233). Athens, GA, October 21-24.

Lohr, L. (2000). Designing the instructional interface. *Computers in Human Behavior, 16,* 61-82.

Lohr, L., & Eikleberry, C. (2001). Learner-centered usability: Tools for creating a learner-friendly instructional environment. *Performance Improvement, 401,* 24-28.

Morrison, G., Ross, S., & Kemp, J. (2004). *Designing effective instruction*. New York: Wiley.

Nielsen, J. (1993). *Usability engineering*. Boston: Academic Press.

Peterson, B. L. (1996). *Using design basics to get creative results*. Cincinnati, OH: North Light Books.

Reigeluth, C. M., & Nelson, L. M. (1997). A new paradigm of ISD. In R. M. Branch & B. B. Minor (Eds.), *Educational media and technology yearbook* (Vol. 22, pp. 24-35). Englewood, CO: Libraries Unlimited.

Smaldino, S., Russell, J., Heinich, R., & Molenda, M. (2004). *Instructional media and technologies for learning* (8th ed). Upper Saddle River, NJ: Prentice Hall.

Smith, P. L., & Ragan, T. J. (2005). *Instructional design*. Upper Saddle River, NJ: Merrill/Prentice Hall.

vonOech, R. (1983). *A whack on the side of the head: How to unlock your mind for innovation*. New York: Warner Books.

Weaver, W. T., & Prince, G. M. (1990). Synectics: Its potential for education. *Phi Delta Kappan, 46(1),* 378-388.

# PART II

# *Principles*

# CHAPTER 5

## Selection Principle: Emphasizing Figure and Ground

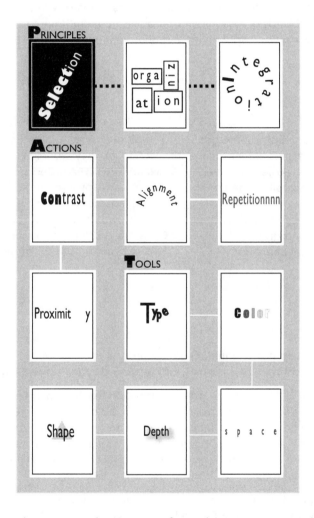

The interior decoration of graphics generates a lot of ink that does not tell the viewer anything new. The purpose of decoration varies to make the graphic appear more scientific and precise, to enliven the display, to give the designer an opportunity to exercise skills. Regardless of its cause, it is all non-data ink or redundant data ink, and it is often chartjunk.

*Edward Tufte*

## NOTES ABOUT THE OPENING VISUAL

The opening visual for this chapter illustrates the selection principle. It was designed in part to emphasize figure and ground. Note how the word *select* stands out (becomes the figure) while the rest of the word becomes the background (or ground). Because the icon representing the chapter topic is black and all the other chapter icons are white, viewers tend to focus on the black, selecting that particular part of the image to process. Since the black topic catches attention, it is considered the figure. Everything else is the ground.

## FOCUS QUESTIONS

- What is figure-ground and why is it associated with selection?
- What kinds of instructional problems relate to figure-ground?
- How do you improve figure-ground perception for instructional information?

## KEY TERMS

**1 + 1 = 3 PHENOMENON**   The theory that two images combined may create a third. Sometimes the third image helps make the overall image easier to understand; other times it may make the overall image more difficult to understand.

**FIGURE-GROUND**   The perception principle that describes the mind's tendency to seek figure and ground distinctions. The figure is typically the information that visual

designers want to stand out, and the ground is the information they want to recede or support the figure.

**GENERATIVE STRATEGIES**   Instructional methods (outlining, concept mapping, drawing, charting, note taking) that require learners to contribute to and construct their own understanding.

**SELECTION**   The cognitive process of attending to particular visual and auditory stimuli.

## INTRODUCTION

Sylvia is helping a mountain bike manufacturer create better repair instructions. She examines an existing repair poster (see **Figure 5–1**) and asks these questions:

- What is the most important information for the repair employees?
- How do I make that information grab the employee's eye?
- How do I make that information easy to refer to when fixing a bike?
- Is a photograph the best way to do the image or would a line drawing be better?
- Is there a way to make several elements seem part of the same focal point to help focus information?

Figure 5-1 shows two possible solutions: one uses a plain white background, another focuses attention on the front wheel with a light gray background and a simplified line drawing of the wheel. Which is better? Sylvia informally tested these two images with nine people, asking the question "Which is better, a line drawing or a realistic image?" She found that seven preferred the simplified line drawing over the light gray background. Such questions have been asked and researched for a long time. During the 1940s and 1950s, realistic instructional images, such as photographs, were favored by research. During the 1960s, however, many researchers agreed that realistic visuals often provided extraneous stimuli that detracted from learning. Simple line drawings were favored because they provided only the essential cues (McIntyre, 1983).

## Revised images

These revised images do a better job of facilitating the selection process than the original image below. The bike part labels and the actual bike parts are easier to see. Notice how the right image allows you to accurately see the bike rim.

 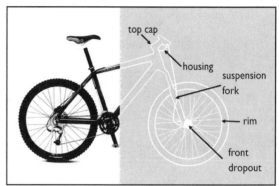

## Original image

This poster has too many visual elements, such as the black boxes, the little bikes, the ghosted label, and the text over the image. These images compete with the bike part labels for attention.

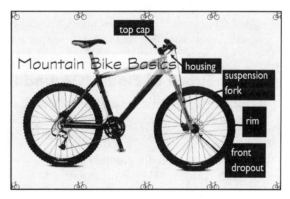

**FIGURE 5–1**   Selection and bike repair

Today the question remains. As with all of the information in this book, the effectiveness of one approach over another often depends on the instructional context. In areas such as medical education and engineering, realistic images are considered more effective because the external stimuli in the images are part of the real-life experience. The purpose of the bike image is not to discuss line versus realistic drawings so much as to introduce the importance of figure-ground considerations when creating visuals. While working with the bike image, Sylvia was attending to the importance of figure-ground in training or support materials. She asked several questions: What information do learners need most? What is the best way to show that information to help them do their task?

# SELECTION AND FIGURE-GROUND

As you learned in Chapter 3, instructional images should help people select, organize, and integrate information in meaningful ways. Mayer (2001) has identified seven characteristics (the 7 c's) of effective instructional visuals: (1) concentrated, (2) concise, (3) correspondent, (4) concrete, (5) coherent, (6) comprehensible, and (7) codable. Of these seven principles, three characteristics—concentrated, concise, and concrete—relate to the cognitive task of **selection.** It is not necessary for each visual to have all characteristics. A visual that facilitates selection may have a concentrated and concise characteristic but lack the concrete characteristic.

"Concentrated" is the first of the three c's and refers to emphasizing key points in both graphics and text elements. "Concise" refers to reducing visual information to its most basic, core level for meaningful learning. "Concrete" refers to elements in the visual that make it easy to visualize.

Many people are surprised by the concise rule, thinking that extraneous information is necessary to make learning more interesting. According to Mayer, learning improves when extraneous information is removed. Motivation may increase, but learning is likely to decrease.

One way to address the three c's is to improve **figure-ground**—a perception principle that explains how the limited information-processing capacity of the human mind forces people to focus on one stimulus at a time rather than several. Figure-ground essentially names the two types of attention: (1) what the learner is paying attention to, or selecting (the figure) and (2) what the learner is not paying attention to (the ground). Implementing figure-ground to improve instruction is simply the act of making the most important information stand out. When you do this, you help the learner focus on what is critical. Using the three c's (concentrated, concise, and concrete) as guidelines will help you achieve optimal figure-ground. By eliminating some of the information that learners immediately pay attention to, you reduce their cognitive load, or the demands placed on their short-term memory. This makes your instruction seem easier and more efficient to the learners.

Tufte (1983) writes about the importance of conserving data ink—"the non-erasable core of a graphic" (p. 93)—for important rather than extraneous information. You can think of data ink as anything that isn't white space. Good use of data ink enhances figure-ground.

## Three Types of Figure-Ground Problems

Creating optimal figure-ground is challenging even when you are aware that your image message should be concentrated, concise, and concrete. Three types of figure-ground combinations or relationships covered in this chapter seem to interfere with the instructional image:

1. The figure and the ground compete.
2. The figure should be the ground and the ground should be the figure.
3. The figure and the ground create an optical illusion.

### Competing Figure and Ground

When figure and ground compete a learner is likely to ask the question "What am I supposed to pay attention to?" Look at the **Figure 5–2,** which presents two sets of original and revised images. The revised images make it easier to understand the main message. The top images show paper based instruction related to career choice. Notice how the after images employ concentrated, concise, and concrete design rules. You can quickly identify the instructional topic and key characteristics.

The tulip bulb example in Figure 5–2 comes from an experience during a second grade field day. The class met outside with another second grade class to plant tulips. The activity took the place of the regular science and math class. Second graders were supposed to mark a Popsicle stick four inches from its end (the math part) and plant it in the ground the right way up (the science part). Since the students were outside near a noisy street, many did not

## Original Image

The figure-ground is not optimal:
1. The text and background blend and obscure the purpose of the document.
2. The text is not chunked into smaller more meaningful units.
3. How does this relate to the reader?

## Revised Image

This image employs the three c's:
*Concentrated:* The topic of careers is emphasized.
*Concise:* Specific job categories are emphasized.
*Concrete:* The message is meaningful to the reader. A Job for YOU!

---

## K–12 Example    Science and Math

## Original Image

The figure-ground is not optimal:
1. Is this a description of Tulip Day or instructions for Tulip Day?
2. What are the most important steps?
3. What tools and measures are needed?

## Revised Image

This image employs the three c's:
*Concentrated:* The title "How to plant tulips" focuses on the main purpose of the document.
*Concise:* There are three precise steps.
*Concrete:* The tulip bulb and Popsicle stick images make visualizing the task easy.

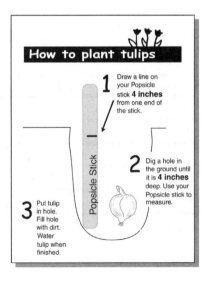

**FIGURE 5–2** Figure-ground competition

## Original Image

The figure-ground is not optimal for the message:
1. The element that should be in the background (the clock) is visually dominant.
2. The text is too small to read. What exactly is important here?
3. The clock image is concrete, but does it convey managing time efficiently?

## Revised Image

This image employs the three c's:

*Concentrated:* The topic of time management is emphasized in several places.

*Concise:* The message space focuses on the purpose of the document.

*Concrete:* Although no images are used, key words are highlighted.

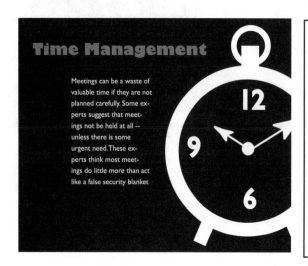

**Time Management**

Meetings can be a waste of valuable time if they are not planned carefully. Some experts suggest that meetings not be held at all -- unless there is some urgent need. These experts think most meetings do little more than act like a false security blanket

*Time Management*

**M**eetings can be a **waste of valuable time** if they are not planned carefully. Some experts suggest that meetings not be held at all, unless an urgent need presents itself. These experts think most meetings do little more than act like a **false security blanket.**

When meetings are a must, several **strategies** may be implemented. First, establish an **agenda** and stick to it. Set time limits for each agenda item. Second, communicate the **focus** early on, making sure that each member of the meeting knows the goals.

### K–12 Example   Science (Chemistry)

## Original Image

The figure-ground is not optimal. Do you notice the lines or the data?

## Revised Image

This image employs the two c's:

*Concise:* The reduction of dark lines helps the message.

*Concrete:* The shading makes the information easier to distinguish.

| Quantum Numbers for Electrons in Atoms | | |
|---|---|---|
| Name | Symbol | Values |
| Principal | n | 1, 2, 3 ... |
| Orbital angular momentum | l | 0, 1 ... n-1 |
| Magnetic | ml | -1 ... 0 ... +1 |
| Spin | ms | +1/2, -1/2 |

| Quantum Numbers for Electrons in Atoms | | |
|---|---|---|
| Name | Symbol | Values |
| Principal | n | 1, 2, 3 ... |
| Orbital angular momentum | l | 0, 1 ... n-1 |
| Magnetic | ml | -1 ... 0 ... +1 |
| Spin | ms | +1/2, -1/2 |

**FIGURE 5–3**   Reversal of figure and ground

hear the teacher's verbal instructions so they picked up the original instructions in Figure 5-2 to figure out what to do.

If you look and read closely, you will see that these instructions have a problem: Both the figure and the ground are competing equally for attention. What happened to the second graders was predictable. Many of them watched what others were doing and tried to copy them. More than half of the students that day did not plant their tulips. The math and science lesson was lost in the confusion. If the second graders had used the revised instructions in Figure 5-2, there might have been much less confusion.

Notice how attention to figure and ground did not stop with a redesign of the graphic elements alone. The writing and sequencing (a hierarchy principle covered in Chapter 5) of the instruction was changed to emphasize the most important information in an organized manner.

## Reversal of Figure and Ground

When figure and ground are reversed, a learner is likely to think "Which message do I pay attention to?" Images with such reversals are common in instructional design. Of all the figure-ground errors, such reversals are the most common among novice designers who "play" with fonts, colors, borders, and clip art. What happens is that these "fun" features often take over visually, making the instruction hard to access. Edward Tufte (1983), in his classic books on information and quantitative design, shows many examples of information or data that are difficult to understand because their display is junked up with graphical embellishment.

In any image where the figure should be the ground and the ground should be the figure the emphasis is in the wrong place. The computer-based training screens on time management in **Figure 5–3** clearly show this type of problem. The original image takes up a lot of space, and the title and text of the unit are hard to read. In the redesign, the instructional text is dominant. Figure 5-3 also shows an original image where heavy lines, rather than data, dominate the table visually. The revised image uses softer lines and subtle shading to keep the focus on the data.

## Figure, Ground, and Optical Illusion

When figure and ground create an optical illusion, the learner is likely to ask "How does this relate to what we are learning?" The Danish psychologist Edgar Rubin made figure-ground experiences notable with his renowned vase/profile illusion (**Figure 5–4**). Look over this image. What do you see? Do you see two human profiles or do you see a vase? When you look at this image, your mind seeks to identify contours that will form into either figure or ground status.

Another widely recognized example of figure-ground can be interpreted from somewhat of an instructional perspective. Imagine now that you are presenting information about the characteristics of elderly women, and you display the female profiles in Figure 5-4. Some in your audience will see an old woman (see the middle profile), while others will see a young woman (see the right profile). They are both seeing correctly. Take a minute and try to see both the young woman and the old woman. Most likely your mind will go back and forth. At some moments you will be focusing on the young woman, who becomes the figure; at other times you will be focusing on the old woman, who then becomes the figure. While you are switching back and forth between the two images, your mind is at work creating those figure-ground distinctions.

Although these images of the two women are an entertaining visual and effectively illustrate the concepts of figure and ground, for most instruction you do not want the learner's mind switching back and forth between figure and ground because it takes too much mental energy. You want the learner to focus easily and quickly on your key message,

What do you see? The vase or the profiles? While you look at this image, your mind may be switching back and forth between the vase and the profiles, trying to establish the contours that identify the figure and ground.

Source: Based on Rubin's Goblet from Archives of the
History of American Psychology. Used with permission.

To help you see the two women, I adjusted the images. To make the old woman more visible, I made her nose more prominent by completely removing the young woman's nose (see middle image). I made the face brighter all over so it would stand out more. These adjustments were done in Adobe PhotoShop with an eraser and a tool that allows you to make a section of an image either darker or lighter. This type of image manipulation takes practice since your goal is to create or adjust images to influence learner perception. You must also be careful that you are not altering copyrighted material without the copyright holder's approval.

**Original image**  **Modified to show old woman**  **Modified to show young woman**

Source: A New Ambiguous Figure, by E.G. Boring, from American Journal of Psychology. Copyright 1930 by the Board of Trustees of the University of Illinois. Used with permission of the University of Illinois Press.

**FIGURE 5–4**   Figure, ground, and optical illusion

the figure. Your design goal is to create a clear figure supported by, but not competing with, the ground.

Another interesting type of optical illusion to watch for is the **1 + 1 = 3 phenomenon**—a theory stating that two figures may combine to form a third, often unanticipated image. **Figure 5–5** illustrates several of these images. The one that is easiest to

When the gray and black bar are placed side by side, you see two bars. When the gray and black bar are separated, you see three bars. (The space becomes a bar—the third element.) Sometimes you will put two elements together like this and unexpectedly get a third.

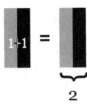          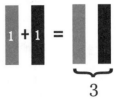

Try to answer the following questions or complete the task. When finished, check the answers at the bottom of this page.

A. Which center dot is larger? The dot in the middle of the left flower, or the right?

B. Are the rows or the columns parallel?

C. Read this carefully. What does it say exactly?

D. Count the black dots.

A. The center dots are equal in size; B. The rows are parallel; C. The word "the" appears twice in the sentence; D. There are no black dots.

**FIGURE 5–5**   The 1 + 1 = 3 phenomenon

relate back to instruction is the "I love Paris in the the Springtime" example. There are so many graphic embellishments in the simple sentence that the eye overlooks what is actually there and the mind does not process all of the information. Poorly designed multimedia instruction often does this by using too many signals: visual, auditory, and motion.

The $1 + 1 = 3$ rule takes place in a lot of poorly designed instruction and information. Rather than seeing the figure supported by the ground, a mixture of the two creates a completely different message than was intended. Tufte (1983, 1990) writes about problems with design that emphasizes the data container instead of the data. An example would be the chemistry table in Figure 5-3. If you look at the original table your eyes are not really drawn to the data, because the data are not emphasized. What is emphasized? The lines, or what Tufte would call the data container. More ink goes into the lines of the chart than into the actual data in the chart. This example is a subtle form of $1 + 1 = 3$ because the visual result of this table is a black and white texture. Try stepping back from the table, perhaps squinting at it. You see more black and white pattern than data. The revised table design takes care of the figure-ground problem by making that data—not the lines of the chart—stand out. Notice how the designer used a soft, less intrusive gray to separate the different rows of information? As a reader, you can see the data easier.

## Figure-Ground and the Novelty Effect

**Figure 5–6** shows how a novel image seizes our interest. For example, this figure presents three images that conflict with what we expect. These types of images may or may not work as intended though. Research shows (Clark and Mayer, 2002; Harp & Mayer, 1998) that novelty itself may take up cognitive resources because learners focus attention on irrelevant rather than relevant information. Cognitive resources might be expended translating what an image means. Such resources might better be left for the content represented or emphasized by the novelty. If you think certain images might enhance your message, however, start collecting them for later use.

## Working with Figure and Ground

As a designer of instructional visuals, your task is to create an optimal figure-ground balance. To do this, you need to create a clear distinction between the figure and the ground and help learners by doing some of their brainwork for them. When a learner sees an image, the brain is working in ways that the learner isn't even aware of, sorting information into figure (important) and ground (supportive) categories. Your job as a designer is to do some of that organizing up front, so the learner does not have to bother with it. By doing so, you make it easier for the learner to access and identify critical information. Wouldn't you rather have the learner expending mental energy on processing or thinking about the content rather than just trying to access and figure out what the content is? The goal of most performance support environments is to help the learner perform a task, not figure out what the task is.

Later in this chapter we look at some situations in which requiring the learner to sort information into figure-ground categories themselves is a good instructional practice. In some situations, requiring learners to consciously organize the information into figure-ground categories actually helps them process the information more deeply and learn more thoroughly. While this may be true in some cases, many more situations benefit from optimal design of figure and ground to facilitate the learning process simply by making the access to instructional information easier.

## K–12 Example    Writing, Language Arts

The novelty of these images makes you notice (select) them. They grab your attention and become the figure of figure-ground. Teachers can use these images to help students generate stories in a creative writing exercise.

Clip art © Dover Images                    Clip art © 1997 RomTech

---

This image is used to generate discussion regarding the tendency for people to see training and instruction as something simply poured into people's brains. The concept of instruction being structured to stimulate thinking is not a common perspective.

**FIGURE 5–6**    Novelty and selection

## K–12 Example    Science, Biology, Health

**Original Image**

What Is a Virus?

A virus is made of membranes, proteins, and one or more DNA or RNA strands. These strands allow the virus to replicate. A virus is "compact, hard, logical, totally selfish, and dedicated to making copies of itself" (Preston, 1994, p. 83). Viruses are parasites; to replicate they must be attached to something else. When a cell comes along, the virus will attach itself to the cell, making the cell its host. When this happens, the cell wraps itself around the virus, drawing it into its system. Once inside the virus begins its work using the cell's structure and energy to duplicate itself with incredible speed.

The page above is ok, but figure-ground is better in the revised image.

Here you see what Clark and Lyons (2004) call "a wall of words." Few actions and tools are used to visually optimize this information.

**Revised Image**

# virusvirusvirus

A virus is made of membranes, proteins, and one or more DNA or RNA strands. These strands allow the virus to replicate. A virus is "compact, hard, logical, totally selfish, and dedicated to making **copies of itself**" (Preston, 1994, p. 83).

Viruses are **parasites;** to replicate they must be attached to something else. When a cell comes along, the virus will attach itself to the cell, making the cell its host. When this happens, the cell wraps itself around the virus, drawing it into its system. Once inside, the virus begins its work using the cell's structure and energy to **duplicate** itself

Ebola Virus

In this revised image you instantly notice the topic of the passage. You see a representation of the Ebola virus and the title stands out clearly.

Actions and tools are used as follows:

### Actions

*Contrast*:  Heading, bold faced words, and image stand out.
*Alignment*: Heading text, and graphics are centered.
*Repetition*: Key words are repeated in bold. The title letters are similar in appearance to the shape of the virus. (Both have a hollow appearance created by parallel lines.) The word "virus" repeats itself to play upon the replication theme.
*Proximity*:  "Ebola virus" is close to the virus image.

### Tools

*Type*:  Typography is used to repeat the "look" of the virus.
*Color*:  Bold type and the virus shape appear in dark contrast to white background, much more than the "wall of grey words" above.
*Shape*: The virus image and background circle create shape.
*Space*: White space surrounding the title makes the title/main theme stand out fom the text.
*Depth*: The leftmost "virus" in the title "pops" or approaches.

**FIGURE 5–7**  Actions and tools for figure/ground

## Actions and Tools

As illustrated in the previous examples, creating the optimal figure-ground balance is challenging. There are no simple rules for achieving the optimal image, but you will find that the actions and tools mentioned in the previous chapters will help you.

You'll mainly use contrast as a way to make important information stand out. Tools that create contrast include type, color, space, shape, and dimension, which you will learn more about in later chapters. For now, be aware that type can be used to create contrast in a variety of ways. It can be bigger or smaller, bolder or softer, closer or far away. Shape can be used to draw the eye, since simple shapes provide easy contours for perceptual recognition. Color can make the elements of a visual more noticeable. Images that are larger or seem to advance use dimension to catch the viewer's attention. White space can direct the eye to what is important. Designers can even create a mental contrast by using images that contrast with expectations.

**Figure 5–7** shows examples using actions and tools to enhance figure and ground. The revised image illustrates how contrast can be very effective in improving figure-ground. Contrast is achieved when two elements are different. The top set of words does not have as much contrast as the bottom and consequently does not look as good together as do the bottom words. Williams (1994) describes effective contrast as elements that are very different: "If the two elements are sort of different, but not really, then you don't have contrast, you have conflict. That's the key—the principle of contrast states that if two items are not exactly the same, then make them different. Really different" (p. 55).

## Improving Selection

**Figures 5–8** through **5–10** show how selection is improved by emphasizing figure and ground in a variety of media formats—from overheads to Web pages to documents and for decorative, representative, organizational, interpretive, and transformative images.

## Generative Strategies

Throughout this book you learn actions and tools that you can put to work to improve learner perception and understanding of instructional visuals. You are doing some of the work for learners by organizing information clearly up front, so their minds do not have to do the work. At times, however, it might be better to make the learner do the organizing work. When your goal is learning oriented, it is time to consider **generative strategies**—techniques that require learners to generate their own meaning by outlining content; creating organizational charts, mental images, and analogies; and summarizing information in their own words (Whittrock, 1989).

These strategies help learners think about information more deeply and learn it more thoroughly. They can also be used to help students distinguish the critical information from the rest. When you use generative strategies, you are requiring the learners to make the figure-ground distinction. **Figure 5–11** illustrates how learners might generate their own figure-ground using mental imagery, adding graphic elements to an image, and selecting or creating an image that summarizes the key point of instruction.

## Overheads/Electronic Slides: An Example of a Decorative Visual

### Original Image

While this owl image looks perfectly fine on paper, it loses much of its clarity when projected.

*Source: Clip art © 1997 RomTech.*

### Revised Image

A rule of thumb for projected displays is to use dark backgrounds. When a room is darkened, dark backgrounds provide greater contrast and legibility.

## Web-based Training: An Example of a Representative Visual

### Original Image

This original Web-based training menu is designed around a photograph. It has a figure-ground problem since the details in the photograph visually interfere with training topics.

### Revised Image

Reducing the clarity of the background image has strengthened the contrast between figure and ground images. Notice how the background net and fabric are less visible in this revision. Typography is less ornate as well. Altogether these changes improve the figure-ground relationship.

*Source: Created by Erin Hunt. Used with permission.*

**FIGURE 5–8**   Figure-ground: Decorative and representative

**Web-based Traning:** An Example of a Representative Visual

## Original Image

The image below is used in training documentation to show where to type a Web address. The problem is that it is too difficult to see. Not only is the address small and slightly illegible, but it gets lost in all of the other information.

## Revised Image

This image is an improvement because it focuses your eye on the important information using a visual magnification strategy. Size is used to create contrast and improve figure-ground distinction in this example.

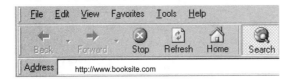

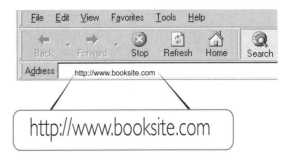

---

**Overheads/Electronic Slides:** An Example of an Organizational Visual

## Original Image

The image below shows a career code based upon Holland's theory of occupational careers. The A, S, E stand for artistic skills, social skills, and entrepreneurial skills, respectively. This image does not do a good job of presenting this information in a way that organizes information for the learner. The occupational code should be presented as a hierarchy to communicate that the first letter is the skill in the greatest demand for that career.

## Revised Image

This image does a better job of showing the relative importance of the occupational codes using novelty, depth (size), and alignment. The initial letters are drawn to represent their meaning (novelty), different sizes represent different degrees of importance, and the stair step alignment represents declining importance.

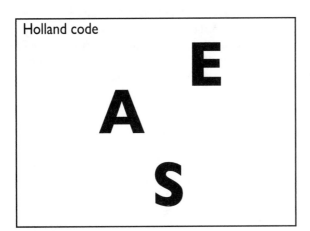

**FIGURE 5–9**  Figure-ground: Representative and organizational

**Paper-based Training:** An Example of an Interpretive Visual

## Original Image

The book graphic below shows hand signals associated with alphabet characters. This figure suffers from Tufte's "chartjunk" because so much of the ink in the image is dedicated to the noninstructional data.

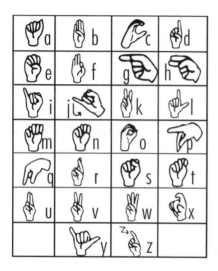

## Revised Image

This revision is an improvement because the chart lines are removed altogether. Each hand is filled with a gray color to help separate the letters. The combination of the gray fill and the white space serves to separate the elements in a way that is less visually intrusive.

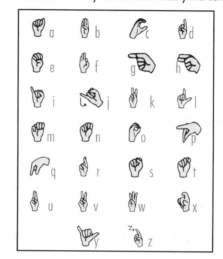

**Computer-based Training:** An Example of a Transformative Visual

## Original Image

These images demonstrate biker position for road and mountain biking. While the angle of the back is easy to see in both bikes, better figure-ground is needed.

## Revised Image

Figure ground is improved using silhouettes. Reduction of unneeded detail focuses attention on the critical information. The dark line emphasizes the angle of the bikers' backs. Making the bikers face the same direction (repetition of direction) and placing them side-by-side (proximity) helps the learner see the distinction.

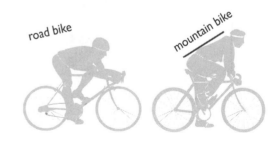

**FIGURE 5–10**   Figure-ground: interpretive and transformative

## K–12 Example   Science
## Mental Imagery

The following passage from The Hot Zone (Preston, 1994) communicates the size and number of viruses present on our planet using mental imagery.

Viruses are too small to be seen. Here is a way to imagine the size of a virus. Consider the island of Manhattan shrunk [to the size of the line you see at the bottom of this paragraph]. This Manhattan could easily hold 9 million viruses. If you could magnify this Manhattan and it were full of viruses, you would see little figures clustered like the lunch crowd on Fifth Avenue. A hundred million crystallized Polio viruses could cover the period at the end of this sentence. There could be two hundred and fifty Woodstock Festivals of viruses on that period—the combined populations of Great Britain and France, and you would never know it. (Preston, 1994, p. 85)

Manhattan

## K–12 Example   Physical Education
## Adding Elements to a Diagram

Ask students to draw where the center of weight falls for different snowboard positions.

Student sees this image

Student draws this image

## K–12 Example   Computer Science
## Generating a Visual Image

A student created these images to help her remember to place a comma inside a parenthesis rather than outside the parenthesis when generating computer code.

## K–12 Example   Languages
## Composing in a Foreign Language

Write a conversation using Spanish vocabulary words learned this week.

**FIGURE 5–11**   Learner-generated figure-ground

## SUMMARY

The previous chapters focused on the importance of visual literacy, related theories, and a recommended design process for creating effective instructional visuals. This chapter begins our focus on the first of the theory-based principles, selection. Selection refers to the mind's tendency to pay attention to what is dominant in an image. Figure-ground distinctions are important to selection processes. Whatever the mind is attending to is the figure, and whatever the mind is not attending to is the ground.

That the mind seeks to find contours and images in visuals has fascinated psychologists for many years. If a contour is associated with more than one image, as in the case of the vase/profile image, the mind tends to perceive both images associated with the contour. What results is a switching back and forth between images, making the vase a figure at one moment and the profiles the figure in the next. This example is important for instruction. Because our goal is usually straightforward communication, we do not want to have the learner expend time trying to find out what the figure is. We want that message to be clear. To achieve this, we then make the figure-ground distinction strong, mostly using the design action contrast, through implementing any of the tools. For instance, type can be made large, bright colors can be used for type or shape, and space and depth can draw the eye to what is important. In the next chapter you learn about the second theory-based principle, organization. Establishing relationships between visual elements is the focus of the next chapter.

## PRACTICE

For additional activities and examples of student work, visit the Companion Website for this book at *http://www.coe.unco.edu/LindaLohr*.

### Resource Activities

Figures R–5, R–6, and R–8, in the Resources section show how to increase figure and ground in photographs. Use these figures as job-aids when creating your visual solution to Chapter 5 Activities. Also consult Figure R–14 for software functions that improve contrast.

### Web Activity

The Web Activity asks you to improve the figure-ground composition in the following information.

### Facts About Tobacco Use

Smoking is the most preventable cause of death in our society. Read below to find out more "tobacco facts."

The earlier people start smoking, the harder it is to quit when they are older. People who start smoking in their teenage years run the risk of becoming lifelong smokers. One-third to one-half of young people who try cigarettes go on to be daily smokers. It takes an average of five attempts for an adult to successfully quit smoking.

A seventh grader's response to this activity is shown here.

### Challenge Activity

The Challenge Activity asks you to modify instruction that you have recently encountered that suffers from figure-ground problems.

This seventh grader created a skull image to emphasize the relationship between smoking and death.

Web Activity solution

## Independent Activitiy

The Independent Activity asks you to pick your own project. You are encouraged to try this one because the information will be more meaningful and thus is likely to be more motivating. Find something from your work or instructional environment that could use better figure-ground distinctions. Create a new visual using the ideas shared in this chapter.

## Justification Activity

Write a justification paper for the activity you select. Describe the following:

- *Your users and the assumptions you make about them (such as age, reading level, and assumed skills).*
- *Why you think your solution will work; include at least two ideas from the book, including page numbers and your interpretation of the passage used.*
- *What you learned from a "user-test" (have someone look at the image and verbalize their thoughts while looking at the image).*
- *The changes you will make based on user comments (or create a revised image).*

## Discussion Questions

1. Find a research article that deals with figure-ground theory. As you are searching for this article, keep in mind that the word "figure-ground" may not help you locate research. Instead, look for articles that emphasize "attention," "motivation," "clarity," "information access," "multiple channel processing," "effectiveness of headings," and other terms that deal with the concept of figure-ground. You can be creative with this search. The idea is to find research that deals with helping people perceive what is important in an image.

2. Discuss the relevance of an article cited in this chapter by Whittrock (1989) to the development of visual instruction. Brainstorm several generative visual strategies similar to those in the textbook.

## K–12 Student Activity

Using the seventh grader's solution to the Web Activity, ask students to create a poster that grabs attention related to tobacco and smoking.

## REFERENCES

Clark, R., & Mayer, R. (2002). *E-Learning and the science of instruction: Proven guidelines for consumers and designers of multimedia training.* San Francisco: Jossey-Bass Pfeiffer.

Harp, S. F., & Mayer, R, E. (1998). How seductive details do their damage: A theory of cognitive interest in science learning. *Journal of Educational Psychology, 90 (3),* 414–434.

Levin, J. R. (1981). On the functions of pictures in prose. In F. J. Pirozzolo & M. C. Wittrock (Eds.), *Neuropsychological and cognitive processes in reading* (pp. 203–228). San Diego: Academic Press.

Mayer, R. E. (2001). *Multimedia learning.* Cambridge, England: University Press.

McIntyre, W. A. (1983). The psychology of visual perception and learning from line drawings: A survey of the research. (ERIC Document Reproduction Service No. ED230901)

Preston, R. (1994). *The hot zone.* New York: Anchor Books.

Tufte, E. (1983). *The visual display of quantitative information.* Cheshire, CT: Graphics Press.

Tufte, E. (1990). *Envisioning information.* Cheshire, CT: Graphics Press.

Whittrock, M. C. (1989). Generative processes of comprehension. *Educational Psychologist, 24,* 345–376.

Williams, R. (1994). *The non-designer's design book: Design and typographic principles for the visual novice.* Berkeley, CA: Addison-Wesley.

# CHAPTER 6

## Organization Principle: Working with Hierarchy

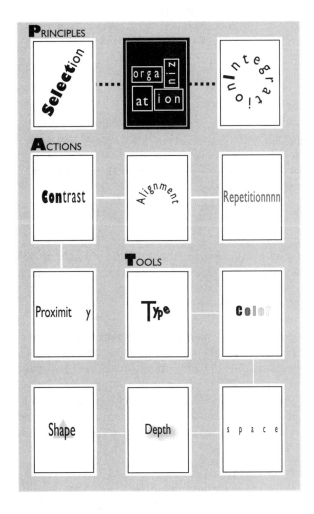

People have no idea of the extent that information structures rule their lives.

*Jenny Robbins*

## Notes About the Opening Visual

The opening visual for this chapter uses organizational design strategies that include methods of establishing information hierarchy. Because organization is one of the most important topics in the book, it is placed on the highest row of the visual. Placing information on the top of a visual space is interpreted by Western cultures as the most important. It is likely that the order in which we read—from top to bottom—establishes this status.

## Focus Questions

- What is hierarchy and how does it relate to organization?
- Do visuals have levels of importance?
- How do you use tools and actions to create visual hierarchy and organization?

## Key Terms

**Chunk**   A unit of information.
**Chunking**   The action of grouping information.
**Cues**   Visual signals that capture and direct attention.
**Hierarchy**   A perception principle that deals with communicating the relative importance of elements in a display.

**Layers**   Different levels of information used for visually stratifying information.
**Planes**   Imaginary or visible lines that form horizontally, vertically, or diagonally.

## Introduction

Sylvia and Zack are redesigning the interface of a parking ticket dispenser. To check out the design, they drive to a parking lot that uses the interface. Like many automated environments, no "live" parking attendant is employed at the site; the dispenser and the person parking the car do all the work.

When Sylvia and Zack encounter the machine, they are aware of three cars waiting behind them so they do not want to take too long to figure out how to get the ticket. The image shown in **Figure 6–1(a)** is what they see. The large circle in the middle catches their attention first because of its highly visible words "Takes Bills Only." When searching through his wallet for the money, Zack realizes he has only quarters, no bills. "Is this the problem with the interface?" he wonders. Upon closer observation he notices an obscure area showing where to insert quarters. Sylvia and Zack agree that many of the drivers probably think they cannot use quarters and start to worry when they realize they do not have any bills.

As Sylvia and Zack analyze the interface they ask these questions:

What is the user trying to do?
What is the user's environment like?
Do any environmental restrictions need to be considered?
Is there a sequential order to information that users should follow?
How do you establish what the user should read first, second, and third?
If there are items of equal importance, how do you communicate this status?

The parking meter redesign shown in **Figure 6–1(b)** considers each question. Since purchasing a parking ticket is the key user task, the words "Pay in Advance Parking" are emphasized in large letters at the top of the display (where Western cultures tend to look first). Minimizing the number of cars waiting in line to buy parking tickets requires that reading time be minimized too. Given that purchases take place from the driver's side of the car, the display is positioned at the correct height, with all typefaces large enough to be readable

## Before and After

These images show how a parking meter was made more user friendly.

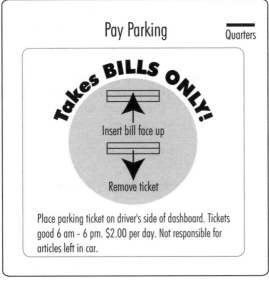

(a)

This seems pretty intuitive, but something is wrong. The machine does take quarters. The first impression you get is that it takes bills ONLY. Placing the quarter slot in the top-right section of the interface makes it hard to notice.

(b)

The option of bills or quarters is more evident here. Notice, too, how the shades of gray move from light to dark, implying a sequence of steps.

(c)

Western cultures read from the top left to the bottom right. Eastern cultures read from the bottom to the top.

**FIGURE 6–1**   Hierarchy and parking meter design

from the driver's seat. Numbering the steps 1 and 2 helps users identify the tasks they must perform. Since the parking ticket dispenser was designed for Western cultures, the steps could be displayed in a left-to-right, top-to-bottom organizational sequence, as shown in **Figure 6–1(c),** which follows the Western culture reading order.

The considerations that Sylvia and Zack made about how the order in which a culture reads information and how sequence and order can best be communicated deal with **hierarchy,** one of the most important organization strategies covered in this chapter. As you read you will notice that hierarchy is mentioned more than organization. Keep in mind that hierarchy is a type of organizational strategy. This chapter shows you how you can make most instruction easier to follow using organization design principles, of which hierarchy is the most prominent.

Hierarchy deals with communicating relative importance between elements in a display. To quickly understand hierarchy, think of an outline for a written composition (see **Figure 6–2**). You have the top levels (see point A), subordinate levels (see point B), and coordinate levels (see point C). Visuals can be made with these same levels of importance. Instead of using numbers and letters, these levels are created using tools (type, shape, color,

## Example 1: The outline

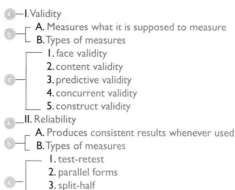

### Validity and Reliability

I. Validity
  A. Measures what it is supposed to measure
  B. Types of measures
    1. face validity
    2. content validity
    3. predictive validity
    4. concurrent validity
    5. construct validity
II. Reliability
  A. Produces consistent results whenever used
  B. Types of measures
    1. test-retest
    2. parallel forms
    3. split-half
    4. internal consistency

This outline has three levels: A, B, & C.

## Example 2: Numbers we live by

| | |
|---|---|
| 4584231 | 458 - 4231 |
| 35A897280 | 35A - 89 - 7280 |

## Example 3: The keypad

**FIGURE 6–2**   Everyday chunking examples

depth, and space) and actions (contrast, alignment, repetition, and proximity). You'll see many applications of these tools and actions in this chapter.

When you create a hierarchy, you are working through several issues:

What do I want the user/learner to look at first, second, and third?
Should I make this big and bold to make people look here first?
If I make this smaller and less bold will people look here next?
Will white space between these elements make them seem distinct and unrelated,
    while at the same time making the clustered elements seem related?
What do I want the learner to compare?

By asking these types of questions, you create what artists and information designers call levels or layers that provide pathways for people to navigate (Mullet & Sano, 1995; Tufte, 1990). In the parking ticket example, the designer of the original interface was probably not aware that the large, brightly colored section of the interface would attract the user's attention first and lead to the mistaken assumption that only bills were required. These dominant features of the interface (the brightly colored circle) created an entry level for reading the interface. Unfortunately, the user's eyes failed to wander, in part because little else caught the user's attention.

When you design for organization, you provide the learner or user with pathways through information. In doing this, you reduce the learner's cognitive load. In the parking ticket example, drivers do not need or want to think through how the information is organized hierarchically; they just want to do a simple task quickly. As with the core idea of selection in Chapter 5, this chapter stresses the importance of organizing information hierarchically up front, saving learners from having to do the work themselves. When you do this, you are essentially reducing intrinsic load.

## WHAT DOES THE RESEARCH SAY ABOUT HIERARCHY?

Creating hierarchy is the act of creating a series of **cues** or signs to direct the eye toward certain information in a certain order. For purposes of this discussion, assume cues and sign mean the same thing; They are both signals that catch the learner's attention. These cues are created using the tools and actions covered later this book. Simple shapes such as lines and arrows, larger or bold typeface, color, use of white space, and elements that create a visual texture or depth all act to direct attention (McIntyre, 1983). Contrast, alignment, and proximity are important actions for creating hierarchy.

While reading this chapter, you may find yourself wondering why some of its content would not be considered for the selection or even integration chapters. If so, your thinking is on track! Some of this information could just as easily have been presented in those chapters. These principles are intertwined and difficult to separate. Figure-ground is important to consider in hierarchy because what you notice first directs you to what you notice next. Figure-ground acts in a larger perspective as a means for providing direction, location, position, motion, and sequence—all hierarchical functions.

A number of researchers support the use of **cues**—a form of hierarchy that uses visuals such as arrows, headings, and lines in instructional materials (Misanchuk, 1992; McIntyre, 1983). Learning materials including signals such as section headings and pointer words generated significantly more student solutions on transfer tests in a study conducted by Mautone and Mayer (2001).

Research consistently finds that visual cueing facilitates learning for low-ability individuals, children, or learners unfamiliar with information. In particular visual cueing is important to people unfamiliar with content, especially when new situations arise (as in the parking ticket example). Other researchers, however, find the usefulness of cues to be questionable. Kennedy (1971) found that students would overlook many signals, such as arrows and headings, that were provided in textbooks. Allen (1975) found that higher-ability students might be handicapped by cues since these students could already focus their attention and the cues just distracted them, perhaps due to extraneous load.

Cues are important, especially in performance environments where part of the goal is to help someone at the moment of need. Just imagine what driving would be like without clear traffic signs or signals. Or think of being in a busy airport trying to catch a plane without visible or well-organized gate numbers or arrival and departure times. Perhaps you can even think of a recent experience in a distance-learning environment where you wanted something as simple as instructions on how to get started. Many students complain when information on a website can be located in multiple places. In part what bothers them is a disrupted hierarchy.

The increase of self-directed learning and performance environments, as in the parking ticket example, requires that information be especially clear and easy to follow. The use of cues to establish hierarchy can be crucial in making information easier to understand and use.

The use of the quote at the beginning of this chapter emphasizes the importance of designing information with hierarchy in mind. People interact with hierarchically arranged information every day. Consider these examples:

- Finding where pasta is in a grocery store by using the store index (information is organized alphabetically)
- Filling your car with gas using the instructions on the pump (information is organized in sequential steps)
- Getting money from the cash machine (information is organized in sequential steps)
- Finding a comedy in your local video rental store (information is organized by emotional categories such as drama, new releases, and horror)
- Registering for classes (information is organized by academic department)
- Locating information on the Internet (information is organized by common search categories such as shopping, travel, and education—though some consider the Internet not organized at all)
- Locating a particular type of store in a mall (information is organized by store type, such as department store, shoe store, home accessories store)

Some of these categories and information structures involve sequence, such as steps in a process or alphabetical ordering, and are clearly hierarchical in nature. Other steps just involve placing things in a category, such as pasta in a grocery store. Pasta is not more or less important than canned vegetables, so how could that be hierarchical? In this chapter, however, categorization is considered a part of hierarchy. It may seem a stretch, and we'll cover it more when we discuss chunking. For now think of it as hierarchical simply because it has to be positioned somewhere and that somewhere usually has a relative position.

Three steps for creating hierarchy are covered in this chapter: (1) chunking information, (2) providing entry points to instruction, and (3) using horizontal and vertical planes. These steps enhance the learner's perception of the hierarchy of an image.

Enhancing hierarchy is similar to enhancing figure-ground. Just as learners will automatically and unconsciously seek figure-ground distinctions, they seek out hierarchical relationships as well. Fleming and Levie (1993) describe the concept this way:

> Early processing organizes perceptual units into groups and the groups into other groups in a hierarchical manner. The way the elements of a message are clustered by the designer may therefore have an important influence on perceptual organization. (p. 63)

As a designer, your job is to identify clusters of information and to arrange them hierarchically. You are likely to ask the following questions, directly corresponding to the three research-based steps mentioned previously:

- How should I chunk (or cluster) the information?
- Where do I want the learner to look first? Should I initially direct the learner's eye to the whole display or just part of the display?
- Where do I position chunks to make the most sense and draw the eye to different parts of the visual?

# HOW SHOULD YOU CHUNK INFORMATION?

Instructional designers call the step of clustering information into related groups **chunking.** Chunks are simply groups of related data. A simple way to envision chunks is to think of the paragraphs on this page. Each paragraph consists of a group of related sentences. You could go a step further and consider each heading section in this chapter a chunk and each chapter in this book a chunk. As a designer, it is up to you how much chunking you want to do.

You might be wondering how chunks fall into the category of hierarchy. Think of chunks as part of a larger hierarchy. A chunk of information usually has some type of hierarchical status. As a designer you continually decide how to chunk information hierarchically. For example, if you were explaining how to make cookies, you might separate the instructions as follows: measuring all of the dry ingredients (flour, sugar, baking powder), measuring the wet ingredients (oil, eggs, milk), preheating the oven, and greasing the pan.

Your dry ingredient instructions would be one chunk, your wet ingredient instructions would be another chunk, preheating the oven and greasing the pan another chunk. You would probably arrange the chunks in a logical order, preheating the oven and greasing the pan being your first chunk, and measuring dry and wet ingredients the second and third chunks.

Your goal when chunking is to help the learner think about information in a meaningful or an efficient way. Information processing theory states that short-term memory can handle seven plus or minus two items at a time (Miller, 1956). Anything over that and the mind is likely to lose pieces of information. This is relevant in our cookie example because there are typically about 14 units of information in a typical cookie recipe.

In the past, most designers used the seven plus or minus two rule for chunking. This rule suggests that no more than seven to nine chunks of information be presented at any one time. Any more than that and the learner would not be able to process the information. Cowan's (2001) recent research makes chunking an even more important strategy for extending memory, suggesting that three to five information chunks as the maximum number for working memory. Did you notice the space-created chunking between paragraphs above? Ask yourself as you read the remainder of this page if more chunking of this nature would help.

Now that those numbers are debated, it appears that we should present fewer, rather than more, chunks of information if we want the learner to be able to work efficiently with that information. Keep in mind that chunk sizes can vary, as discussed in Chapter 3. There may be quite a bit of information in one chunk and very little information in the next. Many factors influence how many units of information a designer might put into a chunk. The information itself, the learning situation, or the expertise level of the learner all influence how you might chunk information. For example, look at a simple recipe for spaghetti. This situation might call for three chunks: the sauce instructions, the pasta instructions, and the assembly and presentation instructions. In this example, the nature of the content influences chunk size.

The expertise level of the learner influences chunking as well, with greater expertise on the part of the learner corresponding to a greater number of information units within a chunk. An advanced cook might need only two or three chunks in the recipe for spaghetti, whereas a beginning cook would likely need more chunks, beginning with a chunk of information on utensils needed and another chunk of information on the spices in the sauce. As a designer, it is up to you to chunk information accordingly.

Let's look at an everyday example of chunking that all of us have experienced—the information shown earlier in example 2 in Figure 6–2. If you shift your attention to the right side of this image, you will notice immediately that the first number is a phone number. Notice how the seven digits have been chunked into two groups. The chunked version seems easier to think about, doesn't it? The second number is a dummy social security number, 35A-89-

7280. Here nine numbers have been chunked into three groups. Chunking must work, or we wouldn't be using it so much.

To emphasize the need for chunking, try this simple exercise. Without looking at your telephone, try to recall which letters on the keypads are associated with which numbers. While you are at it, also try to remember where the #, the operator, and * keys are. If you cannot remember, it is because it is too much information, altogether 26 units of information (see example 3 in Figure 6-2). You have 12 buttons, 24 letters (Q and Z are left off the keypad), 10 numbers, and 2 symbols. This example might not be as effective as it once was though, given the rise in text messaging. Many of us have seen younger people rapidly sending messages with their cell phone keypads.

The keypad's effectiveness, however, is in part based upon the chunking of letters (usually three letters per key) and the mind's ability to remember information in small chunk sizes. When looking for letters on the keypad, the user has an easier time because the alphabet is chunked with three to four letters per key. The keys are in turn chunked in rows of three.

White space emphasizes these chunks. In the telephone number and social security examples in Figure 6-2, white space is used to separate numbers. Increasing the white space between elements makes the elements seem more distinct. Decreasing the white space makes the elements seem more similar. White space is an important tool for creating the appropriate distance (proximity) between information elements.

In whatever you design—whether it is an instructional handout, a document, a Web-based instructional unit, or an electronic presentation—you will find yourself chunking information and then arranging those chunks in ways that you think will make sense to your learner. This arrangement is usually based on some type of hierarchy. Your chunks may be part of something sequential, they may be part of a natural order (you chunk things based on the way they appear in real life), or they may simply be arranged alphabetically. As you arrange the chunks, you must decide where you want the learner to begin, the next step in enhancing the hierarchy of instructional information.

## Where Do You Want Learners to Look First?

The overall arrangement of information chunks influences how a visual is initially perceived. What does a learner look at first in a picture? The whole picture or just part of it? Fleming and Levie (1993) suggest that seeing the "big picture" or the "details in the picture" first depends on the relative size of the image to the space that image takes up in the visual field. Thinking of the visual field as the white space that surrounds an image may help you see the distinction (see **Figure 6–3**). When the visual field is small and the image is large, the learner may be more likely to notice the detail. When the visual field is large and the image is small, the learner may be more likely to notice the big picture. Fleming and Levie (1993) suggest that "typically neither the global (big picture) nor the local (detail) precedence dominates, but rather that people enter the image at a level of detail that is somewhere between the two extremes." (p. 64)

This theory suggests that we manipulate the white space in an image to create an equal perception of the big picture and detail. Likewise, Tufte (1990) recommends that we "create simplicity in the underlying design and complexity in the details." Perhaps the best way to think of this is to turn to another writing analogy. An outline with levels indicated by numbers and letters (I, II, III, A, B, C) provides both a big picture and detail at the same time. Because the outline is brief and displays the key topics, it lets you see the big picture, and each line of the outline lets you see the detail. The heart images in Figure 6-3 also show you both the big picture and the detail. In both images you see the large heart and the details that make up the small hearts.

Providing detail is important since people are attracted to and often motivated by it (Fleming & Levie, 1993; Tufte, 1990). People have been found to choose to study displays that have many rather than few elements and asymmetrical or irregular arrangements (Fleming & Levie, 1978). Advice to keep things simple and sayings such as "less is more" are often misinterpreted as advice to keep out some of the necessary detail. Tufte (1990) describes the unfortunate consequence of such activity as "dummying down" the data.

Where do you look first?

Here you are likely to notice the whole image first (the big heart).

Here you are likely to notice parts of the image first (the individual hearts).

**FIGURE 6-3**   Seeing the big picture and details

To help the learner enter a visual depends in part on how you have dealt with figure and ground. The information on selection in Chapter 5 (providing contrast, emphasizing important information using size, color, and type) can help you make certain areas of a visual be noticed first.

## How Do You Draw the Eye to Different Parts of the Visual?

You have chunked and created a good figure-ground balance to help learners enter a visual. Now you need to think about helping them move through the visual. You need to create paths or layers through which learners can travel. Creating paths is not difficult when you control the sequence in which information is displayed. For example, when you use electronic presentations, movies, and books, the sequence of information is presented very clearly. The learner sees each screen in sequential order starting with the first screen and moving methodically to the last screen. When this is the case, the type of media you use will control the order and sequence of the information and you do not need to worry about how learners will perceive the pathways through the information or where their eyes will move to next.

When this ordering is not controlled, as in some hypertext environments, visual charts, tables, graphs, and diagrams, then you do need to be concerned about how the learner will travel through the information. As is the case with charts and graphs, learners must read information that falls at the intersection of rows and columns. In hypertext settings learners must move through a series of nonlinear links, keeping track of where they have been.

According to Fleming and Levie (1993, p. 69) several attention-drawing principles of design using devices such as "lines, arrows, and the message's composition" can help you control where you direct the learner's attention. You can use these devices to facilitate the mind's natural tendency to react certain ways:

- Organize information on vertical, horizontal, and diagonal planes.
- Respond to different degrees of contrast.
- Perceive relationships based on proximity.

It is interesting to note that these three tendencies rely on three actions: alignment, contrast, and proximity.

## How Do You Use Vertical, Horizontal, and Diagonal Alignment to Improve Hierarchical Organization?

Without thinking, the learner's mind will seek out lines and contours, the figure-ground phenomenon. By placing important information onto either horizontal or vertical alignments, it is more likely to be noticed.

### Vertical Alignment

Horton (1994) suggests that people see items placed on the top part of a vertical plane as being high, powerful, lightweight, light color, spiritual, valuable, rare, primary. Low positions are seen to have these properties: heavy, dark, earthy, common, secondary.

An example of hierarchy can be seen in **Figure 6–4,** which shows signage in a university building. During the period when I served as the department chair, this sign was prominently displayed near the elevator door. Although all three departments, and their chairs, had equal status, this sign made it look like the Statistics department and its chair were the most important.

In general, items on the top are assigned a status of more importance. Consider the two passages shown in **Figure 6–5.** Which is easier to understand? If you think the second example is easier to understand, it is probably because of the arrangement of information. It seems easier to understand that Stephanie is the tallest when her position is also the highest.

### Horizontal Alignment

According to Horton (1985), elements on the left side of the plane have the status of before, cause, primary, problem, crude. Images on the right have the status of after, effect, secondary, solution, refined. Fleming and Levie (1993) make a number of research-based suggestions to show relationships between elements using lines and arrows. They suggest that lines between elements show cause and effect. This perception can be strengthened when the causal element is placed to the left of the element that is affected. Thicker lines between the elements suggest a stronger connection or relationship than do thin lines, and arrows imply an even stronger relationship (Fleming, 1968).

Studies by Winn (1980a, 1980b, 1981, 1982a, 1982b, 1982c, 1983, 1986, 1987) and Winn and Holliday (1985) show how graphics act as strategies that activate learners' cognitive processes along both vertical and horizontal planes. Winn compared learning of evolution-

This signage greeted visitors and students entering the fifth floor of a university building. Which group do you think looks more important?

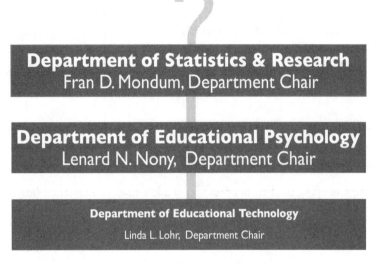

Unfortunately, this is not an exaggeration

This signage would more accurately represent the hierarchical reality of the information.

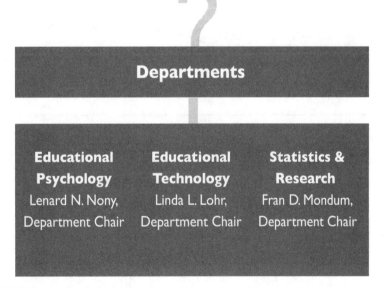

**FIGURE 6–4**   Subtle hierarchical messages

ary sequence using two flow diagrams. One diagram showed evolution of dinosaurs from left to right across the page, and the other showed evolution right to left. Students using the left-to-right diagram learned the category names and numbers better, theoretically because left to right followed the reading sequence where left is first (the oldest) and right is the latest (or youngest).

Figure 6–5 shows evolution in a similar way. Take a moment to study parts (a) and (b). Which part of the figure would help you recall the sequence of evolution most easily? If you

## Vertical alignment

Which passage is easier to understand?

Stephanie is taller than Jackson. Jackson is taller than Nick. Nick is shorter than both Stephanie and Jackson.

Stephanie is taller than Jackson.

Jackson is taller than Nick.

Nick is shorter than Jackson and Stephanie.

## Horizontal alignment

Cause and effect is often understood in a left-to-right sequence (for Western cultures).

(a)

(b)

**FIGURE 6–5**   Vertical and horizontal alignment

preferred the left-to-right sequence in part (b), it might be because you "read" this diagram just as you read most information (in Western cultures). **Figure 6–6** illustrates another example. Which of these diagrams would help you understand the concept of evolution best? If you choose part (b), it may be because you attribute a cause-effect relationship in a left-to-right sequence.

Winn (1981) also conducted a study to teach students the classification of insects at different stages of metamorphosis. Winn suggested that student memory structures (schemas) were activated by a matrix of rows and columns that helped students identify classification categories. Which part of **Figure 6–7** helps you better understand the classification system of wildcats? If you chose part (b), the row and column structure may match your schema for organizing information. The rows and columns provide an organizational structure that adapts easily to how your memory is organized. Part (a) does not help with organization at all. The circle is used to group the wildcat family but does not help as much as the column format. The families *filinae* and *pantherinare* are included in the circle image, but they are more difficult for the learner to group initially.

Which is easier to interpret? Part (b) is easier for Western cultures to understand.

(a)

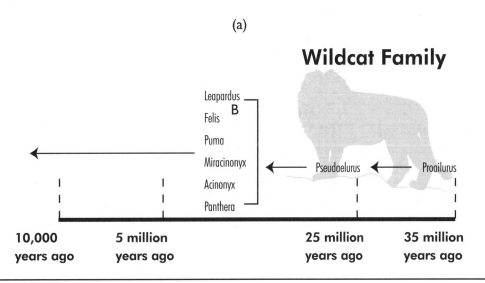

(b)

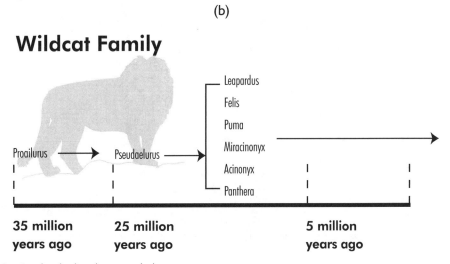

**FIGURE 6–6**   Another look at horizontal alignment

This circular arrangement of the wildcats makes it harder to sort the *Filinae* from the *Pantherinare* family.

(a)

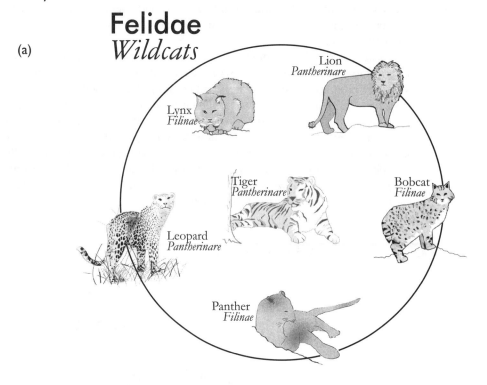

This arrangement makes it much easier to perceive the different cat families.

(b)

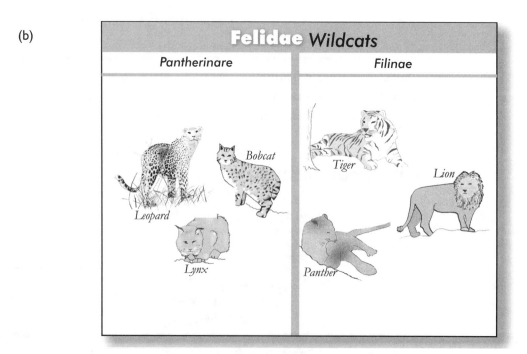

**FIGURE 6–7**   Organizing information: Are circles or columns better?

## Diagonal Alignment

The use of a diagonal alignment to increase perception has not been mentioned frequently in the research literature. Horton (1994) associates information on the diagonal plane near the top of an image with *adventure, far, later, unknown,* and *secondary.* Images at the bottom of a diagonal plane have the status of *near, now* or *soon, familiar, primary, intrusion,* and *involvement.* Many graphic designers recommend that diagonal lines be used to generate excitement and energy in images (Nelson, 1989). My advice is to avoid diagonal alignment unless you want to spend some time. I have observed students struggling to make diagonal arrangements look balanced.

## Reading Order

According to Fleming and Levie (1993), if none of the vertical, horizontal, or diagonal strategies are used, learners will probably resort to their reading order. To tap into this tendency, you need to place the most important items on the top-left area of a display, the next most important items to the immediate right, eventually working toward a lower position on the page, likely starting on the left again. While this left-to-right, top-to-bottom sequencing strategy is an easy way to establish hierarchy, the increase in international audiences will likely make this a less-than-ideal solution, since international audiences may read from right to left or start at the bottom of a page (or display) and move up.

## Proximity

Mayer's proximity principle (2001) is based on a number of research studies showing that text placed close to the image it references is perceived as related. Likewise, text placed close to other text can have the same effect. Consider the example in **Figure 6–8.** In example B, "Turning 40" and "Public speaking" do not appear related to "Events that people worry about." Example A, however, connects "Turning 40" and "Public speaking" to the "Events" label. When the phrases are closer together, as in example A, they are perceived as related.

## Contrast

How do different degrees of contrast convey hierarchical information? Aside from using alignment, hierarchy is perceived through color and size. Images that are brighter or darker are often perceived as more important, dominant, or superordinate. Likewise images that are larger are perceived as more important, powerful, and superordinate to images that are smaller. Shades of color can communicate sequence, time passing, and rates of change. Figure 6–8 shows how shades of gray are used to show the increasing depth of lake water.

# HOW DO YOU USE HIERARCHY TO DESIGN TABLES AND CHARTS?

Hierarchy plays a key role in the design of tables and charts, which rely heavily on hierarchical principles to communicate trends, quantities, summaries, and relationships. This type of data usually involves making comparisons that are hierarchical in nature, such as greater than or less than, bigger or smaller, increased or decreased.

Though easy to format and widely used, tables and charts are often misunderstood by young and old alike (Hartley, 1985; Misanchuk, 1992). Many people have problems with numbers, particularly when they need to locate a number at the intersection of a horizontal or vertical plane, which is the case when reading from tables and charts. The section that follows covers a range of design suggestions to increase the effectiveness of tables and charts.

## Tables

Tables, often the quickest and easiest type of data display to produce, are used to make numerical information easier to understand and to present information when space is limited. Seven heuristics for table design follow.

## Proximity

Notice how the words in example A seem related, whereas the words in example B seem distinct.

| A | B |
|---|---|
| Events that people worry about<br>Turning 40<br>Public speaking | Events that people worry about<br><br>Turning 40<br><br>Public speaking |

## Contrast

Contrasting shades of gray help you see the increasing depth of a lake.

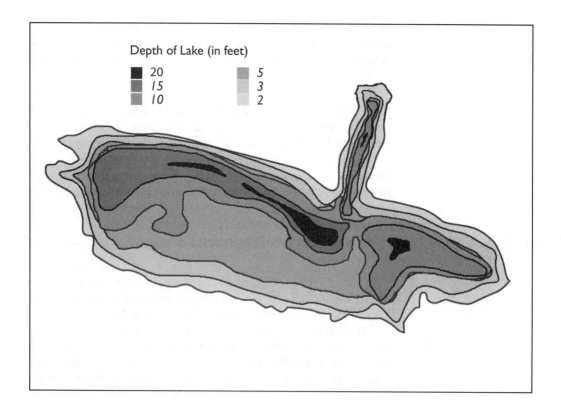

**FIGURE 6–8**  Communicating with proximity and contrast

## 1. Use Tables to Make Information Easier to Understand

Compare the text-based passage to the table displaying the same information in **Figure 6–9.** The table provides a spatial arrangement of data that makes the information easier to comprehend.

Though tables may show the maximum amount of information in the minimum amount of space, they are not always the best way to communicate information. Research shows that people find tables daunting and confusing; tables are perhaps best used with professional audiences when specific quantities are important (Misanchuk, 1992).

### I. Use tables to make information easier to understand.

Compare (a) and (b) below. Does the table help you think about the information more efficiently?

(a)

In Maine, Rhode Island, and Connecticut, the average teaching salary is $45,800. The average salaries for these eastern states are $43,800, $43,100, and $50,000, respectively. Western salaries are lower, with an average of $40,800. Washington, Oregon, and California salaries are $37,900, $41,000, and $43,500, respectively.

(b)

**Side-by-side Teaching Salaries**

| West Coast | | | | East Coast | | | |
|---|---|---|---|---|---|---|---|
| WA | OR | CA | Avg. | ME | RI | CT | Avg. |
| $37,900 | $41,000 | $43,500 | $40,800 | $43,800 | $43,100 | $50,500 | $45,800 |

Design note:

Data are much easier to compare when numbers are side by side. Averages are included as well. Notice, too, how the West Coast is located on the left as it is on most maps.

### 2. Use columns instead of rows when making comparisons.

Most people find it easier to compare side by side than up and down.

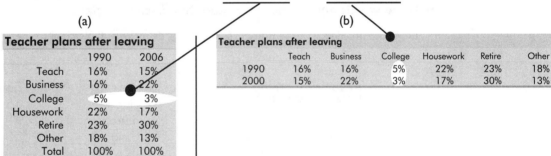

(a)

**Teacher plans after leaving**

| | 1990 | 2006 |
|---|---|---|
| Teach | 16% | 15% |
| Business | 16% | 22% |
| College | 5% | 3% |
| Housework | 22% | 17% |
| Retire | 23% | 30% |
| Other | 18% | 13% |
| Total | 100% | 100% |

(b)

**Teacher plans after leaving**

| | Teach | Business | College | Housework | Retire | Other |
|---|---|---|---|---|---|---|
| 1990 | 16% | 16% | 5% | 22% | 23% | 18% |
| 2000 | 15% | 22% | 3% | 17% | 30% | 13% |

### 3. Use rounded numbers when detail is not needed.

The rounded numbers are easier to think about than the numbers with decimal points.

(a)

**Teacher plans after leaving**

| | 1990 | 2006 |
|---|---|---|
| Teach | 16% | 15% |
| Business | 16% | 22% |
| College | 6% | 3% |
| Housework | 22% | 17% |
| Retire | 23% | 30% |
| Other | 18% | 12% |

(b)

**Teacher plans after leaving**

| | 1990 | 2006 |
|---|---|---|
| Teach | 15.6% | 15.3% |
| Business | 16.2% | 22.1% |
| College | 5.8% | 3.1% |
| Housework | 21.7% | 16.7% |
| Retire | 22.6% | 30.6% |
| Other | 18.1% | 12.2% |

**FIGURE 6–9**   Designing tables: Heuristics 1–3

## 4. Include averages.

Do the averages in part (a) make the table easier to understand?

(a)

### Teaching Salaries

| East Coast | | | |
| --- | --- | --- | --- |
| ME | RI | CT | *Average* |
| $43,800 | $43,100 | $50,500 | **$45,800** |

(b)

### Teaching Salaries

| East Coast | | |
| --- | --- | --- |
| ME | RI | CT |
| $43,800 | $43,100 | $50,500 |

## 5. Place words before numbers.

Does placing the words before the numbers make the table easier to understand?

(a)

| Increase in online holiday shopping | |
| --- | --- |
| Japan | 184% |
| Europe | 96% |
| Asia | 90% |
| N. America | 70% |
| Rest | 188% |

(b)

| Increase in online holiday shopping | |
| --- | --- |
| 184% | Japan |
| 96% | Europe |
| 90% | Asia |
| 70% | N. America |
| 188% | Rest |

## 6. Keep words and numbers a readable distance apart.

Does the proximity of the numbers to the words make a difference?

(a)

| Increase in online holiday shopping | |
| --- | --- |
| Japan | 184% |
| Europe | 96% |
| Asia | 90% |
| N. America | 70% |
| Rest | 188% |

(b)

| Increase in online holiday shopping | |
| --- | --- |
| Japan | 184% |
| Europe | 96% |
| Asia | 90% |
| N. America | 70% |
| Rest | 188% |

Too far for the eye to jump!

**FIGURE 6-10**   Designing tables: Heuristics 4–6

Several perceptually based recommendations in the pages ahead make tables easier to read. In particular, the actions of alignment and proximity play a role in making tables easier to understand.

## 2. Use Columns Instead of Rows When Making Comparisons

Figure 6-9 shows east and west coast salaries side by side. This arrangement places east and west on a coordinate or equal level and makes comparisons easier.

Ehrenberg (1977) suggests using the horizontal rather than the vertical plane when making comparisons. As we have already discussed, if you want to make it easier for the learner

## 7. Create chunks in data to make it easier to read and retrieve information.

Table (a) is easier to scan because the chunking is meaningful. For this task, the alphabetical sequence used in Table (b) is not efficient.

(a)

**Regional Teaching Interest (%)**

| Region | | 1990 | 1995 | 2000 | 2005 |
|---|---|---|---|---|---|
| Far West | AZ | 41 | 39 | 35 | 25 |
| | CA | 33 | 29 | 25 | 27 |
| | ID | 49 | 44 | 37 | 27 |
| | OR | 40 | 39 | 35 | 38 |
| | WA | 48 | 54 | 48 | 38 |
| West | CO | 43 | 38 | 33 | 23 |
| | MT | 45 | 41 | 34 | 24 |
| | NE | 45 | 50 | 44 | 34 |
| | NV | 45 | 43 | 35 | 23 |
| | UT | 44 | 40 | 35 | 25 |
| Midwest | KS | 26 | 30 | 33 | 23 |
| | ND | 52 | 49 | 42 | 32 |
| | OK | 30 | 35 | 30 | 20 |
| | SD | 48 | 45 | 40 | 30 |
| | IA | 35 | 37 | 32 | 22 |
| | MN | 45 | 49 | 42 | 33 |
| | MO | 22 | 27 | 23 | 14 |
| | WI | 44 | 47 | 42 | 44 |
| South | AR | 46 | 49 | 41 | 33 |
| | LA | 49 | 56 | 49 | 37 |
| | NM | 35 | 29 | 24 | 18 |
| | TX | 30 | 37 | 32 | 23 |

(b)

**Regional Teaching Interest (%)**

| | 1990 | 1995 | 2000 | 2005 |
|---|---|---|---|---|
| AR | 46 | 49 | 41 | 33 |
| AZ | 41 | 39 | 35 | 25 |
| CA | 33 | 29 | 25 | 27 |
| CO | 43 | 38 | 33 | 23 |
| ID | 49 | 44 | 37 | 27 |
| IA | 35 | 37 | 32 | 22 |
| KS | 26 | 30 | 33 | 23 |
| LA | 49 | 56 | 49 | 37 |
| MN | 45 | 49 | 42 | 33 |
| MO | 22 | 27 | 23 | 14 |
| MT | 45 | 41 | 34 | 24 |
| NE | 45 | 50 | 44 | 34 |
| ND | 52 | 49 | 42 | 32 |
| NM | 35 | 29 | 24 | 18 |
| NV | 45 | 43 | 35 | 23 |
| OK | 30 | 35 | 30 | 20 |
| OR | 40 | 39 | 35 | 38 |
| SD | 48 | 45 | 40 | 30 |
| TX | 30 | 37 | 32 | 23 |
| UT | 44 | 40 | 35 | 25 |
| WA | 48 | 54 | 48 | 38 |
| WI | 44 | 47 | 42 | 44 |

Highlighting every other row or column helps make data comparisons easier.

(c)

| West States | 1989 | 1999 | 2004 |
|---|---|---|---|
| Arizona | 32,178 | 46,723 | 48,995 |
| Arkansas | 25,395 | 38,663 | 39,945 |
| California | 40,559 | 53,025 | 58,327 |
| Colorado | 35,930 | 55,883 | 58,849 |
| Idaho | 29,472 | 43,490 | 46,586 |
| Iowa | 31,659 | 48,005 | 51,505 |
| Kansas | 32,966 | 49,624 | 53,541 |
| Louisiana | 26,313 | 39,774 | 42,886 |
| Minnesota | 36,916 | 56,874 | 62,538 |
| Missouri | 31,838 | 46,044 | 50,819 |
| Montana | 28,044 | 40,487 | 44,958 |
| Nebraska | 31,634 | 48,032 | 52,472 |
| Nevada | 35,837 | 50,849 | 51,722 |
| New Mexico | 27,623 | 39,425 | 42,240 |
| North Dakota | 28,707 | 43,654 | 51,020 |
| Oklahoma | 28,554 | 40,709 | 44,508 |
| Oregon | 31,553 | 48,680 | 51,011 |
| South Dakota | 27,602 | 43,237 | 49,380 |
| Texas | 31,553 | 45,861 | 49,086 |
| Utah | 33,246 | 51,022 | 52,286 |
| Washington | 36,795 | 53,760 | 57,478 |
| Wyoming | 32,216 | 45,685 | 54,935 |

(d)

| West States | 1989 | 1999 | 2004 |
|---|---|---|---|
| Arizona | 32,178 | 46,723 | 48,995 |
| Arkansas | 25,395 | 38,663 | 39,945 |
| California | 40,559 | 53,025 | 58,327 |
| Colorado | 35,930 | 55,883 | 58,849 |
| Idaho | 29,472 | 43,490 | 46,586 |
| Iowa | 31,659 | 48,005 | 51,505 |
| Kansas | 32,966 | 49,624 | 53,541 |
| Louisiana | 26,313 | 39,774 | 42,886 |
| Minnesota | 36,916 | 56,874 | 62,538 |
| Missouri | 31,838 | 46,044 | 50,819 |
| Montana | 28,044 | 40,487 | 44,958 |
| Nebraska | 31,634 | 48,032 | 52,472 |
| Nevada | 35,837 | 50,849 | 51,722 |
| New Mexico | 27,623 | 39,425 | 42,240 |
| North Dakota | 28,707 | 43,654 | 51,020 |
| Oklahoma | 28,554 | 40,709 | 44,508 |
| Oregon | 31,553 | 48,680 | 51,011 |
| South Dakota | 27,602 | 43,237 | 49,380 |
| Texas | 31,553 | 45,861 | 49,086 |
| Utah | 33,246 | 51,022 | 52,286 |
| Washington | 36,795 | 53,760 | 57,478 |
| Wyoming | 32,216 | 45,685 | 54,935 |

**FIGURE 6–11**   Designing tables: Heuristic 7

## 1. Avoid chartjunk.

Figure (a) has drop shadows, a gray background, thick lines and borders, and images of a dog and cat. Figure (b) minimizes embellishment.

(a)

(b)

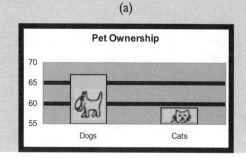

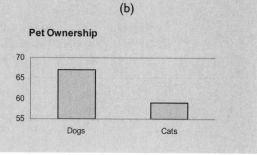

## 2. Use bar charts to display values across categories.

**A.** Vertical and horizontal bar charts tend to be equally effective.

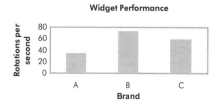

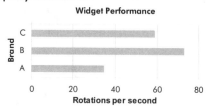

**B.** Some people prefer <u>exact numbers</u> versus <u>nonspecific</u> numbers

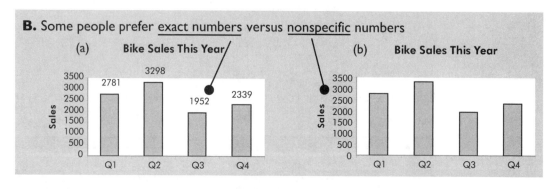

**C.** Tell the truth! Part (a) makes it look like there is a big difference in training preferences between males and females. Part (b) tells it more like it is. There really is not that much of a difference.

(a)

(b)

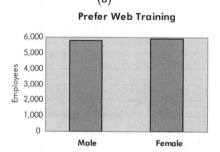

**FIGURE 6–12**   Designing charts: Heuristic 1 and 2

to compare data, put the data side by side. Look at the second heuristic in Figure 6-9. Which table makes it easier to compare teacher plans between 1990 and 2000? Based on Ehrenberg's research, many people would find the data in (a) easier to compare, perhaps because the side-by-side positioning implies a coordinate relationship.

### 3. Use Rounded Numbers When Detail Is Not Needed

Ehrenberg (1977) also suggests that rounded numbers are easier for most people to comprehend. The third heuristic in Figure 6-9 shows rounded percentages. Compare the data in parts (a) and (b). Which is easier for you? Many people would find the rounded numbers in part (a) easier to read and compare.

### 4. Include Averages

Averages should be used when possible to help learners summarize data (Ehrenberg, 1977). **Figure 6–10** part (a) shows a table with an average provided. Notice how the numbers in part (b) are initially more difficult to compare without the average.

### 5. Place Words Before Numbers

Compare the two parts of heuristic 5 in Figure 6-10. Which do you find easier to follow? Many people prefer part (a) because they want to know what they are comparing and prefer to begin reading a chart with words rather than numbers.

### 6. Keep Words and Numbers a Readable Distance Apart

The words and numbers in a table should be kept a readable distance apart. This suggestion employs the proximity action, important for optimizing hierarchy. Elements that are closer together are considered related, whereas elements that are farther apart are not. Compare the two parts of heuristic 6 in Figure 6-10. The numbers are closer to their descriptors in part (a). The eye must travel a greater distance in part (b). Designs such as this are often created because the width of the heading determines where numbers are placed. The heading in part (a) solves this problem by breaking the heading into two lines to avoid a wide spread between the country name and its percentage.

### 7. Create Chunks in Data to Make It Easier to Read and Retrieve Information

Which table in **Figure 6–11** is easiest to scan, part (a) or part (b)? Because part (a) groups information into meaningful categories, most would say that it is the easiest. The shading in parts (c) and (d) can also create chunks. Notice how different types of comparisons are facilitated by the horizontal or vertical direction of the shading shown in Figure 6-11, parts (c) and (d).

## Charts and Graphs

Charts and graphs include many different type of data displays—from bar charts to pie charts to line graphs (or charts), to name a few. Because bar charts and graphs, like tables, can be difficult to understand, it is best to keep their design as simple as possible. The following eight heuristics apply to the design of charts.

### 1. Avoid chartjunk

In this era when people like to play with all the bells and whistles that come with their statistical computer programs, it is important to consider Tufte's (1990) advice related to "chartjunk"—the name used to describe overly embellished statistical information. Think about the lavish charts in bright colors you regularly see in some newspapers, or the graphs that use little pictures, or weather reports that are accompanied by charts with a lot of graphical information in addition to the numbers. Tufte focuses on making the data—not the data container—stand out. The data container is considered anything that is not data. For example, in **Figure 6–12** some of the elements of part (a) in heuristic 1 could be considered chartjunk: the chart lines are not needed, the background shading does not add any information, and the dog and cat icons are not really needed (though many readers liked them). In part (b), the focus is on the data, not everything surrounding the data. However, part (a) might speed up recognition for some and would be more appropriate for young learners.

When there is too much chartjunk, it becomes difficult to determine hierarchy. Consider the visual weight of the different elements in parts (a) and (b). What seems to be the most important? The data comparing dogs and cats in part (a) are hard to separate from the background lines and shading. You can see the hierarchy better in part (b).

## 2. Use Bar Charts to Display Values Across Categories

Bar charts are used when comparisons between two or more variables need to be made or when trends need to be communicated. Both vertical bar charts (also called a column chart) and horizontal bar charts are used with generally equal results (see Figure 6-12, section 2A.) Bar charts are favored over pie and line charts because they allow the reader to see quantitative differences more clearly.

The effectiveness of placing values on the individual bar is debatable. To some, directly labeling the bars [as in section B, part (a) of Figure 6-12] in a bar chart is the best approach; others prefer keeping the data as simple as possible, as in part (b).

Much has been written to show how data displays can distort the truth. Perception plays a large role in this, as viewers often see the gestalt of information rather than the detail. Section C, part (a) of Figure 6-12 uses numbers to emphasize the difference in gender preferences for Web-based training. Because the *y*-axis starts at 5,700, the differences look much larger than they do when the *y*-axis starts at 0. See Tufte's book *The Visual Display of Quantitative Information* (1983) for more information on this topic.

## 3. Focus Attention on the Data, Not the Data Container

In line with all of Tufte's recommendations for the design of information, the data itself needs to be the visual focus, not the data container. To that end, heuristic 3 of **Figure 6–13** is designed to follow Tufte's recommendations. Notice how grid lines are used only when necessary. Tufte also suggests removing the following:

1. Surrounding borders
2. The *y*-axis (but keep the vertical lines)
3. The *x*-axis (or make it a very thin rule)

## 4. Reconsider the Use of Picture/Isotope and Three-Dimensional Charts

What about picture bar charts or isotope charts like the ones shown in newspapers and magazines (see heuristic 4 of Figure 6-13)? While these graphs are often clever, more often than not they are amateurish, may detract from the data, take a lot of time to produce, and often misrepresent the actual data. For instructional materials the rule of thumb is to avoid them. As Tufte (1983) says, the use of pictorial data often dummies down the data and speaks down to the reader at the same time.

What about the effectiveness of three-dimensional charts (see heuristic 4 of Figure 6-13)? Do you think the third dimension for both the bar and pie chart puts the focus on the information? Although three-dimensional charts are easy enough to produce these days, they may not be as effective as simple two-dimensional displays because exact quantities are more difficult to read when data are displayed in perspective.

## 3. Focus attention on the data, not the data container.

Notice the absence of horizontal and vertical axis lines?

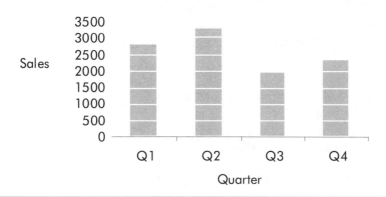

## 4. Reconsider the use of picture isotope and three-dimensional charts.

Isotope or picture graphs take a lot of time to produce and are often an inaccurate representation of data.

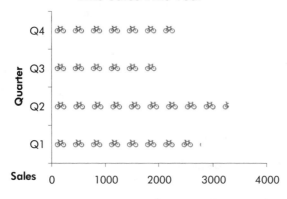

More work is required to figure out the number since your eye has to work with several edges.

What quantity does bar A represent in the chart below? Likewise, what percentage is "All Others" in the pie chart below?

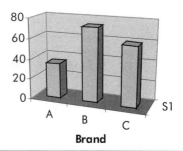

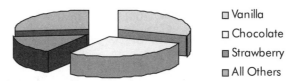

**FIGURE 6-13**  Designing charts: Heuristic 3 and 4

### 5. Use Pie Charts for General Rather than Specific Information

Pie charts show how much each value contributes to a total and are often used to show percentages (see heuristic 5 in **Figure 6–14**). Pie charts are considered easy to understand and thus are widely used. However, using a pie chart presents some real disadvantages. Tufte (1983) has strong opinions along these lines:

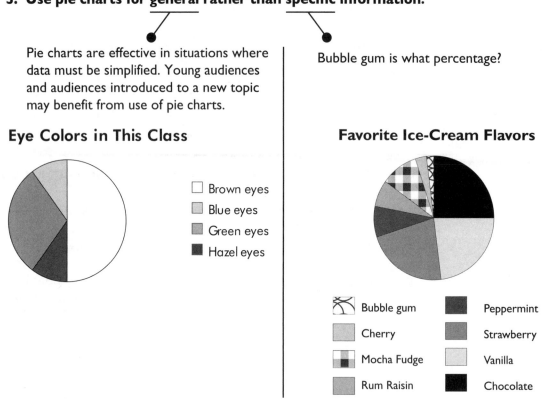

**5. Use pie charts for general rather than specific information.**

Pie charts are effective in situations where data must be simplified. Young audiences and audiences introduced to a new topic may benefit from use of pie charts.

**Eye Colors in This Class**

- ☐ Brown eyes
- ☐ Blue eyes
- ▨ Green eyes
- ■ Hazel eyes

Bubble gum is what percentage?

**Favorite Ice-Cream Flavors**

- ⧖ Bubble gum
- ☐ Cherry
- ▨ Mocha Fudge
- ▨ Rum Raisin
- ■ Peppermint
- ▨ Strawberry
- ☐ Vanilla
- ■ Chocolate

**6. Use line charts to show trends over time.**

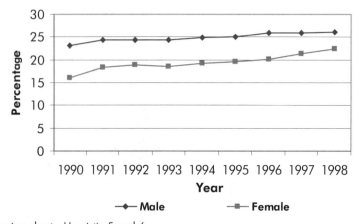

**Received College Diploma**

**FIGURE 6–14**   Designing charts: Heuristic 5 and 6

A table is nearly always better than a dumb pie chart: the only worse design is several of them, for then the viewer is asked to compare quantities located in spatial disarray both within and between pies. Given their low data-density and failure to order numbers along a visual dimension, pie charts should never be used. (p. 178)

Fleming and Levie (1993) are not quite so critical of pie charts, stating that they can be useful where precision is not important. Perhaps the biggest disadvantage of pie charts is that they are not effective for comparing data, especially if more than seven to nine segments of information and small quantities or differences in quantity are involved (see Figure 6-14). The pie shape is not an easy shape to compare because angles are involved. When the goal is marketing a concept or teaching young children (see heuristic 5 in Figure 6-14), pie charts may be the most appropriate choice because they simplify information. For simple data, pie charts are often the most effective way to represent a concept. As with everything else in this book, the "it depends" rule applies. If your audience is a dissertation committee, pie charts may not be specific enough. If your audience is a business crowd, pie charts may be all that is needed to give an overview of a trend. Some household budgeting software programs effectively use pie charts to show how money is allocated, allowing family members to see quickly how they are spending their money.

### 6. Use Line Charts to Show Trends Over Time

If you need to show trends over time (see heuristic 6 in Figure 6-14), use a line chart. Lichty (1989) recommends using a line chart for up to five lines of data.

### 7. Be Cautious with Stacked Area Graphs

Like line charts, stacked area graphs show trends over time. Use of stacked area graphs is discouraged because they are easily misinterpreted. This is a perceptual issue since the quantity of the top value can be perceived to start where the bottom line ends. Relative quantity becomes difficult to determine (see heuristic 7 in **Figure 6–15**).

### 8. Consider Picture Charts When a Picture Does Speak a Thousand Words

As expressed in the opening chapter, pictures can speak a thousand words, and this is true for pictures used in data display as well. Not all pictorial displays of quantitative information dummy down the information. In a fascinating series of books on the subject, Tufte has made Minard's map a classic example of the power of good information design. Minard's map (see heuristic 8 in Figure 6-15) shows in one space how an army the size of 400,000 dwindled to 10,000 during at Napoleon's march to Moscow in 1812. On the map, location (A), direction (B), army size (C), temperature (D), and date (E), are plotted, providing a powerful message about the tragedy of war.

## HIERARCHY IN BOOKS, ELECTRONIC PRESENTATIONS, AND CBT/WBT

Many instructional visuals use a predefined format that has some degree of hierarchy already established. **Figure 6–16(a)** shows the hierarchy of a book chapter. In this graphic, higher levels (Level I, II, III) are assigned to the chapter cover and major topics or sections of the chapter. Lower levels (A, B, C) are assigned to subheadings.

Figure 6-16(b) illustrates electronic slides that show hierarchy. The different layers or levels of information in this display resemble those in the book example.

Figure 6-16(c) shows how computer or web-based training (CBT/WBT) typically uses a hierarchical organization scheme as well. Menus serve as the highest level, units of instruction represent the next level, and instructional content, practice activities, and feedback levels follow. Since CBT and WBT are typically learner controlled, it is important to help the learner see the hierarchical structure of the learning environment.

### 7. Be cautious with stacked area graphs.

Stacked area graphs are difficult to interpret.

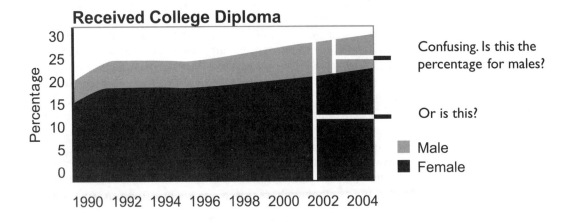

### 8. Consider picture charts when a picture does speak a thousand words.

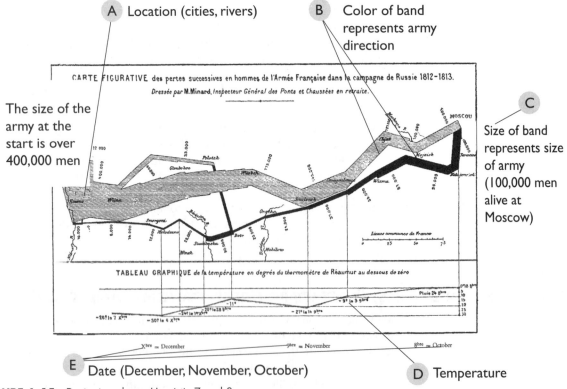

**FIGURE 6–15**    Designing charts: Heuristic 7 and 8

### (a) Books

Here the outline of chapter topics is represented visually. What traditionally would be the topic level in an outline (a Roman numeral, VII) is represented by the chapter cover layout. What traditionally is an A, B, C in an outline is translated visually into headings, for example, Times 24 bold. What usually is a subsection in an outline (numbers 1, 2, 3) are translated into subheadings, such as Times 12 bold.

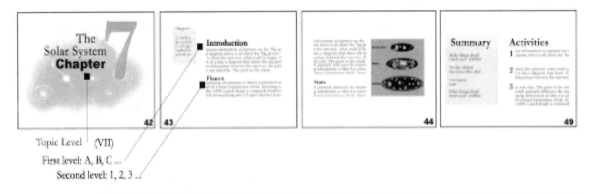

### (b) Slides

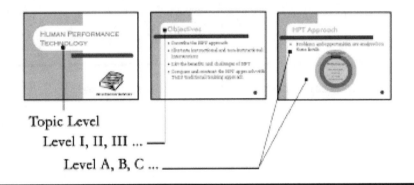

### (c) Computer/Web-Based Training

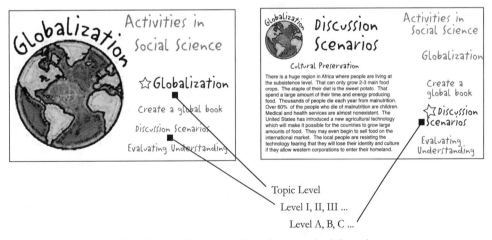

**FIGURE 6–16**   Hierarchy in books, slides, and computer based training/web based training

## Techniques to Show Hierarchy

To increase the hierarchy in your images, try these strategies:

1. Use signal words (see **Figure 6–17**). Morrison, Ross, and Kemp (2004) suggest use of explicit signals to cue the structure of a message. By combining Armbruster's (1986) content structures with Meyer's (1985) signaling words, seven strategies are illustrated.

### I. **Use signal words.**

| Lists | Comparisons | Temporal Sequence | Cause & Effect | Example |
|---|---|---|---|---|
| *Use words like:*<br>First<br>Second<br>Third<br>Subsequent<br>Another | *Use words like:*<br>In comparison<br>However<br>While<br>To distinguish<br>To differentiate | *Use words like:*<br>Beginning with<br>Then<br>After<br>Next<br>First<br>Second | *Use words like:*<br>If<br>Then<br>The reason<br>One explanation | *Use words like:*<br>For example<br>See<br>Include<br>Another |

### 2. **Use numbers or letters to show sequence.**

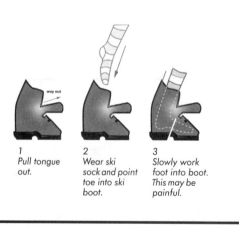

*1*
Pull tongue out.

*2*
Wear ski sock and point toe into ski boot.

*3*
Slowly work foot into boot. This may be painful.

### 3. **Use visual metaphors (high = powerful, low = less powerful) to show relationships.**

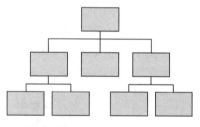

*Flowcharts show hierarchical relationships*

### 4. **Use lines and arrows to  strengthen relationships.**

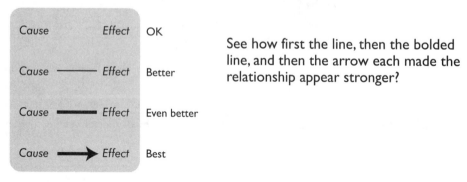

See how first the line, then the bolded line, and then the arrow each made the relationship appear stronger?

**FIGURE 6–17**   Seven techniques to show hierarchy

### 5. Use lines, arrows, and shapes to imply speed.

The tilt, size, and thickness of lines make images appear to be moving faster.

| Fast | *Faster* | **Fastest** |
|------|----------|-------------|
| → | → | → |
| 🏈 | 🏈 | 🏈 |
| ➤ | ➤ | ➤ |
| 🚚 | 🚚 | 🚚 |
| 🦄 | 🦄 | 🦄 |
| 🚒 | 🚒 | 🚒 |

Notice how shapes imply direction.

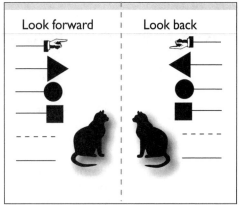

### 6. Use ghost images, small multiples, and numbers or letters to show temporal events.
These images show time passing.

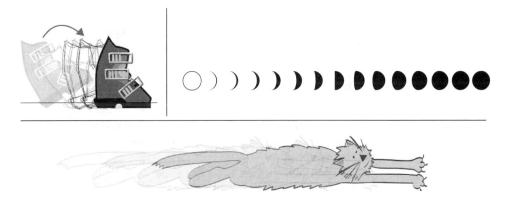

### 7. Use the size of common objects to make comparisons.

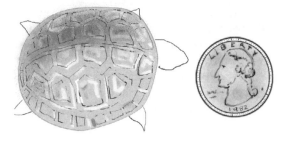

Baby Turtle Shell          Quarter

**FIGURE 6–18**   Seven techniques to show hierarchy (continued)

2. Use numbers or letters to show sequence. (This strategy uses the type tool.)
3. Use Horton's (1994) visual metaphors to show relationships (high = powerful, low = less powerful). (This strategy uses the proximity action.)
4. Use lines and arrows to strengthen relationships. Thicker lines between elements suggest a stronger connection or relationship than do thin lines, and arrows imply an even stronger relationship (Fleming, 1968) (This strategy uses the shape tool.)
5. Use lines, arrows, and shapes to imply speed, and direct attention (see **Figure 6–18**).

6. Use ghost images, small multiples, and numbers or letters to show temporal events. (This strategy uses the color tool.)
7. Use the size of common objects to make comparisons (uses the contrast action).

# How Does Hierarchy Facilitate Different Picture Functions?

At the start of this book you learned about several types of instructional visuals (decorative, representative, explanative, transformative, and organizational). This section of the chapter shows how the principles of hierarchy can be used to improve visuals that represent the following categories: (1) decoration, (2) representation, (3) organization, and (4) explanation.

## Decoration

People and faces are often used as decorative elements in instruction. The top part of **Figure 6–19** shows print-based weight-lifting training. Notice how the image that faces the content (Part A) more effectively directs the eye than the image that faces away (Part B).

## Representation

The purpose of representation is to depict something. Representative images are particularly helpful when used in conjunction with text. The bottom part of Figure 6–19 shows ship images. Part A shows relative ship sizes using line only, and B shows ship size using representative images, which are probably more motivational and interesting than the line representations.

## Organization

Organizational images are useful when temporal and spatial relationships need to be communicated. **Figure 6–20** shows the original recipe (A) without any hierarchical design. The recipe revision (B) uses a title, chunking, numbering, and task orientation that vastly improve the instruction.

The middle image in Figure 6–20 shows a diagram of how the letter J is signed. Here you see the influence of ghosting on the sequence of hand movement.

## Explanation

The purpose of explanation is to clarify often complex and difficult phenomena. Fleming and Levie (1993) recommend adding labels and stripping an image of all unnecessary detail. The bottom part of Figure 6–20 shows an explanation of how the Hawaiian islands have developed over time and are slowly moving in the direction of Japan each year. Using text labels such as "oldest island" and "youngest island" deemphasizes the island names while emphasizing the shift taking place. Although this image is effecive, it could be improved. If you are interested, try to improve this image in your Chapter 6 Challenge Activity.

# How Is Hierarchy Used to Facilitate Generative Strategies?

As stated in the previous chapter, when your goal is more learning-oriented than performance-oriented, it is time to consider generative strategies. To refresh your memory, generative strategies are techniques that require learners to generate their own meaning by outlining content; creating organizational charts, mental images, and analogies; and summarizing information in their own words (Wittrock, 1989). The examples that follow show how learners might generate their own hierarchy using mental imagery, creating an outline and a flowchart that represent content structure, and creating an image that summarizes the key point of instruction.

**1. Decoration**

A.

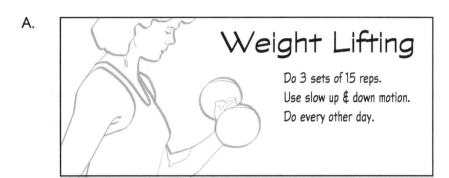

This image directs your eye toward the words.

B.

This image directs your eye away from the words.

**2. Representation**

The ships in B may be more effective because they show more visual details.

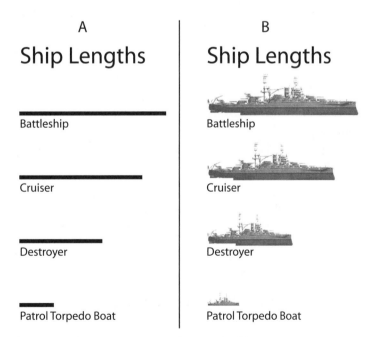

**FIGURE 6–19**   Picture functions and organization principles (part 1 of 2)

## 3. Organization

Recipe A would be hard to follow when making tacos because you would probably lose track of where you left off. Recipe B chunks information hierarchically, and creates superordinate headings for each chunk.

A

Taco recipe

Brown one pound ground beef. Add one package of taco seasoning to water (about 1 cup), then add to browned ground beef. Cut up a tomato, shred lettuce and cheese (1 cup), and cook taco shells on a baking sheet in a 450 degree oven until brown, about 5 minutes. Cook ground beef in seasoning until most of the seasoning evaporates. Spoon ground beef filling into warm taco shells. Add cheese, lettuce, and taco sauce.

B

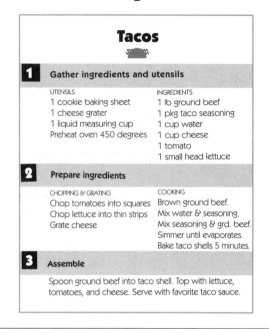

**Tacos**

**1** **Gather ingredients and utensils**

| UTENSILS | INGREDIENTS |
|---|---|
| 1 cookie baking sheet | 1 lb ground beef |
| 1 cheese grater | 1 pkg taco seasoning |
| 1 liquid measuring cup | 1 cup water |
| Preheat oven 450 degrees | 1 cup cheese |
| | 1 tomato |
| | 1 small head lettuce |

**2** **Prepare ingredients**

| CHOPPING & GRATING | COOKING |
|---|---|
| Chop tomatoes into squares | Brown ground beef. |
| Chop lettuce into thin strips | Mix water & seasoning. |
| Grate cheese | Mix seasoning & grd. beef. |
| | Simmer until evaporates. |
| | Bake taco shells 5 minutes. |

**3** **Assemble**

Spoon ground beef into taco shell. Top with lettuce, tomatoes, and cheese. Serve with favorite taco sauce.

A                        B

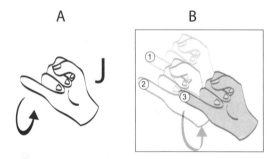

Image A shows the original presentation of how the letter J is signed. The arrow was not enough to show the sequence of the hand movements. Ghosting made the movement order easier to see in image (B).

## 4. Explanation

Arrows show the direction of the plate shift. "Oldest Island" and "Youngest Island" captions imply sequence.

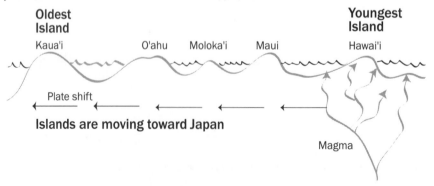

**FIGURE 6–20**  Picture functions and organization principles (part 2 of 2)

Generative strategies require the learner to create meaning. The following examples show learner-generated hierarchical images.

## 1. Mental imagery

Imagine the earth as a little ball one-inch in diameter. On this same scale the moon would be a smaller ball, about a quarter of an inch in diameter, revolving around it at a distance of about 30 inches. The sun would be a sphere about 9 feet in diameter approximately 969 feet from this tiny earth and moon. Jupiter, the largest planet, would be a ball a little over 11 inches in diameter, revolving in an orbit of about 5036 feet (almost a mile). Pluto, the most distant planet known, would be a little object about 3/10 inch in diameter. (Eikleberry, 2000, p. 175)

## 2. Outlines
Creating an outline can help facilitate learning.

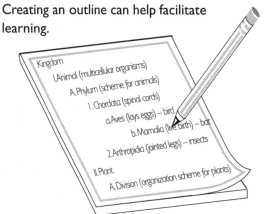

## 3. Concept maps

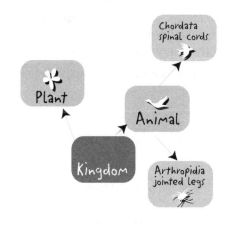

## 4. Image/model

A student-generated image of the information-processing model.

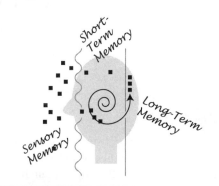

## 5. Flowcharts

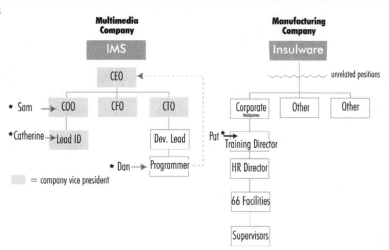

**FIGURE 6–21**   Generative organizational strategies

### Form Mental Images

Mental imagery is a strategy that asks learners to picture something in their minds. In doing so, they create mental representations that help them learn. The first section of **Figure 6–21** includes a mental imagery exercise that helps students gain a perspective on the size of earth in relationship to the sun.

### Create an Outline

A student might be asked to create an outline based upon information related to the classification system for bats, insects, and birds. Concept mapping, flowcharting, and outlining tools, such as Inspiration, Mind Manager, and Smart Draw, can be used to help students organize and arrange ideas and information visually.

### Create a Flowchart

A student might be asked to create a flowchart tracking key players in a case study or story.

### Create an Image or Model

Students might be asked to create an image that helps them understand a concept or process. For example, they might create a drawing similar to the one shown in section 4 of Figure 6–21 in order to understand the following information:

> The information-processing model shows information first perceived, then processed, then encoded into sensory, short-term, and long-term memory.

## SUMMARY

In Chapter 5 you learned the importance of selection—of making the most important information stand out. This chapter takes you a step further by explaining organization—how to move and categorize the most important information. Establishing a hierarchy in your images helps you organize information into layers or levels of superordinate, subordinate, or coordinate status. The easiest way to think of hierarchy in an image is to compare it to a verbal outline with I, II, III, A, B, C levels of importance. Hierarchy is the most referenced organizational strategy in this chapter.

Chunking information is another. Using hierarchical techniques such as spatial analogies and natural reading order helps learners navigate through complex information. Information that is grouped into no more than seven to nine chunks (or three to five depending on whose research you follow) is more likely to be remembered or efficiently used than information that is not chunked.

A designer can use spatial analogies to suggest hierarchy as well (images on the top are considered light, images on the bottom are considered heavy). Charts and graphs are frequently used to display complex content of a hierarchical nature.

Several tools and techniques are used to create hierarchical cues. Lines, arrows, depth, shape, and space can all be manipulated to show relationships between image elements. White space allows similar elements to be grouped together, creating information chunks that are important to the hierarchical concept.

The actions of contrast, alignment, and proximity play an important role in creating hierarchy. Contrast usually provides an entry point into an image. Varying the degree of contrast between elements helps the eye move from the most dominant to the least dominant element. Alignment plays a big role in hierarchy, as the mind tends to seek items along horizontal and vertical planes. Furthermore, unique meanings are often assigned to positions along those planes that can be used to facilitate a message. Proximity, or the degree of distance between elements, is critical for creating not only information chunks but messages about the relationship between chunks.

The next chapter focuses on integration. It combines both selection and organization strategies in a way that helps learners see the big picture.

## PRACTICE

For additional activities and examples of student work, visit the Companion Website for this book at *http://www.coe.unco.edu/LindaLohr.*

## Resource Activity

Skip to the Resources and use Figure R–4 to organize a one- or two-page information display. Projects might include developing an assessment rubric, a resume, or a job-aid.

## Web Activity

The Web Activity asks you to create an image that uses words and symbols to imply hierarchy. The visual shown here illustrates how one student interpreted this activity.

Every element in this visual has some type of hierarchical meaning. Can you spot them all?

Web Activity

## Challenge Activity

The Challenge Activity asks you to use organizational techniques to show how the Hawaiian Islands are growing. This is a difficult task due to the orientation of the islands and the direction of island development (the islands are moving toward Japan). Be sure to include the volcanic activity, plate shifts, labels and other visual and verbal techniques to help the learner. One solution is shown here, but it is flawed in a number of ways. Try to improve it.

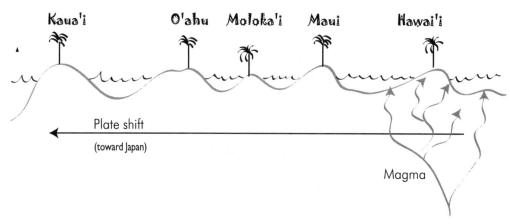

Challenge Activity

# Independent Activity

This activity asks you to pick your own project. You are encouraged to try this one because the information will be more meaningful and thus is likely to be more motivating.

# Justification Activity

Write a justification paper for the activity you select. Describe the following:

- *Your users and the assumptions you make about them (such as age, reading level, and assumed skills).*
- *Why you think your solution will work; include at least two ideas from the book, including page numbers and your interpretation of the passage used.*
- *What you learned from a "user-test" (have someone look at the image and verbalize their thoughts while looking at the image).*
- *The changes you will make based on user comments (or create a revised image.)*

# Discussion Questions

There is some debate over what makes information design effective. Some argue in favor of information graphics such as those that you see in *USA Today* or weekly news-magazines, which employ some degree of embellishment or chart junk. Many adults, seem to like what we call "chart junk." What do you think about the *USA Today* type of data display?

# K–12 Student Activity

The sequence of drawings included here show how a sixth grader generated an organizational image when asked to illustrate prepositions, which are considered hierarchical words because they imply relationships.

Ask students to generate images like this one or to use many of the chapter examples for student projects. Outlining, mental imagery, creating models, and the like can be used as student-generated strategies to help them learn information more deeply.

## K–12 Example

This sixth grader generated a organizational image when asked to illustrate several prepositions. Prepositions are hierarchical words because they show relationships between the words of a sentence. Notice the student's use of arrows  and lines to show sequence.

Activity for K–12 Students

# REFERENCES

Allen, W. H. (1975). Intellectual abilities and instructional media design. *AV Communication Review, 23*, 139–170.

Armbruster, B. B. (1986). Schema theory and the design of content-area textbooks. *Educational Psychology, 21*, 253–267.

Cowan, N. (2001). The magical number four in short-term memory: A reconsideration of mental storage capacity. *Behavioral and Brain Sciences, 24*, 87–114.

Ehrenberg, A. S. (1977). Rudiments of numeracy. *Journal of Royal Statistical Society A, 140*, 227–297.

Fleming, M. L. (1968). Message design: The temporal dimension of message structure. *USOE Final Report*, NEDA Title VII Project 1401.

Fleming, M., & Levie, H. (1978). *Instructional message design.* Englewood Cliffs, NJ: Educational Technology Publications.

Fleming, M., & Levie, H. (1993). *Instructional message design* (2nd ed.). Englewood Cliffs, NJ: Educational Technology Publications.

Hartley, J. (1985). *Designing instructional text.* New York: Nichols.

Horton, W. K. (1994). *The icon book: Visual symbols for computer systems and documentation.* New York: Wiley.

Kemp, J. E., Morrison, G. R., & Ross, S. M. (2004). *Designing effective instruction.* Upper Saddle River, NJ: Prentice Hall.

Kennedy, L. D. (1971). Textbook usage in the intermediate-upper grades. *The Reading Teacher, 24*, 723–729.

Lichty, T. (1989). *Design principles for desktop publishers.* Glenview, IL: Scott Foresman.

Mautone, P. D., & Mayer, R. E. (2001). Signaling as a cognitive guide in multimedia learning. *Journal of Educational Psychology, 93(2)*, 377–389.

Mayer, R. E. (2001). *Multimedia learning.* Cambridge, England: University Press.

McIntyre, W. A. (1983). *The psychology of visual perception and learning from line drawings: A survey of the research literature.* Eric Document Reproduction Service No. ED 230 901.

Meyer, B. J. (1985). Signaling the structure of text. In D. J. Jonassen (Ed.), *The technology of text* (Vol. 2, pp. 64–89). Englewood Cliffs, NJ: Educational Technology Publications.

Miller, G. A. (1956). The magic number seven, plus or minus two: Some limits on our capacity for processing information. *Psychological Review, 63*, 81–97.

Misanchuk, E. R. (1992). *Preparing instructional text: Document design using desktop publishing.* Englewood Cliffs, NJ: Educational Technology Publications.

Morrison, G. R., Ross, S. M., & Kemp, J. E. (2004). *Designing effective instruction* (3rd ed.). New York: Wiley.

Mullet, K., & Sano, D. (1995). *Designing visual interfaces: Communication oriented techniques.* Englewood Cliffs, NJ: Sunsoft Press.

Nelson, R. P. (1989). *The design of advertising.* Dubuque, IA: Wm. C. Brown.

Tufte, E. (1983). *The visual display of quantitative information.* Cheshire, CT: Graphics Press.

Tufte, E. R. (1990). *Envisioning information.* Cheshire, CT: Graphics Press.

Winn, W. D. (1980a). The effect of block-word diagrams on the structuring of concepts as a function of general ability. *Journal of Research in Science Teaching, 17*, 201–211.

Winn, W. D. (1980b). Visual information processing: A pragmatic approach to the imagery question. *Educational Communication and Technology Journal, 28(2)*, 120–133.

Winn, W. D. (1981). The effect of attribute highlighting and spatial organization on Identification and classification. *Journal of Research in Science Teaching, 17*, 201–211.

Winn, W. D. (1982a). The role of diagrammatic representation in learning sequences: Identification and classification as a function of verbal and spatial ability. *Journal of Research in Science Teaching, 19*, 79–89.

Winn, W. D. (1982b, May). Status and trends in information processing. Paper presented at the Annual Meeting of the Association for Educational Communications and Technology, Research and Theory Division, Dallas, TX. (Eric Document Reproduction Service No. ED223236)

Winn, W. D. (1982c). Visualization in learning and instruction: A cognitive approach. *Educational Communication and Technology Journal, 30(1)*, 3–25.

Winn, W. D. (1983, April). Processing and interpreting spatial information represented graphically. Paper presented at the Annual Conference of the American Educational Research Association, Montreal (Eric Document Reproduction Service No. ED223236)

Winn, W. D. (1986, April). Simultaneous and successive processing of circuit diagrams having different amounts of detail. Paper presented at the Annual Conference of the American Educational Research Association, San Francisco. (ERIC Document Reproduction Service No. ED270305

Winn, W. D. (1987, April) Graphic design as instructional design: Towards a syntax for computer graphics. Paper presented at the Annual Conference of the American Educational Research Association, Washington, DC.

Winn, W. D., & Holliday, W. (1985). Design principles for diagrams and charts. In D. H. Jonassen (Ed.), *The technology of text* (Vol. 2, pp. 277–299). Englewood Cliffs, NJ: Educational Technology Publications.

Wittrock, M. C. (1989). Generative processes of comprehension. *Educational Psychologists, 24*, 345–376.

# CHAPTER 7

## *Integration Principle: Gestalt*

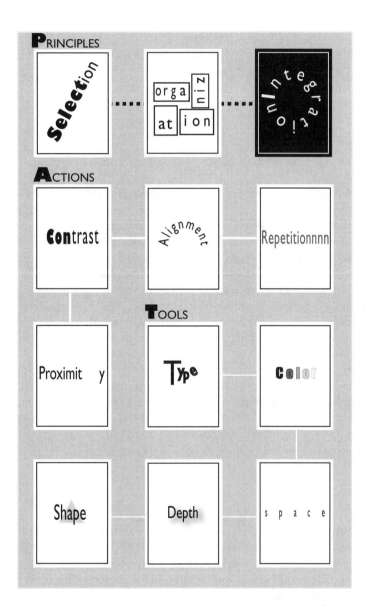

Simplicity in the underlying message, complexity in the details.

*Edward Tufte*

## NOTES ABOUT THE OPENING VISUAL

The opening visual for this chapter employs the gestalt principle of design to enhance perception, which is commonly defined as the whole being greater than the sum of its parts. The large rectangle (the whole, which represents the book) encloses all the book icons (the parts, which represent major topics in the book). The placement of each icon suggests its relationship to the other topics within the book.

## FOCUS QUESTIONS

- Why are figure/ground and hierarchy considered gestalt principles?
- How does improving the gestalt of an instructional message help the learner?
- How do you enhance gestalt?

## KEY TERMS

**ASYMMETRY**  A form that does not have balanced proportions.

**BALANCE**  An even and aesthetically pleasing distribution of elements.

**CLOSURE**  The mind's tendency to seek completion.

**CONTIGUITY**  The mind's tendency to seek a direction to follow and continue to follow based on directional cues.

**GESTALT**  A principle of perception stating that the whole is greater than the sum of its parts. Effective instructional visuals depend on creating gestalt, a total learning or performance environment (the whole) based upon the successful design and integration of all visual and instructional elements (the parts).

**GOLDEN RECTANGLE**  Any rectangle with sides that have a ratio of 5 to 8. This ratio is believed to produce a balanced and pleasing (golden) image or to evoke from the viewer a sense of harmony.

**GRID SYSTEM**  A set of intersecting lines used to align objects. If the grid is on as you draw or move objects, their corners align on the nearest intersection on the grid.

**PREVIOUS EXPERIENCE**  A gestalt principle that explains the importance of helping the learner relate new information to previous knowledge and experience.

**PROXIMITY**  The mind's tendency to group elements based on their closeness to each other.

**RULE OF THIRDS**  A technique that distributes the elements of a display along the intersection of imaginary lines that divide an image into thirds.

**SIMILARITY**  The mind's tendency to group items based on likeness; the action of repetition facilitates this grouping.

**SYMMETRY**  Beauty of form arising from balanced proportions.

**WHITE SPACE**  A graphic element that can be thought of as the plain background of an image. Even though it is called "white" space, it can be whatever color the background is.

## INTRODUCTION

A big, brightly colored poster of the writer's wheel (**Figure 7–1a**) is prominently posted in a classroom where Antonio, the sixth grade teacher introduced in Chapter 1, is teaching students the process approach to writing. The five key stages of the writing process—brainstorming, writing, conferencing, editing, and revising—are represented by color-coded, pie-shaped wedges. Each student has a writing notebook (**Figure 7–1b**), a folder with the writer's wheel on the cover, with a movable pointer showing which stage of the writing process the student is taking part in.

This writer's wheel is an example of effectively using the integration principle, the topic of this chapter. The wheel shows the big picture of writing as a circular shape that makes it immediately apparent that writing is a cyclical process. The pie-shaped wedges show the individual components that make up writing. Students can thus easily envision the writing process as the sum of individual steps.

(a)                                                                  (b)

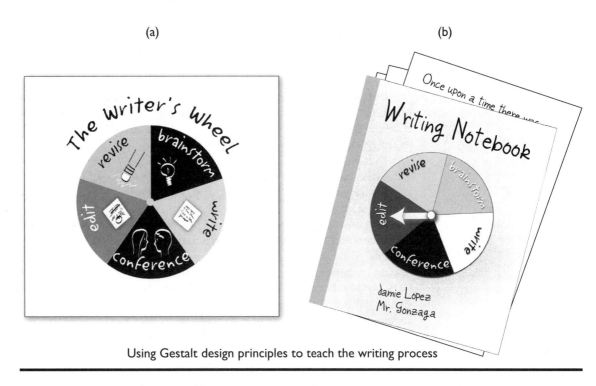

Using Gestalt design principles to teach the writing process

(c)

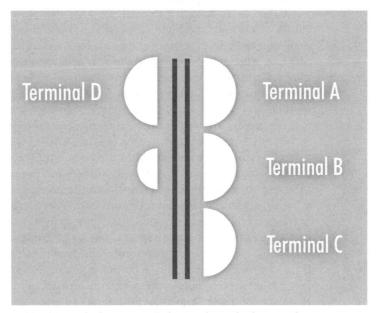

Using gestalt design principles to show the layout of an airport

**FIGURE 7-1**   Gestalt examples

When creating the writer's wheel, Antonio asked these questions:

- How can I show the underlying structure of writing?
- How can I show the elements of writing in the context of the underlying structure?
- How can I make the image simple yet instructional?
- How can I make this look approachable, even fun?

These questions address integration issues since they focus on the big picture—the **gestalt.** Just as the selection chapter focused on figure and ground, and the orientation chapter focused on hierarchy, this chapter focuses on integration and on gestalt. Gestalt involves the psychology of perception, a branch of psychology started by Max Wertheimer (1880–1943) around 1910. The underlying belief of gestalt is that individuals are predisposed to organize information in particular ways. According to Mullet and Sano (1995), the rules derived from gestalt studies provide useful insight into what makes images work effectively, a belief in harmony with the message of this book.

That integration is the final perception principle covered in this book is no accident. It is last because gestalt is the all-encompassing principle of perception. Every tool, action, and principle covered here can be applied to improving or enhancing integration. Even though selection and organization were treated as separate perception principles, they are actually considered gestalt principles. They were treated separately only because of their importance to the design of instructional materials.

The gestalt branch of psychology proposes that individuals construct representations that do not always reflect reality, an idea that should seem familiar. As you learned in Chapter 5, the mind unconsciously separates elements into figure and ground categories and assigns a status of importance to elements perceived as the figure. As a designer, you can take advantage of this phenomenon by making the elements you want to emphasize stand out from other elements, thereby increasing the odds that your audience will see the central message. Likewise, in Chapter 6, you learned that the mind tends to categorize and create hierarchies of information, especially grouping together elements that fall on horizontal or vertical planes. When you want certain items to be associated, you place them along a similar plane (which explains why alignment is considered an important design action).

Other ideas related to gestalt include the phi phenomenon, the law of Pragnanz (Koffka, 1935), and the importance of context. Wertheimer (1959) discovered the phi phenomenon using an experiment in which two blinking lights, switching on and off at a particular rate, were perceived as one. The law of Pragnanz, which emphasizes precision or simplicity (Ormrod, 1990), explains how individuals may see one thing (such as imperfect circles, squares, and lines) yet remember another (circles with perfect symmetry, squares with 90 degree angles, and straight lines).

Gestaltists also believed in the importance of presenting information within as opposed to isolated from its natural context. Antonio's writer's wheel is a good example of how information can be presented within the context of the whole. Rather than teaching individual elements of the writing process, Antonio focuses on the whole process of writing. The meaning of gestalt, in fact, relates to the importance of context, since gestalt stands for whole, shape, form, configuration, and even essence. Gestalt psychologists noted that early in the perception process individual elements in an image were often perceived as a group or a form rather than as individual elements (Wertheimer, 1959).

Think of gestalt as the relationship of parts to whole. As you may already have gleaned from this overview, when you optimize gestalt in instruction, you are essentially helping learners to see the big picture without overloading their short-term memory. An easy way to think of designing for gestalt is to think of a map. City maps show the relationship of parts (symbols for streets, blocks, buildings) to the whole (the layout of the city). Shopping mall maps show the relationship of individual stores, restaurants, and restrooms to the layout of the mall. The airport maps shown in Figure 7–1(c) illustrate the relationship of terminals, concourses, and gates to the layout of the airport.

# Five Gestalt Principles

This chapter covers five gestalt principles important to the design of instructional information, as shown in **Figure 7–2**: (1) closure, (2) contiguity, (3) similarity, (4) proximity, and (5) previous experience. The first four are widely recognized principles, and we have already

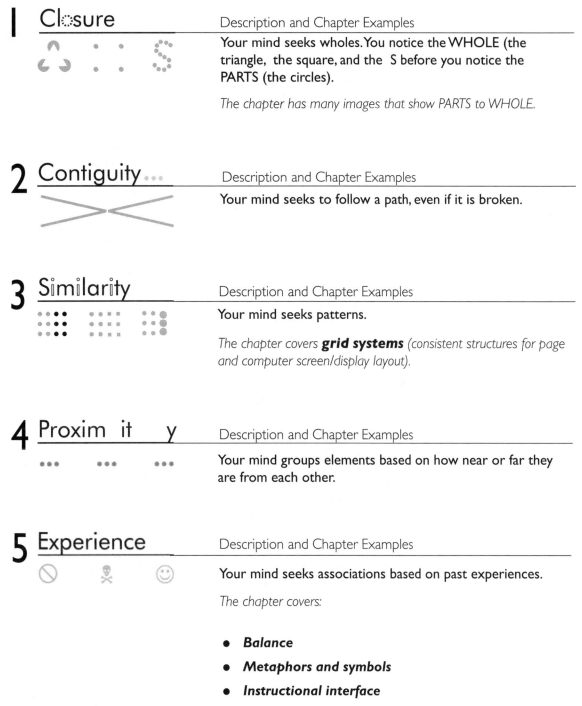

**FIGURE 7-2**  The five gestalt principles

discussed proximity and similarity (what this book refers to as repetition). The fifth principle, previous experience (Ormrod, 1990; Pettersson, 1993), has been added because it is critical for creating a big-picture understanding of effective instructional visuals. This principle contributes most to the task of helping the learner integrate information in a meaningful way. As discussed earlier, instructional images should help learners select, organize, and integrate information. It is the integration task that we try to facilitate when we focus on improving or optimizing gestalt.

# Closure

The principle of **closure** describes how the mind seeks completion. **Figure 7–3** presents four examples of this phenomenon. First, look at the word *closure*. Notice how the letter *o* is not a complete circle? Your mind automatically filled that circle in and interpreted it as an *o*. Do you see a triangle in the left image? Do you see a square formed by the four dots? Does the letter *S* stand out? In all of these cases, there are no lines to define the shapes. Your mind filled in the lines because it wanted the big picture. Closure relates to the need for the mind to have a general understanding. According to Luchins and Luchins (1959), closure is a key factor in cognitive organization. Extracting meaning and deriving conclusions is the function of closure. As learners, we often walk away from a learning situation with an overall impression or feeling but lack awareness of the details. This phenomenon is related to closure, the mind's unconscious and continual effort to create meaning.

For a designer of instructional visuals, this phenomenon suggests some basic directions. First, you can simplify your designs since you do not always need to include a complete image. Figure 7-3 shows a string with a ball attached to it dangling from a finger. The image does not need to show the entire body of the person. The arm and hand are enough to communicate. This simplification helps the mind summarize the critical attributes of a message. Second, when you include some gaps in your design, you allow learners to fill in their own information. For example, if the arm in Figure 7-3 relates to instructions you need to follow, the incomplete image might help you to imagine yourself performing the step.

# Contiguity

The principle of **contiguity,** also called the theory of direction, states that the mind will seek a direction to follow and will continue to follow directional cues. You learned the role of contiguity in Chapter 6, when the directive effects of arrows, lines, and shapes were used to establish order and hierarchy. When you have a strong line or plane in an image, the eye wants to follow—and to continue to follow—that line. Look now at Figure 7-3 and notice how your eye tends to travel on one of the diagonal lines. When it gets to the halfway point of the image, the eye seems to prefer to continue traveling on that line. Notice how the image is really two arrows facing each other. Your mind does not seem to see the arrow shapes distinctly as it sees the long diagonal lines formed by the two images together. When you create instructional images you can use the principle of contiguity to direct your eye, just as it does in the Statue of Liberty image in Figure 7-3. Chapter 6 covered in detail how you can use lines and shapes to establish direction.

# Similarity

The principle of **similarity** is close to the design action of repetition. When similarity is addressed in gestalt, it refers to the mind's tendency to group items based on likeness. **Figure 7–4** shows an image with 12 dots, but your eye is more likely to see a group of gray dots and a group of black dots. The center image shows six dots and six squares, but your mind is more likely to see a group of circles and a group of squares. The rightmost image shows six small dots and three large dots, but your mind is more likely to see a group of small dots and a group of large dots. In these examples elements in the image were grouped based on the similarity of color, shape, and size. By grouping elements, the mind is automatically reducing the cognitive load placed on memory.

Similarity is an important element in instructional development, particularly in hypermedia environments such as electronic displays and computer-based and Web-based training. In hypermedia environments, learners move between screens of information, often in a nonlinear order. Marking their positions in these environments is difficult to do. Disorientation and a feeling of being lost are frequent complaints about these experiences. Books are

Principle **1**:

You see a PART (the arm), but your mind tells you that the part belongs to a WHOLE (the person).

Using the closure principle to imply "person"

---

Principle **2**:

Your eye will follow an implied path. Here the arm of the statue directs your eye to the words.

In 1886, France gave
the United States the Statue of
Liberty, a national monument
symbolizing , democracy,
friendship and freedom.

Using the contiguity principle to focus attention

**FIGURE 7–3**   Closure and contiguity examples

*Source: Click art © 1997 RomTech.*

Principle **3**: <u>Similarity</u>

(a) **Using a grid to provide consistency (maintain similarity).**
Many layout programs make it very easy to work within a grid, as you see in the electronic slide presentation below.

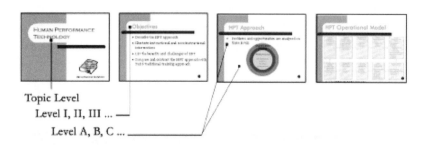

(b) **Deviating from the grid.**
Notice how the right-hand screen deviates from the grid in the image below. The text passage here is lengthy and consequently the margins have been increased. Also, the navigation bar that is part of the other screens has been removed since the only direction to go from this screen is back. It is OK to work outside of the grid once in a while, especially if your content demands it. When you continually change content to match a grid, however, you need to rethink the grid.

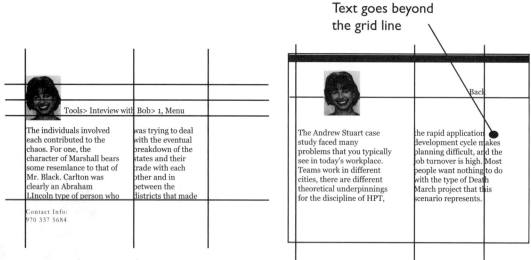

**FIGURE 7–4**    Similarity examples

easy for learners to thumb through and establish their positions, but this is not always the case in hypermedia environments. It then becomes important for learners to establish a "lay of the land" (Kristof & Satran, 1995).

### Grid Systems

Creating a lay of the land is often accomplished through the use of a **grid system**—a set of intersecting lines used to align objects and provide consistency throughout instruction. When you create a grid, you create a specific place for specific items. These places are repeated from page to page or from screen to screen. This repetition makes a grid fall under the category of similarity.

Grids are easy to create since most software programs allow you to turn a grid background on or off and to use rulers and guidelines to establish horizontal and vertical placement lines that can be used to create consistency throughout an instructional document or environment. (See Figure R–9 in the Resources for instructions.)

You may be wondering if a template is a grid system. Think of a template as a format for documents, presentations, and Web pages that establishes a grid system in addition to other design conventions such as size and style of typeface, color of typeface and background. Templates relate more to the total design of an instructional environment whereas a grid mostly defines horizontal and vertical borders for text and images. **Figure 7–5** is a grid system for Web-based training (WBT) with five designated areas: (1) orientation, (2) navigation,

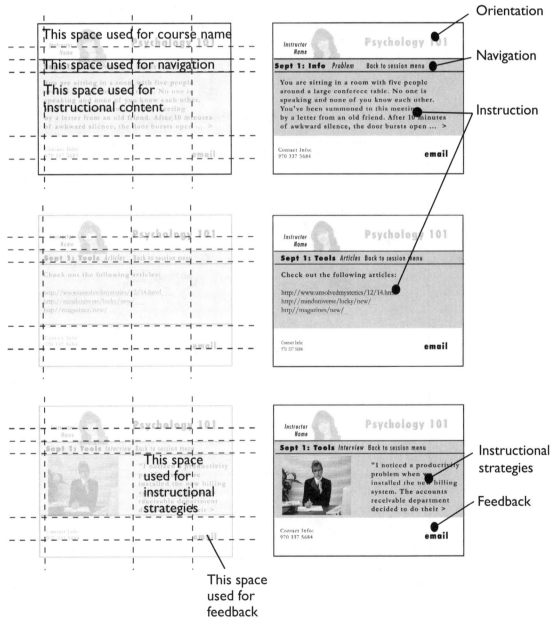

**FIGURE 7–5**   A Web-based training (WBT) grid with five designated areas

(3) instruction, (4) instructional strategies, and (5) feedback. Books and electronic presentations use grid systems as well (see **Figure 7–6**). Mullet and Sano (1995) consider grid-based design essential to any large-scale information system: "By structuring each presentation along similar lines, the grid ensures that users will benefit from experience with the system as they learn to predict where a particular piece of information will be found" (p. 134).

It is the predictive value of a grid that has merit for the design of instructional materials. When you provide a consistent layout, you theoretically reduce cognitive load. Users do not have to relearn the layout when they move from screen to screen or page to page. They know where to find specific information, and they can make distinctions between types of informational content. For example, if the right-hand column of a Web-based training environment is designated for outside links, the learner reading for only the most critical information will learn to skip the information in that column. Learners who want additional detail, however, may find themselves looking in the right-hand column.

Grids do not need to be followed all the time. Misanchuk (1992) gives refreshing advice by emphasizing that grids be allowed to vary. At times, following a grid just does not work for the instructional content. Many designers find themselves changing content to accommodate a grid. This can be done easily in some situations, but when it cannot, it is probably time to consider changing the grid.

Each page looks different but follows the underlying grid.

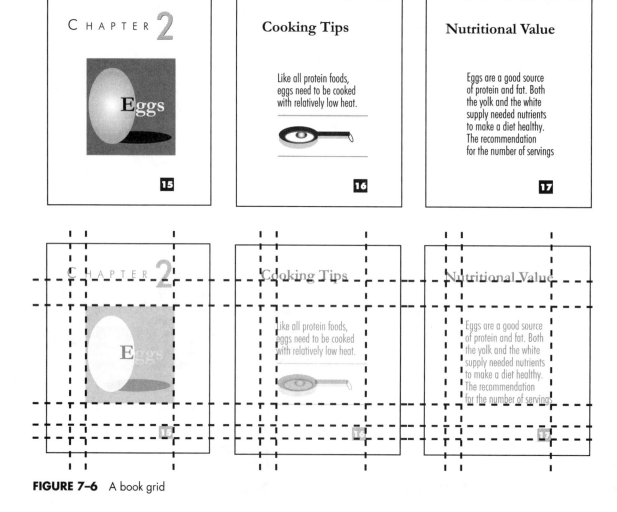

**FIGURE 7–6**   A book grid

## Proximity

The rule of **proximity** states that the mind will group elements based on their closeness to each other. If you look at **Figure 7–7,** you see three groups of three dots rather than nine distinct dots. As with the other rules of gestalt, when the mind groups things, it reduces the load placed on short-term memory.

Principle **4**: <u>Proxim  it    y</u>

### K–12 Example

Math

By placing the numbers close to the pie shapes, part (b) teaches geometry more effectively than does part (a). The parts to whole relationship is easier to perceive.

(a)

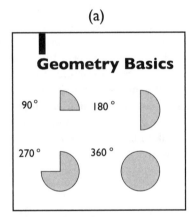

(b)

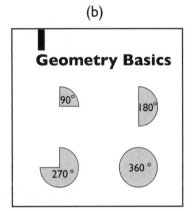

### K–12 Example

Nutrition

By placing the instructional steps close to the images, part (b) teaches cooking information more effectively than does part (a). The parts to whole relationship is easier to perceive.

(c)

(d)

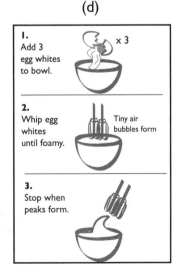

**FIGURE 7–7**   Proximity examples

Using the proximity rule can help you make instructional information easier to understand. Part (a) of Figure 7–7 does not have the optimal proximity between the shaded area of
the circle and the number of degrees. The pie-shaped area on the top left could be associated
with either 90 degrees or 180 degrees. Part (b) shows an improved display, removing all doubt
about the number of degrees associated with the shaded areas. The closer the numbers are
to the area, the easier it is to understand the image.

I had a dentist who cleverly used proximity to teach dental care. He met with each
new patient and presented a short slide presentation on healthy gums and teeth. In this
presentation he pointed out various features of strong teeth and gums using a photograph of a perfect set of teeth. He then showed a side-by-side display of the patient's X-
ray next to the healthy gum image. He concluded his instruction by showing the healthy
gums superimposed over the patient's X-ray. Having the healthy gums in such close proximity to the patient's X-ray made it easy for the patient to compare his or her teeth to
ideal teeth.

Mayer's (2001) work is related to this proximity issue. Mayer and Sims (1994) find that
inexperienced students gained the most from instruction where visual and verbal explanations were presented concurrently (in close proximity). They explain this finding using their
dual coding theory of multimedia, which suggests that the concurrent presentation of visual
and verbal descriptions increases the likelihood of internal connections (in the mind of the
learner) between visual and verbal representations of those descriptions.

Mayer et al. (1996) show that the best illustrations for summarizing scientific content
are made up of a series of frames illustrating the major steps in a process. The whole (the
process) is in constant view of the parts (the individual steps). Figure 7–7(c) and (d) presents a series of frames that show how to whip egg whites. Each frame illustrates the context
(the bowl) and the changes that take place in the context of that bowl from step to step.
The parts are in proximity with the whole.

## Previous Experience

The principle of **previous experience** states that new impressions are influenced by previous experiences or by the immediate context. How the learner analyzes and interprets
new information depends in part on a range of learner experiences, emotions, and the pre-
vailing situation (Pettersson, 1993).

The previous experience principle is explained by information processing theory, as described in Chapter 3. The ability to keep information alive in short-term memory is increased when learners can associate that information with what they already know. For example, if you are trying to teach the circulatory system, you might help learners by
comparing the circulatory system with their plumbing system at home. When learners can
associate this new information about the circulatory system with old information about
plumbing, they are able to remember it better, because their mind already has a schema set
up for plumbing. This all depends, of course, on whether learners understand the plumbing
in their house.

Recently, a student was creating a lesson on downhill skiing and right of way. The rule is
that the skier higher on the hill must yield to the skier lower on the hill. She taught this rule
using a driving analogy. When traveling on an interstate highway, the cars in the rear must yield
to the cars in the front. Since most people drive on highways, this analogy was effective.

### Symbols, Icons, and Metaphors

Symbols, icons and metaphors are widely used in instruction because of the power of the
previous experience rule. **Figure 7–8** illustrates some generally recognized symbols. The circle with a diagonal slash means *no* or *forbidden*; the skull and crossbones is a symbol of
death; the smiley face is a symbol of friendliness or happiness. When people encounter these
symbols, they quickly understand their meaning.

# Principle 5: Experience

The meaning of symbols and icons vary from culture to culture.

**Universal Meaning**          **Culturally Specific Meaning**

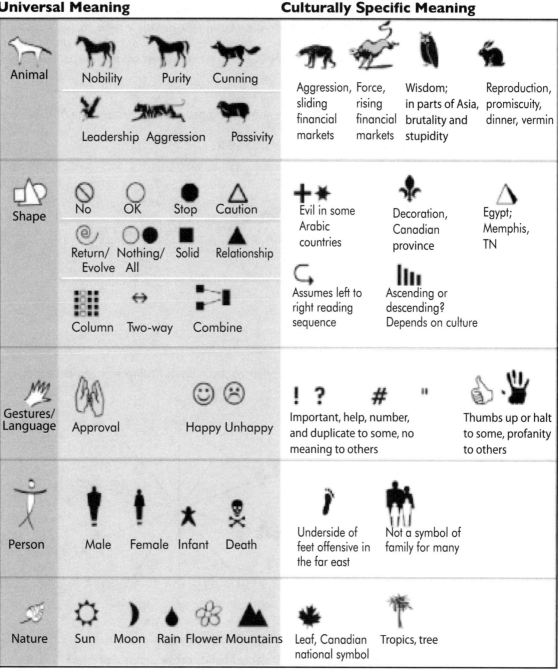

**FIGURE 7–8** Experience examples

Figure 7–8 uses the five symbol categories identified by Miller, Brown, and Cullen (2000): (1) animal, (2) shape, (3) gestures/language, (4) person, and (5) nature. The chart in Figure 7–8 is not extensive as many symbol families range from professionally specific symbols (electrical circuitry) to symbols that have universal meaning (traffic signs). For additional information on this topic, consult the *Symbol Source Book: An Authoritative Guide to International Graphic Symbols* by Henry Dreyfus, or contact consulate offices in major cities around the world for more information about culture and customs.

Symbols, icons, and metaphors are widely used in software applications, computer-based training, and Web-based training environments to help people learn new tasks or information [see **Figure 7–9(a)**]. An eraser symbol means that information can be deleted, an

(a) Non-English-speaking cultures cannot be expected to understand the ABC symbol of spell checking.

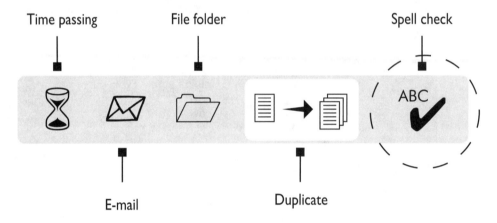

(b) Depending on your culture (experience) these pointing fingers mean direction or dismemberment.

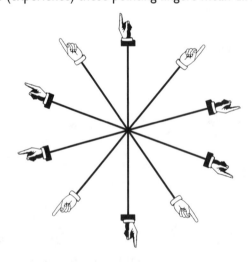

(c) Depending on your culture (experience) hands mean yes or worthless

**FIGURE 7–9**    Same symbols, different meanings

envelope means you can send an e-mail message, a small disk means you can save a file on a floppy disk, and a check mark with letters above it means you can ask to have your spelling checked. Because hourglasses, envelopes, file folders, and pages are fairly universal in appearance, these icons are likely to be quickly understood. However, the spell check symbol with the letters ABC would not work in cultures that do not use these letters in their alphabets.

Although it might seem that visual images have a universal appeal, this really is not the case, as many cultures interpret such images differently. The interpretation of symbols and colors is highly dependent on experiences, culture, and previous knowledge. If you are creating instruction for a specific audience and are familiar with their customs and culture, you can use your knowledge of their culture to help strengthen learning since you are tapping into what learners already know.

In China and other cultures, a snake is a good thing (Miller, Brown, and Cullen, 2000), a symbol of birth and renewal. In Western cultures, however, snakes are likely to be associated with deception or evil (Horton, 1994). A person from a Western culture looking at the hands in Figure 7–9(b) would see a finger pointing out a direction, whereas a person in a different culture might interpret the pointing finger as a symbol of dismemberment, since it is a body part without the rest of the body shown. In general, use of body part icons or images with international audiences is considered risky. Likewise in Figure 7–9(c) the hand symbol used to show "yes" or "OK" in the United States means zero or worthless in France and has even more insulting connotations in other cultures.

Colors have different meanings across cultures as well. In Western cultures red often means danger, but in China it means joy and festivity. White is often associated with purity and virtue in Western cultures but means death and mourning in Eastern cultures (Horton, 1994). In general, it is important to test your design with a representative audience in order to identify any potential cultural sensitivity.

## Instructional Interfaces

With more and more instruction taking place in a distance learning environment where a teacher may not be physically present in a classroom setting, communicating clearly with visuals becomes more important than ever. When no one is available to provide directions, the instructional interface must do so. Such an interface can be considered to be all of the elements in an instructional environment that help the learner go about the task of learning (Lohr, 2000). For example, menus, buttons, navigational cues, and the like are typical components of an instructional interface.

**Four Instructional Interface Metaphors**   Instructional interface metaphors, which rely heavily on previously presented learning gestalt principles, fall into four categories: (1) the outline metaphor, (2) the book metaphor, (3) the desktop metaphor, and (4) the syllabus metaphor (see **Figure 7–10**).

***Outline and Book Metaphors***   Outlines are frequently used to organize computer-based learning and serve as an interface format. Book metaphors with a table of contents and the display of instructional information against the backdrop of pages are common as well.

***Desktop Metaphor***   The desktop metaphor organizes a learning environment around desktop elements. Important learning documents can be linked to images of file folders, computer screens, and desktop reference books. Many Web-based training settings make extensive use of file folder organization. The user simply clicks on file folder tabs to move to different content.

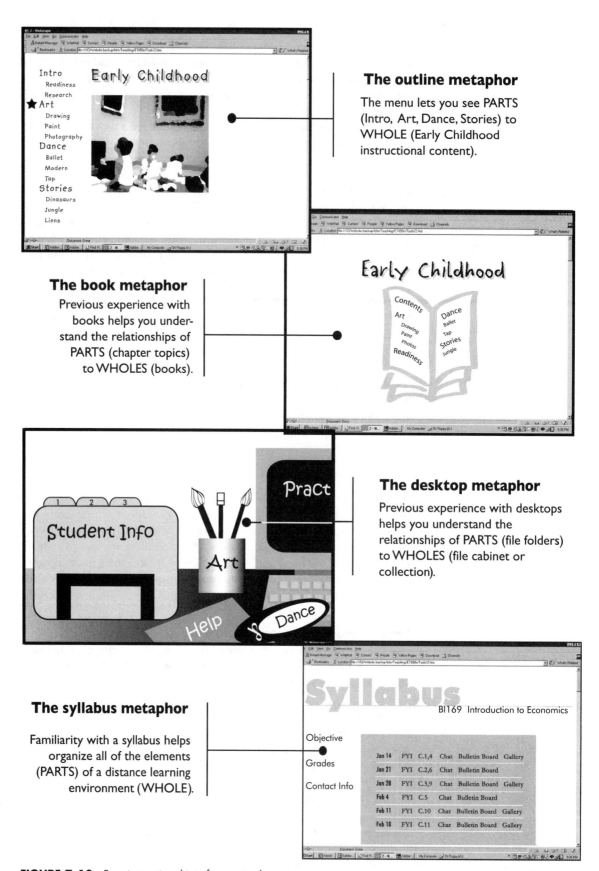

**The outline metaphor**

The menu lets you see PARTS (Intro, Art, Dance, Stories) to WHOLE (Early Childhood instructional content).

**The book metaphor**

Previous experience with books helps you understand the relationships of PARTS (chapter topics) to WHOLES (books).

**The desktop metaphor**

Previous experience with desktops helps you understand the relationships of PARTS (file folders) to WHOLES (file cabinet or collection).

**The syllabus metaphor**

Familiarity with a syllabus helps organize all of the elements (PARTS) of a distance learning environment (WHOLE).

**FIGURE 7-10** Four instructional interface metaphors

***Syllabus Metaphor***   The syllabus metaphor is often used in distance learning environments. Such courses are often organized around the familiar structure of a course syllabus. Objectives, grading policies, contact information, and other components of a course are linked with the syllabus page.

**Template Interfaces**   Instructional interface metaphors are useful, but as with grid systems, metaphors may not work optimally with the structure of the content. Another problem is that people do not always have the previous experience required to interpret metaphors.

Many templates are now available for interface design. Large course management systems such as Blackboard, eCollege, and WebCT provide a precoded shell that allows an instructor simply to insert content into the appropriate section of the interface. These templates employ grid systems that designate where all types of content are to be placed. Many of these templates are fine but some reflect the mind-set of the programmer, making the interface technocentric and hard to follow. A recent study found that even simple modification of these interfaces increased student acceptance of the learning environment (Lohr et al., 2006).

**Design Based on Student and Teacher Tasks**   A good way to check the instructional effectiveness of a template or to design an instructional interface from scratch is to consider the tasks of both teachers and learners and how these are made visual in the interface. When considering the teaching role, it is best to think more of a facilitator or someone who helps provide access to information but is not always the source of information.

An important question to ask is whether your interface is performing the many functions of a responsive teacher/facilitator. Does it anticipate the types of questions learners typically have when taking part in any type of training environment? For instance, does the interface answer questions such as these: Am I being graded? What am I supposed to do? Am I doing things the right way? Lohr (2000) suggests that designers and usability experts do a quick run-through of an interface to see if it is addressing some of the most basic types of learner questions (see **Figure 7–11**):

1. Does the learner feel comfortable and welcome? Look for or create these elements:
   - Warm colors
   - "Welcome" page
   - Picture of the instructor
   - Pictures of other students
   - Information that is chunked to reduce cognitive overload
2. Does the learner know how to move through the environment? Look for these elements:
   - Extra help
   - Ways to backtrack and exit
   - Assessment checklists
   - Link descriptions
3. Is there support for the learning process? Look for these elements:
   - Visual overviews
   - Options to skip information or to go into greater detail
   - Opportunities for practice/rehearsal/application
   - Case studies that provoke deeper thinking
   - Collaborative learning activities such as chat sessions and threaded discussions
4. Does the learner receive adequate feedback? Look for these elements:
   - Progress report with current grade
   - Hints to help learners focus
   - Feedback from fellow students
   - Sample projects

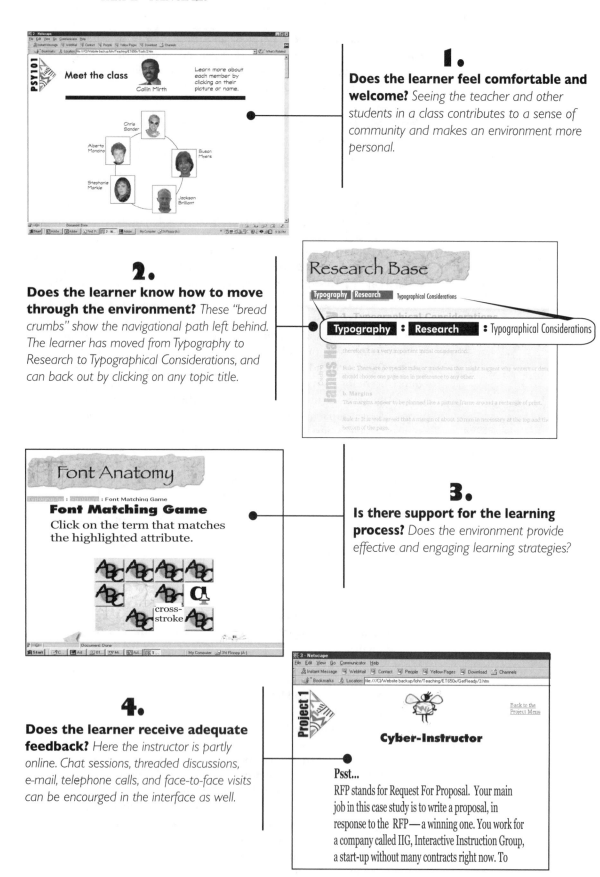

**1.**

**Does the learner feel comfortable and welcome?** *Seeing the teacher and other students in a class contributes to a sense of community and makes an environment more personal.*

**2.**

**Does the learner know how to move through the environment?** *These "bread crumbs" show the navigational path left behind. The learner has moved from Typography to Research to Typographical Considerations, and can back out by clicking on any topic title.*

**3.**

**Is there support for the learning process?** *Does the environment provide effective and engaging learning strategies?*

**4.**

**Does the learner receive adequate feedback?** *Here the instructor is partly online. Chat sessions, threaded discussions, e-mail, telephone calls, and face-to-face visits can be encourged in the interface as well.*

**FIGURE 7–11**   A learner-friendly interface: Four questions

As you can see, the possibilities are endless. Designing the interface is a complex undertaking when you consider all of the learning tasks that must be supported.

**Figure 7–12** shows an interface for open-ended learning environments. To address the unique tasks of learning in such an environment, the interface is divided into five sections: (1) problem, (2) course information, (3) tools sections, (4) assess, and (5) explore. Open-ended learning environments encompass a variety of self-directed learning approaches for ill-structured content, or content that you might consider to be more gray than black or white. For this particular unit, the learner is given a rather vague request for proposal (RFP) and is asked to write a proposal response. The interface provides space for the learner to explore the history behind the RFP and some of the challenges in writing it. For these kinds of learning environments, there really is not a clear solution to a problem.

Sometimes the interfaces you design are based more on information than on instruction, as is often the case in Web-based documents. Lynch and Horton (1999) suggest you put header and footer information on each page since you can never be sure how viewers found their way to your page. They may have come from your main menu, but then again they may have been provided only with a link to a specific page. Therefore it is important to provide author name or institution, an informative title, a creation/revision date, and one link to the document's home page. This information is usually found at the bottom of the Web page.

**General Interface Design Guidelines**   Many of the steps for interface design for websites are similar to those covered previously. Lynch and Horton (1999) and Nielsen (2000) consider the following seven items important:

1.  Know your users. (Are they advanced users or novices?)
2.  Keep navigation clear. (Make sure users know where they are, where they came from, how to back out or exit if needed, and how to get back to a home page.)
3.  Provide one menu with many links rather than many menus and submenus of fewer links. Get people to the information as quickly as possible. Users would rather have one menu with many selections available rather than several menus with few selections.
4.  Keep the time it takes to load your Web page to a minimum by using few graphics and animations or audio. (Users get frustrated when loading takes longer than 10 seconds.)
5.  Design for simplicity, using the same grid structures and layouts.
6.  Make sure you give visual feedback to any actions users take. (If they click to go somewhere new, make sure it looks new.)
7.  Make sure you consider handicapped users. (Provide text-based descriptions of your graphics.)

## Using Tools and Actions to Increase Gestalt

As with figure/ground and hierarchy, your job is to do some of the organizational work up front in order to save the learner's mind from having to do unnecessary work. The human mind makes a continual effort to impose order and create meaning. The more you accelerate that process, the more you help the learner's mind. By thinking about the five gestalt principles presented in this chapter and by employing the tools and actions that follow, you are working to control the big picture that learners see while helping them keep track of the details as well.

### Type

Typesetting and typefaces are integration tools that can be used to strengthen a message. In **Figure 7–13(a)** the words "Fit in" look like they are squeezed into the available space, emphasizing the message that creative people do not "fit in." The type chapter ahead explores additional ways type can be used to echo a message. For example the word wave can be distorted to look wavy.

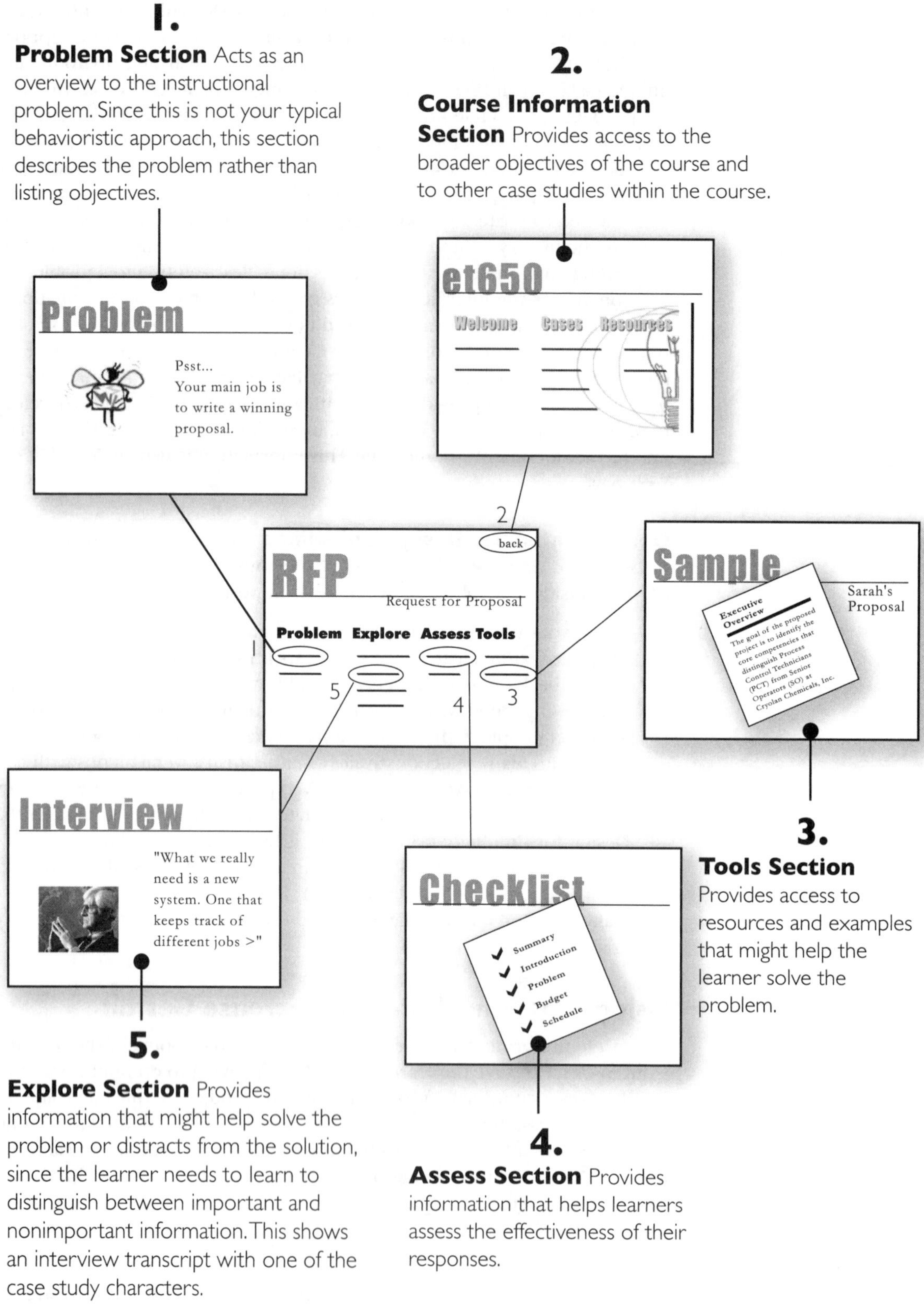

**1.**

**Problem Section** Acts as an overview to the instructional problem. Since this is not your typical behavioristic approach, this section describes the problem rather than listing objectives.

**2.**

**Course Information Section** Provides access to the broader objectives of the course and to other case studies within the course.

### Problem

Psst...
Your main job is to write a winning proposal.

### et650

Welcome    Cases    Resources

### RFP

back

Request for Proposal

**Problem  Explore  Assess Tools**

1          5        4      3

2

### Sample

Sarah's Proposal

Executive Overview
The goal of the proposed project is to identify the core competencies that distinguish Process Control Technicians (PCT) from Senior Operators (SO) at Cryolan Chemicals, Inc.

### Interview

"What we really need is a new system. One that keeps track of different jobs >"

**5.**

**Explore Section** Provides information that might help solve the problem or distracts from the solution, since the learner needs to learn to distinguish between important and nonimportant information. This shows an interview transcript with one of the case study characters.

### Checklist

✓ Summary
✓ Introduction
✓ Problem
✓ Budget
✓ Schedule

**4.**

**Assess Section** Provides information that helps learners assess the effectiveness of their responses.

**3.**

**Tools Section** Provides access to resources and examples that might help the learner solve the problem.

**FIGURE 7–12**  The five parts of an active learning interface

(a) Type is used to create a visual metaphor (an integration strategy). The words "Fit in" are squeezed into the available space, emphasizing the message that creative people do not "fit in."

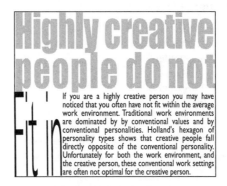

(b) Shapes are used to represent the seven information structures that show parts to whole.

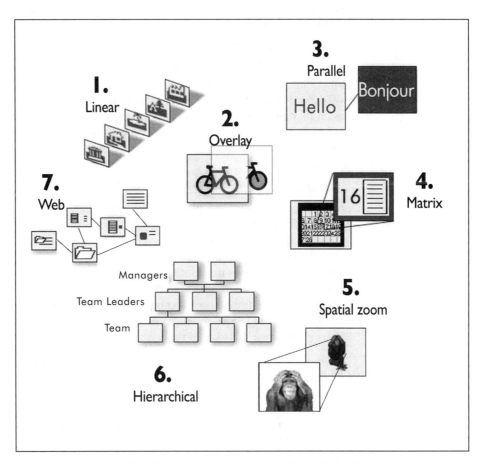

*Source:* Adapted from C. Mok (1996). *Designing business: Multiple media, multiple disciplines.* San Jose, CA: Adobe Press.

**FIGURE 7–13**   Integration tools: Type and shape

## Shape and Proximity

Mok (1996) identifies seven universal data organizational structures or shapes, illustrated in Figure 7-13(b):

1. Linear
2. Overlay
3. Parallel
4. Matrix
5. Spatial zoom
6. Hierarchical
7. Web

Notice how these structures consist of mostly lines and squares and how the closeness (proximity) of the elements increases a sense of relatedness.

A sense of gestalt is facilitated when images look balanced. One way to achieve quick balance is to use images that fit the display size and orientation. For example, the tall Egyptian figure in **Figure 7–14(a)** is particularly suitable for a display size that is taller than it is wide. If you were limited to a display that was wider than it was tall, you might use an image that is also wider than it is tall for that space, as shown in Figure 7-14(b).

## Color and Repetition

Color coding is used to help people associate information. **Figure 7–15(a)** shows a general view of the Hawaiian Islands in which the island of Kauai is shaded a light gray, as is a blowup diagram of Kauai. Since both elements in the display have the same color, the learner perceives them to be connected. This uses both color and repetition (similarity) to improve the learner's sense of gestalt.

## Depth and Contrast

Depth and contrast help people sense the gestalt of an image. Figure 7-15(b) shows a photograph of wheat placed in the background of the food pyramid. The opacity of the wheat photograph has been reduced to 40 percent so that the wheat image becomes a background element and does not compete with the pyramid text.

Many artists use this technique of blurring the background (reducing contrast) or using dull or cool colors because these actions create the illusion of depth. Next time you see a landscape painting, notice how the background consists of dull colors and the foreground consists of brighter colors and sharper images. Notice how depth is also created in Figure 7-15 by shading the left side of the triangle black.

## Space

**White space** is a powerful tool for facilitating gestalt. Covered in greater detail in Chapter 11, it is considered a graphic element. You can think of white space as the plain background of an image, as if the image alone is sitting on a piece of blank paper. Even though it is called "white" space, it can be whatever color the background is, such as gray space, blue space, or orange space.

White space helps create a sense of **balance**—the sense of harmony achieved when all of the elements in a display work together. By this definition, balance is a manifestation of gestalt. Three strategies for creating balance are found in **Figure 7–16.**

### Identifying the Type of Balance to Use (Symmetrical or Asymmetrical)

**Symmetry** is achieved when all elements in a display are centered. If you are not sure, imagine the image on a piece of paper and mentally fold the paper in half. Do you see the same image on both sides of the page? If so, you have symmetrical balance. Symmetrical balance is considered to be formal, conventional, and calm. Consider a painting such as

White space is a powerful tool for facilitating integration of instructional images, mostly by creating balance. Balance can be thought of as the harmony achieved when all of the elements of a display work together. Although the images below use white space differently, they look balanced. You have a sense of harmony. The WHOLE seems related to the PARTS.

(a)

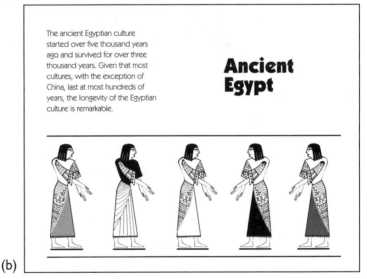

(b)

**FIGURE 7–14**   Integration tools: Space

(a) Color (gray) and repetition (similarity) facilitate integration by separating parts (Kauai) within the context of the whole (Hawaiian Islands).

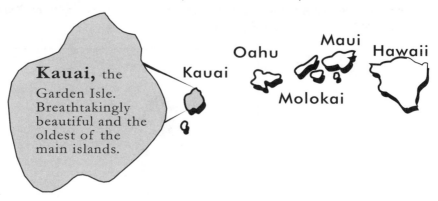

(b) Depth facilitates integration here by creating a contrast between the breads and grains section (part) of the pyramid and the other sections (whole). Photographic images tend to evoke a sense of depth.

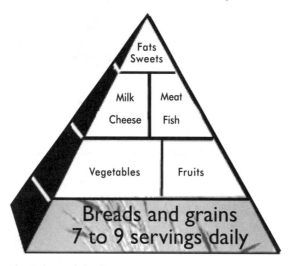

**FIGURE 7–15**   Integration tools: Color and depth

*American Gothic* by Grant Wood, which shows a farmer holding a pitchfork next to his sister. Both figures are centered in the painting (Peterson, 1996). Although the image would not be exactly the same if you were to fold it in half (the farmer is on one half and his sister on the other), it is still considered symmetrical because the weight of the visual elements is roughly equal. Symmetrical balance is easy to create and works well in many instructional situations. Keep in mind, though, that symmetrical balance can become tedious if it is overdone.

**Asymmetry** is form that does not have balanced proportions. Asymmetrical balance is achieved when all elements in a display are in harmony, but the elements are not symmetrical (as in the art and math example of Figure 7–16). If you imagine Part B on a piece of paper and mentally fold the paper in half, you would not see the same image on both sides of the page. Asymmetrical balance is often used to create interest, excitement, and mystery. Consider the painting *Starry Night* by Vincent van Gogh. Although this image is not

## K–12 Example
Art and Math

(a) Identify type of balance to use (symmetrical or asymetrical).

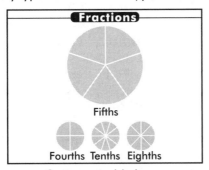

Symmetrical balance

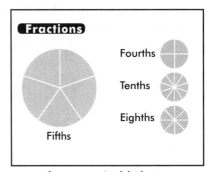

Asymmetrical balance

(b) Consider the rule of thirds. Position important information at the intersection of imaginary lines that break the image into thirds.

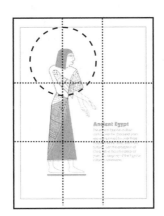

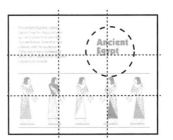

(c) Consider the golden rectangle.

**When the longer sides of a rectangle are 1.6 times the length of the other side, the rectangle tends to have a pleasing appearance.**

**You can also figure out this proportion by making two sides 8 units and the other sides 5 units.**

**This image shows several rectangles with these proportions. The 8 to 5 ratio can be any measure — inches, points, or centimeters, for example.**

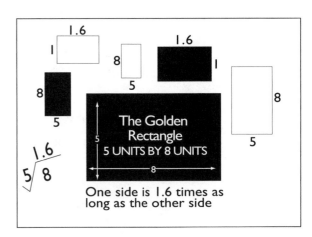

**FIGURE 7-16**   Three strategies for creating balance

symmetrical, the painting is balanced. The random shifts of emphasis all over the canvas create an interesting, energetic, and mysterious display. Unlike symmetrical balance, asymmetrical balance is more difficult to master. You will find occasions that warrant the effort, though, particularly when an instructional message is unconventional or when you need visual interest or energy.

**The Rule of Thirds**    The **rule of thirds** suggests you divide the visual elements of a display along the intersection of imaginary lines that divide an image into thirds. Placing the focal point near the intersection of these lines can be particularly effective. Notice how your eye is drawn to the intersections of the images in Figure 7–16(b). The rule of thirds is a nice rule of thumb, but that does not mean you will use it in all situations.

You will also find that you do not always want to place the elements of a display exactly on the lines or intersections. You may prefer something a little more to the right or left, or top or bottom. There is always a degree of judgment involved with all these rules. That is why we often call design rules heuristics, or rules of thumb that do not apply to all situations. The rule of thirds might best be called the rule of approximate thirds, given how it is applied and interpreted by designers. The rule of thirds, however, can be useful when you are assessing your layout.

**The Golden Rectangle**    Another helpful technique is to employ the proportions of the **golden rectangle**—any rectangle with sides that have a ratio of 5 to 8. This ratio is believed to produce a balanced and pleasing (golden) image or to evoke from the viewer a sense of harmony. Another way to think of the 5 to 8 proportions is to use the ratio 1 to 1.6. That is, the long sides of a rectangle are 1.6 times as long as the shorter sides. Figure 7–16(c) illustrates several versions of the 5 × 8 proportion.

Like the rule of thirds, the golden rectangle will not work all of the time. To suggest that you specifically create rectangles with golden proportions in all of your work is impractical. Consider the standard page size of 8.5" ×11"; these dimensions do not have golden proportions. Golden proportions would be 5" × 8", 8.5" × 13.6" (8.5 × 1.6 = 13.6), and other sizes. Given that it is impractical and costly to change paper size, you would bypass the golden rectangle heuristic. It is useful to know that you could experiment with those proportions if needed, though.

## How Does Gestalt Facilitate Different Picture Functions?

Chapter 1 discussed several types of instructional visuals (decorative, representative, organizational, interpretive, and transformative). This section shows how principles of gestalt have been used to improve visuals that represent these different categories.

### Decorative

Look over **Figure 7–17(a)**. Which image has more harmony or unity? It is a tough call, but I think the right image is the better of the two and thus achieves a greater sense of gestalt. The box around the left image separates the visual design from the content, making it seem less unified as a whole.

I used this particular image for three reasons. First, I find that boxing images in, particularly when the image shows a whole body, whole building, or whole anything, is not always a good idea, especially if you want to create a sense of relatedness or gestalt. Boxes often work better when you have used a section of an image. They act to visually define the edge if one is not supplied. Since the statue is whole, there is no need to define edges.

(a) Decorative image

## K–12 Example
Art

The box in (a) separates elements (PARTS) of this image, making it look a little chopped up. The curved lines and the direction of the statue in (b) make the image seem more unified (WHOLE).

**Assignment**
Find a statue in the museum and make a pencil sketch. Focus on capturing depth and movement.

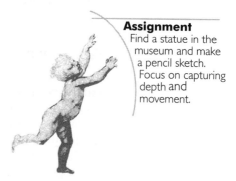

**Assignment**
Find a statue in the museum and make a pencil sketch. Focus on capturing depth and movement.

*Source:* Click art ©1997 RomTech.

(b) Representative image

## K–12 Example
Science
This image allows you to see parts to whole.    In this image you see mostly parts.

(a)

(b)

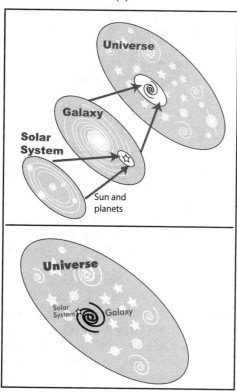

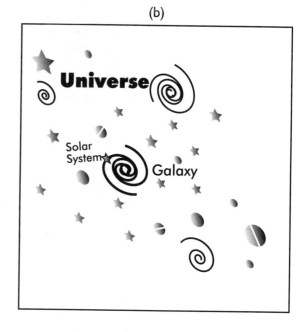

**FIGURE 7–17**   Picture functions and integration principles

Second, you will see that the statue on the left points to the edge of the display, away from the text, making it seem even more disconnected from the words. Given that the statue is likely to grab your attention first (it is the biggest element), it should direct you toward the content rather than off the edge of the display.

Third, aligning text to an image creates gestalt. In the right image, the instructional text could be aligned along a number of places—the leg, the belly, the hands. Creating a thin curved rule, aligning the text to the rule, and placing the text and rule in close proximity to the image, helped the overall gestalt. This position works since the statue is now pointing toward the text. Notice how design actions of contrast, alignment, proximity, shape, and type were used.

### Representative

If your goal is to help people learn the general characteristics of the solar system, the galaxy, and the universe, as well as the relationship between these, which part of Figure 7–17(b) would you use? Most people would consider that the left image does a better job of representing the instructional content since it provides information about each entity (notice the sun and planets in the solar system) as well as their relationship to each other. Although the typeface size in the right image shows a hierarchical relationship (the word *Universe* is largest), each element is ill defined. You see the whole but do not get a clear picture of how the parts relate to the whole.

### Organizational

Have you ever sat through an electronic presentation that seemed like a stream of unending bullets (see **Figure 7–18,** top image)? During such presentations, it is easy to stop paying attention. The problem is that when you do start paying attention again, you have no idea where you are because each screen looks the same.

A greater sense of gestalt, or of understanding where you are in the larger context, is achieved in the figure below the top image in Figure 7–18. This presentation design employs a number of visual cues to mark your location. Notice the side panel that shows your location in the presentation. From any screen you see a representation of all future slides. All in all this figure provides visual cues to help summarize, categorize, and keep content active in short-term memory. Keep in mind, however, that these visual cues may not be needed and may even detract when the subject is easy to understand and the presentation is short.

### Interpretive

Compare the two parts at the bottom of Figure 7–18 and identify which one you think is best. Would grade schoolers have a better chance of interpreting the assignment correctly if they were given the worksheet in part (a) or (b)?

Gestalt is a parts-to-whole relationship. Consider the whole in both parts as practicing the process of addition; consider the parts as the sections of the worksheet that help the learner practice. Which image does the best job of helping the learner practice addition?

From a gestalt perspective, part (a) is better since it clearly identifies and separates the example section of the worksheet from the practice section. The two headings make the student task clear. Although part (b) also provides practice, the expectation is less clear since the example and the practice sections are positioned so close together.

Notice how proximity is effectively used in part (a). By positioning the example and practice activities further apart, the learner can more easily distinguish the difference between the two. Figure and ground are balanced as well by the clear headings.

## Organizational images

### K–12 Example
Health

Slide by slide you see only PARTS; you don't see the big picture (WHOLE).

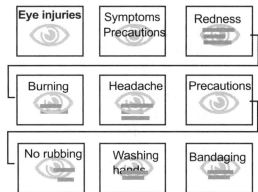

The menu on the left side as well as the visual cues help you stay connected to the WHOLE and understand the organization.

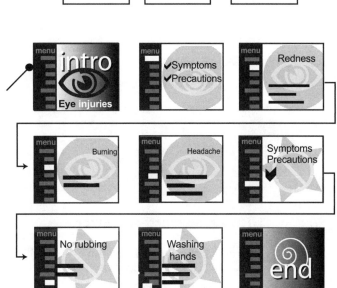

Interpretive images

### K–12 Example
Math

In part (b) everything runs together: you do not see the important sections (PARTS) as clearly as in (a).

(a)                    (b)

**Addition**

Example
2 + 3 = 5

You try it
4 + 5 = ?

**Addition**

2 + 3 = 5

4 + 5 = ?

**FIGURE 7–18**   Picture functions and integration principles

## (a) A visual analogy

### K–12 Example
Business
Economics

Ask learners to create visual analogies as a strategy for problem identification. Here a student compares a faulty billing system to a leaky pipe.

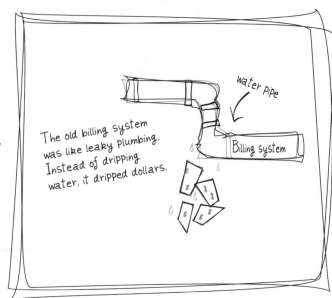

## (b) An advance organizer

Drawing this type of diagram is a good way to help organize thoughts (PARTS) into a meaningful message (WHOLE). Here a student creates a map of the concept "needs assessment."

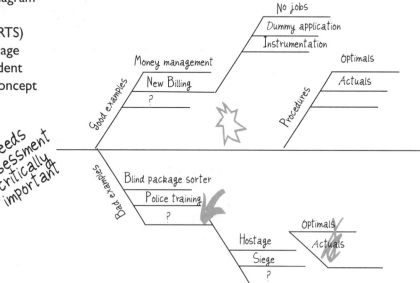

**FIGURE 7–19**   Generative strategies and integration

## How to Design Generative Strategies with Gestalt in Mind

As in the last two chapters, we'll shift direction and look at generative strategies that explore gestalt. When your goal is more oriented to long-term learning, it is time to consider generative strategies—techniques that require learners to generate their own meaning. Generative strategies for integrating information in meaningful ways include using metaphors or analogies, outlining content, creating charts, using mental images and analogies, summarizing information in one's own words, and telling stories (Wittrock, 1989). By doing these things, the learner thinks about the information more deeply and learns it more thoroughly.

Generative strategies can be used to help understand relationships between different elements. The following examples show you how learners might be able to use visuals to help them integrate information in ways that are meaningful and allow them to understand the big picture, or gestalt.

### Analogy

Have the learner create a visual analogy of the overall instructional message (gestalt). The learner might be asked to draw an analogy of a topic. For instance, after a discussion of a faulty billing system, students are asked to illustrate the problem. **Figure 7–19(a)** shows how a student completed this assignment: by drawing a leaky pipe that is dripping dollar bills. This image clearly conveys the message that a faulty billing system wastes money.

### Advance Organizer

Have learners create a diagram using any shapes they want to represent their thoughts on a topic and how they see parts fitting into a whole. Figure 7-19(b) shows the learner's initial ideas in illustrating the importance of needs assessment.

## SUMMARY

Everything in this book relates to the topic of integration, which is the focus of this chapter. This is fitting because the word *integration* implies the assimilation of information. Overall, this chapter explains the importance of facilitating learner integration through visual cues designed to emphasize a parts-to-whole relationship. When Edward Tufte (1990) describes good design as "simplicity in the underlying message, complexity in the detail," he is addressing gestalt, a German word that roughly translates as "whole" or "form" and involves the belief that the whole is greater than the sum of its parts. As designers, our goal is not only to help learners see the underlying message but to provide clear access to critical supportive information as well.

The five principles of gestalt were explained: (1) closure, (2) contiguity, (3) similarity, (4) proximity, and (5) previous experience. Each of these laws describes how the mind, when presented with information, works to generate understanding. As designers, our job is to accelerate that process if possible.

The law of closure describes how the mind fills in gaps. For designers this means we may not need to supply all of the information. If we show part of an image rather than the whole image, the mind is likely to fill in the rest. By leaving out some of the information, we are reducing cognitive load, or the amount of information learners must process at any one time.

The law of contiguity tells us that the mind tries to follow a path or plane. Once it is started along that path, the mind wants to continue. As designers we want to take advantage of that momentum. By directing the eye along a path, we can control the sequence and ease in which information is processed. Chapter 6 covered the law of contiguity in detail.

The principle of similarity explains how the mind groups information it perceives to be related. By using or repeating similar elements (colors, shapes, fonts), designers can simplify data since the mind groups like elements, in turn reducing cognitive load. The action of repetition allows the mind to see these patterns and simplify information.

The principle of proximity explains how items that are placed close together are perceived as related and how those that are far apart are perceived as unrelated. Removing distance between elements facilitates the mind's grouping of information into similar categories, making information easier to remember and understand. Increasing this distance facilitates the perception of separate categories. Elements that are far apart are seen as distinct and unrelated.

The principle of previous experience explains the importance of helping the learner relate new information to previous knowledge and experience. As designers we want to draw from the previous meanings of colors and symbols to enhance the meaning of our content. For example, if we want to convey extreme danger, we could use a skull and and crossbones image because it is a universal symbol of death. By using visual elements that already have meaning, we can reduce a learner's cognitive load.

Computer-based training environments rely heavily upon effective use of gestalt principles, especially in the design of grid systems—underlying structures that provide consistency throughout instruction—and interfaces—the communication devices between a product and a system. An instructional interface consists of all the visual, verbal, and auditory cues that help learners go about the task of learning. Grids are typically built into interfaces.

The principles of gestalt relate clearly to the design of grids and interfaces because they address the task of reducing complexity and overload, an important consideration when dealing with the many functions of an instructional interface. The tools and actions that facilitate gestalt are described in the chapters that follow.

## PRACTICE

For additional activities and examples of student work, visit the Companion Website for this book at *http://www.coe.unco.edu/LindaLohr*.

### Resource Activities

Use Figures R–4, R–5, R–6, R–7, and R–9 from the Resources to help you complete the activities below.

### Web Activity

The Web Activity asks you to create an interface for an instructional unit to help a learner see how the parts of a lesson relate to the whole. One solution to this activity is presented here.

This solution shows how the overall topic (the whole — nutrition) is covered using an organizational structure that shows the different topic levels (the parts — plant subdivided into fruits, vegetables and legumes).

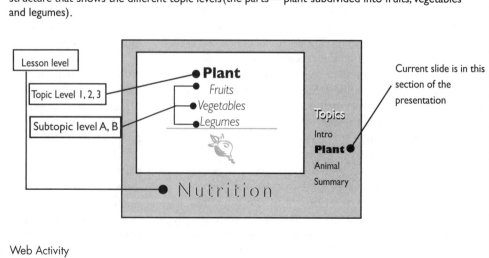

Web Activity

## Challenge Activity

The Challenge Activity asks you to create an instructional presentation and practice activity that addresses one or more of the gestalt principles. One solution to this activity is presented here.

This example shows how the principle of **similarity** is integrated in both the content presentation and practice display. The consistent use of the skeleton and muscle between lesson content and practice helps the learner connect information to a novel situation, showing transfer of knowledge.

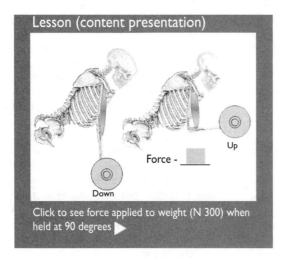

Lesson (content presentation)

Force -  _____

Up

Down

Click to see force applied to weight (N 300) when held at 90 degrees ▶

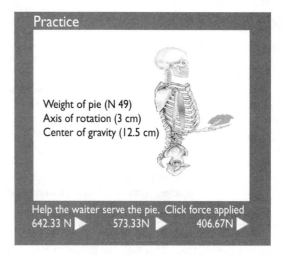

Practice

Weight of pie (N 49)
Axis of rotation (3 cm)
Center of gravity (12.5 cm)

Help the waiter serve the pie.  Click force applied
642.33 N ▶        573.33N ▶        406.67N ▶

Challenge Activity

## Independent Activity

The Chapter 7 Independent Activity asks you to pick one of the following projects.

1. Take photographs using the 10 composition tips job aid (Figures R–4 and R–5).
2. Create workshop materials that coordinate different instructional materials (similar worksheets, documents, electronic slides).
3. Create a portfolio interface for job-hunting or personal assessment.

## Justification Activity

Write a justification paper for the activity you select. Describe the following:

- ■ *Your users and the assumptions you make about them (such as age, reading level, and assumed skills).*
- ■ *Why you think your solution will work; include at least two ideas from the book, including page numbers and your interpretation of the passage used.*
- ■ *What you learned from a "user-test" (have someone look at the image and verbalize their thoughts while looking at the image).*
- ■ *The changes you will make based on user comments (or create a revised image).*

## Discussion Questions

An interface is defined as the cues that communicate between a user and a system. Based on this definition, identify as many interfaces as you can. Is an airport an interface? Do books have an interface? How about a theater? For each example you come up with, identify criteria that make the interface effective. Discuss similarities and differences.

# K-12 Student Activities

1. Create a theme-based event for members of your class or school. Make signage, promotions, job aids, etc., that match the theme.
2. Create instructional materials for the local animal shelter, YMCA, or community organization. Create materials with gestalt in mind.

## REFERENCES

Dreyfus, H. (1984). *Symbol source book: An authoritative guide to international graphic symbols*. New York: Van Nostrand Reinhold.

Gestalt Psychology. (2000). Microsoft Encarta Online Encyclopedia. Retrieved from *http://encarta.msn.com*.

Horton, W. K. (1994). *The icon book: Visual symbols for computer systems and documentation*. New York: Wiley.

Koffka, K. (1935). *Principles of gestalt psychology*. New York: Harcourt, Brace.

Kristof, R., & Satran, A. (1995). *Interactivity by design: Creating and communicating with new media*. Mountain View, CA: Adobe Press.

Lohr, L. (2000). Designing the instructional interface. *Computers in Human Behavior, 16(2)*, 161–182.

Lohr, L., Falvo, D., Hunt, E., & Johnson, B. (2007). Improving the usability of web learning through template modification. In B. Kahn (Ed.), *Flexible learning* (pp. 186–197). London: Information Science Publishing.

Luchins, A. S., & Luchins, E. H. (1959). *Rigidity of behavior—A variational approach to the effect of einstellung*. Eugene, OR: University of Oregon Books. Retrieved from *http://www.enabling.org/ia/gestalt/gerhards/closure.html*.

Lynch, P. J., & Horton, S. (1999). *Web style guide: Basic design principles for creating web sites*. New Haven, CT: Yale University Press.

Mayer, R. E. (2001). *Multimedia learning*. Cambridge, England: Cambridge University Press.

Mayer, R. E., Bove, W., Bryman, A., Mars, R., & Tapangco, L. (1996). When less is more: Meaningful learning from visual and verbal summaries of science textbook lessons. *Journal of Educational Psychology, 88(1)*, 64–73.

Mayer, R. E., & Sims, V. K. (1994). For whom is a picture worth a thousand words? Extension of a dual-coding theory of multimedia learning. *Journal of Educational Psychology, 86(3)*, 389–401.

Miller, A. R., Brown, J. M., & Cullen, C. D. (2000). *Global graphics: Designing with symbols for an international market*. Gloucester, MA: Rockport Publishers.

Misanchuk, E. R. (1992). *Preparing instructional text: Document design using desktop publishing*. Englewood Cliffs, NJ: Educational Technology Publications.

Mok, C. (1996). *Designing business: Multiple media, multiple disciplines*. San Jose, CA: Adobe Press.

Mullet, K., & Sano, D. (1995). *Designing visual interfaces: Communication oriented techniques*. Englewood Cliffs, NJ: Prentice Hall.

Nielsen, J. (2000). *Designing web usability: The practice of simplicity*. Indianapolis, IN: New Riders Publishing.

Ormrod, J. (1990). *Human learning: Theories, principles, and educational applications*. Upper Saddle River, NJ: Merrill/Prentice Hall.

Peterson, B. L. (1996). *Using design basics to get creative results*. Cincinnati, OH: North Light Books.

Pettersson, R. (1993). *Visual information*. Englewood Cliffs, NJ: Educational Technology Publications.

Tufte, E. (1990). *Envisioning information*. Cheshire, CT: Graphics Press.

Wertheimer, M. (1959). Principles of perceptual organization. In D.C. Beardslee & M. Wertheimer (Eds.), *Readings in perception* (pp. 115–135). Princeton, NJ: Van Nostrand.

Wittrock, M. C. (1989). Generative processes of comprehension. *Educational Psychologist, 24*, 345–376.

# PART III

## Actions and Tools

# CHAPTER 8

## Actions: Contrast, Alignment, Repetition, and Proximity

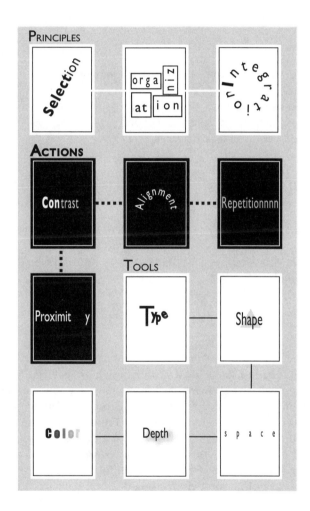

[Contrast, alignment, repetition, and proximity] won't make you a brilliant designer, and they won't land you $20,000 web designer contracts, but they will keep you from embarrassing yourself in front of millions of people.

*Robin Williams and John Tollett*

Due to cost, pictures and images may not always be on the same page.
Whenever possible, images are placed as close to their reference as possible.

## Notes About the Opening Visual

This chapter explains the critical role that contrast, alignment, repetition, and proximity play in instructional visuals. The opening visual uses all of these actions. Try to guess where each action took place and if it served any instructional purpose, then compare your thoughts to **Figure 8–1.**

Although the chapter opening visual uses all four actions, you do not need to use all of these in an image. Sometimes you will use only one or two, because that is all you need. In many images the actions overlap. For example, you might align a word with another word using an alignment tool like the one shown in Figure 8–1. If you find that after aligning the words, they make a bigger, bolder impact, you have also created contrast. The point is that these tools overlap quite a bit.

## Focus Questions

- Why are the concepts of contrast, alignment, repetition, and proximity considered actions?
- Do you use all four actions in every visual?
- Do these actions improve instruction?
- How do you use these actions?

## Key Terms

**ALIGNMENT** Lining up visual elements along an edge or imaginary path.
**CONTRAST** Making the components of a visual image—for example, shape and color—different.

**PROXIMITY** The positioning of elements close together or far apart.
**REPETITION** Reusing elements or using similar elements.

## Introduction

Sylvia has just been asked to do a small redesign project for a local paint company that wants to encourage sales by showing customers how to apply faux paint finishes to walls, furniture, and anything else that might benefit from a decorative look. The store owner shows Sylvia a flyer she thinks might work (see **Figure 8–2**). "Of course," she says, "we're hiring YOU to redo this because we think you can turn this into something better." Sylvia asks the owner, "Who will be using this? Is there any particular group of people you want to attract?" The owner thinks for a few seconds, then replies, "I'd say artsy/craftsy types. You can make the flyer look fun, but don't go overboard."

As Sylvia looks over the flyer she asks herself these questions:

- How do I make people notice the different painting techniques?
- How do I make the information look organized?
- How do I rewrite this so the information is organized and helpful?
- How can I make the page unified when there are so many techniques and descriptions?

Sylvia has just asked four questions that are related to the design actions covered in this chapter. Her first question deals with the importance of contrast, the second deals with alignment, the third repetition, and the fourth repetition and proximity.

### Alignment

The icons are aligned with the edges of the light gray background and with each other. *Instructional benefit? All icons appear to be connected by invisible lines.*

### Contrast

Each Action is on a highly contrasting black background, which clearly separates it from the Tools and Perception icons. *Instructional benefit? The action icons grab your attention. You see where they fit within the bigger picture.*

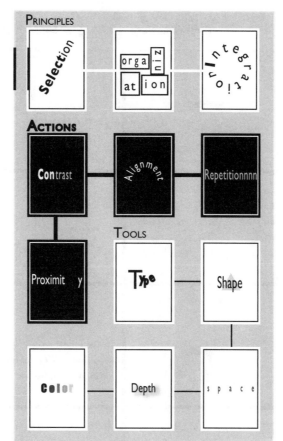

### Repetition

Each icon uses typography to express its meaning. *Instructional benefit? The simplicity of the design makes the topic easier to grasp.*

### Proximity

Related icons are close together. *Instructional benefit? The learner sees groupings.*

These symbols represent computer alignment icons. Selecting all objects and clicking on one of these icons will align the objects accordingly.

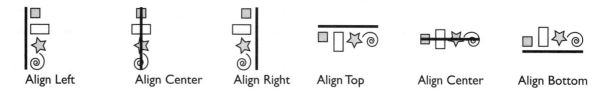

| Align Left | Align Center | Align Right | Align Top | Align Center | Align Bottom |

**FIGURE 8-1**   CARP in the cover graphic

Contrast, alignment, repetition, and proximity are all considered design actions because they require that you do something to one or more elements of a visual. When you create contrast, you make two or more elements very different from each other by manipulating them to increase the difference in size, color, or shape, among other things. When you align, you move elements around to line up on various edges. When you take an element and recreate

# Materials for Faux Painting

| | | |
|---|---|---|
| **Paint** | Paint is the primary ingredient in all of the faux techniques. | The most important thing to consider when dealing with paint is the color. Use either complementary or contrasting colors to achieve your desired look. |
| If you are using a latex glaze, mix it with a colored paint, 4 parts glaze to 1 part paint. If you are glazing over that, next use 8 parts glaze to 1 part paint. | Glaze is used to create translucent effects in many techniques including color washing, sponging, ragging, etc. | **Glaze** |
| **Brush** | Brushes are especially important in the color wash painting techniques. | If you are color washing, first cover wall with a coat of paint. Then, dip your brush in glaze and randomly brush in crisscross strokes across your wall. |
| To create a faux technique with rollers, roll different colors in horizontal stripes vertically on your wall. Let the different colors "bleed" into each other at the edges. | Rollers are necessary for many techniques that need a base color before applying the technique. However, they can also be used to create effects. | **Roller** |
| **Sponge** | Sponging is one of the most common paint techniques. It is also one of the easiest for the novice to achieve. | First, have a base coat on your wall. Then, dip sponge in another paint color or glaze mixture and distress wall. |
| Ragging is used to achieve a variety of effects depending on the fabric used in the technique. | **Rag** | Either bunch rag up or twist into roll. Dip in paint and either distress or roll across your wall. |

**FIGURE 8–2**   Original flyer
*Source: Erin Hunt. Used with permission.*

some aspect of it, you are using the repetition action—repeating color, typeface, shapes, and other things. When you move elements close together or far apart, you are using the proximity action.

Look at the flyer and guess where contrast, alignment, repetition, and proximity could be improved (**Figure 8–2** and **Figure 8–3**). After you look this over, look at Sylvia's redesign (**Figure 8–4**).

Contrast, alignment, repetition, and proximity problems.

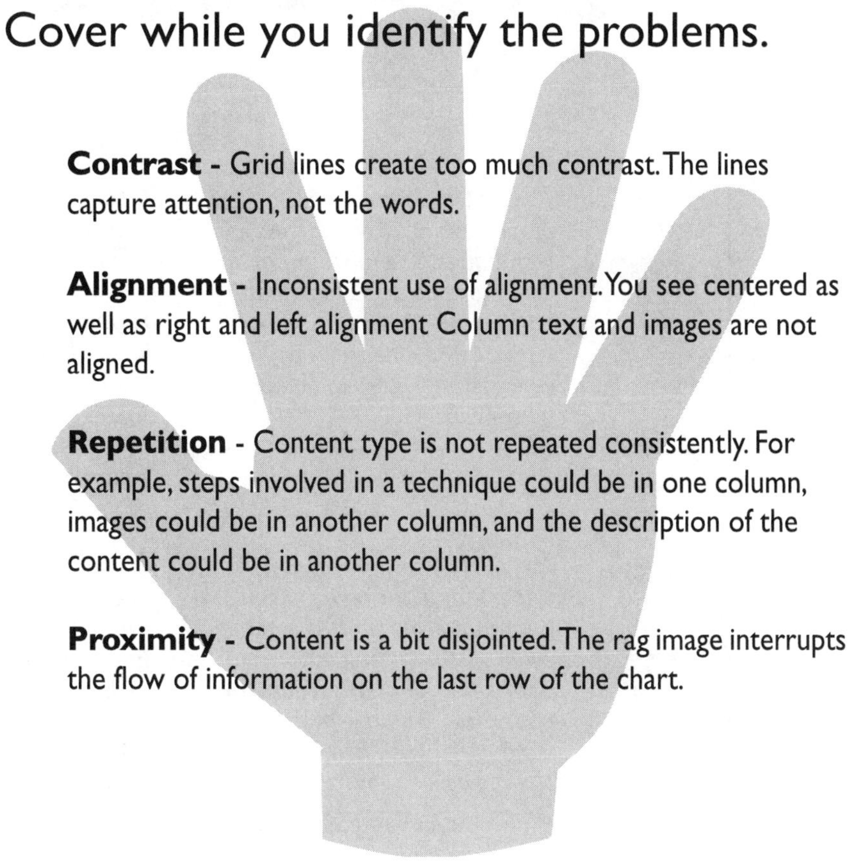

# Cover while you identify the problems.

**Contrast -** Grid lines create too much contrast. The lines capture attention, not the words.

**Alignment -** Inconsistent use of alignment. You see centered as well as right and left alignment Column text and images are not aligned.

**Repetition** - Content type is not repeated consistently. For example, steps involved in a technique could be in one column, images could be in another column, and the description of the content could be in another column.

**Proximity** - Content is a bit disjointed. The rag image interrupts the flow of information on the last row of the chart.

**FIGURE 8-3** Problems with the original flyer

# Faux Painting Materials

**Paint** *is the primary ingredient in all of the faux techniques. The most important thing to consider when dealing with paint is the color. Use either complementary or contrasting colors to achieve your desired look.*

**Glaze** *is used to create translucent effects in many techniques, including color washing, sponging, and ragging. If you are using a latex glaze, mix it with a colored paint, 4 parts glaze to 1 part paint. If you are glazing over that, use 8 parts glaze to 1 part paint.*

**Brushes** *are especially important in the color wash painting techniques. If you are color washing, first cover wall with a coat of paint. Then, dip your brush in glaze and randomly brush in crisscross strokes across your wall.*

**Rollers** *are necessary for many techniques that need a base color before applying the technique. However, they can also be used to create effects. To create a faux technique with rollers, roll different colors in horizontal stripes then roll vertically on your wall. Let the different colors "bleed" into each other at the edges.*

**Sponging** *is one of the most common paint techniques. It is also one of the easiest for the novice to achieve. First, have a base coat on your wall. Then, dip sponge in another paint color or glaze mixture and distress wall.*

**Ragging** *can achieve a variety of effects depending on the fabric used in the technique. Either bunch rag up or twist it into roll. Dip in paint and either distress or roll across your wall.*

**FIGURE 8–4**   Revised flyer
*Source: Erin Hunt. Used with permission*

# THE RESEARCH ON CARP

The research behind the instructional effectiveness of contrast, alignment, repetition, and proximity (CARP) is limited. Most of the literature describing the merits of CARP focus on aesthetic design principles that are not based on experimental research. **Table 8–1** presents a few experimentally based studies that address each CARP element individually. Of all the CARP actions, contrast and proximity appear to have the strongest research base.

**TABLE 8–1**   *Research on Contrast, Alignment, Repetition, and Proximity*

| CARP Action | Key Word | Multimedia Principle Description | Related Research |
|---|---|---|---|
| Contrast | Coherence | "Students learn better when extraneous material is excluded rather than included." P. 113 In other words, focus on what is important by removing what is not important. | S. F. Harp & R. E. Mayer (1998). How seductive details do their damage: A theory of cognitive interest in science learning. *Journal of Educational Psychology, 90,* 414–434. R.E. Mayer, W. Bove, A. Bryman, R. Mars, & L. Tapangco (1996). When less is more: Meaningful learning from visual and verbal summaries of science textbook lessons. *Journal of Educational Psychology, 88,* 64–73. |
| Alignment | Chunking | Research on chunking is indirectly related to alignment because aligning items tends to group items perceptually. Thus, what might be considered several distinct elements is instead perceived as one element. In other words, a new schema may be created by a chunk, which becomes the basis for expanding memory or the ability to reduce cognitive load. | F. Paas, A. Renkl, & J. Sweller (2003). Cognitive load theory and instructional design: Recent developments. *Educational Psychologist, 38 (1),* 1–4. |
| Repetition | Rehearsal Chunking | *Rehearsal* is the act of repeating information in memory and can significantly increase retention. Repeating tools (color, line, shape, color, depth, and space) tend to create perceptual associations, or chunks (see *Alignment*). | J. E. Ormrod (2004). *Human learning.* (4th ed.) Upper Saddle River, NJ: Pearson. |
| Proximity | Contiguity | "Students learn better when corresponding words and pictures are presented near rather than far from each other on the page or screen." P. 81 | P. Chandler & J. Sweller (1991). Cognitive load theory and the format of instruction.*Cognition and Instruction, 8,* 293–392. R. Mayer (2001). *Multimedia learning.* Cambridge, England: Cambridge University Press. |

Text blocks B and C have enough contrast to make you notice the heading; however, image C is the best. Look for typefaces that include light, regular, **bold,** and **ultra bold** (as in this Gill Sans typeface).

A

**This heading has contrast**
but the contrast is not strong. There isn't that much of a difference in the heading and this body text.

B

**This heading has**
more contrast. The typeface in the heading is bigger than the body text. The contrast here is adequate, but not optimal.

C

**This heading has**
the most contrast. Not only is the typeface bolder than this body text, but the typeface is from a different type family as well.

There is some contrast here between heading and content. The flowers create the most contrast.

Whiskey Barrel Flowers

Fill the whiskey barrel or plastic insert with potting soil. If you are working with old dirt, dig through it until the large clumps are broken.

Place your plants in the pot so they are just sitting on the top of your soil. Work from the middle of the whiskey barrel to the outside edges, putting your tallest plants in the middle and your shortest plants on the edges. Be sure to place any flowers or plants that droop on the edges too, since these will look nice draping over the edges of the whiskey barrel. Use tall grass, fern and ivy as fillers.

Dig a hole about the width and length of each flower. Before putting the flower in, sprinkle a few beads of fertilizer into the hole. Pack the dirt around the flower. When finished lightly sprinkle the beaded fertilizer over the top surface. Water liberally.

This image has the most contrast on the page. It may be fun to look at, but try following the instructions. You see a big gray block of text. You'd perform one of the steps, and when the step was completed you'd probably have to read through everything again just to find where you left off.

This image does a better job of creating contrast. Instruction is broken into smaller instructional chunks. White space and large numbers call attention to the three overall steps of planting flowers.

# Whiskey Barrel Flowers

Fill the whiskey barrel or plastic insert with potting soil. If you are working with old dirt, dig through it until the large clumps are broken. Place your plants in the pot so they are just sitting on the top of your soil. Work from the middle of the whiskey barrel to the outside edges, putting your tallest plants in the middle and your shortest plants on the edges. Be sure to place any flowers or plants that droop on the edges too, since these will look nice draping over the edges of the whiskey barrel. Use tall grass, fern and ivy as fillers. Dig a hole about the width and length of each flower. Before putting the flower in, sprinkle a few beads of fertilizer into the hole. Pack the dirt around the flower. When finished lightly sprinkle the beaded fertilizer over the top surface. Water liberally.

## *Whiskey Barrel Flowers*

1  Fill the whiskey barrel or plastic insert with potting soil. If you are working with old dirt, dig through it until the large clumps are broken.

2  Place your plants in the pot so they are just sitting on the top of your soil. Work from the middle of the whiskey barrel to the outside edges, putting your tallest plants in the middle and your shortest plants on the edges. Be sure to place any flowers or plants that droop on the edges too, since these will look nice draping over the edges of the whiskey barrel. Use tall grass, fern and ivy as fillers.

3  Dig a hole about the width and length of each flower. Before putting the flower in, sprinkle a few beads of fertilizer into the hole. Pack the dirt around the flower. When finished lightly sprinkle the beaded fertilizer over the top surface. Water liberally.

**FIGURE 8–5**  Contrast

# A Review of Each Action

Following the same organizational approach as the research, this chapter will also present information about each action individually.

## Contrast

You create **contrast** by establishing differences between elements in a visual. How much of a difference do you need to create? Create more than you think you need. Most people, especially educators, are way too timid. As Robin Williams (1994) advises, make things really different. Look quickly at **Figure 8–5.** Try not to read the words, but do try to determine which text block–A, B, or C–has the optimal contrast. Text blocks B and C have enough contrast to make you notice the heading; however, C is the best.

### The Book Icon for Contrast

The *contrast* icon in the chapter opening visual uses dark and wide letters adjacent to light and thin letters. It is fairly easy to do this when you have a typeface that is packaged with a variety of heavy and thin fonts. For the icon, Futura Heavy was used with Futura Condensed Light. Futura also has fonts that are called Black (not as bold as Heavy), Black Italics, Book (a reading weight), and others. It is a good idea to have at least one serif and sans serif typeface in a variety of weights because it is a quick and effective way to create contrast. To emphasize, make sure you have at least one really "fat" font and one really skinny font.

### Sylvia's Use of Contrast

Look again at Sylvia's redesign (Figure 8-4) to see if you can identify where contrast was employed. Notice how Sylvia used contrast with type and space:

- In the title
- In the headings
- Between the body text and the headings
- Between the text chunks

### Another Example of Contrast

Figure 8-5 shows three sets of instructions for creating whiskey barrel flower arrangements. Which do you think has the optimum contrast for helping someone perform the task of potting a plant? If you imagine yourself potting plants, you might see why the bottom right set of instructions is best. It calls attention to the three overall steps, which might help people potting the plants keep track of where they are in the process.

## Alignment

When you line things up along an edge or some type of imaginary line or path, you are using **alignment. Figure 8–6** illustrates a variety of alignments—from vertical to circular to centered. One of the most important things to remember about alignment is that text should be left-aligned for easier reading (in western cultures). You learn more about this in the next chapter.

One instructional benefit of alignment relates to the perception that aligned items are related. The images that are aligned form a perceptual chunk that can be used to reduce cognitive load.

### Sylvia's Use of Alignment

The lower section of Figure 8-6 shows a number of alignment actions applied to the painting flyer: shape, right, left, top, center, and bottom alignment.

Text aligned to a shape is rarely easy to read.

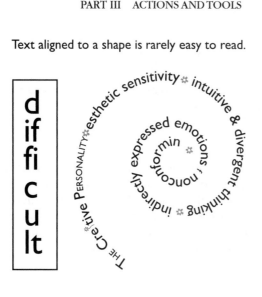

The
CREATIVE PERSONALITY

esthetic sensitivity
intuitive & divergent thinking
indirectly expressed emotions
nonconforming behavior

*Centered text is formal.*

The
CREATIVE PERSONALITY

esthetic sensitivity
intuitive & divergent thinking
indirectly expressed emotions
nonconforming behavior

*Left aligned text is easiest to read.*

CREATIVE PERSONALITY The

esthetic sensitivity
intuitive & divergent thinking
indirectly expressed emotions
nonconforming behavior

*Right aligned text is difficult to read.*

This painting flyer effectively uses many types of alignment, including shape, right, left, top, and bottom alignment.

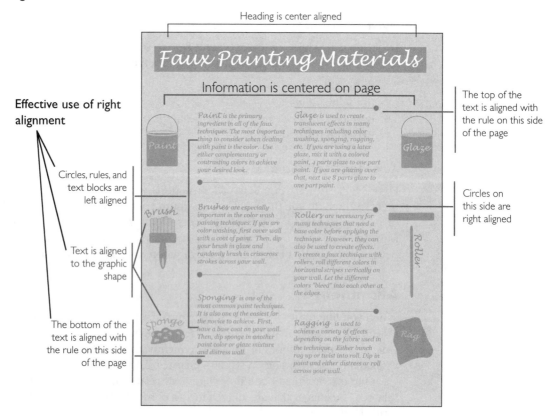

**FIGURE 8–6**   Alignment

### The Book Icon for Alignment

The alignment icon in the chapter opening visual shows the word *alignment* curving around the top half of a circle. Each letter aligns to a corresponding part of the circle edge. You can create these types of alignments in software programs such as Adobe Illustrator, where you create the shape (for example, the half-circle), then click on the edges of the shape with a text alignment icon, and type. As you type, you see the letters align themselves to the shape.

### Another Example of Alignment

A historical example of alignment and relationships is illustrated in **Figure 8–7.** The 2000 presidential elections were controversial because the candidates' names did not align with the ballot holes.

## Repetition

When you employ **repetition,** you take some element of a visual and use it again. Repetition can create a sense of harmony and unity. When you repeat similar colors in a display, or similar typefaces, you imply relationships. One of the reasons why too many typefaces in a document are distracting is that each typeface creates a slightly different message. With too many messages going on, things can get confusing.

### The Book Icon for Repetition

The icon for alignment in the chapter opening visual shows the letter *n* repeated many times. You will find that repetition is one of the easiest actions to perform because you just have to duplicate something, or some aspect of something. For example, the repetition icon could just as easily have been the word *repetition* duplicated three or four times. Notice how all of the book's icons repeat something? They each show their meaning using words only. This repetition makes them seem related, and at the same time it simplifies the overall message.

### Sylvia's Use of Repetition

The lower half of **Figure 8–8** shows the number of ways Sylvia effectively repeated color, typeface, image size, shapes, and even white space in the painting flyer.

### Another Example of Repetition

The upper half of Figure 8-8 shows examples of a computer-based training on clouds. Which example do you think uses repetition most effectively? Can you identify any repetition problems in any of the images? The leftmost image uses conflicting types of cloud images for buttons. The cartoon cloud does not work effectively with the photograph images of clouds, and the cloud inside the pointing finger is not even visible. The rightmost image effectively repeats the shape of the cloud with the shape of the buttons. Additionally, the typeface has a cloudlike appearance.

## Proximity

Working with **proximity** involves moving visual elements close together or far apart. When elements are close together, they seem related; when they are far apart, they seem unrelated. In the top left image of **Figure 8–9** notice that the duck on the left is separated by space from the ducks on the right. This positioning makes the duck seem independent or isolated. The other duck image has the opposite effect. When the ducks are all positioned close to one another, they seem related, as if they are one family.

### The Book Icon for Proximity

The proximity icon in the chapter opening visual separates the letter *y* from the other letters using space. Doesn't the letter *y* in the icon look a little bit like that independent duck?

**K–12 Example** Social Studies, History, Publications

The 2000 election will be remembered as the election with the Florida Ballot problem. Votes counted for Pat Buchanan and Ezola Foster may have been meant for Al Gore and Joe Lieberman. People who read from the top to bottom, rather than right to left, may have punched the second hole down, thinking they were voting for Al Gore. Since the ballot was meant to be followed left to right, their punch counted as a vote for Pat Buchanan rather than Al Gore. The poor alignment of the rules separating candidates contributed to the problem.

The ballots also have serious contrast problems. The use of all capital letters makes it hard to distinguish individual letters and words. (You learn more about this in Chapter 9.) In addition, if the numbers had been larger, there might have been a greater chance of voter accuracy.

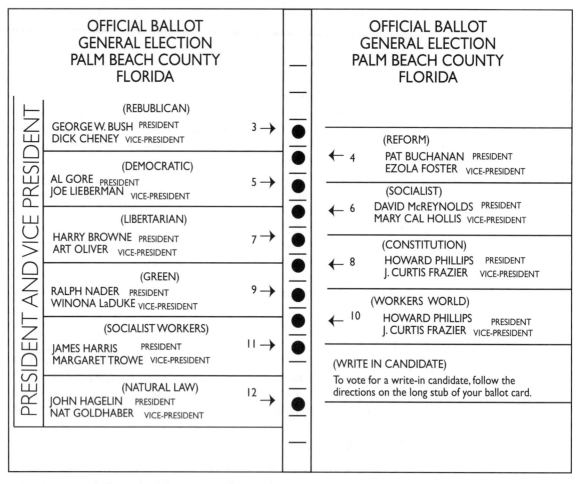

**FIGURE 8–7**   A ballot and its alignment problems

And don't the other letters look like the duck family? As you can see, just moving things close or apart can make a difference.

## Sylvia's Use of Proximity

If you look back at the original painting flyer image (Figure 8–2), you will notice two columns of information were used to describe each paint technique. Sylvia strengthened the connection

## K–12 Example Science

This web training page lacks repetition. Notice four different fonts used. The type of images used are different as well with line drawings, clip art, and realistic images.

Here repetition is used effectively. The font (Curlz) matches the cloud shape. Furthermore, the buttons look like clouds. All cloud images are realistic. Additionally the background border has tiny swirls that echo the typeface and cloud images.

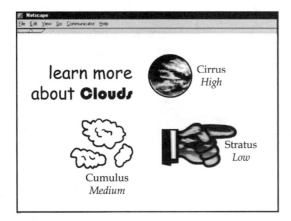

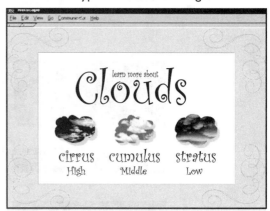

This painting flyer repeats a number of elements.

The typeface (Lucida Handwriting) for headings and subheadings is repeated

Image size is repeated

The left and right sides of the page have approximately the same amount of white space

The same color is used in the heading and graphics

Small circles and thin rules are repeated

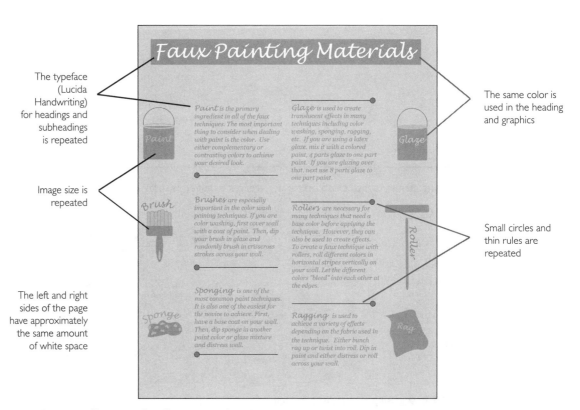

**FIGURE 8–8** Effective and ineffective use of repetition

## K–12 Example Many topics

The grouping of ducks far apart or close together contributes to the message of either being part of something or independent. Typography also contributes to this message.

## K–12 Example Math

Worksheet 1 shows three math problems, numbered 1, 2, and 3. These numbers, however, are positioned too closely to the first equation number. The learner is likely to read the first equation as 12 + _____ = 20, not as 2 + _____ = 20. Worksheet 3 uses letters for the different math problems, eliminating the problem of mixing numbers.

Here the word *Independence* is in proximity with only one duck and looks disassociated with the other ducks.

The word *Teamwork* centered over the ducks strengthens the message of unity/togetherness.

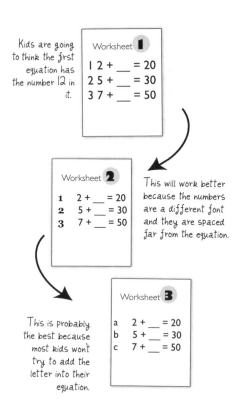

Kids are going to think the first equation has the number 12 in it.

**Worksheet 1**

1 2 + ___ = 20
2 5 + ___ = 30
3 7 + ___ = 50

This will work better because the numbers are a different font and they are spaced far from the equation.

**Worksheet 2**

1   2 + ___ = 20
2   5 + ___ = 30
3   7 + ___ = 50

This is probably the best because most kids won't try to add the letter into their equation.

**Worksheet 3**

a   2 + ___ = 20
b   5 + ___ = 30
c   7 + ___ = 50

Putting elements into close proximity creates a unified message.

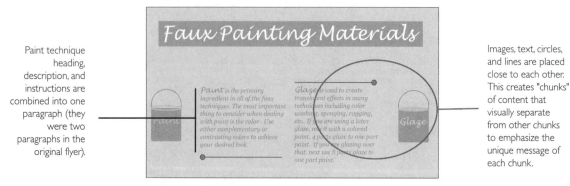

Paint technique heading, description, and instructions are combined into one paragraph (they were two paragraphs in the original flyer).

Images, text, circles, and lines are placed close to each other. This creates "chunks" of content that visually separate from other chunks to emphasize the unique message of each chunk.

**FIGURE 8–9**   Using the proximity principle.

between the two columns by combining them. She also moved the heading closer to the text and made the two seem more related. White space was used as well, as seen in the chunks of information that make up each paint technique. The white space surrounding the information helps create the chunk. Each of these chunks is moved far enough away from the other techniques to set them apart. In these examples, moving elements close together made them seem more related (as in the title and text) and moving elements apart (as in the individual chunks of information) made them seem more distinct. The shaded remake of the flyer shown in Figure 8-9 highlights Sylvia's use of proximity.

### Another Example of Proximity

I have often noticed a proximity problem with the math worksheets my daughter brings home from school (see the top right image in Figure 8-9). The top worksheet shows three math problems, numbered 1, 2, and 3. These numbers, however, are positioned too closely to the first equation number. The learner is likely to read the first equation as $12 + \_\_\_\_ = 20$, not as $2 + \_\_\_\_ = 20$. The second worksheet is better because the item numbers are positioned farther away from the equations. The last worksheet is even better because it uses letters for the different math problems, eliminating the problem of mixing numbers (a solution that would not work as well for algebraic equations).

## SUMMARY

In the previous chapters you learned about the importance of design that facilitates learner selection, organization, and integration. This chapter explains how contrast, alignment, repetition, and proximity can be used to help make this happen. Although simple, these actions can make the difference between something that is and is not instructionally useful. Contrast, alignment, repetition, and proximity are all called design actions because they describe something that you do with design elements related to type, shape, color, dimension, and space.

When you work with contrast, you create strong differences in typefaces, shapes, and colors. You resize images or give them shadowing or text to make them appear to come forward or fall back. Contrast is the action that helps learners see the main point; thus it is important for enhancing learner selection.

When you align type, shapes, and even space, you help establish unity among different elements and establish hierarchies of information, improving the organization of information.

When you repeat type, shapes, color, size, and spatial arrangements, you likewise help the learner make connections. Color-coding is an example of assigning a color to similar items to show their relationship. Consider shopping mall maps that show store levels and codes using the same color.

When you move items close together to make them seem to be part of the same message or when you move things apart to make them seem to be different messages, you are working with the power of proximity. Moving headings closer to the subordinate content often improves a learner's understanding of the information.

Altogether contrast, alignment, repetition, and proximity are powerful actions because they influence learner perception. You will manipulate these actions in endless ways, using the information from the chapters that follow on type, shape, color, depth and space to improve your instructional message.

## PRACTICE

For additional activities and examples of student work, visit the Companion Website for this book at *http://www.coe.unco.edu/LindaLohr.*

## Resource Activity

Use Figures R-4, R-9, R-14, and R-15 from the Resources to help you complete the chapter activities below.

# Web Activity

> The Web Activity asks you to create your own icons for contrast, alignment, repetition, and proximity.

# Challenge Activity

The Challenge Activity asks you to use contrast, alignment, repetition, and proximity in a poster advertising facts about pit vipers. One student's solution is presented here.

### K–12 Example   Biology

This student responded to the Chapter 8 Challenge Activity by illustrating information about pit vipers using contrast, alignment, repetition, and proximity. The large viper image contrasts with the relatively small type. White type on the dark gray background also provides contrast. The words *Pit Viper Venom* are shape-aligned since they fit within the viper jaw. The strong *V* letters in *viper* and *venom* repeat the shape of the jaw opening and teeth. Labels are in close proximity to what they define.

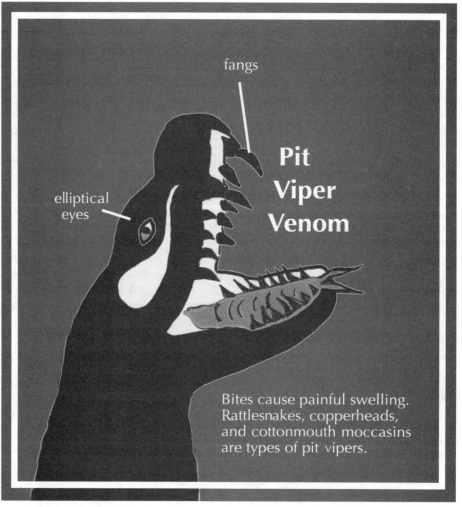

Challenge Activity

## Independent Activity

The Independent Activity asks you to pick your own project. You are encouraged to try this one because the information will be more meaningful and thus is likely to be more motivating. Some ideas include reformatting papers, posters, job aids, charts, and tables to include contrast, alignment, repetition, and proximity.

## Justification Activity

Write a justification paper for the activity you select. Describe the following:

- *Your users and the assumptions you make about them (such as age, reading level, and assumed skills).*
- *Why you think your solution will work; include at least two ideas from the book, including page numbers and your interpretation of the passage used.*
- *What you learned from a "user-test" (have someone look at the image and verbalize their thoughts while looking at the image).*
- *The changes you will make based on user comments (or create a revised image).*

## Discussion Questions

The previous chapter explored integration and five gestalt principles: closure, contiguity, similarity, proximity, and previous experience. Which of these principles are similar to contrast, alignment, repetition, and proximity?

## K–12 Student Activity

Ask students to do activities similar to the Challenge Activity, incorporating contrast, alignment, repetition, and proximity into an instructional image.

## REFERENCES

Harp, S. F., & Mayer, R. E. (1998). How seductive details do their damage: A theory of cognitive interest in science learning. *Journal of Educational Psychology, 90,* 414-434.

Mayer, R.E., Bove, W., Bryman, A., Mars, R., & Tapangco, L., (1996). When less is more: Meaningful learning from visual and verbal summaries of science textbook lessons. *Journal of Educational Psychology, 88,* 64-73.

Williams, R. (1994). *The non-designer's design book: Design and typographic principles for the visual novice.* Berkeley, CA: Peachpit Press.

Williams, R., & Tollett, J. (1998). *The non-designer's web book: An easy guide to creating, designing, and posting your own web site.* Berkeley, CA: Peachpit Press.

# CHAPTER 9

## *From Type to Typography*

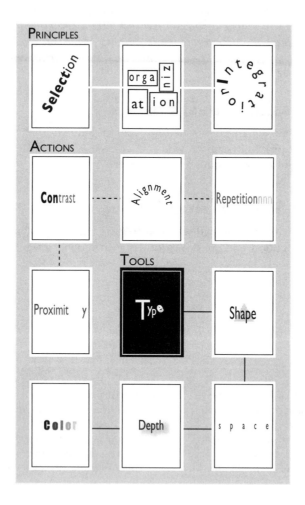

Type is everywhere. Type exists. It is a fundamental part of our lives. These simple facts are essential to understanding how to communicate more effectively.

*Erik Spiekermann and E. M. Ginger*

Due to cost, pictures and images may not always be on the same page. Whenever possible, images are placed as close to their reference as possible.

## Notes About the Opening Visual

Notice how the words alone on this opening visual communicate the meaning of different tools, actions, and perceptions. For example, the word *Type* is made up of letters that look different and are arranged so that they are not aligned evenly. This display shows you that type can change and that letters can be manipulated to express a message. The word *Color* shows each letter in a different shade of gray, illustrating how type can express color as well, even if in black and white. In the word *selection*, another word—*select*—appears to move forward because it is in a bold dark color and has a drop shadow behind it. All of these actions show how type can be used to convey meaning.

## Focus Questions

- What is a font?
- Are there rules of thumb for using type?
- Are serifs better than sans serifs for reading?

## Key Terms

**FONT**   A computer-generated typeface for a specific point size. For example, Times New Roman 12-point is a font, as is Times New Roman 14-point. Bookman 8-point is a font, as is Bookman 72-point. The meaning of font has changed in the last decade to mean typeface.

**INSTRUCTIONAL TYPOGRAPHY**   The art and science of using individual letters, words, and passages of text to convey an instructional message.

**KERNING**   The action of increasing or decreasing the horizontal letter spacing between individual characters or letters in a word.

**LEGIBILITY**   The ease with which short bursts of text can be read (Williams & Tollett, 1998).

**READABILITY**   The ease with which long passages of text can be read (Williams, 1998).

**SANS SERIF**   A typeface having characters without any small strokes at the end of each line.

**SERIF**   A typeface having characters with small strokes at the end of each line.

**TEXT**   The main body of written or printed material, as opposed to display matter, footnotes, appendixes, etc. (Carter, Day, & Meggs, 1985, p. 247).

**TYPE**   Synonymous with typography in this book.

**TYPEFACE**   The formal definition of alphabetical and numerical characters that are unified by consistent visual properties (Meggs & McKelvey, 2000). Times New Roman, Arial, and Bookman are examples of the thousands of typefaces in existence.

**TYPE FAMILY**   All the varieties of a particular typeface, such as Arial Extra Bold, Arial Bold, Arial Narrow, Arial, and Arial Narrow Italics.

**TYPOGRAPHY**   The art of the letterform (Carter, Day, & Meggs, 1985); typography involves composing the letterform (Meggs & McKelvey, 2000)

**X-HEIGHT**   The height of a typeface's lowercase letters.

## Introduction

Latisha, the community college instructor introduced in Chapter 1, is working on her fall semester syllabus. A syllabus template has been provided for her to complete. After using the template however, Latisha is dissatisfied with its appearance (see **Figure 9–1**). She finds the syllabus hard to follow and cannot help but think that if she finds it confusing, the students will find it even more so.

As she looks over the syllabus, Latisha thinks, "Everything on the syllabus looks like one big gray box of text! Things aren't broken into visual groups. Assignments are mixed with

**Original Syllabus**

# Syllabus
ED670,
Special Education Litigation
Time: M, W, F 2:00 - 3:00 pm
Location: Beady Hall

This course covers legal issues relating to school accountability for the growth and development of special needs learners. The student learns by participating in weekly case studies that replicate real-world events.

Evaluation is based on meeting course objectives which include: active participation in each class meeting; preparation for case-studies that show analysis and creative thinking; and completion of a paper for conference or journal submission. Attendance is mandatory. Missing more than one class will automatically reduce your grade by one letter. Grade scale of 90 (A), 80 (B), 70 (C), 60 (D) is used. Required readings include packets available at the bookstore. In addition, each student will acquire copies of the following and/or other materials pertinent to their area of interest for a reference collection:
1. National Administration of the Exceptional Children's Educational Act, 2 .US.

> *In accordance with the Americans with Disabilities Act, reasonable accommodations will be made for individuals with special needs in order that they may receive educational benefit from this course. Please discuss your needs with your instructor as soon as possible.*

This is just too hard to read. There are not any breaks in the text, making it what Clark and Lyons (2004) call "a wall of words."

**Revised Syllabus**

# ED670:
# Special Ed. Litigation
2:00 - 3:00  M, W, F   Beady Hall, 113

## Course Goal
You will learn legal issues relating to school accountability for the growth and development of special needs learners.

## Objectives
You will participate in weekly case studies that replicate real-world events. Readings include packets available at the bookstore and copies of the following :

1. National Administration of the ECEA
2. US. Supreme Court Cases
3. State and other cases pertinent to your specific area of learning.

## Evaluation
Evaluation is based on meeting course objectives which include: active participation in each class meeting;

In this "chunked" version, the important words stand out, making the syllabus easy to scan, locate, and retrieve information.

**Chunked type**

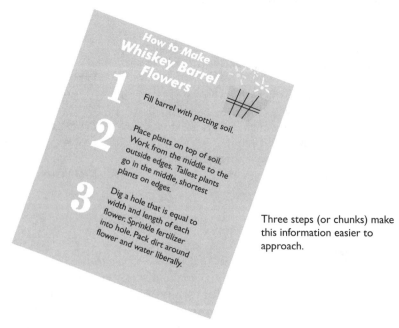

Three steps (or chunks) make this information easier to approach.

**FIGURE 9–1** Using type to chunk content

course objectives and evaluation criteria. The typeface seems overly formal and distant. I want my students to feel comfortable and welcome."

Latisha has these questions:

- What font should I use to make the syllabus friendly?
- Should I change the way this is written?
- Should I use more than one font?
- Will inserting spaces here and there help students organize the information?
- How can I use headings to make the information more understandable?

Latisha wonders, however, if she would be breaking the rules by not following the template. On the one hand, she thinks, "The department wants the syllabi to be consistent. I'd be breaking rules." On the other hand, she thinks, "This syllabus doesn't communicate."

In the end Latisha decides to create a new syllabus format that is easy for the students to understand (see Figure 9-1). Several days after turning in her syllabus, her department chair stops her in the hallway. "Latisha, your syllabus is great. I'm surprised that just moving the text around makes it so much easier to read."

Latisha's department chair is experiencing the power of typography. Of all of the tools in this book, type is likely to influence your work the most. Unlike clip art and photographic images, type is a graphic tool easily accessible to everyone who has a computer. It is also a graphic tool that is copyright free, so unlike using other graphic forms, you do not need to obtain any permission when you use type to enhance visual instruction.

There are countless books on typography, filled with appealing and motivating images. This chapter distills much of the information contained in these books into instructionally relevant topics, including basic typography definitions, the use of type as a unique instructional tool, classification schemes for type, the anatomy of type, and basic computer skills for working with type (see the Resources for more information).

## WHY IS TYPE POWERFUL?

**Type** is perhaps the most versatile tool in this book. You can use type simply to create chunks of information that make following instructions easier, as in Figure 9-1. Or you can get complex with type, using it to express emotion or to enhance a message, as in **Figure 9–2.**

Careful choice of type is important. Compare the match between **typeface** and message in the bottom half of Figure 9-2. In one image the words *War Declared* are set in an elegant typeface, while *Delicate Flowers* are set in a bold typeface. It becomes clear that the right message will be conveyed if *War Declared* is set in the typeface that *Delicate Flowers* is set in, and vice versa.

You can see some of the organizational and communicative power of type in **Figure 9–3.** Type facilitates all the tools as well as all the actions covered in this book.

## WHAT ARE THE CATEGORIES OF TYPE?

Most studies of type begin with learning about the different categories of type and the names of available typefaces—a nearly endless selection ranging from Arial, Futura, Garamond, and Bodoni to Dingbats, Webdings, Old English, and Techno. To help organize the wide assortment of **fonts,** type is classified into categories based on characteristics of their anatomy. As you read through these different font groups, notice that the tools and mediums available during the time in history they were developed determined the appearance of new type families. "The history of type is a history of technical constraints" (Spiekermann & Ginger, 1993, p. 115).

Although type has many different taxonomies or classification schemes, we'll use the scheme that groups type into the following six groups: (1) Black Letter, (2) Roman,

This typeface looks festive.

This typeface looks proper and formal.

This typeface looks friendly.

This typeface looks businesslike.

**These typefaces conflict with the meaning of the words.**

**These typefaces complement the meaning of the words.**

*War Declared*

Supreme Court Ruling

**DELICATE FLOWERS**

*Delicate Flowers*

Supreme Court Ruling

**WAR DECLARED**

**FIGURE 9-2**   Using Type to Express Meaning
*Source: Created by Clark Parsons. Used with permission.*

(3) Square Serif, (4) Sans Serif, (5) Script, and (6) Decorative. (see **Figures 9–4** through **9–12.**) Most people learning about type start the process unable to see much of a difference between the different groups. As you learn subtle variances in type groups, you will become more discerning with type selection from both an aesthetic and instructional perspective. As it turns out, typefaces from all of the groups can be used to enhance instruction. Knowing the different families can also help you select typefaces when faced with typeface names you do not recognize. By knowing that the edges of Square Serifs look blocky, you can look for a Square Serif substitute if you do not have access to any of the classic Square Serifs.

Type can be thick or thin, dark or light to create **contrast.**

Contrast

Type can be **aligned** to the edges of lines, shapes and pictures.

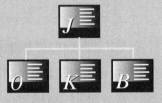

Type can be **repeated** to create harmony. The boxes seem related because large letters are repeated.

Type can be in close **proximity** to show relationships. Type can be far apart, to show differences.

This sentence and the sentence below it look like they belong together.

This sentence looks like it belongs to the sentence above, even though it is in a different typeface.

Type that is far apart

seems unrelated. Even though this sentence is in the same typeface as the top sentence, it still seems unrelated.

Type can be an organizing **shape.** The letter Z acts as a sequential path.

*Your path to better sleep*

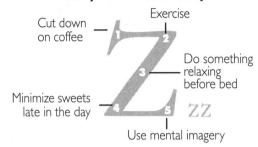

Type can be any **color** on the color wheel.

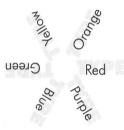

Type can show dimension and **depth**. Notice how the drop shadows make the words appear to move forward.

Type can be **spaced** so that chunks of information are created. These chunks make reading easier.

**FIGURE 9-3**  Manipulating type with actions and tools

## Instructional Application

The Black Letter typeface has **limited application in instruction** and is usually only used for **decoration** — on training certificates, awards, and documents in drop-letter caps, as you can see in the examples column.

One could argue that small applications of Black Letter typefaces might be effective in creating a certain look and feel for a piece, perhaps giving it a timeless look or a formality. Drop cap applications can direct attention, too, which you will learn more about in chapters on figure/ground and hierarchy.

Though beautiful, it is **too difficult to read** when there are more than a couple of words, as you can see in the longer sentence at the end of the right column.

**Some History**
The Black Letter type family is one of the oldest typefaces, used in the days of Gutenberg. An elaborate, hand-drawn appearance characterizes Black Letter typefaces.

## Examples

**Frank typeface**

Ornate hand drawn appearance

Good for certificates and other ornate documents.

The National Institue
of Consulting Professionals
formally recognizes

**John Smith**

**Certified Consultant**

Drop cap is good for directing attention.

An inadequate world-view can leave a person or a population unable to make solid and workable decisions. Problems cannot be solved, and the resulting environment is not conducive to either lasting success or satisfaction. There is little doubt that many of the failed or failing policies in todays society are like bedroom doors installed in a house with a faulty foundation.

### A Black Letter Typeface

Frank is used in this sentence.

*A longer sentence set in Frank:*

An inadequate world-view can leave a person or a population unable to make solid and workable decisions (Eikleberry, 2000).

**FIGURE 9–4**   Black Letter

## Instructional Application

Old Style typefaces are **widely used in instructional materials.** Considered **very easy to read,** they are characterized by tapered or slanted serifs and inclined counters (you learn more about counters in the pages that follow).

**Some History**
The Roman typeface appeared in the days that Roman stonecutters chiseled letters into stone. Serifs (the cross strokes at the ends of letter forms) were used to keep the stone from chipping when the cutters ended the strokes.

There are three types of Roman type: Old style, Modern, and Transitional. This page shows examples of Old Style typefaces.

## Examples

**Times New Roman typeface**

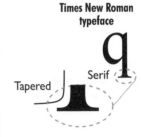

Slanted

Inclined

## Some Old Style Typefaces

Garamond is used in this sentence.

Times New Roman is used in this sentence.

*A longer sentence set in Times New Roman typeface:*
An inadequate world-view can leave a person or a population unable to make solid and workable decisions (Eikleberry, 2000).

**FIGURE 9–5**   Roman: Old Style

## Instructional Application

Modern Roman typefaces have
perpendicular serifs, upright counters, and
often high contrast between lines. Although
**striking in appearance**, they are considered
**difficult to read** when there is moderate to
large amount of body text.

## Examples

Bodoni
typeface

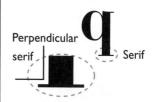

Perpendicular
serif                         Serif

Very thin strokes

Very
thick
strokes

Upright
counter

### A Modern Typeface

Bodoni is used in this sentence.

*A longer sentence set in Bodoni typeface:*
An inadequate world-view can leave a person or a
population unable to make solid and workable
decisions (Eikleberry, 2000).

**FIGURE 9–6**   Roman: Modern

## Instructional Application

Transitional typefaces have some characteristics of both Modern and Old Style. They may have perpendicular serifs and low contrast between the lines. Or they may have tapered, slanted serifs with high contrast and upright counters. They are difficult to classify because of their combining attributes. Transitional typefaces are **considered very readable**.

## Examples

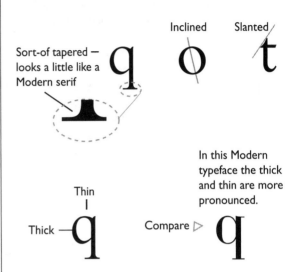

## Some Transitional Typefaces

Bembo is used in this sentence.

Caslon is used in this sentence.

Centaur is used in this sentence.

*A longer sentence set in Bembo typeface:*
An inadequate world-view can leave a person or a population unable to make solid and workable decisions (Eikleberry, 2000).

**FIGURE 9–7**    Roman: Transitional

## Instructional Application

Square serifs, like Roman typefaces, are **widely used in educational materials** since they are considered **highly readable**. This typeface is **often found in children's books** for this reason. The typeface is often darker than the others, a quality some research finds to improve readability and to be preferred by readers. A new Web-based Square serif typeface, Georgia, has been designed specifically to optimize screen reading.

## Examples

Clarendon typeface

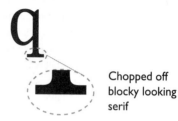

Chopped off blocky looking serif

### Some Square Serif Typefaces

Century is used in this sentence.

Clarendon is used in this sentence.

Georgia is used in this sentence. Georgia is a typeface designed for the Web.

*A longer sentence set in Clarendon typeface:*
An inadequate world-view can leave a person or a population unable to make solid and workable decisions (Eikleberry, 2000).

**FIGURE 9–8**   Square Serif

## Instructional Application

Sans serif means "without serifs." Sans Serif typefaces do not have the little extensions at the end of characters.

Many consider Sans Serif type more **legible for computer-based instruction or presentation**, since the resolution of computer monitors is often not great enough to show serifs, making serif typefaces lose their legibility. This is a debated claim since there is not a large body of research to support such statements. Regardless of proof, Sans Serif typefaces are frequently **used as headings** in all types of instructional materials.

Two new Sans Serif typefaces have been designed to optimize screen display: Trebuchet and Verdana.

**Some History**
Fonts without wings are called "sans serifs." Some of the earliest sans serif fonts were cut in Italy in the early 1500s.

## Examples

Univers typeface

No serif

### Some Sans Serif Typefaces

**Franklin Gothic is used in this sentence.**

Futura is used in this sentence.

Helvetica is used in this sentence.

Trebuchet is used in this sentence.

Univers is used in this sentence.

Verdana is used in this sentence.

*A longer sentence set in Franklin Gothic typeface:*

**An inadequate world-view can leave a person or a population unable to make solid and workable decisions (Eikleberry, 2000).**

**FIGURE 9–9**   Sans Serif

## Instructional Application

Like Black Letter type, Script and Cursive type have **limited** application in instructional materials since they can be difficult to read in text of any length. They are often used to designate different voice (as I do in this sentence with this ruleswriting typeface.) As with Black Letter, script typefaces are used frequently in certificates, to designate a historical period of time, and in small places where ornamentation may be desired.

Script forms were considered "gimmick" fonts because they looked handwritten. Cursive (another word for Script) forms, however, go back to the earliest days of printing when monks used cursive forms to write. As printing caught on and spread, the monks adopted faster forms to keep up with the increased pace of their writing.

## Examples

Brush Script Typeface

## Some Script Typefaces

Brush Script is used in this sentence.

Lucida handwriting is used in this sentence.

Freestyle script is used in this sentence.

A longer sentence set in Brush Script typeface:
An inadequate world-view can leave a person or a population unable to make solid and workable decisions (Eikleberry, 2000).

**FIGURE 9–10**   Script

## Instructional Application

Symbol typefaces and Dingbats **provide access to a variety of images that can be used for instructional purposes**. For example, if you were teaching keyboarding, you might make the image to the right that shows the middle row keys. These keys come from the Qwerty typeface, a symbol typeface. The bottom image on the right shows you Webdings, another symbol typeface.

## Examples

Qwerty typeface

Middle row keys:

The keyboard image comes from typing the the letters *a, s, d, f, g, h, j, k, l* and *;*

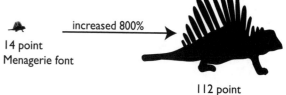

14 point
Menagerie font

increased 800%

112 point
Menagerie font

## Some Symbol Typefaces

Moonphases

Menagerie Dingbats

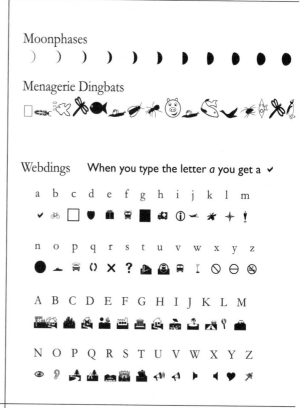

Webdings      When you type the letter *a* you get a ✔

| a | b | c | d | e | f | g | h | i | j | k | l | m |
|---|---|---|---|---|---|---|---|---|---|---|---|---|

| n | o | p | q | r | s | t | u | v | w | x | y | z |
|---|---|---|---|---|---|---|---|---|---|---|---|---|

| A | B | C | D | E | F | G | H | I | J | K | L | M |
|---|---|---|---|---|---|---|---|---|---|---|---|---|

| N | O | P | Q | R | S | T | U | V | W | X | Y | Z |
|---|---|---|---|---|---|---|---|---|---|---|---|---|

**FIGURE 9–11**   Decorative: Symbol

## Instructional Application

Decorative typefaces are often **used for titles, headings, and other display purposes** because they are **tiring to read for anything that is very lengthy.**

While extensive use of decorative typefaces is generally discouraged in instructional materials, they can be used quite effectively in small amounts to **create a mood** or act in part as a **metaphor** for a topic

### Some History

Decorative typefaces (also called Ornamentals) have been around since the 1800s. Recently the World Wide Web and the proliferation of digital type tools have made Decorative fonts some of the most developed fonts today. Even though there are a large number of these Decorative fonts, they do not share the widespread acceptance of the older more classic typefaces.

Decorative typefaces are categorized into two groups: display and symbol. This page covers display typefaces.

## Examples

Really Bad Typewriter typeface

Some call these
Grunge typefaces

The E drops out of the title. It is absent, making the type in the title reflect the title's meaning.

## Some Display Typefaces

Really Bad Typewriter is used in this sentence.

**Ravie is used in this sentence.**

Litterbox is used in this sentence.

*A longer sentence set in Really Bad Typewriter typeface:* An inadequate world-view can leave a person or a population unable to make solid and workable decisions(Eikleberry, 2000).

**FIGURE 9–12**   Decorative: Display

# WHICH TYPE IS BEST FOR INSTRUCTION?

After reading the last few pages you may be asking, "But which typefaces tend to be best for instruction?" The answer to that question is found in the "It Depends" rule (see **Figure 9–13a**.) Like all design choices, a selection or action is accompanied by consideration of many different elements, all of them interacting to create a whole that is greater than the sum of the parts.

A variety of factors interact—from the characteristics of the instructional content and learners to delivery format and even colors of other elements in a learning environment—creating a variety of interaction effects that can all influence the selection of typeface. A learner-centered methodology for making decisions of this nature is described in Chapter 4. The "ACE it" approach explains a process for involving the learner in design decisions. Hartley (2004) has several good suggestions, including the recommendation that type decisions for instruction be made heuristically. Since individuals have widely varying opinions on typefaces (Misanchuk, 1992), Hartley provides a practical option: "It may be wiser to stick to conventional and familiar typefaces than to employ idiosyncratic ones" (p. 798).

## Classic Typefaces

Some typefaces have stood the test of time and are considered classics. Steven Heller describes classic typeface this way, "In addition to all the functional and esthetic concerns, a typeface that continues to be used beyond its period of fashion, in my book that is a classic" (Meggs & McKelvey, 2000, prologue). Classic typefaces (see Figure 9–13b) are grouped into **serif** (characters with small strokes at the end of each line) and **sans serif** (characters without the small strokes) categories.

## Unique Typefaces

Black (1990) suggests that the unique properties of instruction be your guide to instructional typeface selection. If special character sets are needed, such as unique accents or mathematical symbols (see again **Figure 9–14a**), then a typeface that either provides these or works well with another typeface that does should be considered. If an instructional piece must be copied many times, then a typeface that maintains its legibility over frequent copies would be considered.

## Serif Versus Sans Serif

For most people, decisions about type boil down to the decision of whether to use serif or sans serif typefaces. There is a widespread belief that most people prefer reading body text set in a serif typeface. Popular books such as *The Non-Designer's Web Book* (Williams & Tollett, 1998), recommend a serif typeface for extended text, suggesting that serifs are most appropriate when readability is a concern. **Readability** is defined as "how easy it is to read a lot of text, extended text, pages and pages of text" (Williams & Tollett, 1998, p. 214). Figure 9-14 presents descriptions and images of legibility and readability.

Arditi and Cho (2005), White (1988), and Hartley (2004) are not as directive, citing research that fails to find any significant difference between serif and sans serif text related to readability. While White (1988) suggests that reading ease may be improved because the serif leads the eye from one letter to the next, this proposition has not been substantiated by research.

### (a) The "It Depends" Rule

What should you do? It depends . . . on the learner, the content, the task, the environment, other elements in the visual, and your level of skill. Design decisions do not take a cookbook approach. That is why design is considered an art and a science.

---

**Classic Typefaces**

| Serif | Sans Serif |
|---|---|
| Baskerville | **Franklin Gothic** |
| Bembo | Futura |
| Bodoni | **Futura Black** |
| Caslon | Helvetica |
| Centaur | Univers |
| Century | |
| Clarendon | |
| Garamond | |
| Times New Roman | |

**Symbol Typefaces**

a b c d e f g h i
α β χ δ ε φ γ η ι

j k l m n o p q r
φ κ λ μ ν ο π θ ρ

s t u v w x y z
σ τ υ ϖ ω ξ ψ ζ

---

### (b) Mixing Classic and Sans Serif Typefaces

This would be easy for children to read because of the Clarendon typeface.

## Franklin Gothic

Clarendon body text is used here to show you what it looks like when combined with the Franklin Gothic typeface as a heading.

Many people have these typefaces so you will see this combination a lot.

## Helvetica

Times New Roman body text is used here to show you what it looks like when combined with the Helvetica typeface as a heading.

## Futura

Bodoni body text is used here to show you what it looks like when combined with the Futura typeface as a heading.

## Univers

Caslon body text is used here to show you what it looks like when combined with the Univers typeface as a heading.

This looks elegant but works best when body text is minimal.

This looks elegant but does not lose any readability.

**FIGURE 9–13**  Some type considerations

What is the difference between legibility and readability? Williams and Tollet (1998) define the difference below.

# Legibility
is defined as how easy it is to read **short bursts of text,** such as headlines, bullets, and signs. Sans Serif typefaces are preferred when legibility is the goal.

# Readability
is defined as how easy it is to read a lot of text, or long passages of text. Serif typefaces are preferred when readability is the goal.

Notice the contrast between heading and body text

## Look here

This body text does not have much contrast with the heading.

## **Look here**

This body text has more contrast with the heading.

This example shows one type of contrast. Bold headings are contrasted with a regular typeface.

## Look here

This body text does not have much contrast with the heading.

## **Look here**

This body text has more contrast with the heading.

This example shows two types of contrast:
- Sans serif headings are contrasted with serif body text.
- Bold headings are contrasted with a regular typeface.

**FIGURE 9–14**  Legibility and readability (definitions and strategies)

## Legibility and Readability

On the other hand, sans serif fonts have a reputation for clarity. Williams and Tollett (1998) suggest using a sans serif type to improve legibility. **Legibility** is defined as the ease with which readers will recognize short bursts of **text** such as headlines and titles (Williams & Tollett, 1998). Many consider sans serif type more legible for computer-based instruction or presentation, since the resolution of computer monitors is often not great enough to show the serifs, making the typeface, especially when it is small, difficult to read. Again, as with the readability literature, there is not a large body of research that substantiates these claims.

Miles Tinker (1963), who has done extensive research on typefaces, considers legibility and readability to be the same. Tinker investigated legibility by measuring speed of perception, perceptibility at a distance, perceptibility in peripheral vision, visibility, eye movements, and other similar calculations. In Tinker's research, Roman typefaces had the best legibility and Black Letter the least, as measured by learner speed. The difference between Roman, Square Serif, and Sans Serif typefaces, however, was not significantly different. Black Letter typefaces were significantly linked to decreased reading speed. Even though reading speeds were higher for some Roman typeface (Garamond and Times New Roman), learners preferred the Square Serifs typeface Chelthenham, indicating preference for typefaces that are heavier in appearance. Black Letter typefaces were considered the hardest to read quickly and were the only typefaces where speed of reading and learner preference results matched.

What does this mean for you? First, since research shows no significant readability and legibility differences between serifs and sans serifs, you can feel free to use what you and your audience prefer. Williams (1994) offers this suggestion: "If the only sans serifs you have in your font family are Helvetica and Avant Garde, the best thing you can do for your pages is invest in a sans serif family that includes a strong, heavy black face" (p. 87). In other words, learn to use a big, wide sans serif typeface in combination with a lighter font. Try this strategy and you will see your pages or screen designs come alive with headings that are especially bold, making a nice contrast with body text that is lighter and more elegant (see again Figure 9-16). Also consider using a serif typeface in the body text to provide extra contrast with the serif heading shown in the bottom right side of Figure 9-14.

## Take a Type Test

Test your knowledge of typefaces by taking the test in **Figure 9–15.** Match the typeface with its description by drawing lines or filling in the blanks. The correct answers can be found at the bottom of the figure. **Figure 9–16** presents a quick overview of the type families and their recommended use for instructional materials.

In the sections that follow you will find other important information about type for instructional purposes, such as attributes of type that make a difference in readability. For example, a lowercase letter that is a little taller and wider than normal is considered easier to read. Additionally, several layout characteristics related to text are important to educators.

# CAN YOU TALK TYPE?

"I'm not so sure about using Paris for instruction. Verdana's x-height is better."
"Paris is elegant, but I agree, we need something more readable for training."

What are these people talking about? You'll learn in the pages ahead that **x-height** refers to the height of a typeface's lowercase letters. Things like x-height and serifs are responsible

Match type category name with the correct description on the right.

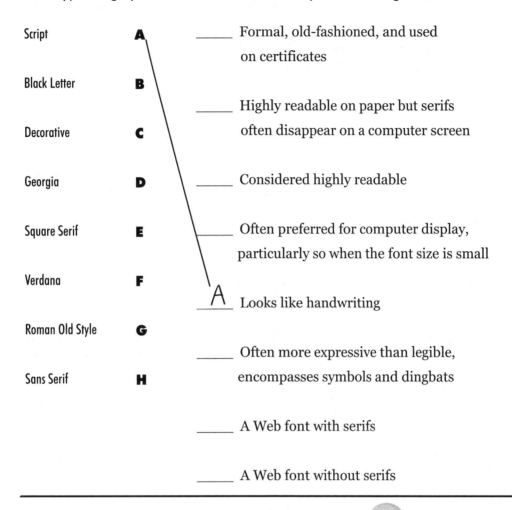

Script                        **A**        _____ Formal, old-fashioned, and used
                                                           on certificates

Black Letter                  **B**
                                           _____ Highly readable on paper but serifs
                                                           often disappear on a computer screen

Decorative                    **C**
                                           _____ Considered highly readable

Georgia                       **D**
                                           _____ Often preferred for computer display,
                                                           particularly so when the font size is small

Square Serif                  **E**
                                           __A___ Looks like handwriting

Verdana                       **F**
                                           _____ Often more expressive than legible,
                                                           encompasses symbols and dingbats

Roman Old Style               **G**

Sans Serif                    **H**        _____ A Web font with serifs

                                           _____ A Web font without serifs

# Answers:
Cover these up while you take
the test.

A. Script = Handwriting
B. Black Letter = Formal
C. Decorative = More Expressive
D. Georgia = A web font with serifs
E. Square Serif = Considered highly readable
F. Verdana = A web font without serifs
G. Roman Old Style = Highly readable on paper
H. Sans Serif = Often used for computer display

**FIGURE 9–15**   Test yourself

| Family | Classics | Application |
|--------|----------|-------------|
| Black Letter | No identified classic<br>Old English typeface | Drop caps, directing attention, historical emphasis, certificates |
| Roman: *Old Style* | Garamond, Times New Roman | Very readable |
| Roman: *Modern* | Bodoni | Elegant, but can be difficult to read in long passages |
| Roman: *Transitional* | Bembo, Caslon, Centaur | Very readable |
| Square Serif | Century, Clarendon, Georgia | Very readable |
| Sans Serif | **Franklin Gothic**, Futura, Helvetica, Trebuchet, Univers, Verdana | Very legible, bold versions especially good for headings |
| Script | No identified classic<br>Kunstler Script | Can seem approachable or formal |
| Decorative: *Display* | No identified classic<br>Kristen typeface | Good for establishing mood |
| Decorative: *Symbol* | No identified classic<br>Webdings | Good for symbols and images |

**FIGURE 9–16**   Instructional applications of type

for giving each typeface its type attributes—its unique appearance (see **Figure 9–17**). Not all of these attributes have an instructional impact (though x-height does!), but those that do will be described in some detail after we have identified all of the type attributes.

## WHICH TYPE ATTRIBUTES ARE IMPORTANT FOR INSTRUCTION?

Of the attributes discussed earlier, five are important for instructional visuals: (1) x-height, (2) serifs, (3) counters, (4) leading, and (5) kerning.

### X-Height

**Figure 9–18** shows how taller x-heights are easier for children to read. When the lowercase letters are larger, their distinguishing attributes are easier to see.

**Cross stroke:** The horizontal stroke that crosses the vertical stroke of a type character.

**Ascender:** The part of a character that rises above its body. The letters *b, d, f, h, k, l,* and *t* have ascenders.

**Descender:** The part of a character that falls below its baseline. The letters *g, j, p,* and *y* have descenders.

**Caps height:** The height of an uppercase letter measured from the baseline.

**Ascender height:** The height of the tallest part of a letter.

**Bowl:** The curved portion of a character that encloses a counter (the enclosed or partially enclosed area of a type character). The letters *a, b, c, d, e, g, h, m, n, o, p, q,* have bowls.

**Baseline:** The line on which the bases of upper- and lowercase letters rest, not including descenders.

An inadequate World-view can leave a person or a population unable to make solid decisions.

**Leading:** The vertical space between lines of text, called line spacing in some computer programs.

**Counter:** The enclosed or partially enclosed area of a type character, including the letters *a, b, c, d, e, g, h, m, n, o, p* and *q*. Readability is thought to increase with wider counters.

**Kerning:** The horizontal space between individual characters or letters in a word.

**Serif:** The small end strokes on a character. Most people seem to perfer serif type for reading large bodies of text.

**X-height:** The height of a lowercase letter without ascenders or descenders. The height of the letters *x* (or *a, c, e, i, m, n, o, r, s, u, v, w, z*) gives you the x-height of a typeface. In terms of instructional impact, generally speaking, letters with larger x-heights are considered easier to read.

**FIGURE 9–17**   The anatomy of type

**X - Height:** The height of a lowercase letter without ascenders or descenders.

Taller x-heights in text passages can be easier for people to read because the additional height emphasizes the lowercase letters. The two *x*'s below both have an x-height of 50 points. Verdana's x-height is twice as tall as Paris's x-height.

All of the typefaces below are 15 points. Clarendon is has the tallest typeface.

X ----- X

A Verdana lowercase *x*, 50 points

A Paris lowercase *x*, 50 points

Bodoni Georgia Clarendon

A teacher creating instruction for children would be wise to choose a typeface with a larger x-height. The x-height for Paris shown below is one half as tall as Clarion, making Clarion a better choice for children.

The planets in our solar system are Mercury, Venus, Earth, Mars, Jupiter, Saturn, Uranus, and Neptune. To help you remember these names try to remember this sentence: My Very Earthy Mother Just Served Us Nachos.

The planets in our solar system are Mercury, Venus, Earth, Mars, Jupiter, Saturn, Uranus and Neptune.
To help you remember these names try to remember this sentence: My Very Earthy Mother Just Served Us Nachos.

Paris typeface

Clarion typeface

**FIGURE 9–18** Type attributes for instruction: X-height

## Serif or Sans Serif?

As previously discussed, one widely held belief is that using a serif typeface is better for long passages of paper-based text, and using sans serif typeface is best for computer displays and headings. Instructional technology research, however, has found no significant difference when comparing the effectiveness of serifs versus sans serifs for instructional materials, with one exception. The use of very small (under 10 points) serif typefaces is discouraged for computer displays because the serifs disappear (see **Figure 9–19**).

## Serif

Some say that serifs are more readable on paper and sans serifs are more readable on a computer screen. There is no evidence that supports these claims other than the research that shows that any serif type 10 points and lower can be difficult to read on a computer screen.

Garamond type. 18 point and 9 point.

## Sans Serif

Some say that serifs are more readable on paper and sans serifs are more readable on a computer screen. There is no evidence that supports these claims other than the research that shows that any serif type 10 points and lower can be difficult to read on a computer screen.

Franklin type. 18 point and 9 point.

### Web typefaces

There are three typefaces designed for a computer or Web display: (1) Georgia, (2) Trebuchet, and (3) Verdana. Most people have these typefaces on their computer system.

Georgia is a serif typeface designed for electronic viewing.

Trebuchet is a sans serif typeface designed for electronic viewing.

Verdana is a sans serif typeface designed for electronic viewing.

**FIGURE 9–19** Type attributes for instruction: Serifs and sans serifs

Where does that leave you? Does this mean anything goes? To be safe, experiment with both serif and sans serif typefaces and test them out with representatives of your learner audience. Don't be too shy about using serifs on the Web either, particularly when you use the Georgia typeface designed specifically for the Web (see again Figure 9-19). Two sans serif typefaces that work well on the Web are Verdana and Trebuchet.

## Counters

There are two major differences between counters and x-heights. Whereas x-heights are the height of a lowercase letter, counters (see **Figure 9–20**) are the width of the enclosed part of uppercase letters (*A*, *B*, *D*, *O*, *P*, *Q*) and lowercase letters (*a*, *b*, *d*, *g*, *o*, *p*, *q*). Some consider wide counters to improve legibility and readability. Figure 9-20 displays the difference in counter widths for the Kabel and Futura Light Condensed typefaces, and it shows the effect of counter size on similar text passages. All in all, narrow counters are difficult to read, as both of these examples show. At times, however, narrow counters are helpful for squeezing words into tight places.

## Leading

When you change leading, you either increase or decrease the vertical space between lines of text (see **Figure 9–21**). Usually the leading is automatically set to be 20 percent larger than the point size of the text font. Therefore, if you have set your font size to 12, your leading will be approximately 20 percent larger, or 14.4. As a rule of thumb, the longer the line of text, the greater the leading should be.

By adjusting leading, you can subtly change the look and feel of instruction. For example, if you want to make your instruction seem more approachable to a group of people who typically do not like reading, try increasing the leading. They will see more white space and may be less intimidated by the amount of text they need to read.

Leading is often used to adjust the spacing of text lines in projected slide displays. The software often sets the leading too high, as in Figure 9-21. Decreasing the leading separates the title more distinctly from the bullet points and groups both the title and bullet points.

Keep in mind that leading in either extreme (low or high) is not optimal for readability. Figure 9-21 shows different leading combinations.

In his review of design guidelines for screen-based programs (computer-based training), Rimar (1996) suggests that readability and comprehension increases as leading increases. Double spacing, as opposed to single spacing, is recommended. More information about leading is discussed in the layout section of this chapter. Tinker (1983) suggests the following leading values for text that spans between 2 and 5 inches.

- For 6 to 9 point text, use leading up to 4 points higher. For example, 6 point text would use leading between 7 and 10 points.
- For 10 to 12 point text, use leading up to 5 points higher. For example, 10 point text would use leading between 11 and 15 points.

## Kerning

"Type from a computer is ugly," a typography instructor informs his class. He then adds, "To make type look good, you need to letter space." This instructor is talking about **kerning**—the action of increasing or decreasing the horizontal letter spacing between individual characters or letters in a word. By kerning, you can make words look better

 **Counter:** The width of of the enclosed part of uppercase letters and lowercase letters.

Some consider wide counters to improve legibility and readability. The image below shows the effect of counter size on similar text passages. All in all, narrow counters are difficult to read. At times, however, narrow counters are helpful for squeezing words into tight places.

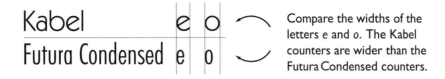

Compare the widths of the letters *e* and *o*. The Kabel counters are wider than the Futura Condensed counters.

**Kabel** An inadequate world-view can leave a person or a population unable to make solid and workable decisions. Problems cannot be solved,

**Futura Condensed** An inadequate world-view can leave a person or a population unable to make solid and workable decisions. Problems cannot be solved, and the resulting environment is not

**18 point Univers**
This is a text passage with large counters. You might try using large counters when you need text to be especially legible.

**18 point Onyx**
This is a text passage with small counters. You might try using small counters when you need text to fit into a narrow space.

Suppose you just want to type extensive and interesting information into a restricted space.

**Wide counter**
Kabel

Suppose you just want to type extensive and interesting information into a restricted space. Typefaces with narrow counters help you!

**Narrow counter**
Futura Light Condensed

Which side holds more words?

**FIGURE 9–20**   Type attributes for instruction: Counters

popul ↕ 11. Leading
make

**Importance of World-View**

- Decisions

- Problem-solving

- Satisfaction

**Importance of World-View**

- Decisions
- Problem-solving
- Satisfaction

Too much leading here. The words in the title do not seem to belong together.

Leading has been decreased here. Notice how the words in the title seem to belong together now. The same thing happens with the bullet points.

---

## 11 point text with 7 point leading:

Leading is too small here.

An inadequate world-view can leave a person or a population unable to make workable decisions. Problems cannot be solved, and the resulting environment is not conducive to either lasting success or satisfaction.

## 11 point text with 18 point leading:

Leading is too large here.

An inadequate world-view can leave a person or a population unable to make

workable decisions. Problems cannot be solved, and the resulting environment

is not conducive to either lasting success or satisfaction.

**FIGURE 9–21**   Type attributes for instruction: Leading

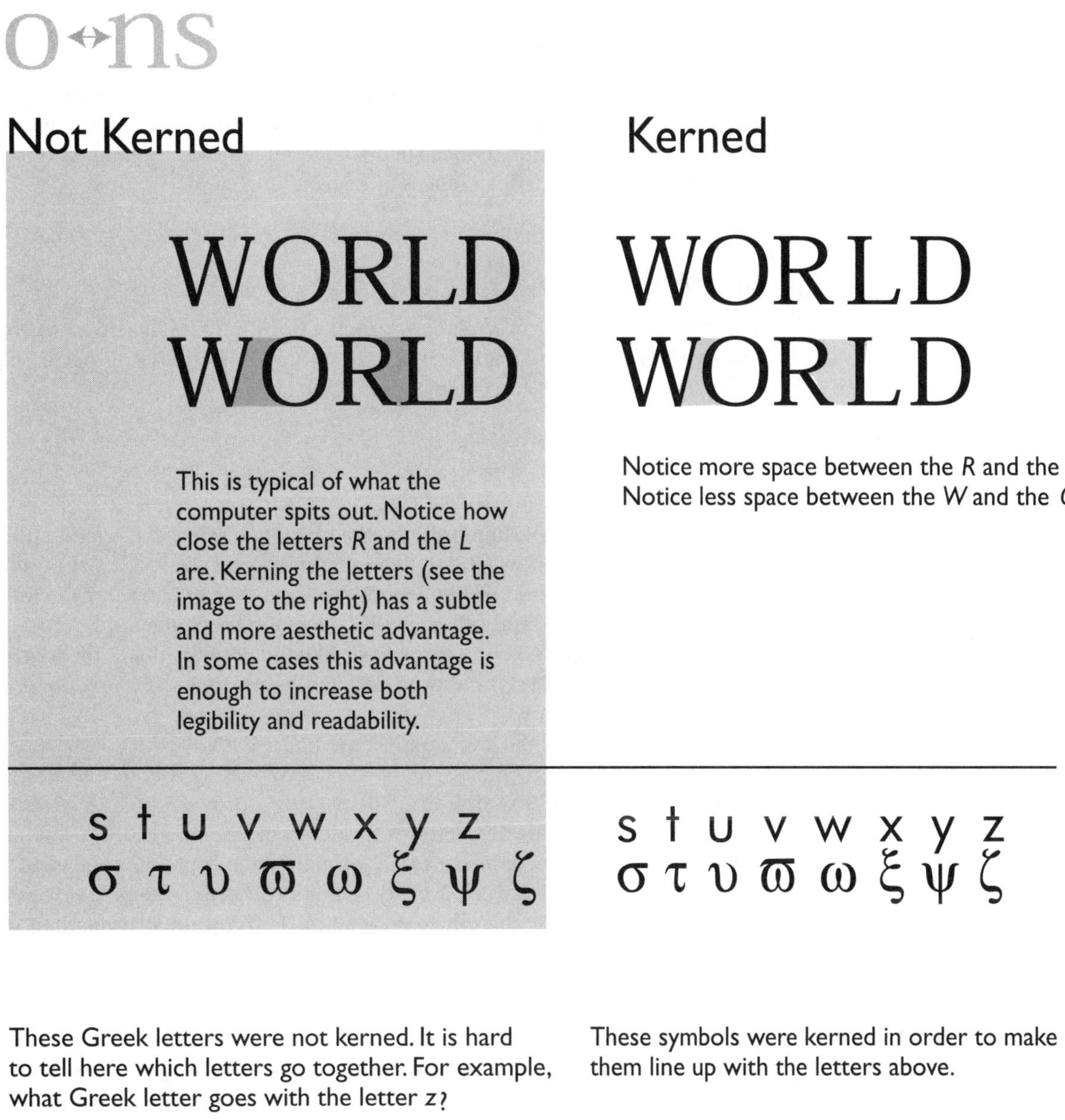

O⟷ns

## Not Kerned

WORLD
WORLD

This is typical of what the
computer spits out. Notice how
close the letters *R* and the *L*
are. Kerning the letters (see the
image to the right) has a subtle
and more aesthetic advantage.
In some cases this advantage is
enough to increase both
legibility and readability.

## Kerned

WORLD
WORLD

Notice more space between the *R* and the *L*.
Notice less space between the *W* and the *O*.

s t u v w x y z
σ τ υ ϖ ω ξ ψ ζ

s t u v w x y z
σ τ υ ϖ ω ξ ψ ζ

These Greek letters were not kerned. It is hard
to tell here which letters go together. For example,
what Greek letter goes with the letter *z*?

These symbols were kerned in order to make
them line up with the letters above.

**FIGURE 9–22**   Type attributes for instruction: Kerning

(see **Figure 9–22**). Used mostly for type sizes larger than 30 points, kerning is generally
performed to improve the appearance of a heading. In Figure 9-22 notice how the appearance of the word *WORLD* is improved by decreasing the kerning between the letters *W* and *O* and increasing the kerning between the letters L and D. Some research supports kerning. According to Rivlin, Lewis, and Davies-Cooper (1990), applying proper
kerning improves appearance. Varying the width between letters, if done correctly, can
also increase readability (Lynch 1994).

Kerning can also make things fit better. For example Figure 9-22 shows the correspon-
dence between letters of the alphabet and symbol characters. Some computer programs
have a kerning option that helps you change the space between letters. Without kerning,
the last letters in the list are not aligned, making the symbol for *x* look like it is the symbol
for *y*.

# How Does Type Affect Layouts?

According to Hartley (2004), the way a designer uses space on a page greatly affects how easily the reader can understand and retrieve information. This theory applies equally to screen-based information. Issues such as text alignment, line length, type size, and cueing devices all impact the effectiveness of instruction.

## Text Alignment

Text alignment refers to the place where the body of text lines up along the edge of a page, screen, shape, or image. **Figure 9–23** shows the four different types of alignment: (1) left, (2) right, (3) centered, and (4) justified.

## Line Length

There are many rules of thumb that should help you select the length and size of your text. Optimal line length follows the "it depends" rule. Point size, page size, direction, and leading all play into the selection of line length (see bottom of Figure 9–23). Different rules apply for text, screen, paper, and other media. Generally speaking, if a typeface is small, the line length should be short. People tend to dislike line lengths that are very short or very long. According to Tinker (1963), children under 10 years are most comfortable with line lengths between 2 and 3 inches.

Some suggest optimal line lengths based on the number of characters in the line—ranging from 35 to 75 characters. Given that leading plays a role in line length decision, these guidelines have limited usefulness. Tinker (1963) provides research-based guidelines that help you figure ideal leading settings for different line width and point size combinations. For example, Tinker recommends that for a line length of 5.5 inches and 12-point text the leading should be set between 13 and 16 points. To make things easy to remember, you can also use the following guideline: Set leading 1 to 5 points larger than text when text is between 6 and 12 points.

Another rule of thumb for remembering an acceptable width of 4 to 5 inches is to use your palm as a guide (a technique similar to using your foot to measure length in feet). Measure your palm until you have a good idea of where 4 to 5 inches falls (see **Figure 9–24,** bottom right image). This method comes in handy when you do not have a ruler nearby or when you simply need to eyeball whether something will fit within a column of text.

Left-aligned text is considered the easiest to read.

Text where the **left** edge is **aligned**, leaving the right edge to fall unevenly from line to line, is considered ragged right, or left aligned. This is considered to be the most readable and is highly encouraged for long instructional text passages over all other alignment types.

This is a ragged right edge.

This is a ragged left edge.

**Right-aligned text** does the opposite, like this paragraph. Here, the right side is aligned and the left side is ragged. Right-aligned text can be difficult to read in long passages so should be avoided in lengthy instructional text. Right aligned text, however, can add an element of interest and at times is useful when aligning text to a graphic or another column of text.

Right-aligned text is considered hard to read.

Centered text is the most formal, but it can be hard to read because of the ragged edges.

Text that is **centered** in a document falls exactly in the middle for each line of text. While it may be a quick way to create balance on a page (everything is centered evenly), it is hard to read, and it can look boring. Novice designers tend to overdo centered text for that reason. These designers think centered text improves the appearance of their work, when in reality it makes their work look less, rather than more, professional. Sometimes, however, centered text in instructional materials is perfectly appropriate, (especially when used for short segments of text, such as a title page) since centered text is often more formal.

Justified text is aligned on both edges, causing small gaps between letters. These small gaps can strain the eyes.

Text where both the right and left edges of text line up is considered **justified**. This type of alignment is usually avoided in instructional text since the small gaps created within the lines can be difficult to read. The learner's eyes will eventually get tired of the irregular spaces — between — words — (exaggerated — here — for — effect.)

## Line length

Notice how small the typeface is in this paragraph. It is 8-points, about as small as you can reduce a typeface and have it remain legible. It is much harder to read in long lines than short lines. Compare this paragraph with the one below. Which paragraph is harder to read because your eye doesn't get a break?

Notice how small the typeface is in this paragraph. It is 8-points, about as small as you can reduce a typeface and have it remain legible. It is much harder to read in long lines than short lines. Compare this paragraph with the one above. The top paragraph is harder to read because your eye doesn't get a break.

This shows how small type is easier to read when the line length is short.

**FIGURE 9–23**   Text alignment

# These are rules of thumb that do not apply to all situations.

**For a projected visual, set type 1/2 inch for every 10 feet.**

**For slides and transparencies, set type so it is legible at an arm's length.**

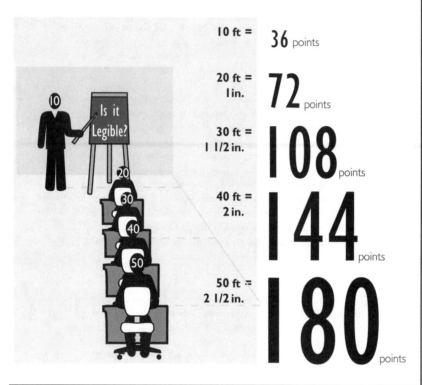

| | |
|---|---|
| 10 ft = | 36 points |
| 20 ft = 1 in. | 72 points |
| 30 ft = 1 1/2 in. | 108 points |
| 40 ft = 2 in. | 144 points |
| 50 ft = 2 1/2 in. | 180 points |

**For slides and transparencies, set type so it is legible 6 feet from the computer screen.**

**For printed or computer-based training set type 3 to 5 inches, or approximately the width of your palm.**

6 feet from computer screen

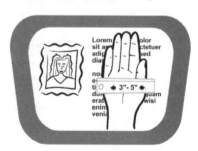

**FIGURE 9–24**   Heuristics for choosing type size

Other good advice related to optimal line length comes from Hartley (2004), who recommends that you break a line of text when it makes sense, based upon content and not some formula. For example, rather than conventional formatting in which text spans the length of a column or width of the page, text instead spans the length of an idea or thought. For example, look at the following passage:

> My mother's parents were named Alonzo and Louise. My mother has two brothers: Frank Junior and Gene. Frank Junior and his wife Christy have two children: Stephanie and Brock. Gene and his wife Maggie have three children: Johnny, Janice, and Keighley. My mother's immediate family is made up of her husband Jackson and her three daughters: Carrie, Lazlo, and Bea.

Notice how much easier it is to understand the text when lines are broken as follows:

> My mother's parents were named Alonzo and Louiseo
> She also has two brothers: Frank Junior and Gene.
>    Frank Junior and his wife Christy have two children:
>       Stephanie and
>       Brock.
>    Gene and his wife Maggie have three children:
>       Johnny,
>       Janice, and
>       Keighley.
> My mother's immediate family is made up of her husband Jackson and her three daughters:
>    Carrie, Lazlo, and Bea.

Hartley also suggests a floating baseline—that is, breaking the bottom edge of text according to the content. Rather than filling up all of the pages, the text stops or breaks when the content warrants it.

## Type Size

The distance from the lowest point of the longest descender to the highest point of the tallest ascender is considered the type size—what is called point size in computer applications. There are about 36 points in ½ inch and 72 points in 1 inch. Notice how some typefaces are the same point size, but they look either larger or smaller based on x-height or counter size (see again Figure 9–18).

Many other general rules address appropriate point sizes for legibility of different formats (projected presentations, computer-based training, and print-based instruction). Given the considerable difference in equal point sizes of different typefaces, these rules may or may not apply.

For printed text and computer-based instruction, the most commonly recommended point size is 12 points. According to Tinker (1963), the type size in most textbooks falls between 10 and 12 points, with 11 being the most popular. Headings are generally sized 14 points and higher.

For projected displays, a common guide is the $6 \times 6$ rule, which states that an overhead transparency should have no more than six lines of text and no more than six words in each line. Another guideline, the 6w $\times$ 2w rule, states that text must be legible a maximum of six screen widths distance and a minimum of two screen widths distance. Another recommendation is to hold your slide at arm's length from your face (see Figure 9–24, top-right image). If you can read the text easily, the slide will probably be legible when projected.

If you are evaluating a slide from a computer screen, display the slide at 100 percent and back 6 feet away from the front of the screen (see Figure 9–24, bottom-left image). If you can read the text from this distance, it will most likely be visible when projected.

A more scientific approach (Heinich, Molenda, & Russell, 1993) is to consider the dimensions of the room (see Figure 9–24, top-left image). Estimate the furthest distance from which your slide will be viewed. For every 10 feet, increase the typeface ½ inch (remember 36 points is approximately ½ inch for many typefaces).

## Cueing Devices

Cueing devices are used to signal or cue readers to a change in message. Changing colors, using all caps, bolding, changing size or typeface, increasing or decreasing leading, underlining, and italicizing are all examples of this practice.

One rule of thumb for typography is to limit the number of cues to one or at the most two combinations. (*Notice* HOW **confusing** THIS <u>sentence</u> **IS** *to READ*.) Hartley (2004) suggests a rule of thumb to avoid using three or more additional cues when one or two at most will do. The research on the effectiveness of cueing or directing information is contradictory: Some researchers have found learning gains from cues (Croft & Burton, 1995) while others have found impairment (Rivlin et al., 1990). Rimar (1996) states that to date there is minimal solid research on appropriate cueing methods.

Many novices use all capital letters to emphasize information, not realizing that ALL CAPITAL LETTERS ARE DIFFICULT TO READ, AS YOU CAN SEE IN THIS SHORT SENTENCE—AND IN THE SENTENCES THAT FOLLOW. AFTER A WHILE YOUR EYES BECOME TIRED. HAVE YOU EVER NOTICED HOW HARD IT IS TO READ FOOD LABELS THAT ARE SET IN ALL CAPS? A rule of thumb is to avoid using all caps, unless you are dealing with mathematics (Tinker, 1963) or are working with only a few words.

Problems with readability associated with all caps can be explained in part by gestalt theory, which was discussed earlier in this book. In all caps text, the eye tends to pass quickly over a word since all of the letters are the same height. Individual letters are not perceived as distinctly because they are not that different from each other (see **Figure 9–25**). Notice how the top half of the word *millennium* is easier to figure out than the bottom half. You can also see how difficult it is to read the word *millennium* when the dots over the *i*'s are missing.

The all-caps rule holds for italics as well. According to Raines (1989), italics should not be used for emphasis because people ignore them. *Avoid setting long lines of text in italics. Italics are very difficult to read, as you can see in this short sentence and the sentences that follow. After a while your eyes become tired.* Although this is good advice, I do believe that italics can be used effectively to highlight certain words occasionally.

Other types of cues include headings, such as the Summary heading that follows below. Headings are also used to help learners understand the organization of content. Misanchuk (1992) recommends using no more than four levels of headings. If you have more than four, you might consider restructuring your content. Three or fewer levels of headings are more effective, according to research by Lang (1987) and Miles (1987). Learners may have difficulty understanding the organization of text when more than three headings are used.

## SUMMARY

Prior to reading this chapter, you learned about a perception, actions, tools (PAT) approach to designing instructional visuals. The idea behind PAT is reflected in the five tools that influence learner perception: (1) type, (2) shape, (3) color, (4) depth, and (5) space.

In this book the word *type* is synonymous with *typography*. Instructional typography is defined as the art and science of using individual letters, words, and passages of text to convey an instructional message. Although type is only one of the five essential tools for creating instructional visuals, it is perhaps the most powerful tool. Type can increase the organization of information and also communicate emotion. Not only can type be used to enhance the other tools such as shape, color, depth, and space, it can be manipulated by actions of contrast, alignment, repetition, and proximity as well. You can select from any number of typefaces to enhance an instructional message; thousands are available for use.

Typefaces are classified into six categories: (1) Black Letter, (2) Roman, (3) Square Serif, (4) Sans Serif, (5) Script, and (6) Decorative. Some categories, such as serif typefaces (Roman and Square Serif) and sans serif typefaces, have a preferred but not researched-based place in instructional materials. Serif typefaces are preferred for reading large passages of text, but there is no research to strongly support this preference. Likewise, sans serif typefaces are preferred for headings and computer displays, but again research does not strongly support or explain this preference either. Some characteristics of type, such as x-height and counter width, have some implications for instructional design, with larger x-heights and wider counters considered easier to read.

All uppercase letters are difficult to read.

Would you recognize this word without the dots?

See  how helpful a mix of uppercase and lowercase letters is? You can figure out the word even when the bottom half is missing. Most people would have difficulty if all they saw was the bottom half.

**FIGURE 9–25**   Uppercase and lowercase readability

The "it depends" rule influences decisions about type. It recommends that designers consider the learner, the context, other elements in the visual, and the message as they make typeface selections. A few other guidelines have been proposed, such as avoiding too many cueing devices, using classic typefaces, and considering the unique properties of the instructional unit prior to selecting a typeface.

The next chapter will discuss shape, the second tool for creating visuals. Like type, shape is an easy tool to use and is copyright free, and it can be used to make instruction easier to understand.

# PRACTICE

For additional activities and examples of student work, visit the companion website for this book at *http://www.coe.unco.edu/LindaLohr.*

## Resource Activity

Use Figures R–11, R–12, and R–13 in the Resources section as job aids for the chapter activities.

## Web Activity

The Web Activity for this chapter focuses on type as a tool for expression. The activity requires that you use just letters (no clip art) to describe the following words: *collaboration, synergy, alienation,* and *bossiness* (see the example shown here).

### Use typography (black and white only) to express the words
*collaboration, alienation, synergy,* and *bossiness.*

Collaboration

Synergy

Alienation

Bossiness

Web Activity

The first Challenge Activity asks you to match letter forms with architecture.

(a)

---

The second Challenge Activity asks you to design words to express their meaning.

(b)

Challenge Activity

## Challenge Activities

The first Challenge Activity asks you to match letter forms with architecture, as shown in image (a). The second Challenge Activity asks you to design words to express their meaning, as shown in image (b).

## Independent Activity

The Independent Activity asks you to revise an existing instructional document. Use type to improve the document's appearance, readability, and legibility.

## Justification Activity

Write a justification paper for the activity you select. Describe the following:

- *Your users and the assumptions you make about them (such as age, reading level, and assumed skills).*
- *Why you think your solution will work; include at least two ideas from the book, including page numbers and your interpretation of the passage used.*
- *What you learned from a "user-test" (have someone look at the image and verbalize their thoughts while looking at the image).*
- *The changes you will make based on user comments (or create a revised image).*

## Discussion Questions

"The Crystal Goblet" is an essay using a crystal goblet as a metaphor for good typography. It was originally published in 1929 by Beatrice Warde, who used the masculine pseudonym "Paul Grandjean" at that time. The piece was later published under her own name in 1957. Warde adhered to the philosophy that the best design was a transparent design. In her essay, Warde asks the reader to choose a crystal or a gold goblet for the sake of tasting a wine. Based on a person's choice, she will know whether that person is a connoiseur of wine. To read her essay, visit http://www.coe.unco.edu/Typography/Sections/CrystalGoblet/index.htm. Discuss what transparent design means for a typographer.

## K–12 Student Activities

Use the website and Challenge Activities to generate similar ideas for use with K–12 students. Learn with them as they use type to create signage around the school or in individual classrooms. Use type to express the meaning of words—for example, set the word *thin* in a light and narrow typeface.

## REFERENCES

Arditi, A., & Cho, J. (2005). Serifs and font legibility. *Vision Research, (45),* 2926-2933.

Black, A. (1990). *Typefaces for desktop publishing: A user guide.* London: Architecture Design and Technology Press.

Carter, R., Day, B., & Meggs, P. (1985). *Typographic design: Form and communication.* New York: Van Nostrand Reinhold.

Clark, R. C., & Lyons, C. (2004). *Graphics for learning: Proven guidelines for planning, designing, and evaluating visuals in training materials.* San Francisco. Pfeiffer

Croft, R. S., & Burton, J. K. (1995). Toward a new theory for selecting instructional visuals (Report No. IR 016 996). In *Imagery and Visual Literacy, Annual Conference of the International Visual Literacy Association,* Tempe, AZ. (ERIC Document Reproduction Service No. ED 380 075)

Hartley, J. (1985). *Designing instructional text.* London: Kogan Page.

Hartley, J. (2004). Text design. In D. H. Jonassen (Ed.), *Handbook of research for educational communications and technology* (2nd ed.). Englewood Cliffs, NJ: Educational Technology Publications.

Heinich, R., Molenda, M., & Russell, J. D. (1993). *Instructional media and the new technologies of instruction.* New York: Macmillan.

Lang, K. (1987). *The writer's guide to desktop publishing.* London: Academic Press.

Lynch, P. J. (1994). Visual design for the user interface. *Journal of Biocommunications, 21 (1),* 22-30.

Meggs, P. B., & McKelvey, R. (2000). *Revival of the fittest: Digital versions of classic typefaces.* New York: RC Publications.

Miles, J. (1987). *Design for desktop publishing.* San Francisco: Chronicle Books.

Misanchuk, E. R. (1992). *Preparing instructional text: Document design using desktop publishing.* Englewood Cliffs, NJ: Educational Technology Publications.

Raines, C. (1989). *Visual aids in business: A guide for effective presentations.* Los Altos, CA: Crisp Publications.

Rimar, G. I. (1996). Message design guidelines for screen-based programs. *Journal of Computer Assisted Learning, 12,* 245-256.

Rivlin, C., Lewis, R., & Davies-Cooper, R. (1990). *Guidelines for screen design.* Oxford, England: Blackwell Scientific Publications.

Spiekermann, E., & Ginger, E. M. (1993). *Stop stealing sheep and find out how type works.* Mountain View, CA: Adobe Press.

Tinker, M. A. (1963). *Legibility of print.* Ames: Iowa State University Press.

Tinker, M. A. (1965). *Bases for effective reading.* Ames: Iowa State University Press.

White, J. V. (1988). *Graphic design for the electronic age: The manual for traditional and desktop publishing.* New York: Watson-Guptill Publications.

Williams, R. (1994). *The non-designer's design book.* Berkeley, CA: Peachpit Press.

Williams, R., & Tollett, J. (1998). *The non-designer's web book: An easy guide to creating, designing, and posting your own web site.* Berkeley, CA: Peachpit Press.

# CHAPTER *10*

## *Shape Tools*

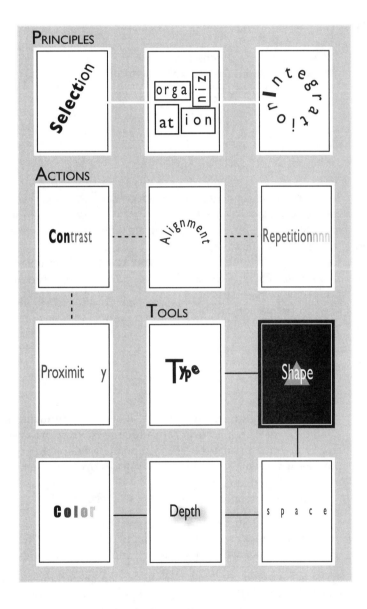

Get into shape.

## NOTES ABOUT THE OPENING VISUAL

Notice how most of the opening visual is made up of a simple **shape,** the rectangle. The underlying shape of the image is a rectangle, the elements on the shape are rectangles, and even the page is a rectangle. When creating this design, I wanted to convey the idea of building blocks. Squares might have worked since they would be more representative of building blocks, but I liked the harmony created with the rectangles. In this chapter you learn to use basic shapes in instructional visuals.

## FOCUS QUESTIONS

- Are meanings attached to shapes?
- Can shapes be used to enhance learning?
- What is the display shape?

## KEY TERMS

**COMPUTER-BASED SUPPORT SYSTEM**   Just-in-time assistance for the user of a system; also called *electronic performance support system (EPSS)*.

**DISPLAY SHAPE**   The shape of the background upon which an image is placed for viewing.

**JUST IN TIME**   Information that is made available at the time of need rather than in a formal training session; information that does not need to be memorized but needs to be available during a task.

**PROTOTYPE**   A quickly constructed example of something that is not yet fully created.

**SHAPE**   Elements used to create form (Peterson, 1997, p. 38).

**STORYBOARD**   A visual outline; used to plan out the appearance of a product.

## INTRODUCTION

Sylvia and Zack, the instructional designer and graphic artist/programmer introduced in Chapter 1, are working on a **computer-based support system** and have only one day to come up with a **prototype.** The computer-based training will include lessons for new employees in a restaurant chain. Sylvia watches over Zack's shoulder as they brainstorm what the menu should look like.

While he is working, Zack has these questions:

- What shapes should I use?
- Which shapes can I combine effectively?
- Which shapes will help me group and separate information?

Sylvia is amazed when Zack comes up with an elegant solution (see **Figure 10–1**) based mostly on shapes: lines, rectangles, ellipses, circles, and brackets.

Sylvia has learned an important design lesson. Simple shapes are often incredibly effective, both from a functional and aesthetic perspective. Like type, they are easy for the designer to use. She watches Zack as he changes the sizes and arrangements of the shapes until the image looks balanced (you learned about balance in Chapter 7). No doubt Zack's skill helps him accomplish the task quicker than Sylvia could, but she is right when she thinks, "I could do that."

## Simple shapes at work in Zack's support tool

Use shape to group or separate information. Design an overall shape that reads as a unit when you want something read as a unit. Likewise use shapes to divide information when you want information to be seen differently.

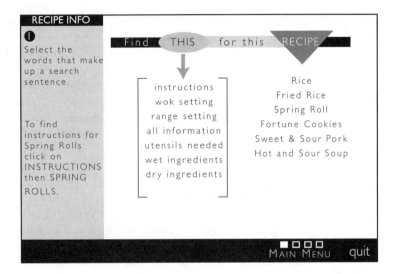

Notice how different information zones (see A, B, and C to the right) are set up by Zack's use of rectangles. Zack wants instructional information (section A) to be kept separate from navigational information (sections B and C). Navigation related to a cooking topic (section B) is also separated from navigation of the whole performance support environment (section C).

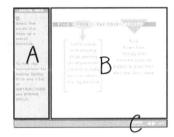

---

## Why shapes work perceptually

This experiment showed how the mind automatically creates perceptual groupings.

When people saw either
      two end parentheses ( (
      or left and right parentheses ( )
they grouped them as one unit; they saw the ( ( as one unit and the ( ) as one unit, even though each of these perceived units was actually composed of two distinct elements.

When these people saw the two elements displayed (see image) they did not perceive them as one element but two, most likely because the underlying shape did not seem like one shape.

| What is presented | What is perceived | |
|---|---|---|
| ( ( | ( ( | One unit is perceived. People see one shape. |
| ( ) | ( ) | One unit is perceived. People see one shape. |
| ( ∩ | ( ∩ | One unit is perceived. People see one shape. |

**FIGURE 10-1**   Simple shapes and why they work perceptually

*Source: Adapted from Attention and Object Perception by J. R. Pomeratz, E.A. Pristach, & C. E. Carson. In B. E. Shepp & S. Ballestero's (Eds.). Object Perception, Structure and Process (pp. 35–90) Hillsdale, NJ: Lawrence Erlbaum Associates.*

Simple shapes are about as versatile as typography. This is why they are introduced as the second design tool: Next to typography they are a designer's most useful tool. You will find in many instructional situations that all you need to use is type and shape. Together they are powerful. Make a point to find and study images that rely mostly on shape—corporate logos, business card design, brochures, wrapping paper, websites, and even design on coffee cups. Shapes are everywhere and are often stunningly simple.

Shape is formally defined as "any element that is used to give or determine form" (Peterson, 1997, p. 38). The form-giving function of shape explains its influence on learning. People tend to perceive shapes as wholes (or gestalt). Gestalt is often defined as shape. A shape is seen as a unit, and anything superimposed on a shape, or aligned to it, is likely to be seen as part of that unit. Therefore, a shape can be an effective way of presenting related but distinct information as one unit, as explained in the research by Pomeratz, Pristach, and Carson (1989). (See the lower image in Figure 10-1.)

## THE INSTRUCTIONAL FUNCTION OF SHAPE

In the pages ahead, you will see how a variety of shapes are used to improve instruction. Like type, most computer programs allow you access to drawing tools with which you can quickly create lines, circles, arrows, and boxes with minimal effort. Though common, these shapes have a timeless appeal. Just think about their use in many corporate logos and national flags.

### Simple Shapes

Shapes offer designers more than classic appearance. Hansen (1999) lists a variety of instructional attributes for circles, ovals, squares, rectangles, and lines. Circles and ovals (see **Figure 10–2**) are used to show unity, imply harmony, show processes, focus attention, and show elements of systems or subsystems. Since circles create a natural balance, they are easy elements for a beginner to use. Squares and rectangles (see **Figure 10–3**) can contain information, facilitate comparisons, focus attention, and show hierarchy. Lines (see **Figure 10–4**) are used to separate and define, show motion and direction, make connections, show a process, and convey emotion and volume.

### Common and Complex Shapes

Common shapes (see **Figure 10–5**), including triangles, stars, swirls, arrows, brackets, and more, are used to provide direction, imply motion, organize and unify, make something look engaging or fun, and make connections (join items). More complex shapes come from clip art and digital images (images that have been converted to a digital form to be used on a computer).

## IDENTIFYING THE DISPLAY SHAPE

A good place to start a design is to determine the underlying shape of your document (known as the **display shape**). Elizabeth Boling (Smaldino, Molenda, Heinich, and Russell, 2005) suggests that early in the design process you identify the underlying shape for your instructional visual and then arrange your type and other design elements around that shape. Part of what determines that underlying shape is the display shape. Are you using a standard computer screen, a standard page size, or a nonstandard size? Hartley (1985, 1996) suggests that your design decisions start and revolve around this issue of display size. **Figure 10–6** provides some useful dimensions for display shapes used when storyboarding a project. This figure also shows how Hartley's advice was used for this book and its original website.

## Show Unity

The oval shapes unify the lessons on the training menu. Compare the top menu to the bottom menu.

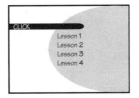

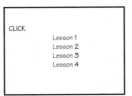

Japanese Flag

## Imply Harmony
### K–12 Example Literature/Reading

## Show Processes
### K–12 Example Science

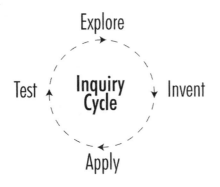

## Show Systems

## Focus Attention
### K–12 Example Literature/Reading

**FIGURE 10–2**   Circle shapes

## Contain Information

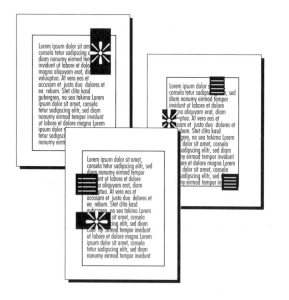

## Facilitate Comparisons

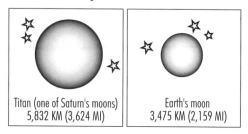

## K–12 Example *Earth Sciences*

## Focus Attention

## K–12 Example History

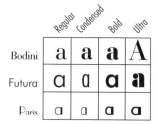

## Show Hierarchy
## K–12 Example Health

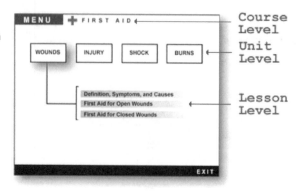

**FIGURE 10–3**  Rectangle and square shapes

**Separate and Define**
**K–12 Example** Earth Sciences

| The Universe | Stars | Galaxies | Solar Systems |
|---|---|---|---|
| | *Matter* | *Milky Way* | *Mercury* |
| | *Space* | *Quasars* | *Venus and Mars* |
| | *Sun* | *Active Galaxies* | *Jupiter* |
| | | | *Saturn* |
| | | | *Uranus* |
| | | | *Neptune* |
| | | | *Pluto* |

**Show Motion and Direction**
**K–12 Example** Chemistry

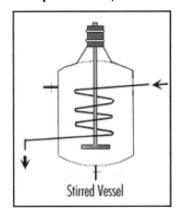

*Source: Clip art  © 1997 Rom Tech*

**Make Connections**

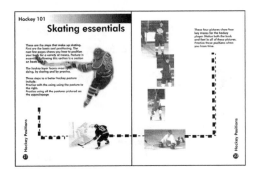

**Show a Process**

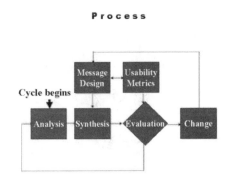

**Convey Emotion and Volume**

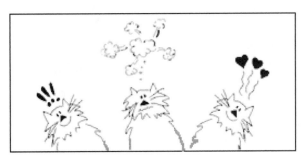

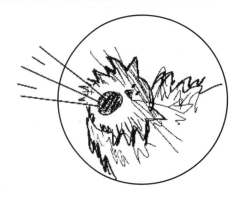

**FIGURE 10–4**  Lines

**Provide Direction**

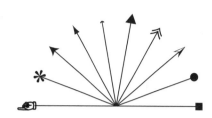

**Imply Motion**
**K–12 Example** Earth Sciences

Magnetic pull

No magnetic pull

**Look Engaging**

**Organize and Unify**

**K–12 Example** Consumer Sciences

Estate
Planning
**Distribution**

Investments
Home Equity
**Accumulation**

Emergency Cash
**Protection**

**Financial Pyramid**

**Make Connections**

Assemble
these
items
{ Pyrex beaker
Alum
Insulated cooking mitt
Washer
Pencil
Clear glass bowl
White distilled vinegar
Food coloring

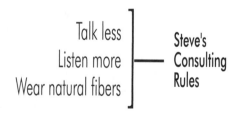

Talk less
Listen more
Wear natural fibers
] Steve's
Consulting
Rules

**FIGURE 10–5**   Common shapes

**Use these ratios when storyboarding different media formats.**

**This is a sample storyboard. Most storyboards have a unique appearance.**

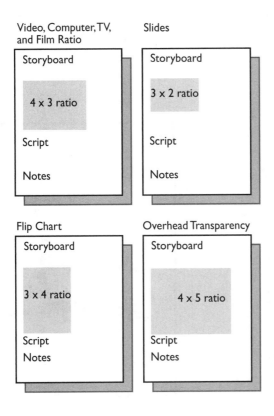

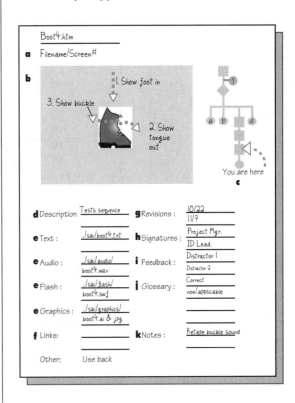

When I created the opening visuals for all the chapters in this book, I considered what the end product would look like. Anything I created needed to work for both the book and the book's website.

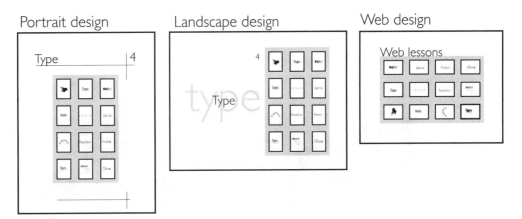

**FIGURE 10–6**  Planning the display shape

## Shapes to Fit the Display

You have just learned that the underlying shape of your display will be an important determinant in your eventual design. Generally speaking, you will choose shapes and layouts that complement the underlying display shape. For now, consider the rules of thumb shown in **Figure 10–7**. Long and narrow displays require long and/or narrow graphics or a layout that complements the shape of the background. Perfectly square displays tend to work well with

If you have an elongated display shape, use a long and narrow image.

If you have a symmetrical or balanced image, use a symmetrical display like this square.

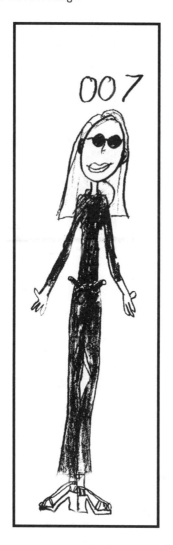

If you have a wide and short image, use a wide and short display shape.

**FIGURE 10–7**   Matching images to the display shape

symmetrical arrangements, and wide and shallow displays work well with images that have either wide or shallow (or both wide and shallow) attributes. Though they are oversimplified, these guidelines are satisfactory for the purposes of this chapter.

## Cartoon Shapes

There are times when it helps to use cartoon characters in instructional materials. You might use them to show a dialog between several people or to identify who is speaking. In distance classes, for example, it is sometimes challenging to separate your comments as the instructor from other comments, perhaps the comments of an expert, or the comments from an author. Showing who is speaking via a cartoon is often an effective means of establishing and clarifying the voices in a lesson (see **Figure 10–8**). Anybody can create cartoons using simple shapes, lines, circles, and squares that can be easily manipulated.

**A.** Start with a male face.

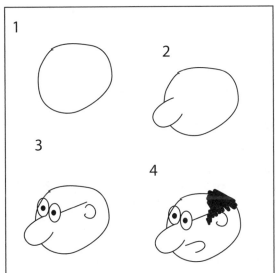

**B.** Now try a female face. Add emotion.

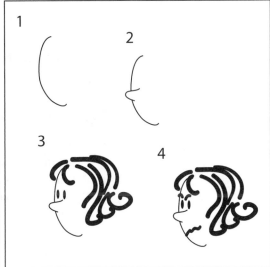

**C.** Now draw the body.

**D.** Complete the drawing.

**FIGURE 10–8**   Creating a cartoon: Using simple shapes and lines

## SUMMARY

Shape is the second of five tools (type, shape, color, dimension, and space) used to create effective instruction. Many designers recommend starting a design project by first thinking about the overall shape of the project—a square or rectangular page, for example—and the underlying shape that goes onto the page.

The importance of shape is often overlooked. Shape can be used to communicate instructional information.

Simple shapes such as circles, squares, and lines help learners see relationships, direction, and sequence. Common shapes such as swirls, stars, arrows, and brackets help communicate emotion, imagination, and groupings. Complex shapes such as digital images and photographs can add realism to a design.

## PRACTICE

For additional activities and examples of student work, visit the Companion Website for this book at *http://www.coe.unco.edu/LindaLohr.*

### Resource Activity

Use Figures R–11, R–12, and R–13 in the Resources as job aids for the chapter activities.

### Web Activity

Using the line tool in PowerPoint or some other program, create a self-portrait using five lines. An example of a five-line face is shown here. One tip: Double-click to "stop" the line tool. Some programs keep drawing the line after you have finished the shape. When that happens, just double-click.

Draw yourself using five lines or less. Circle shapes should be drawn like this:

You should see both end points

Web Activity

### Challenge Activities

The following activities ask you to create an instructional image for the content described. Focus on using shape tools—lines, squares, circles, etc.—to complete this activity.

1. Groups go through the four stages in their development: (1) forming: generally a stage of energy and excitement; (2) storming: the stage when personalities clash; (3) norming:

the stage when individuals in the group learn how to adjust to each other's work styles and personalities; (4) performing: the stage when the group is productive. An example of the student's solution is shown here.

2. A butterfly starts out as an egg, what looks like a tiny round or oval bead. The egg contains microscopic elements, such as ribs and eyes, that will form the adult butterfly. Eggs are usually attached to a leaf or some other part of a plant, and laid next to food that will eventually be eaten by the caterpillar (or larva), the long wormlike stage of the butterfly. If you look closely, you will see that the worm is covered with patterns and stripes and even small hairs. The caterpillar is busy feeding and growing during this stage.

   This is followed by the chrysalis (or pupa) stage, the time when the caterpillar tissues change into insect structures. Because the chrysalis is brown or green, it blends into nature while it makes this transformation.

   During the adult (or imago) stage, the colorful butterfly that we are all familiar with emerges and can take part in creating eggs of its own. Butterflies have courtship, mating, and egg-laying rituals. The adult butterfly may also change locations and start breeding butterflies in a new habitat.

This is one student's solution to the challenge to draw the four stages of team development using simple shapes such as squares, circles, triangles, and arrows.

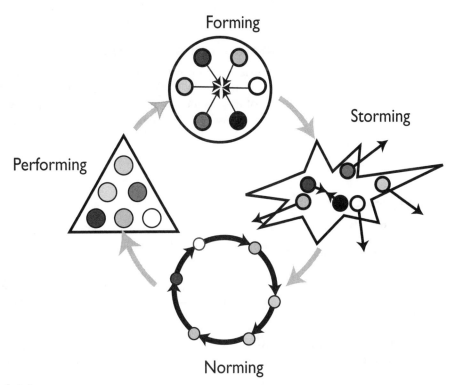

Challenge Activity

## **Independent Activity**

Choose a project that incorporates a shape that will facilitate the instructional message into its design.

## Justification Activity

Write a justification paper for the activity you select. Describe the following:

- *Your users and the assumptions you make about them (such as age, reading level, and assumed skills).*
- *Why you think your solution will work; include at least two ideas from the book, including page numbers and your interpretation of the passage used.*
- *What you learned from a "user-test" (have someone look at the image and verbalize their thoughts while looking at the image).*
- *The changes you will make based on user comments (or create a revised image).*

## Discussion Questions

A number of famous logos consist of basic shapes—for example, the symbol for the Olympics is a series of overlapping circles. Discuss the advantages of simple shapes in this type of design. Provide new examples. Are there any disadvantages or challenges associated with using simple shapes for icons and other designs?

## K-12 Student Activities

Ask students to portray the life of a famous person using shapes. For example, see how students can unscramble the information below about Thomas Jefferson to create a coherent message. Encourage students to rewrite sections of the passage or the entire passage. Emphasize the importance of making this information easy to understand and remember.

### About Thomas Jefferson

Thomas Jefferson was born in Albermarle County, Virginia, in 1743. He died at Monticello on July 4, 1846. In 1772 he married Martha Wayles Skelton. In 1776 he drafted the Declaration of Independence. Jefferson served as the governor of Virginia from 1779 to 1781. He was president of the United States from 1801 to 1809.

## REFERENCES

Hansen, M. (1999). *Visualization tools for thinking, planning, and problem solving.* Cambridge, MA: MIT Press.

Hartley, J. (1985). *Designing instructional text.* London: Kogan Page.

Hartley, J. (1996). Text design. In D. H. Jonassen (Ed.), *Handbook of research for educational communications and technology* (pp. 795-820). New York: Simon & Schuster Macmillan.

Peterson, B. L. (1997). *Using design basics to get creative results.* Cincinnati, OH: North Light Books.

Pomeratz, J. R., Pristach, E. A., & Carson, C. E. (1989). Attention and object perception. In B. E. Shepp & S. Ballestero (Eds.), *Object perception: Structure and process* (pp. 35-90). Hillsdale, NJ: Lawrence Erlbaum.

Smaldino, S. E., Molenda, M., Heinich, R., Molenda, M., & Russell, J. D. (2005). *Instructional media and the new technologies of instruction.* New York: Macmillan.

Smaldino, S. E., Russell, J. D., Heinich, R., and Molenda, M. (2005). *Instructional media and technologies for learning.* Upper Saddle River, NJ: Prentice Hall.

# CHAPTER *11*

## *Color, Depth, and Space*

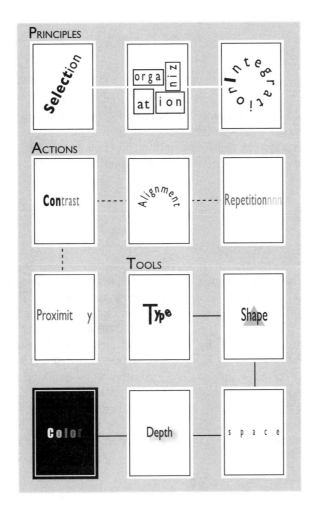

All communication between the readers of an image and the makers of an image must now take place on a two-dimensional surface. Escaping this flatland is the essential task of envisioning information—for all the interesting worlds (physical, biological, imaginary, human) that we seek to understand are inevitably and happily multivariate in nature. Not flatlands.

*Edward Tufte*

Due to cost, pictures and images may not always be on the same page.
Whenever possible, images are placed as close to their reference as possible.

**261**

## NOTES ABOUT THE OPENING VISUAL

The opening visual for this chapter uses color, depth, and space as design tools. Black, white, and gray show color contrast; depth is achieved with drop shadowing; and space is used to position type and shapes.

Though working with color, depth, and space takes practice, there are quick ways to use these tools effectively.

For one, a white or gray background always looks good with small areas of bright color; you can hardly go wrong with this approach. If you want more visual or instructional emphasis, you might try drop shadows for depth since they make images look like they are floating above the paper.

## FOCUS QUESTIONS

- How do I choose colors for instructional purposes?
- Should I base decisions on the psychology of color?
- Can color improve instruction?
- What is depth? Does it have an instructional impact?
- What is white space? Is it always white?

## KEY TERMS

**COLOR** A visual quality of something based upon how light is reflected or emitted. Color imparts a hue such as red, green, or violet.

**COLOR CONTRAST** The relative brightness of two colors.

**COLOR SPECTRUM** The range of colors produced by passing white light through a prism (see color insert 1).

**COLOR WHEEL** A visual representation of color theory explaining how colors are created and combined in aesthetic schemes (see color insert 1).

**DEPTH** The degree to which something can be measured in terms of size, dimension, and texture.

**HUE** An attribute that describes colors such as red, green, and violet; we tend to use the word *color* instead of *hue.*

**LEARNING ATTRIBUTES** The role of color in attention, search tasks, and retention.

**PHYSIOLOGICAL ATTRIBUTES** The physical impact of color, including adaption, arousal, and acuity.

**PSYCHOLOGICAL ATTRIBUTES** Preferences, meanings, and harmony assigned to color.

**SATURATION** The depth or intensity of a color; also called *chroma.* If a color is saturated, the hue is strong.

**VALUE** The intensity of white in a color; also known as *brightness* and *luminance.*

## INTRODUCTION

Latisha, the community college instructor and part-time technical writer introduced in Chapter 1, has been asked by a local hospital to redo some print materials, among them a daily menu design (**Figure 11–1**).

Latisha has these questions when she sets out to redesign the materials:

- How can I use **color** to separate or chunk information?
- Which colors should I use?
- Should I use drop shadowing or images that have some depth to them?
- How can I use space to make the information easier to read?

Analyze Latisha's new design and how she employed color, depth, and space to improve the menu. All three of these tools are generally used to focus attention, provide direction, and help the learner see the big picture.

Color (black and white), depth, and space are used to redesign the hospital menu below.

| **Original Menu** | **Original Menu as Seen by Patient on Painkillers** |
|---|---|

Even a healthy person would find this menu too hard to read. The black and white bars create a distracting, almost vibrating, visual.

**Improved Menu**

**Depth**
Drop shadows create the illusion of depth, making the time stand out.

**Space**
White space is used to chunk menu information into breakfast, lunch, and dinner.

**Salida City Hospital Daily Menu**
Order up to three items per meal

**Breakfast**
6 - 9 a.m.

Scrambled eggs
French toast
Pancakes with syrup
Yogurt

**Lunch**
11 a.m. -
1 p.m.

Pizza
Turkey sandwich
Yogurt with fruit

**Dinner**
6 - 8 p.m.

Soup (vegetable, chicken
  noodle, broccoli)
Macaroni and cheese
Lasagna
Clam spaghetti
Pudding

**Color**
Black, white, and gray are used in the redesign. Black is used for critical content; white is used as a spatial element; and gray is used as a decorative element in the rising, full, and setting sun images.

**FIGURE 11-1**   Redesign using color, depth, and space

# COLOR OVERVIEW

If you are like most people, it is appealing to think about creating instructional visuals that use **color**—a tool of instruction that can make or break the appearance and effectiveness of a document or image. With the accessibility of affordable printers, projection devices, and software, the ability to create color-enhanced visuals is easier now than ever. Used effectively, color can enhance both the aesthetic and instructional quality of educational or support materials.

Before getting started, you may want to locate the four-page color insert in this book, which shows examples of color wheels as well as strategies on using color to improve learner selection, organization, and integration.

## What Is Color?

Color is created by the interactions of white light upon an object and how receptors in the eye perceive the object. Different wavelengths create different colors. When a white light passes through a prism, the different wavelengths create a color spectrum (see Color Insert 1).

The color wheel (also on Color Insert 1) is another organization scheme for color that displays how countless colors emerge from the mix of red, yellow, and blue hues known as the primary colors. You will see here a number of different color schemes that can be used to display color effectively.

## Characteristics of Color for Visual Instruction

Color is complex, and knowing how to work with it effectively depends on an understanding of hue, value, and saturation, important characteristics that can help us identify precisely the conditions under which color has an impact.

### Hue and Value

The word **hue** is synonymous with the word *color* and is used to identify color as we know it—for example, red, blue, and green. There are two qualities of hue that impact perception and must be taken into consideration when using color in instructional materials: (1) value and (2) saturation. **Value** is synonymous with brightness and refers to the degree of light that a color emanates. A high value is very bright; a low value is very dark. **Saturation** is synonymous with chroma and refers to the depth or intensity of color. (See the butterfly on Color Insert 2.) There are two heuristics for value and saturation: (1) increase saturation to make instructional information advance, and (2) decrease the hue or value when the instructional information takes up a large space and diverts the eyes from what is important.

### Physiological, Psychological, and Learning-Related Attributes of Color

Pett and Wilson (1996) encourage designers to pay attention to three attributes of color: (1) physiological, (2) psychological, and (3) learning related. The physiological attribute of color defines the phenomenon of color perception based on physical properties related to the viewing environment. Color varies according to our expectations. We may see clouds as white, but if we look closely we will see many colors, including blues, grays, and browns. Our eyes adapt to color when entering or exiting a bright or dark room. Afterimages appear when we shift our focus away from color, producing different colors. Colors change according to the colors around them. The green color in the leaf of a tree will look one way when placed on a blue background and another when placed on a red background. (See the leaves in Color Insert 2.) Some colors at the extremes of the spectrum (violet, red) are focused in different places of the eye and tend to advance while other colors in the middle of the spectrum (green, yellow) tend to recede. Psychological aspects of color are related to age, gender, and cultural preferences. There are many widely held beliefs about color:

- Children prefer bright primary colors.
- Blue and green relate to aloofness and freshness.
- Orange and red are associated with excitement.

Colors of high value (more white) are considered light and airy as compared to colors of low value (more black, less white). Low value (more black) are considered heavy and somber. Many meanings associated with color are learned, as explained by the color white representing purity in one culture and death in another.

The instructional functions of color refer to the use of color in educational situations, a topic discussed in the next section.

## Four Instructional Functions of Color

Edward Tufte (1990) describes four functions of color, or hue, in information design: (1) labeling, (2) identifying quantity and measurement, (3) representing reality, and (4) creating aesthetic appeal.

**Labeling**   The first function of color is to label or differentiate information. Maps often make extensive use of color. A subway map might use blue to designate the location of restrooms, red to designate all stops on a particular line, and green to identify where tokens can be purchased. The blue colored lines in many road maps are used to identify two-lane back roads that distinguish these "blue highways" from the red or black interstate highways. Ski areas label the difficulty of different runs using color and shape. A green circle means "easy" or "for beginners," a blue square means "intermediate," and a black diamond means "for experts only."

**Identifying Quantity and Measurement**   The second function of color is to show quantity or measurement. In a pie chart, colors are often used in pieces of the pie, showing the relative percentages of certain items. Island maps use different saturations of blue to designate deep and shallow areas, with deeper areas colored a stronger, deeper blue. A diagram showing the spread of AIDS over time uses a stronger saturation of color to show a greater number of causalities (see Color Insert 3).

**Representing Reality**   The third function of color is to represent reality. For example, medical illustrations show the color of healthy versus unhealthy fingernails. A dentist may have posters showing examples of healthy versus unhealthy gums. If you were in a wine-tasting class, you would learn the difference between chardonnays and cabernets by their red and white colors. Architects use colored pencils on blueprints to help clients visualize the sections or details of a plan. A wardrobe planner uses colored fabric swatches to help a client choose clothing.

**Creating Aesthetic Appeal**   The fourth function of color is to create decoration or aesthetic appeal. We see this function of color every day on television, in printed materials, and on the Web. Color is used because people tend to prefer color to black and white, finding color motivating, soothing, stimulating, and capable of evoking emotions (Misanchuk, Schwier, & Boling 2000).

## Research on Color and Learning

Pett and Wilson (1996) describe color and its research-based impact on instructional materials design. They cover a wide range of color applications and conclude that the effect of color on learning is slight. Despite the enthusiasm and high regard educators tend to have regarding color, the research on learning from color is mixed. Some researchers have found that the use of color facilitates cognitive processes involved in learning, such as memory support, recall of information, and promotion of interaction between learners and content (Misanchuk et al., 2000), but others report that color can be distracting and inhibit performance (Shneiderman, 1992). Regardless of mixed findings, the simple fact that learners prefer color materials makes it important for us to learn what we can about using color effectively. In addition, color can help learners locate information quickly, thus increasing the usability of instructional materials as well as their effectiveness, efficiency, and appeal.

You might be surprised, too, that there are almost as many research-based reasons against the use of color in instruction as there are for it (Misanchuk et al., 2000). In their review of the literature, Misanchuk, Schwier, and Boling (2000) list reasons why color is and is not considered instructionally beneficial.

## Reasons for Using Color

There are many reasons to use color:

- Color may be necessary (medical students need to know the color of healthy versus unhealthy tissue, jewelry students need to know the correct color of a soldering flame and color of metal when heated correctly).
- There are many research-based advantages for color. Misanchuk et al. (2000) list 19 references in all, only a few of which are listed here. These include the ability to "attract and control attention, add visual cues, locate information, link logically related data, show associations, tie together related items that are scattered, aid in differentiation and discrimination among elements, facilitate subtle discriminations in complex displays, help interpret related and unrelated information, facilitate identification, speed searches for objects, increase task speed, express quality or quantity, rank items, highlight student errors, differentiate between required and optional data, aid decision making."
- Learners prefer color.

## Reasons Against Using Color

There are many reasons against using color:

- Color may not be necessary.
- Researchers have found color to be distracting (Horton, 1991; Livingston, 1991) and confusing (Shneiderman, 1992). Chapman (1993) contends, "If color is added to a presentation and not functionally related to the task, its presence can act as a deterrent to performance" (p. 14).
- Learners may not have the technology to access color adequately.

You may have noticed that the necessity of color topped both of the lists. In a review of the research by Dwyer and Lamberski (1983), the influence of color on learning was highly dependent on the learning task at hand. This finding is in harmony with Tufte's (1990) recommendation to use color to represent reality. For the designer this means using color when color is a critical element of the learning or performance context. For example, if you were creating a job aid for inserting a colored ink cartridge into a printer, you would probably use black and white for everything else but the location of the cartridge. If you were teaching people to identify the perfect color of green for fresh broccoli, you would be smart to use the same green in your instruction. If you were teaching a group of medical students the color of a particular skin rash, you would need to show it. If you were teaching about color, you should use color.

Dwyer and Lamberski (1983) also found time and age to influence the power of color as an instructional tool. In their research, the effectiveness of color cues in instruction was dependent in part on the time available to learners to process those cues. Learners who have more time to study a color-coded visual are more likely to see why and how the various color codes have been used.

## Choosing Color for Instruction

If you decide to use color, you might find choosing and making it work well a challenge. Unless you have worked with color extensively, it is a good idea to leave complex color design to the experts. The encouraging news is that black, white, gray, simple primary colors (red, blue, and yellow), or secondary colors (purple, green, and orange) are amazingly versatile and effective in instruction and are easy for most people to use. Color Insert 1 illustrates how each color wheel is made up of small dots of bright colors surrounded by white space. Color wheels are a great tool, but they do not work for all situations. How do you decide on color the rest of the time? Principles of selection, organization, and integration learned in the previous chapters will help you.

### *Selection*

Choose colors to make important information stand out and improve learner selection (figure/ground). By facilitating the use of contrast, color can help the learner differentiate between important and less important information. There are two color schemes that are particularly important for visual acuity and perception: (1) the spectral scheme, and (2) the warm and cool color scheme (see Color Insert 1) that divides the color wheel in half. Acuity refers to the preciseness of perception and the ability to distinguish between different elements and is important for figure/ground distinctions.

There are two heuristics (rules of thumb that do not apply to all situations) for the spectral and warm and cool color schemes:

1.   Colors that fall in the middle of the color spectrum—yellow, green, white, and blue—are associated with greater acuity. Experiments measuring acuity examine how well these colors facilitate recognition and perception. In general, middle spectrum backgrounds (such as a white or yellow paper background with black text) are more effective than extreme spectrum backgrounds (such as violet or red backgrounds with black text). Room lighting also plays a role with middle spectrum text more visible against a black background than extreme spectrum text. This makes intuitive sense because books have long been printed with black text on a white page with success. Many of the studies related to color and acuity focus more on hue though than on value or saturation. For example an extreme spectrum color such as violet, with high value (bright violet) may be highly visible. Pett and Wilson (1996) recommend attention to the characteristics of saturation.

2.   Warm colors (yellows, reds, and oranges) tend to advance while cool colors (blues, greens, violets) tend to recede. To make an element noticeable, or move to the figure area of a figure-ground arrangement, a designer might consider using warm colors. As with the previous rule, however, color value needs to be considered as well. Lower values (darker colors) tend to stand out more than lighter values (lighter colors). For example, a low value (darker) yellow might stand out more than a high value (lighter) blue.

Black, white, and gray can be used effectively to facilitate selection. A rule of thumb is to use darker background colors when the overall area is small (see **Figure 11–2**). Although a dark background might improve selection in a small space (notice the effective contrast in the 100 percent black swatch and Idaho images in Figure 11–2), its effectiveness decreases as visual space increases.

### *Organization*

Choose color that will establish an order of importance (hierarchy). Color can suggest a ranking or sequential order (Horton, 1994). Color facilitates hierarchy through the creation of separate categories or layers of information. These categories can show levels of importance or the progression of data. You can use dark-to-light or dull-to-bright sequences to show increasing significance or importance. For example, in a table of contents, book parts might be set in the highest chroma color, book chapters in a mid-chroma color, and chapter

## Consider contrast...

White text is most visible on darker backgrounds (60% black or higher).

100% black
90% black
80% black
70% black
60% black

Black text is most visible on lighter backgrounds (50% black or lower).

50% black
40% black
30% black
20% black
10% black

} A background lower than 20% black will not copy well on a photocopier

## But also consider space, too...

Although contrast here is strong, the passage is not easy to read. A strong contrast covering a large area is often not optimal for design purposes. While the 100% black swatch above might seem the strongest contrast, it doesn't work well when the area covered is large, as in this block of text below.

Contrast here is better for reading. Here a lighter background is more effective in a larger space.

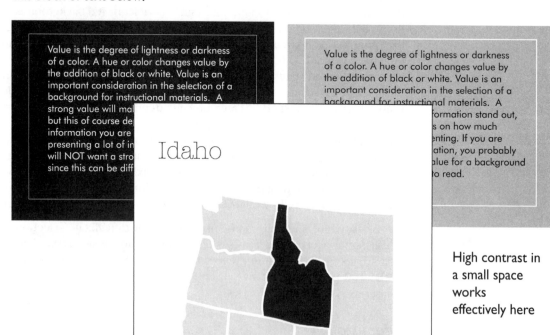

Value is the degree of lightness or darkness of a color. A hue or color changes value by the addition of black or white. Value is an important consideration in the selection of a background for instructional materials.  A strong value will mal... but this of course de... information you are... presenting a lot of in... will NOT want a stro... since this can be diff...

Value is the degree of lightness or darkness of a color. A hue or color changes value by the addition of black or white. Value is an important consideration in the selection of a background for instructional materials.  A ...formation stand out, ...s on how much ...enting. If you are ...ation, you probably ...lue for a background ...to read.

Idaho

High contrast in a small space works effectively here

**FIGURE 11-2**  Contrast using black, white, and gray

sections in a low chroma color fill (see Color Insert 3). If you do not have color, shades of black (see Figure 11-2) can be used to suggest sequential order.

## Integration

Choose colors that help the learner see the big picture (gestalt). As discussed at the beginning of this chapter, color can tie complex information together in aesthetic, organizational, and psychological ways. A variety of color selection schemes can contribute to the learner's sense of gestalt. The following section describes four types of color selection schemes, based on (1) the color wheel, (2) inspiration from nature or art, (3) custom palettes provided with templates, and (4) psychological associations.

**Choose Color Based on the Color Wheel**    Color Insert 1 shows a number of color wheel schemes, including warm and cool color schemes, analogous schemes, complementary schemes, and more. These schemes help you pick colors that work well together. Often the schemes are limited to two colors (complementary), or three colors (split-complementary). The advantage of this approach is that you are able to work effectively with fewer colors, which can translate into fewer mistakes given the limitation of color interactions.

**Choose Color Based on Inspiration from Nature and Art**    Tufte (1990) suggests using colors found in nature, especially those on the lighter side, such as the blues, yellows, and grays of sky and shadow. He recommends using large background areas in muted colors to allow brighter colors to stand out more vividly. He also advises distributing colors throughout a work to give it better unity.

An approach that I like to use involves finding color combinations from works of art, the Internet, advertisements, and design books. For example, I have a poster of Vincent van Gogh's *The Chair* above my desk. The colors I initially see are complementary golds, terra-cottas, and blues. But when I compare the colors to the paint chips in my computer programs, I find that the colors are usually very grayish, or as Tufte says, muted. These are colors I would not have picked without the help of van Gogh's painting.

**Choose Color Based on Color Palettes Found in Templates**    Several books suggest artist-created color schemes (see the Resources). These books provide specific values that you can use to duplicate colors exactly as shown on your computer. These color schemes are a great help, but they do not completely take care of everything for you. You still need to spend time with them. You may be given the right colors, but you must figure out how much of each color to use. In recent years, art-related books also provide relatively sized paint chips that allow you to get a sense of how much of any one color to use within a suggested color scheme. For example, if a text passage calls for a turquoise and terra-cotta orange color scheme, you would see not only a turquoise chip and a terra-cotta orange color chip but also the percentage or ratio of terra-cotta orange versus turquoise. The text might suggest using 90 percent terra-cotta orange and 10 percent turquoise. The color chip for terra-cotta would be nine times as large as the turquoise chip.

The same can be said for the custom palettes that are part of software programs. These palettes have predetermined color schemes for background colors, text, drop shadows, and highlights. Even though the software companies claim that artists designed these color sets, they are not effort-free and require a user's judgment, as some of the combinations lead to questionable results.

**Choose Color Based on Psychological Associations**    Colors evoke emotional responses (Horton, 1994). Walking into a room with blue walls can seem cold and somewhat formal. Blue, green, and some shades of purple are considered cold colors and can be used to calm, soothe, and reassure. Walking into a room with soft yellow walls can do the

**TABLE 11–1**   *Color and Mood/Meaning*

| Color | Meaning/Mood |
|---|---|
| *Red* | Passion, power, zeal, happiness, aggression, impulsiveness (the American Automobile Association considers red-car drivers more accident-prone because of their carefree natures, according to Nelson, 1989), danger, shame, optimism, warmth, extroversion, fire, bloodshed; can evoke a fight or flight response (Boyle, 2001). |
| *Orange* | Often misunderstood and misused; popular with children, but considered a least favorite color along with yellow by adults; energetic, festive, good for celebrations and happy events, knowledge, civilization, friendliness, deference, pride, warmth, gregariousness. |
| *Yellow* | Warmth, cowardice, intelligence, brightness, clarity (in Western cultures), sacredness — as it approaches the color of gold (in the Orient and Europe, according to Nelson, 1989), treachery, novelty, idealism, introspection (Horton, 1994), madness (Vincent van Gogh used a lot of yellow), good cheer; bright yellow is the most visible color (Boyle, 2001) and is considered a least favorite color along with orange; provokes irritability in architectural settings. |
| *Green* | Growth, freshness, health, hope, but also associated with guilt, disease, nausea, terror (Nelson, 1989); among the most cited favorite colors (Boyle, 2001). |
| *Blue* | Serenity, tranquility, dependability ("true blue"), constancy, used in many logos (Boyle, 2001), aloofness ("blue-blood"), sobriety, fear, sky, water, ice (transparent) (Nelson, 1989), depression |
| *Violet* | Considered both a warm and cold color (red brings out the warmth, blue the coolness), royalty (in some countries only royalty could wear—and afford—purple), nobility, sorrow, loneliness, vanity, nostalgia, wit, spirituality, regret (Horton, 1994); good for targeting creative types (Boyle, 2001) |
| *White* | Purity, truth, in the Orient used for mourning (Nelson, 1989), bland |
| *Black* | Depression, sorrow, gloom, death, sensuality, elegance, sophistication, elite, sin, dignity, morbidity, sinister |
| *Brown* | Earth, dirt, chocolate, coffee (Boyle, 2001), duty, parsimony, reliability, bareness, poverty (Horton, 1994) |

opposite, creating a background that feels warm and inviting. Yellow, orange, and red colors are considered warm colors and can be used to arouse, alert, and excite. Many of these emotional reactions to color depend upon color values and saturations. For example, although a soft yellow may be inviting and soothing, other yellows are known to provoke irritability in architectural settings.

In addition to influencing moods, colors also have symbolic meaning, often related to cultural background (Nelson, 1989). White is associated with weddings in Western cultures but with mourning in some Eastern cultures. **Table 11–1** describes how the same color can mean many things. For example, green is associated with both growth and disease, blue with dependability and transparency, and red with happiness and bloodshed. Although some of the associations in the table may be more common than others, they are clearly not universal and with other elements on a page are often not even influential. For example, a black background with bright vibrant colors would hardly be considered sinister; nor would a white background with vibrant colors be considered bland.

# DEPTH

In this book depth refers to scale, dimension, and texture (see **Figure 11–3**). Depth plays a critical role in making information stand out (facilitating selection).

# Enhancing instruction with color: *Basics*

The Color Spectrum ▲

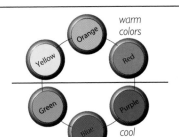

**The color wheel** is a combination of warm and cool colors. Use a warm color with a cool color to create a contrast. Warm colors **advance** (become the figure) and cool colors **recede** (become the ground).

**Primary colors** create all other colors. Use primary colors with other primary colors. Use all three to illustrate three aspects of something. Use **in children's materials** or when bright colors are important.

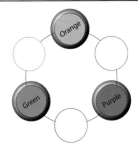

**Secondary colors** are created from mixing two primary colors—for example, yellow + red = orange. Use all three colors to illustrate three aspects of something.

**Tertiary colors** are created from a mix of adjacent primary and secondary colors. Use together to enhance aesthetics.

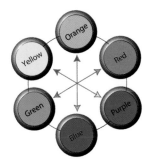

**Complementary colors** fall directly opposite each other on the color wheel. Use when you want to create a contrast. Try unequal percentages—20% yellow and 80% purple, for example. Can be jarring in equal percentages.

*versus*

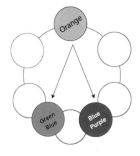

**Split-complementary colors** fall to each side of a color's complement. Use for three aspects of something and for situations with two subordinates.

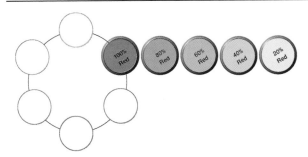

**Monochromatic colors** are different shades of the same hue. A tint is created with different percentages of white, a shade is created with different percentages of gray. Use to show increasing or decreasing levels of something. These are easy for a novice to use but care must be taken to ensure enough contrast.

**Analogous colors** are next to each other on the color wheel. Use to show changing levels of something. These are easy for a novice to use and usually provide enough contrast.

# Color for learner selection (figure/ground)

## Exaggerate saturation and value to increase acuity

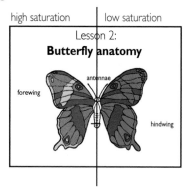

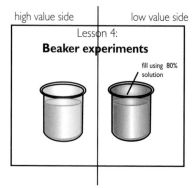

If highly saturated colors are used, images are easier to perceive since they advance.

High value images (high brightness) are more difficult to perceive. (Stand back and squint—which side advances?)

## Contrast backgrounds and foregrounds carefully

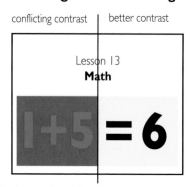

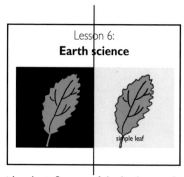

Avoid background and foreground combinations that use the same degree of value (brightness) or saturation. Also avoid colors close to each other on the color wheel. Here the green and blue have a similar level of brightness and they are also next to each other on the color wheel.

Consider the influence of the background color on the foreground color. The leaf against the black background looks brighter than the leaf against the gray background, but both leaves are the same color.

### Working with complementary colors

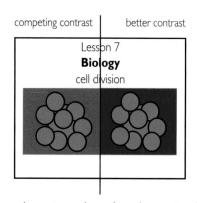

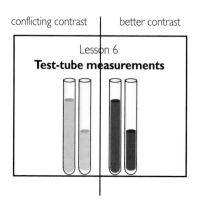

Avoid complementary colors of equal saturation (intensity). Contrast the value (brightness) of foreground and background

# Color for learner organization (hierarchy)

Chapter 6, Organization Principle: Working with Hierarchy, covers methods for showing sequence, direction, and change as well as subordinate, superordinate, and coordinate relationships. Notice how color coding is used to link the words above to the map examples below.

**Use increasingly dark or intense color to show spread/growth of AIDS.**

SPREAD OF AIDS IN AFRICA

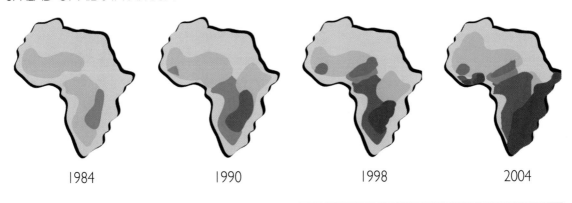

| 1984 | 1990 | 1998 | 2004 |

**Use the same color to chunk/group content.**
In the map below, each state and arrow pair use the same color in order to group them visually, making it easier for learners to fill in the blank.

In the table of contents below, Parts 1 and 2 use the same color to show their coordinate status. The content sections are also highlighted in the same color, making it easier to pair them visually.

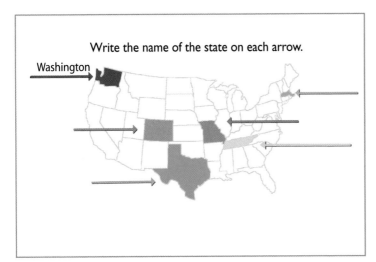

Contents

Part 1 Composing
Position ———— 2
Balance ———— 4
Dimension ———— 8
Lighting ———— 12

Part 2 Printing
Effects ———— 14
Printing ———— 16

**Use different colors to separate content.** In the map above, states are shown in different colors to make comparisons of shape, size, and location easier. In the table of contents different colors are used to show the superordinate status of the parts to the subordinate levels (topics).

4

# Color for learner integration (gestalt)

Chapter 7, Integration Principle: Gestalt, covers methods for achieving gestalt in instructional materials. Gestalt takes place when the whole is perceived as greater than the sum of its parts.

## Use color to connect parts to whole.

Report

Contents

Part 1
Part 2
Part 3
Part 4

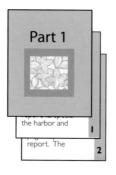
Part 1 — the harbor and ... report. The 1 2

Part 2 — the land of sun and ... report. Its special According to Miller 5 6

Part 3 — is important to visit the Plaza when the ... Kansas City haunts 9 10

Part 4 — status is achieved through ... old money marks 11 12

## Use color to match mood.

The color used in children's books is carefully chosen to match the story mood.

Energy, impulsiveness, and cheer tend to be associated with orange, red, and yellow, respectively.

Freshness, aloofness, and loneliness tend to be associated with green, blue, and purple, respectively.

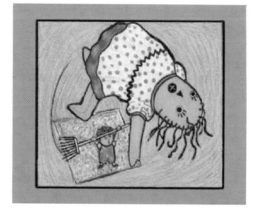

The story character sees this bowl of strawberries and decides to eat some while her grandma is not looking.

The story character flings her doll into the air when she feels ignored by her mother.

## Use color schemes to create harmony and balance (see example on color insert 1).

**Scale** established with weight and relative proportions

# Important
Not important

This is the actual size of a microchip. Putting it next to a penny helps you see its relative size.

**Dimension** created through shadowing

**Drop Shadow**
**No Drop Shadow**

Too many drop shadows can be distracting and hard to read.

**Texture** created by detail

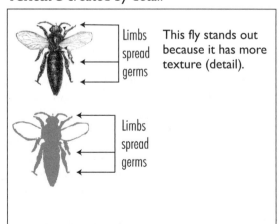

This fly stands out because it has more texture (detail).

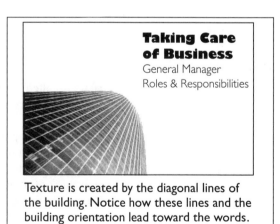

Texture is created by the diagonal lines of the building. Notice how these lines and the building orientation lead toward the words.

**FIGURE 11–3**   Depth: Scale, dimension, and texture

## Scale

Scale, or relative proportions of objects, communicates relative importance and creates an element of complexity or detail that signify depth, as you see in the Figure 11-3 images. The word *Important* has greater size due to the weight of the font. The size of the microchip is communicated more clearly when placed next to an image of a penny. Comparisons of this nature are helpful because you help learners assimilate new information by using what is already in memory.

## Dimension

Shadows give an image dimension, or depth, as in *Drop Shadow* in Figure 11-3. When too many elements use drop shadowing, the technique loses its impact, as shown in the "meeting-only" image in Figure 11-3. You can also use shading and figure shadowing, as seen as well in Figure 11-3. Notice how shadows can be stark or light (and from different light sources).

## Texture

Texture—the presence of a rough or patterned surface—adds depth and makes items stand out. For example, sand is textured, water is not. Corduroy is textured, satin is not. Notice how the top fly image in Figure 11-3 stands out more than the fly at the bottom. The detail provided in the top image provides the sense of depth. Perspective creates depth. If you ever find yourself with a boring image, just use perspective to liven things up. Diagonal alignment also adds texture and energy to an image. The building shown from an unusual perspective in Figure 11-3 helps the message stand out because it points diagonally to the title.

Photographs are an easy way to employ perspective along with detail. Another way to add depth and increase texture is to use the three-dimensional tools now offered in many presentation packages. Overall, photographs can be used to increase depth and texture in instructional materials because they provide an immediate way to see relative sizes, dimension, and texture. The Resources section presents ten composition tips that you will find useful when composing images with a camera (see Figures R-5 and R-6 in the Resources section). Note that scale, dimension, and texture are addressed in these ten composition tips.

## SPACE

Space—called white space, negative space, counter space, and trapped space—is a design tool that is often not recognized as such. **Figure 11–4** illustrates how white space can be used to divide text and graphics and how a page with a gray background can still be said to have white space. Although space is the area between visual elements that is often ignored, it has an important role in instructional visuals. Space can direct the eye to important information by chunking and separating instructional elements, as in Figure 11-4. A design rule of thumb is to avoid trapped space, as illustrated by the CD training image also in Figure 11-4. Trapped space refers to any place in an image that draws the eye and locks it in a dead or empty area.

Hartley (1985, p. 27) considers space an important tool for clarifying text. It is space that separates letters from each other. It is space (with punctuation) that separates phrases, clauses, and paragraphs from each other; and it is space (with headings and subheadings) that separates subsections and chapters from one another.

## White space

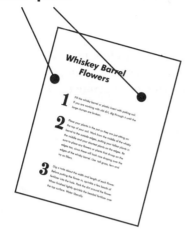

## Gray space

This same document is printed on gray paper. The white space is still called white space, even though it is actually "gray" in color.

## Trapped space

This doesn't look right. The area traps the eye in a meaningless place.

Corrected to eliminate trapped space.

## Another example of trapped space

Space here is purposefully trapped to emphasize a point. This concretely shows space as a river. The term *river of white space* refers to the illusion of a river running through text, generally an unwanted effect.

## Using space to show intervals of time

From *The Flight of the Bumble-Bee* by N. Rimskij-Korsakov (1844–1908)

**FIGURE 11–4**  Types of space

## Space as a Tool for Clarifying Text

Hartley (1985) maintains that the consistent use of space has three instructionally related benefits:

1. It increases the rate of reading because readers are more able to see redundancies.
2. It helps readers access the more personally relevant pieces of information.
3. It enables readers to see the structure of a document.

Symmetrical shapes look balanced. Both halves of an image look equal.

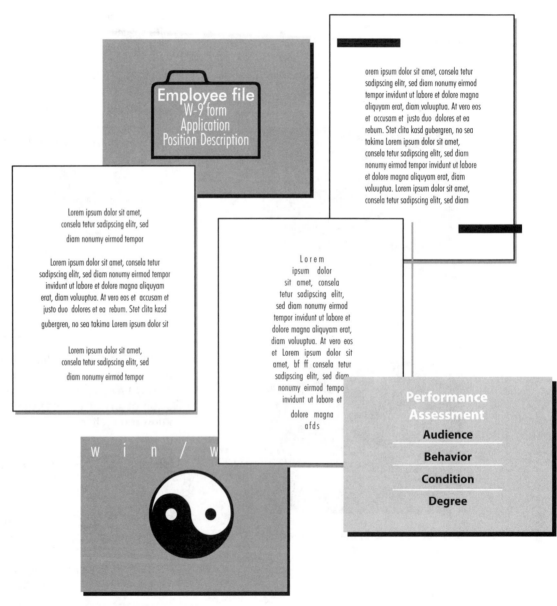

**FIGURE 11–5** Symmetrical shapes

As discussed in Chapter 9, Hartley (1985) recommends a "floating page," a page that ends not according to a predetermined bottom margin but according to where the content naturally ends.

## Space and Perception of Time

Space can impart a sense of timing, with items that are spaced further apart communicating distance in time. Consider the arrangement of musical notes in Figure 11-4.

## Space and Balance

Space also helps balance images on a page or screen. Balance is considered the distribution of information, or the achievement of equilibrium. You use space to work with balance by moving information into places to achieve either a symmetrical or an asymmetrical arrangement.

### Symmetry

Symmetry is a visual arrangement in which everything is in equilibrium; all elements are equal. It often conveys a sense of calm and professionalism (see **Figure 11–5**). Symmetrical arrangements, however, can be static and boring.

### Asymmetry

Asymmetry is a visual arrangement in which elements appear to be thrown off balance. Asymetrical designs tend to create more visual interest (see **Figure 11–6**).

### White Space

What's the best way to work with white space? White space is challenging at first because it is hard to "see." Yet to work effectively with white space, you must see it. One technique to try is to stand back from a design and look at it while squinting. Squinting allows the white space to be viewed as a separate visual element. If the white space looks odd, perhaps there are areas of trapped white space or rivers of space (as discussed earlier in Figure 11-4). The goal is to create a good balance between the white space and the other elements that make up the visual. With practice, you will eventually develop a good eye for white space.

## SUMMARY

This chapter concludes our look at design tools by describing and demonstrating how color, depth, and space enhance instructional visuals. Color has aesthetic as well as instructional impact and is useful for creating a mood, drawing attention, and organizing information into groups. Though color takes time to master, there are some easy and effective ways for nonartists to use color. Using white backgrounds with a small amount of primary color is easy for most people. Color schemes, colors from nature, and color combinations found in artwork are effective ways to select color combinations as well.

Depth is a tool that uses scale, and dimension to direct learner attention. Diagonal shapes instantly add energy to an image. Photographs and other images that have a textured, detailed, or shaded appearance create an illusion of depth and often create more visual interest or direct learner attention.

White space (or a background color) is the final tool covered in this chapter. Though often ignored, unused space is considered a design tool as important as type, shape, color, and depth. Space can direct a learner's attention and create symmetrical or asymmetrical balance. Many learners prefer images and text passages that use plenty of white space because they feel less overwhelmed by the volume of information presented.

Text and images are not centered here, but they look balanced.

**FIGURE 11–6**  Asymmetrical shapes

## PRACTICE

For additional activities and examples of student work, visit the Companion Website for this book at *http://www.coe.unco.edu/LindaLohr*.

### Resource Activity

Use the job aids in the Resources (see Figure R–5 through Figure R–8) to help you complete the chapter activities.

### Web Activity

The Web Activity asks you to take an image and revise it using color, depth, and space. One student's solution is shown here.

Below are good examples of the Chapter 11 Web and Challenge Activities, which asked students to create an instructional image using color, depth, or space.

Here a student uses color (shades of black), and texture (the edge of the stars), and space to depict the Big Dipper constellation.

The Web Activity

## Challenge Activity

The Challenge Activity asks you to create an image and experiment with changing its appearance with depth, color, and space. Two students' solutions are shown here.

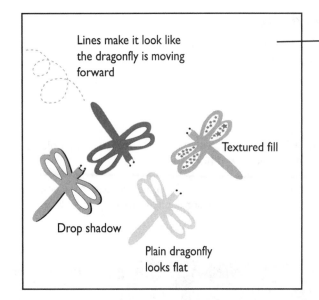

Lines make it look like the dragonfly is moving forward

Textured fill

Drop shadow

Plain dragonfly looks flat

This student uses line, shadow, and textured fill to create depth in the dragonfly images.

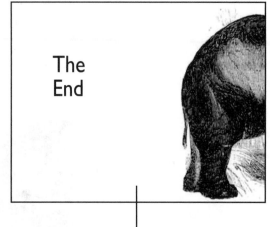

The End

This student uses texture (the detailed line drawing), and white space to communicate "the end" of a slide presentation.

The Challenge Activity

## Independent Activity

The Independent Activity asks you to pick your own project. You are encouraged to try this one because the information will be more meaningful and thus is likely to be more motivating. Some ideas include color-coding an organizational image, reformatting a document to make effective use of space (don't forget Hartley's "floating" page suggestion to make page breaks when content changes), adding texture to an image that seems flat and uninteresting.

## Justification Activity

Write a justification paper. Describe the following:

- *Your users and the assumptions you make about them (such as age, reading level, and assumed skills).*
- *Why you think your solution will work; include at least two ideas from the book, including page numbers and your interpretation of the passage used.*
- *What you learned from a "user-test" (have someone look at the image and verbalize their thoughts while looking at the image).*
- *The changes you will make based on user comments (or create a revised image).*

## K–12 Student Activity

Organize a series of photography lessons. For one lesson ask students to take pictures that incorporate texture—for example, students can take pictures of a similar object but each student would find a different way to incorporate texture into their composition. Continue this strategy with color, dimension, and space. Ask students to critique each other's work.

## REFERENCES

Boyle, C. (2001). *Color harmony for the web: A guide for creating great color schemes on-line*. Gloucester, MA: Rockport Publishers.

Chapman, W. (1993). Color coding and the interactivity of multimedia. *Journal of Educational Multimedia and Hypermedia, 2(1)*, 3–23.

Dwyer, F. M., & Lamberski, R. J. (1983). A review of the research on the effects of the use of color in the teaching–learning process. *International Journal of Instructional Media, 10*, 303–328.

Hartley, J. (1985). *Designing instructional text*. New York: Nichols.

Horton, W. (1991). Overcoming chromophobia: A guide to the confident and appropriate use of color. *IEEE Transactions on Professional Communication, 34(3)*, 160–171.

Horton, W. K. (1994). *The icon book: Visual symbols for computer systems and documentation*. New York: Wiley.

Livingston, L. A. (1991). The effect of color on performance in an instructional gaming environment. *Journal of Research on Computing in Education, 24*, 246–253.

Misanchuk, E., Schwier, R., & Boling, E. (2000). *CD-ROM, Visual design for instructional multimedia*. Self-published.

Nelson, R. P. (1989). *The design of advertising*. Dubuque, IA: William C. Brown.

Pett, D., & Wilson, T. (1996). Color research and its application to the design of instructional materials. *Educational Technology Research and Development, 44 (3)*, 19–35.

Shneiderman, B. (1992). *Designing the user interface: Strategies for effective human-computer interaction* (2nd ed.). Reading, MA: Addison-Wesley.

Tufte, E. R. (1990). *Envisioning information*. Cheshire, CT: Graphics Press.

# RESOURCES

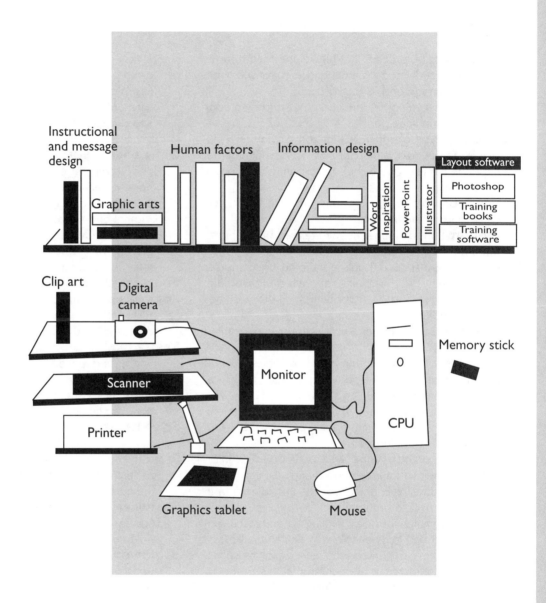

"I get by with a little help from my friends."

*The Beatles*

## NOTES ABOUT THE OPENING VISUAL

The opening visual shows a cartoon sketch of all the "things" you might want to have around as you create instructional visuals—from reference books and software to your computer and computer peripherals such as cameras, scanners, and printers. This visual is essentially an overview of the key topics covered in the chapter.

## KEY TERMS

**ANTI-ALIASING** A process that blends the rough edges of a rasterized image, creating a soft transition between the image and its background.

**BIT** The smallest unit of information processed by a computer; a computer signal.

**BROWSER** A type of software that can display information (graphics, text, animation) on the Internet; Internet Explorer, Firefox, and Safari are currently three popular browsers.

**CLIP ART** Line art or photographs found in books, on disks, and on the Internet.

**COLOR-DEPTH** The number of color-related bits (1-bit, 4-bit, 8-bit, 16-bit, and 24-bit) a pixel can store.

**COMPUTER GRAPHICS** Visuals generated by computer software with draw or paint capabilities. PowerPoint and Word have draw capabilities; Photoshop has paint capabilities.

**COPYRIGHT** Legal rights for reproducing a work granted by its creator.

**GRAPHIC FILE EXTENSION** The last three characters in a file name that designate a particular type of graphic format (for example, .bmp, .jpg, .eps, .tif, wmf).

**HARDWARE** The physical equipment—such as the monitor, central processing unit, printer, and scanner—that makes up a computer system.

**INTERNET AND WORLD WIDE WEB (WWW)** The information highway that is composed of a vast network of computers; the Web is the part of the Internet with which most people are familiar.

**LISTSERV** A commercial e-mail mailing list and discussion group subscribed to by people with similar interests; all members of the group receive the same e-mail messages.

**MEMORY** A computer component that stores data; examples of types of memory include RAM (random access memory), which provides temporary memory to run programs such as Microsoft Word and Adobe Illustrator, and ROM (read-only memory), used to store prerecorded data on computer chips and compact discs (as in CD-ROMs, DVDs, and other storage devices).

**OPEN SOURCE SOFTWARE** Software that can be downloaded without charge by those who want to use it (nonexperts) and those who want to revise it (programming experts). The term *open source* refers to the original code behind the software. Because programmers are allowed to modify it for specific purposes the software programs evolve into products believed to be better than traditional closed software.

**PIXEL** An abbreviation for picture element.

**PORT** A device that accepts data transferred to the computer, including wireless transfer as well as serial, parallel, USB, and IEEE 1394 transfer using cables.

**RASTER GRAPHICS** Graphics made up of a collection of pixels, and edited by changing pixels; also called *bitmap graphics*.

**RESOLUTION** Visual quality based on the number of pixels along the height and width of an image or display.

**SCANNER** A device that passes a light-emitting element across an image to capture it in digital format.

**SEARCH ENGINE** A program that finds information on the Internet based on keywords typed into a browser. The most notable examples are Google and Yahoo.

**SOFTWARE** Computer programs, like Microsoft Word or Adobe Illustrator, that provide the instructions that make the hardware work.

**VECTOR GRAPHICS** Graphics formed by vectors (mathematical formulas) and edited by changing the outlines and fills of a shape.

## INTRODUCTION

In the Practice activities that conclude each of the chapters in this book you will see references to the Resources section—a helpful guide to basic information on hardware, software, and other training resources. **Figure R–1** provides a good overview of topics and the chapters associated with them. The information in this chapter is more technical than the information provided in the other chapters. Specific information and "how to" instructions are found in two sections:

Part 1: The website activities: Five frequently asked questions (See Figure R–1 through Figure R–15)

| Question: | Use Figure: | Used for End-of-Chapter Activity |
|---|---|---|
| **1** What software programs should I use? | **R-2** | Chapter 1* |
| **2** What computer skills should I work on first? | | |
| ■ Learn to find and use Internet images. | **R-3** | Chapter 2* |
| ■ Learn to create tables. | **R-4** | Chapters 3, 6, 8 |
| ■ Learn to use simple shapes and graphic images. | **R-5** | |
| *Try ten composition tips.* | **R-6** | Chapters 5, 7, 11* |
| *Understand digital resolution, cameras, and scanners.* | **R-7** | Chapters 7, 10, 11* |
| *Learn to crop and adjust photos.* | **R-8** | Chapters 5, 11 |
| *Learn to use grids.* | **R-9** | Chapters 6, 7, 8* |
| *Learn to use and modify clip art.* | **R-10** | Chapters 5, 10* |
| ■ Learn to use type. | | |
| *Use text boxes.* | **R-11** | Chapter 9* |
| *Do text box project.* | **R-12** | Chapter 9 |
| *Avoid the font problem.* | **R-13** | Chapters 4, 9* |
| ■ Learn common computer toolbox icons | | |
| *Use toolbox icons for CARP.* | **R-14** | Chapters 4, 8, 11* |
| *Use the 80/20 rule to create CARP.* | **R-15** | Chapters 4, 8* |
| **3** How do I post my work in a distributed environment? (Later in this chapter) | No figure | |
| **4** How do I get help with the software? (Later in this chapter) | No figure | |
| **5** What do I need to know about copyright? (Later in this chapter) | No figure | |

* Information from figure will be applied in most activities.

**FIGURE R-1** Web Activity FAQs

# PART 1: THE WEBSITE ACTIVITIES: FIVE FREQUENTLY ASKED QUESTIONS

This section covers basic information to help you complete the book's website activities. Use Figure R-1 to quickly identify and scan information related to five frequently asked questions. Additional information is provided in the text below as well.

## Question 1. What software programs (PowerPoint, Illustrator, Word, Photoshop) should I use?

Figure R–2 shows a variety of graphic software programs and describes the differences between Draw, Paint, and Layout programs. Educator discounts allow you to purchase these programs at significantly reduced prices. If your resources are limited and you do not mind learning on your own, you might try the open source graphics programs listed as alternative options in Figure R-2. Open source programs are free and can be located using an Internet search engine.

Recently Smart Draw, a new software program for PCs, enables you to bypass both Draw and Paint programs when you design instructional materials. To learn more about the product, try a free trial version at *http://www.smartdraw.com/specials/education.asp,* and explore the options for receiving an educator discount.

Knowing which graphics program to learn and use depends on how much skill you currently have and how much skill you need to develop. If you are new to computers and visual design, consider using PowerPoint or Microsoft Word or try the trial version of Smart Draw. If you have some experience and want to learn skills that will allow you to do more advanced work with greater flexibility, consider learning Adobe Illustrator, Adobe Photoshop, and Macromedia Flash (for animation). It is beyond the scope of this book to teach you how to use these programs, but the Companion Website for this book does have a "Links" page that will direct you to self-paced instructional tutorials.

## Question 2. Which computer design skills should I work on first?

Figure R-3 through Figure R-15 address how to obtain information for the following five computer skills.

1. Finding and using Internet images
2. Creating tables
3. Using simple shapes and graphic images
4. Using type
5. Using common computer toolbox icons

These figures cover most of what you will need to complete the chapter activities. Some of these topics however need more information and are covered below.

### Using Type

As you read in Chapter 9, one of the quickest most visual tools that is easy to learn, copyright free, and at your disposal is type. Learn how to use text blocks (sometimes called text boxes) right away. All graphics programs have a text block/box tool. When you type words into text boxes, you can easily move them around wherever you want. This gives you visual power because you can control spatial arrangements. The ability to "A"lign information and change the "P"roximity of text (the A and P of CARP), allows you to create stronger messages (review Chapter 8, which discusses CARP, for more information). PowerPoint and Illustrator are good tools for learning how to use text blocks because they allow you to create them quickly. You can also use text blocks in page layout programs with similar ease. At the bottom of Figure R-11 you find a practice activity asking you to arrange three text blocks.

### Understanding Resolution, Digital Cameras, and Scanners

Resolution becomes important not only for scanners and digital cameras but for any type of computer display. Some projects such as printed documents, require a high resolution in order to look good. Other projects, such as websites, look fine with a low resolution.

The number of pixels measured across the width and length of an image determines resolution. An image with a resolution of 1,280 pixels $\times$ 1,280 pixels has a total of more than 1 million pixels (1,280 pixels $\times$ 1,280 pixels = 1,305,600 pixels) and is measured in megapixels. An image with 2 million pixels has a resolution of 2 megapixels, and so on. The more pixels that make up an image, the better the image quality.

It might help to think of pixels this way. Imagine that you are holding up a wire mesh screen. Wherever wire threads intersect, you have a square. Think of each square as a pixel. Consider that you have two types of screens, one with 100 squares, and another with 200 squares. Suppose you are looking through these two screens at the same marble (see Figure R-7). Each square in the 200-wire mesh screen captures a smaller unit of detail in the marble than does the other screen. The same thing happens when images are digitized. When you are able to capture a dark blue in one square and a light blue in the one next to it, your final picture will have more precision than if you capture a blend of the two, which is what happens with digital cameras and other imaging devices. The quality of your output is dependent on how many pixels your digital device can capture. The more pixels you have, the better your display quality.

How much resolution you need is determined by how you plan to display images. If you intend to use your images for the Internet, your resolution does not need to exceed much more than 72 to 96 pixels per inch (PPI), since higher resolution is matched by longer load times that are generally disliked in online settings. Printed images need higher resolution and are measured in dots per inch (DPI), which refers to the number of dots of ink used to print text and graphics; the more dots, the better and sharper the image. For most print applications, a 600 DPI or higher is the new standard. Pixels per inch and dots per inch are many times used interchangeably and both measure image resolution—how a device, such as a monitor, displays an image. The quality of the image on screen is determined by the number of pixels that can be displayed in a given area. For our purpose, DPI and PPI are the same thing, they are the number of little dots that make up the image. To put in perspective, if you want to shoot a 4 $\times$ 6 inch photo that is print quality (300 DPI), you will need 300 pixels for every inch of output. You will need a 1200 (3 $\times$ 400) $\times$ 1800 (6 $\times$ 300) pixel image. If you multiply the two numbers you get the resolution you will need from a digital camera: 1200 $\times$ 1800 = 2,160,000 pixels, or 2.16 megapixels. You will want a digital camera with at least 2.6 megapixels to make a 4 $\times$ 6 inch photo.

### Scanners and Digital Cameras

Scanners and digital cameras make more sense when you understand resolution. There are many useful and creative ways that these tools can be used. Your scanner can create images from a number of things:

- photographs
- drawings
- sketches
- objects like pencils, fabrics, nails, and more

Scanners are a good way to add visual depth to your instructional materials. By depth I mean the detail and shadows that can make information look real or more noticeable. When you scan, you are essentially taking a picture of the object you are scanning, and in the process you get a lot of visual detail.

Digital cameras are also a good way to add visuals to your instruction, and they are particularly handy for personalizing instruction. Not only can you take pictures of the exact training or school environment, but you can take pictures of the trainees or students, too.

Digital cameras operate like scanners. You take a picture (the scan) and then move the picture from the scan into your computer. There are several ways to do this, and it is getting easier as the technology improves. The oldest method is to hook the camera up to the computer using a cable that uploads (sends the image from the camera to the computer) using one of several ports (devices that accept the image data). The most common ports are serial ports (older and slower); parallel ports (commonly used for printers); universal serial bus (USB) ports, which are newer and faster; wireless ports (transferred using infrared technology); and IEEE 1394 ports. Depending upon the camera, you either operate software that transfers the images from the camera to the computer or the technology does this for you with the press of a button. Printers today are accepting images directly from camera disks, making it easy to print images.

Most new cameras allow you to save your images directly onto removable disks (also called removable memory), which include inch computer disks, CD-ROMs, DVDs, smaller camera-specific disks (also called cards), and memory sticks. When removed, these disks fit into a CD-ROM drive, or some type of peripheral designed specifically for the card, or into a USB port.

Digital images are saved in a number of different formats. Table R–1 lists some common formats by their graphic file extension and where they are used.

**TABLE R–1**   *Some Common File Extensions and Their Uses*

| Extension | Name | Used in |
|---|---|---|
| .bmp | Bitmap | **Electronic presentations** (Microsoft PowerPoint) |
| | | **Documents** (Microsoft Word) |
| | | **CD-ROMs** and multimedia not used over the Internet |
| .eps | Encapsulated PostScript | **Print publications and illustrations** |
| .gif | Graphics Interchange Format | **Web-based documents** for images that have a continuous or flat color |
| .jpeg | Joint Photographic Experts Group | **Web-based documents** for photographic images or images that have noncontinuous colors and a variety of shades or gradations |
| .png | Portable Network Graphics | **Web-based documents** for images similar to .gif files but without any copyright/licensing issues |
| .pdf | Portable Document Format | **Electronic** documents for both computer screen and page output; maintains the "look" of the original document by embedding fonts |
| .tiff | Tagged Image File Format | **Print documents** when high quality and precision is required; tiff files can be changed (made either larger or smaller) without losing precision |

*Note:* Consider investing in clip art, just to make it easy for yourself to find images. You often pay very little for thousands of images.

## Question 3. How do I turn in projects in a distributed learning environment (BlackBoard, ECollege, WebCT and the like?)

Generally you turn in your visual projects by attaching them to a message or thread. If your files have a .gif or .jpg extension, everyone will be able to view them. Remember that the other people in the class may need to have the same software you used to create the images in order to look at them. Most people learn this when they use an unusual font in a presentation and find out that none of their classmates can see the font they chose. This happens when class members do not have that particular font resident in their system. The five things you can do to amend the problem are included in Figure R–13.

## Question 4. How do I get help using software?

Use the help file for your application! Even though people say "help files aren't helpful," they can lead you to solutions, even if it does not happen as fast as you would like. Help files allow you to search using an index or by typing in a search term. You will probably jump from topic to topic to locate an exact answer. Sometimes it is a good idea to move on, and do something else, because eventually you will stumble into the answer. You can also call or email the software's technical support center. Try typing the software name in a search engine. You can also refer to books mentioned in Figure R–16.

## Question 5. What do I need to know about copyright?

The most accurate source of information regarding copyright can be found at the Library of Congress website *lcWeb.loc.gov/copyright/circs/circ21.pdf*. Copyright is a very difficult topic to discuss with any certainty and this government publication does the best job of describing the issues and their complexity.

The easiest way to understand copyright is to imagine yourself as someone who has created something that others want. Do you want your work to be used by others or not? Do you want to give others the permission to copy and redistribute your work? Do you want to be financially compensated or recognized? Copyright laws allow you to legally make these decisions and to seek compensation when others use your work without permission. Copyright is a form of protection provided by the laws of the United States to creators of original works of authorship. When you copyright your work, you alone can authorize the reproduction of any type of instruction (print, video, images, etc.) you create. You can protect yourself in the event that people try to use your work without permission.

You may be surprised to learn that anything you create is automatically considered copyright protected the moment it is created. Copyright is secured when your work becomes concrete, either visually or aurally (through some type of auditory device), including images, books, manuals, computer training videos, and computer-based training units. You do not have to mark your work with a copyright symbol or register your work with the U.S. Copyright Office to gain protection. You do, however, have the option of including a copyright symbol or notice on your work. The copyright notice basically informs the public that your work is copyrighted. You also may choose to register your copyright with the U.S. Copyright Office (*www. loc.gov/copyright*). The key advantage to including a copyright notice and registering your copyright is extra legal protection.

If you are confused at this point about what you have to gain from copyright protection, you are not alone. Copyright laws are somewhat ambiguous. On the one hand the law states that anything you create is considered copyrighted, which means you are automatically legally protected the moment you create something. You do not need to mark it with copyright symbols or register it with the U.S. Copyright Office for the materials to be considered legally protected. On the other hand, however, the U.S. Copyright Office suggests registering the copyright for extra security in a court of law. By registering your copyright you make it part of public record and secure extra protection in a court of law. The exact value of a copyright seems somewhat vague. One wonders about the legal strength of an unregistered copyright. Perhaps the best advice is to play it safe and include a copyright notice and register the copyright when warranted.

You might also wonder what is and is not considered copyrighted. The following are copyrightable:

- literary works
- musical works
- dramatic works
- pantomimes and choreographic works
- pictorial, graphic, and sculptural works
- motion pictures and other audiovisual works
- sound recordings
- architectural works

The following are not copyrightable:

- nontangible work (work that is not visible, recorded, or aural)
- titles, names, short phrases, and slogans
- familiar symbols or designs
- mere variations of typographic ornamentation, lettering, or coloring
- mere listings of ingredients or contents
- ideas, procedures, methods, systems, processes, concepts, principles, discoveries, or devices, as distinguished from a description, explanation, or illustration
- common information (for example, standard calendars, height and weight charts, tape measures and rulers, and lists or tables taken from public documents or other common sources)

## Following Copyright Laws When Creating Not-for-Profit Work

Although copyright owners have the power to limit use of their work, a "fair use" exemption to the copyright law allows educators and students a looser interpretation of the law if the materials they use promote learning, scholarly activity, and free speech or discussion, and if they meet certain conditions. The law lists the following factors as critical for determining whether a particular use of a copyrighted work is a permitted fair use:

- the purpose and character of the use, including whether such use is of a commercial nature or is for nonprofit educational purposes;
- the nature of the copyrighted work;
- the amount and substantiality of the portion used in relation to the copyrighted work as a whole; and
- the effect of the use upon the potential market for or value of the copyrighted work. (See the copyright and fair use website at Stanford University, *www.fairuse.stanford. edu.*)

This fair use exemption, like the rest of the copyright law, is quite vague and open to interpretation. In order to help educators be adequately sure that they are not in violation of the copyright law, various groups of publishers and educators (the consortium of College and University Multimedia Centers, for one) have assembled to create a set of fair use guidelines. If educators stay within these guidelines, they can be reasonably sure they are acting legally and have the backing of this large group of publishers and educators. In a nutshell, nonconsumable materials (nonprofit) have the following fair use guidelines:

## Print Materials

Teachers or trainers are generally allowed the following:

- a single copy of any type of print materials (an article, a poem, an illustration)
- multiple copies (not exceeding the number of students in the class) only when a spontaneity condition is met (the teacher uses the materials at the "last minute")
- a limit of 250 words for a poem that is distributed under the spontaneity exception
- 10 percent (or a maximum of 1,000 words) of prose distributed under the spontaneity exception.

If in doubt, seek copyright permission from the publisher of the work. A form is available for requests at the Copyright Clearance Center; you can call (978) 750-8400 or go to *www.copyright. com*. You will need to specify the title, author, and/or editor, and edition, the exact number of pages and copies, page numbers and chapters used, how you plan to use the information, what form it will be in (classroom handout, newsletter, etc.), and whether the material will be sold.

## Software

One backup of a computer program is permitted; language modification is approved if a language-specific program is not available. A copy of software is not permitted over a network nor is making multiple backups.

## Multimedia

Students and teachers may use copyrighted multimedia materials that are referenced and included under the fair use exemption of the U.S. Copyright law. Copyrighted materials may be used for education, portfolios for future employment, or evaluation materials. Educators and students may use the following:

- materials for up to two years after the first instructional use without receiving permission to use the copyrighted material
- 10 percent or 3 minutes of motion media
- 30 seconds of music
- Five images per artist
- 2,500 fields in a database

These rules apply to distance learning environments as well. For example, if a person wants to post several paintings on his website, the fair use law allows him legally to do that if he meets all the criteria; he should use no more than five images per artist and show the images no longer than two years. Since the person is not using the images to make a profit, his reproductions of those works should be permitted.

## For-Profit Work

If you are creating instructional material for profit, you are advised to consider carefully the copyright laws and receive permission of the copyright owner to do any of the following:

- reproduce the work
- prepare derivatives of the work
- distribute copies of the work
- display the work publicly

In general, if a work has been in the public domain for more than 75 years, it is considered legal to use without a fee. As with all the copyright provisions, however, the rules are difficult to interpret, and it may be hard to determine the age of an image or its copyright status without a great deal of work. If the image is in a book that is more than 75 years old, then the image could be assumed to be copyright free, unless some organization or individual who has extended the copyright status assumes that image's copyright. For example, if the book is 75 years old, but the creator of the image is still alive, then the image would not be considered copyright free.

In many cases, you may not know when the work was created, who created the image, whether the creator or creators registered the image, and whether the creator or creators are still alive. Copyright laws are based upon whether the image was created before or after January 1, 1978, and whether the creator was an individual, several individuals, or a sponsoring organization or party. In addition to these facts, in order to determine copyright status, you must know whether the work was registered and by what date, as well as if the authors are still alive.

Works originally created on or after January 1, 1978, are copyright protected from the moment of creation plus an additional 70 years after the author's death. Stanford University's copyright and fair use website (*www.fairuse.stanford.edu*) offers this guideline: In the case of "a joint work prepared by two or more authors who did not work for hire," the term lasts for 70 years after the last surviving author's death. For works made for hire, and for anonymous and pseudonymous works (unless the author's identity is revealed in Copyright Office records), the duration of copyright will be 95 years from publication or 120 years from creation, whichever is shorter.

Works originally created before January 1, 1978, but not published or registered by that date are now given federal copyright protection: the life-plus-70 or 95/120-year terms stated previously apply to them as well. The law provides that in no case will the term of copyright for works in this category expire before December 31, 2002, and for works published on or before December 31, 2002, the term of copyright will not expire before December 31, 2047.

The laws for copyright for works that were created and copyright registered prior to January 1, 1978, are somewhat difficult to interpret. Copyright status can last anywhere from 28 years to a total term protection of 95 years, based upon renewal extension status. Most works are copyright protected for at least 75 years, but under certain conditions a total protection of 95 years applies. Therefore, it can be difficult for an individual to determine.

Because of the potential risk, the advice is to use only images you know to be copyright free. Since this book in part teaches you how to use digital technology to create instructional visuals, you are more than aware of the ease in which you can revise an original work beyond recognition. It is fairly easy to scan a photograph out of a magazine and make enough changes to make the work unrecognizable even to the original artist/creator. Most individuals feel that in altering an image, a new and completely different image has been created, thus justifying the practice. In the end, the decision to alter or not becomes one that is often made in the context of expedience. You must get a project done quickly and to do so requires a little "cheating." In all likelihood, you will not be sued for changing an image beyond recognition; however, I urge you to avoid the temptation. Plenty of available copyright-free images can be modified beyond recognition. It is always best to err on the side of caution.

You should also be aware that some clip art is not as "free" as it may appear. Be sure to read the fine print that accompanies clip art to make sure it is also royalty free, meaning you do not have to pay to use it. You will often find the fine print on the CD-ROM envelope or jacket cover. Some clip art companies require their permission to use their images in for-profit endeavors, even if they are educational. For example, a clip art manufacturer is not likely to give you permission to create a website where people can download their clip art. Some clip art manufacturers also will not let their clip art make up a substantial portion of your product.

# PART 2: RESOURCES FOR DEVELOPMENT OF INSTRUCTIONAL MATERIALS

Part 2 is divided into two sections: (1) training resources, and (2) understanding the computer and its peripherals. The figures that accompany these sections are self explanatory. See Figure R-16 for a list of books and training materials related to the information covered in this textbook. See Figures R-17 and R-18 to review basic information about computers and input and output devices.

*This list of software represents the most widely used layout programs. Other programs are available but are not as well known.*

# Draw Software

Adobe Illustrator, CorelDraw, Freehand, Macromedia Flash, and Microsoft Word art tools, as well as flowchart/idea mapping programs, such as Inspiration that allow you to create and easily adjust logical and conceptual visualizations. Inkscape, an open source program, is another draw program that you can download for free from the Internet.

# Paint Software

Adobe Photoshop, Corel Painter, Paint Shop Pro. GIMP is an open source paint program that you can download for free from the Internet. Photo-editing software also falls in this category.

## Image Characteristics

Like a line drawing, very clear edges.

Like a photograph. fuzzy edges. If you look closely at the edges of the graphic, you see pixel edges, called "jaggies" because of their zigzag appearance.

## When to Use

Draw programs create vector/object oriented graphics, good for typography, shapes, and line artwork, especially when printing and resizing is needed.

Paint programs create bitmap/raster graphics, good for showing lots of detail (as in photographs) and for having very small file sizes when saved in .jpeg and .gif formats. Bitmap images are not as good as vector images for printing, and they do not resize well when increased.

## How to Create

You create vector graphics by drawing outlines. These outlines are based upon mathematical formulas.

You create raster/bitmap images with a digitized paintbrush.

## How to Edit

Vector graphics are edited by changing the edges of the outline. Some skill is required to work with the Bezier curves and handles that allow you to make these changes.

Raster graphics are edited using erasers, paintbrushes, and smudge tools that are used to edit the image's pixels. Editing with these tools is fairly intuitive, working much like real-world pencils and paintbrushes. A feature called anti-aliasing removes some of the jagged edges of raster images by creating a soft transition between an image and its background.

## How to Save

Save images as file.eps, file.wmf, file.pict, file.cdr *(see Table R-1)*.

Save images as file.bmp, file.tiff, file.pcx, file.pct, file.pnt *(see Table R-1)*.

# Layout Software for Draw and Paint Images

These programs make it easy to combine text and graphics for print publications (PageMaker, QuarkXPress, Microsoft Publisher, Adobe InDesign). Web and computer based presentation layout programs include FrontPage, Dreamweaver, Authorware, Illustrator, Freehand, CorelDraw. "Scribus" is an open source desktop publishing program that you can download free from the Internet. With all of these layout programs, you import text and images and adjust their layout and the order of presentation.

**FIGURE R–2** What software programs should I use?

*Instructions will vary depending upon software, computer system, and browser type.

## How do you find images on the Internet?

**1**. Use a search engine that has an image search. Try www.Google.com and others.

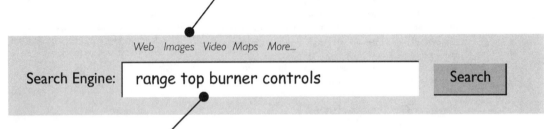

Web  *Images  Video  Maps  More...*

Search Engine:  range top burner controls     Search

**2**. Type in your search term.

**3**. Select the image you want, right click (control right click for Mac) and save the file to your computer desktop.

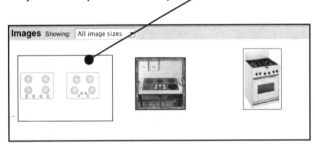

**Images** Showing: All image sizes

## How do you place images in your document?

**4**. Open your document and select Insert > Picture > From File **from the drop-down menu.**

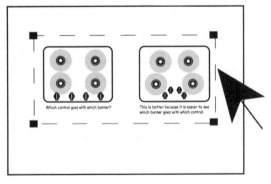

Select the image and move it where you like. (This is easier to do in PowerPoint than in Word.)

**FIGURE R-3**  Finding and using internet images*

Displaying information in tables is an excellent way to organize data hierarchically. The horizontal (rows) and vertical (columns) planes allow you to format information in superordinate, subordinate, and coordinate formats. Six steps for creating a table in a word processing program follow. Word processing programs will vary, so consult the Help file in your software program when needed.

**I.** Analyze your data. Identify superordinate, coordinate, and subordinate levels of information.

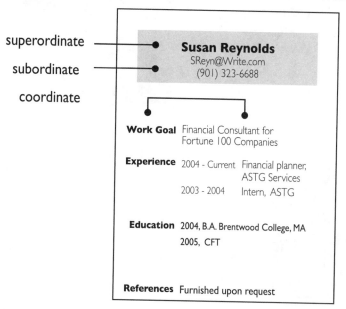

**2.** Sketch out table to estimate the number of rows and columns needed. (*Note*: You can easily add or delete rows or columns later.)

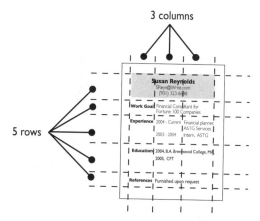

**3.** Create the table by entering the number of rows and columns needed. To do this, select Table > Insert > Table from the drop-down menu. When prompted, enter the number of rows and columns needed.

**4.** Type information into the rows and columns.

**5.** Add or delete rows or columns by selecting Table > Insert/Delete > Columns/Rows from the drop-down menu.

**6.** Add rules and shading if needed, by selecting Select Format > Border and then choosing bordered or shaded areas when prompted.

**FIGURE R–4**  *Learning to create tables*

These tips will help you compose any visual, not just photographs. Rarely will you be able to apply all ten tips in any one image.

## 1. Capture relative size

Here the image helps you see the respective sizes of the baby and Mickey Mouse.

1/3    1/3    1/3

1/3

1/3

1/3

## 2. Use the two-thirds rule

Focus your image near the imagined intersection of horizontal and vertical lines that divide your image into thirds.

## 3. Consider background

Pay attention to background objects that might create a distraction. Here the two bikers look like two elk. The father/daughter image on the left does a better job of establishing a background.

## 4. Get close

Zoom in on the subjects of interest. The photographer considers the father, daughter, and azaleas important in the image above. The photographer focuses attention on the baseball player in the image below.

## 5. Capture depth

Find foreground and background compositions. Here the chain-link fence communicates the distance between the child and fence. Use diagonals when possible, as you see here in the lines of the fence.

**FIGURE R–5**    Ten composition tips

## 6. Capture color contrast

Here the bird and seashore create a good contrast to the dark color of the sand.

## 7. Use lighting

Take pictures that show contrast in light and dark colors. Early morning and late afternoon are good times to take pictures because shadows and light work together to create contrasts and depth.

## 8. Capture natural poses

This image is interesting because it captures a young girl as she is running. A posed picture would be much less effective.

## 9. Find frames

Here a window (in the process of construction) frames a view of the backyard.

## 10. Use texture

The grass surrounding the cow provides a textured background, and creates interest and depth.

**FIGURE R–6**  Ten composition tips

# Resolution

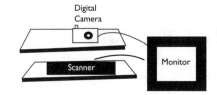

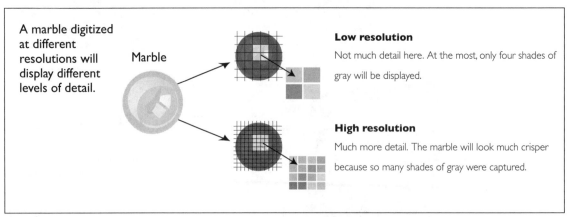

A marble digitized at different resolutions will display different levels of detail.

Marble

**Low resolution**

Not much detail here. At the most, only four shades of gray will be displayed.

**High resolution**

Much more detail. The marble will look much crisper because so many shades of gray were captured.

# Scanners

General Instructions (check your scanner manual for specific information)

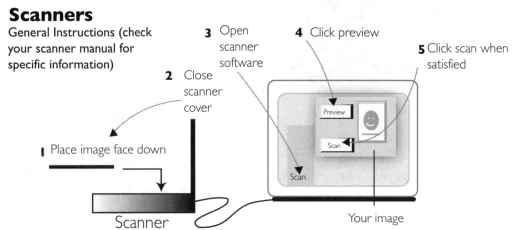

**1** Place image face down

**2** Close scanner cover

**3** Open scanner software

**4** Click preview

**5** Click scan when satisfied

Scanner

Your image

# Digital Cameras

General Instructions (check your digital camera manual for specific information)

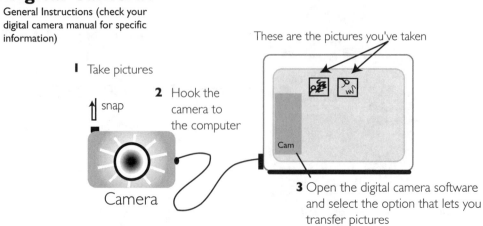

**1** Take pictures

snap

**2** Hook the camera to the computer

Camera

These are the pictures you've taken

Cam

**3** Open the digital camera software and select the option that lets you transfer pictures

**FIGURE R–7**   Resolution, digital cameras, and scanners

You can facilitate **learner selection** by focusing attention on the most important part of an image and by increasing the contrast between figure/ground images. Most photo editing programs have crop and adjustment tools to help you do this. The icons and palettes shown below may not look identical to those in your program, but they will share similar features. Search "crop" or "adjust" in your Help file for specific instructions.

| The crop tool | The adjustment tool |
|---|---|

The crop tool lets you select a section of your photo that you want the learner to focus on. Everything outside of the selection edges is removed.

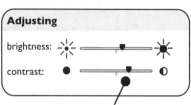

Moving the sliders will change the degree of brightness and contrast in an image.

**FIGURE R–8**    Learning to crop and adjust photos

## Use Help

Type "grid" in your software program Help file to learn how to align text and objects along grid lines. By default, objects and text will "snap" to the lines of an invisible grid. Try the following for additional support.

### For word processing programs*

1. On the Drawing toolbar, click **Draw**, and then click **Grid.**

2. Do one of the following:

   - To automatically align objects on an invisible grid, select the **Snap objects to grid** check box.

   - To automatically align objects with grid lines that go through the vertical and horizontal edges of other shapes, select the **Snap objects to other objects** check box.

### For electronic presentation programs*

1. On the Drawing toolbar, click **Draw,** and then point to **Snap.**

2. Do one of the following:

   - To automatically align objects on a grid, **point to Grid, and check to see that it is selected** (it will have a check mark next to it).

   - To automatically align objects with grid lines that go through the vertical and horizontal edges of other shapes, click **To Shape.**

### For drawing programs*

1. On the View toolbar, click **Show Grid** or **Snap to Grid.**

2. Do one of the following:

   - On the View toolbar, click **Show Rulers.**
   - On the View toolbar, click **Show Guides.**
   - Click on ruler edge, hold down and drag guideline onto page.

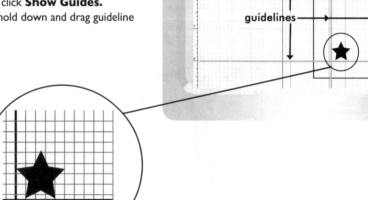

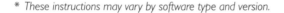

\* *These instructions may vary by software type and version.*

**FIGURE R–9**　Learning to use grids

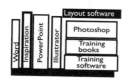

# How do you customize images?

recolor, duplicate, resize

add a drop shadow

distort

frame and rotate

add emotions

You can easily change clip art to match your instructional purpose. In addition to the images you see on the right, you can try different fills and filter effects (making strokes look like they are paint, crayon, pastels, for example). Use the words above as search terms in Paint and Draw program Help files.

## K–12 Example  Geography

A teacher created this graphic to emphasize the distance between Australia and North America.

**1** Clip-art is located.

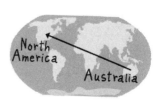

**2** Distracting information is eliminated. Use the eraser icon, paintbrush icon, or magic wand icon.

**3** An arrow and the words *Australia* and *North America* are added.

**FIGURE R–10**  Learning to use and modify clip art

Learn to use text boxes, a feature that allows you to place text anywhere on a page, screen, or slide.
Text boxes allow you to create customized and more effective images. The following instructions are generic for
Illustrator,[T] Photoshop, and Word[T]. These instructions may need to be altered based on the particular version of
the software package that you use. If you cannot find these tools, use your Help file and do searches on the words
"Text," "Toolbar," and "Selection."

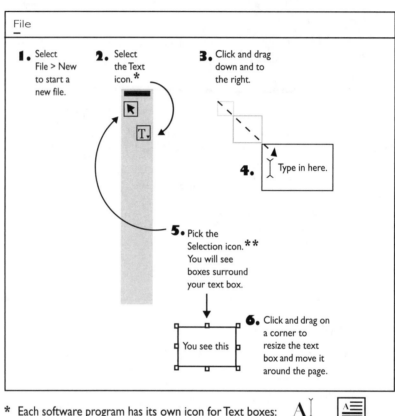

* Each software program has its own icon for Text boxes:

** Each software program has its own Selection icon:

**Exercise**
Use three text boxes to create this image.

**FIGURE R–11**   Using text boxes

These are some of the basic steps for completing the Chapter 9 Web Activity in PowerPoint.

## Completed Project

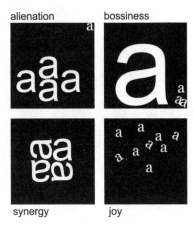

alienation          bossiness

synergy          joy

## Step 1:
### Start with a blank PowerPoint template.

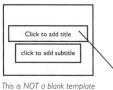

*This is NOT a blank template because it has textblocks.*

You will not be using any of the fields or textblocks that automatically show up when you open a PowerPoint file. The te field/blocks will get in the way of your design because they limit your ability to place things.

Select (click on) each textblock and delet the field.

## Step 2:
### Draw 4 black boxes.

*Note: The tools can be tricky to find. Try the View > Toolbars pulldown menu. Also use the program's Help file and search on words like Paint Bucket, or Square.*

Draw one box using the square tool. Hold down the Shift key to make the box a true square.

Make sure box is selected and click the paint bucket icon to make one black square.

Select the black square

Copy it. Paste it three times to make three more boxes.

Align the four boxes to look like the image on the left.

Group the boxes using the group tool.

## Step 3:
### Add type inside box.

alienation

Select type tool. A

Type title (alienation).

While selected, choose font and size.

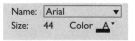

| Name: | Arial | ▼ |
|---|---|---|
| Size: | 44 | Color A ▼ |

Arrange with selection tool.

Type letter. Use paint bucket to paint letter white.

Copy and paste as needed.

Group your work.

Repeat process to complete work.

**FIGURE R-12**   Practicing: A text box project

## The problem

Sometimes your font does not show up for other people.

| **This is what you want people to see...** | **...but this may be what they actually see:** |
|---|---|
|  | 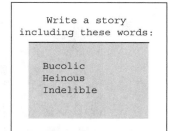 |
| You used the fonts Gill Sans, Harrington, Chiller, and Broadway. | The computer substituted the Courier font because it could not find the fonts you used. |

## Five Solutions: From easiest to most difficult

**1.** Use fonts that are resident on all (PCs and Macintosh) computers: Georgia, Verdana, Trebuchet.

**2.** Save your file in a PDF format or embed fonts in the presentation (available as a "Save As" option in some programs).

**3.** Take your text and images into a more powerful graphics program (such as Photoshop) and convert them to raster (bitmap) images. Some programs have an "Outline" or "Rasterize" feature that changes fonts into bitmaps that everyone can view.

**4.** Take a snapshot of your image using the Print Screen key (PC, top row of keyboard) or the Grab Utility (Macintosh, use Find to locate the Grab utility). After you have captured the image, open your document and "Paste." You may want to use a crop tool to remove sections of your image.

**5.** E-mail the font. You must find a way to download the font and attach it to an e-mail.

**FIGURE R–13**   Posting your projects: Avoiding the "font" problem

## K–12 Example Language Arts

Basic toolbox icons are used to create a slide that teaches the role of adjectives in modifying nouns.

### Step 1

Use type and selection icons to create box.

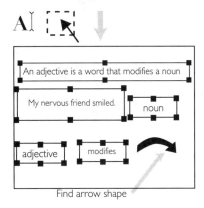

Find arrow shape

### Step 2 **A**lignment

Use the center alignment icon.

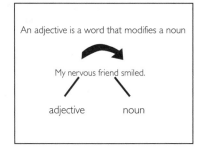

### Step 3 **R**epetition

Use type tool to type individual letters of "modify" that can be aligned to arrow curve (repeats shape of curve).

Repeat use of ALL CAPS on "adjective" and "noun" (to convey their equal status).

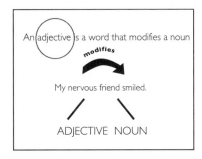

### Step 4 **P**roximity

Use selection to move "adjective" and "noun" closer to "nervous" and "friend".

### Step 5 **C**ontrast

Use the paint bucket tool to create dark grey rectangle and darker gray circle.

Select **Object > Arrange > Send to back** to move gray rectangle to bottom layer (so words and other elements are on top).

Use character palette to change fonts and colors as shown in image below.

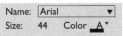

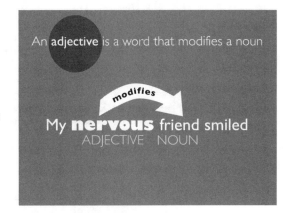

**FIGURE R-14**   Using toolbox icons for CARP

You use 20 percent of the items on a drawing toolbar 80 percent of the time. Those toolbar items are ones that help you contrast align, repeat, and move things close or far away (proximity). Keep in mind that icons will not look the same from application to application. In general, the icons below are similar to what you find in most graphic software programs.

# Contrast

■ *Contrast type*
Use the type icon and character panel to change words and letters.

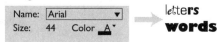

■ *Contrast color*
Use the bucket icon to change colors.

■ *Contrast size*
Use the Shift key on the keyboard with selection icon. Shift, select object, and drag to change sizes.

■ *Contrast shape*
Use different shapes to change form.

# Alignment

■ Use the alignment icons to line things up along horizontal and vertical planes.

■ Use rulers, grids, and guidelines.

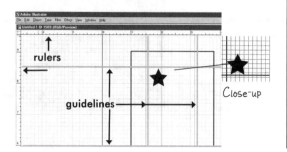

# Repetition

■ *Repeat shapes, type, and colors.*
Use the copy and paste icons.

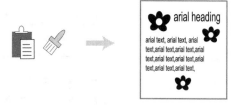

# Proximity

■ *Move related items close together and unrelated items apart.*
Use the selection icon and move images (text and graphics) close or far apart.

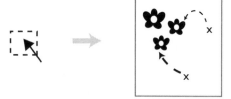

Use text boxes.

1. Type words with type icon.

   words words

2. Select words with selection icon.

3. Select text box and move it.

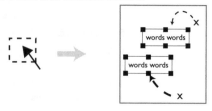

**FIGURE R-15**  Using the 80/20 rule for CARP

Part 2: Resources for development of instructional materials (Figure R–16 through Figure R–18)

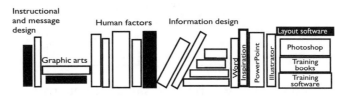

# Further Reading *Listed in alphabetical order by category*

## Psychology

The Psychology of Graphic Images: Seeing, Drawing, Communicating, 2002
Manfredo Massironi
London: Lawrence Erlbaum Associates
Overview: Intensive examination of graphics and perceptual/cognitive processes

## Human Factors

Don't Make Me Think, 2005
Steven Krug
Indianapolis, IN: city, state: New Rider's Press
Overview: A book you will easily understand and will use immediately

Designing Web Usability, 2000
J. Nielson
New Riders Publishing
Overview: Teaches the importance of simplicity; though written for the Web, applies to most design

Envisioning Information, 1990
Edward Tufte
Cheshire, CT: Graphics Press
Overview: Timeless information design advice; beautiful book design

The Design of Everyday Things, 1988
D.A. Norman
New York: Doubleday
Overview: You'll see the world (especially doors) differently after reading this book

The Cognitive Style of PowerPoint: Pitching Out Corrupts Within, 2006
Edward Tufte www.edwardtufte.com
Cheshire, CT: Graphics Press
Overview: Provoking commentary on thoughtless use of slideware

The Visual Display of Quantitative Information, 1983
Edward Tufte
Cheshire, CT: Graphics Press
Overview: The book on data integrity

Universal Principles of Design: 100 Ways to Enhance Usability, Influence Perception, Increase Appeal, Make Better Design Decisions, and Teach Through Design, 2003
W. Lidwell, K. Holden, and J. Butler
Gloucester, MA.: Rockport Publications
Overview: The title says it all.

Visual Explanations: Images and Quantities, Evidence and Narrative, 1997
Edward Tufte
Cheshire, CT: Graphics Press
Overview: Gripping information design examples and analysis

## Graphic Arts

Color Harmony for the Web, 2001
C. Boyle
Gloucester, MA: Rockport Publishers
Overview: You will keep this book by your computer. Great color combinations!

The Non-Designer's Design Book: Design and Typographic Principles for the Visual Novice, 1994
R. Williams
Berkeley, CA: Addison-Wesley
Overview: A classic on the simple power of contrast, alignment, repetition, and proximity

Understanding Comics: The Invisible Art, 1993
S. McLoud
New York: HarperPerrennial
Overview: Scott McLoud comes as close as anyone to describing a visual language. Written in a comic book style, each frame speaks a thousand words

## Education

Graphics for Learning, 2004
Ruth Clark and Chopeta Lyons
New York: Wiley
Overview: Integrates visual design into the broader context of Instructional Development, particularly applicable to business contexts

Multimedia Learning, 2001
Richard Mayer
Cambridge, England: Cambridge University Press
Overview: Shares seven research based multimedia principles

## Training (books)

"Hand's On" training series by Lynda Weinman
"Classroom Book" series by Adobe

## Training (tutorials)

Search www.adobe.com; www.macromedia.com; www.corel.com; www.microsoft.com
Search "(software name) tutorials" in search engine

## Websites

http://www.copyright.gov/circs/circ21.pdf (for fair use guidelines)

### Professional Organizations*

International Visual Literacy Association (IVLA)  www.ivla.org
A not-for-profit association of educators, artists, and researchers dedicated to the principles of visual literacy.

American Institute of Graphic Arts (AIGA)  www.aiga.org
A place professionals turn to exchange ideas and information, participate in critical analysis and research, and advance education and ethical practice.

Human Computer Interaction International (HCII)
www.hci-international.org
A conference series related to  human computer interaction and information society technologies.

* Join organization LISTSERVS to learn more and meet other professionals who share your interests.

**FIGURE R-16**  Books and training

 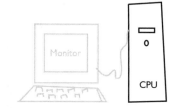

Would you know what the sales tag means?

Let's take it line by line:

### 3.6 GHz Processor

This refers to the speed of the CPU — the core of your computer system, often called the system's brain. Speed is measured in megahertz and gigahertz, which refer to the number of bytes processed per cycle.

### 500 GB Hard Drive

This tells you how much information you can save or store on your hard drive. Your computer programs will take up some of this space, along with the files you create. The table below explains kilobytes, megabytes, and gigabytes.

> 1 Kilobyte (KB) = 1,000 bytes
> The text-only version of this chapter is approximately 45 KB
>
> 1 Megabyte (MB) = 1,000 KB
> The 300 dpi version of this page (an Adobe Illustrator file) is 4 MB
>
> 1 Gigabyte (GB)= 1,000 MB
> The combination of all of the black and white 300 DPI .tif extension graphic files in this book (approximately 500 images) take up approximately 1 GB of memory.

### 128 Mb RAM

This tells you that the computer has 128 MB of random access memory (RAM)— what makes your programs run effectively when you are working with them. When a program seems to be running slowly, it may be because there is not enough RAM.

### DVD

A removable disc with a storage capacity of 4.7 to 17 GB of memory. The chart below shows you other types of removable memory.

**Types of Removable Memory Storage Capacity**

| | |
|---|---|
| Memory stick | > 1 GB |
| CDROM | 700 MB |
| Zip disk | > 1 GB |

### Answers to Common Questions

**How much RAM and hard drive do I need?** As much as you can afford. Both graphic programs and the images they create require plenty of RAM and storage space.

**How big are graphic files?**
The size of graphic files depends on several things: the resolution of the color, the resolution of the image, the width and height measurements of the image, and the format in which the image is stored. Black, white, and gray images that are small (about 1" x 1") and saved in a .gif or .jpeg format are about 1 or 2 KB. Color images that are the same size, saved as 300 DPI, and stored in a .tif format are about 160 KB. When you increase color resolution and image size and use a .tif or .eps format, your files can be several megabytes.

**FIGURE R-17**   Understanding the computer

## SUMMARY

The previous chapters describe how to design instructional visuals; the Resources section identifies the tools you need to actually create something. Knowing the requirements and types of hardware and software is important; therefore some of the basic jargon and software products useful for visual design are introduced. Since most designers are inspired by

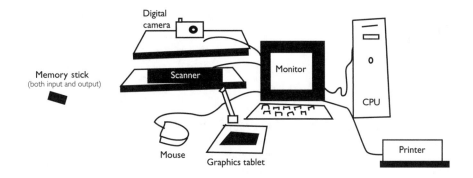

# What are the most common devices to help capture, create, and display visuals?

## Input

**Digital cameras** are good for keeping up-to-date, last-minute, realistic, emotion-provoking images. They operate like any camera, but store the photograph as a digital file that you upload to your computer. Since the technology for digital cameras has advanced and prices have dropped, they have become a "must have."

**Scanners** allow you to copy all kinds of images into a digital format including documents, sketches, objects, and fabrics.

**Graphics tablets** are useful if you like to draw or trace images, but find the mouse limits your ability to do so. Though a tablet works like a mouse, it feels like a pen, capturing different pressures and creating lines of different widths, making drawings look more realistic and less mechanical.

## Output

**Laser printers** produce high quality black and white or color documents at 300, 600, and 1,200 DPI and are reasonably affordable.

**Professional printing companies** produce top-quality print jobs that may require color separations. You work with a service bureau (the printer usually recommends one) to prepare your files for this type of printing.

**Inkjet printers** produce a lower quality document and, given the dropping price of laser printers may be used on a less frequent basis.

**Monitors** display images in relatively low resolutions and thus lose some of the crispness found in print publications. Because of the lower resolution requirements, however, image file sizes for monitor viewing can be much smaller, making them easier to manage.

**FIGURE R-18**   Input and output devices

others, a list of exceptional reference books from instructional message design, graphic arts, human factors, and information design are listed for your reference and inspiration.

This also marks the end of this book. I hope you have discovered that developing instructional visuals is not only challenging but fun, and something you will continue to learn and explore. By helping your learners select, organize, and integrate information, you will undoubtedly improve their learning experience. Good design will influence the future, so be part of it!

# INDEX